Praise for Learn Enc

"I have nothing but fantastic things to say about @LearnEnough courses. I am just about finished with the #javascript course. I must say, the videos are mandatory because @mhartl will play the novice, and share in the joy of having something you wrote actually work!"
— Claudia Vizena

"I must say, this Learn Enough series is a masterpiece of education. Thank you for this incredible work!"
— Michael King

"I want to thank you for the amazing job you have done with the tutorials. They are likely the best tutorials I have ever read."
— Pedro Iatzky

Learn Enough HTML, CSS and Layout to Be Dangerous

LEARN ENOUGH HTML, CSS AND LAYOUT TO BE DANGEROUS

An Introduction to Modern Website Creation and Templating Systems

Lee Donahoe

Michael Hartl

✦✦ Addison-Wesley

Boston • Columbus • New York • San Francisco • Amsterdam • Cape Town
Dubai • London • Madrid • Milan • Munich • Paris • Montreal • Toronto • Delhi • Mexico City
São Paulo • Sydney • Hong Kong • Seoul • Singapore • Taipei • Tokyo

Cover image: smalvik/Shutterstock
Figures 1.5-1.7, 5.7, 9.2(b), 16.11: GitHub, Inc.
Figures 1.8, 1.10, 3.2, 13.8, 13.9, 14.12, 15.29(b), 17.1, 17.3-17.5: Google LLC
Figures 1.9, 1.12, 1.13, 2.1-2.7, 2.9-2.11, 3.1, 3.3-3.5, 3.8-3.10, 4.1-4.4, 4.6, 4.7, 4.9-4.16, 5.6, 5.10, 6.1-6.5, 7.4, 7.5, 7.9-7.17, 7.20-7.23, 8.2-8.4, 8.6, 8.8-8.14, 8.18-8.25, 8.27-8.33, 8.36, 8.38, 9.3, 9.6, 9.7, 9.9-9.11, 9.14, 9.16-9.20, 9.29-9.39, 9.43, 9.44, 10.3-10.8, 10.10, 10.11, 10.13, 10.14, 10.17, 10.18, 11.08, 11.12, 11.15-11.22, 12.2, 12.5, 12.6, 12.8, 12.9-12.13, 13.3-13.7, 13.11-13.16, 13.20, 13.22, 13.23, 14.3, 14.4, 14.8-14.10, 14.13, 14.14, 14.17, 15.29(a), 17.6-17.8: Apple Inc.
Figure 4.15, page 92: Icon courtesy of Twitter, Inc.
Figures 5.4, 14.1: Microsoft
Figures 8.15, 9.4, 9.15, 9.42, 13.19: Amazon.com, Inc.
Figure 15.46: Caniuse.com
Figure 16.1: Hover
Figures 16.8-16.10, 17.2: Cloudflare, Inc.

Many of the designations used by manufacturers and sellers to distinguish their products are claimed as trademarks. Where those designations appear in this book, and the publisher was aware of a trademark claim, the designations have been printed with initial capital letters or in all capitals.

The authors and publisher have taken care in the preparation of this book, but make no expressed or implied warranty of any kind and assume no responsibility for errors or omissions. No liability is assumed for incidental or consequential damages in connection with or arising out of the use of the information or programs contained herein.

For information about buying this title in bulk quantities, or for special sales opportunities (which may include electronic versions; custom cover designs; and content particular to your business, training goals, marketing focus, or branding interests), please contact our corporate sales department at corpsales@pearsoned.com or (800) 382-3419.

For government sales inquiries, please contact governmentsales@pearsoned.com.

For questions about sales outside the U.S., please contact intlcs@pearson.com.

Visit us on the Web: informit.com/aw

Library of Congress Control Number: 2022935502

ISBN-13: 978-0-13-784310-7
ISBN-10: 0-13-784310-0

1 2022

Contents

Preface

Learn Enough HTML, CSS and Layout to Be Dangerous teaches you how to make modern websites using HyperText Markup Language (HTML) and Cascading Style Sheets (CSS). This tutorial includes several much-neglected yet essential techniques for page layout, including more advanced CSS techniques like flexbox and grid. It also covers the use of a static site generator to make websites that are easy to maintain and update. Finally, this tutorial shows you how to register and configure custom domains, including both custom URLs and custom email addresses. You can think of *Learn Enough HTML, CSS and Layout to Be Dangerous* as "a website in a box": everything you need (and nothing you don't) to design, build, and deploy modern, professional-grade websites.

The only prerequisites for *Learn Enough HTML, CSS and Layout to Be Dangerous* are knowledge of the Unix command line, a text editor, and version control with Git (as covered, for example, by *Learn Enough Developer Tools to Be Dangerous*). These prerequisites allow us to use good software development practices throughout the tutorial. This includes using a text editor to ensure readable code formatting and using version control to track changes in our projects. It also enables frequent deployment to production (for free!) using GitHub Pages.

The skills you'll develop in this tutorial are valuable whether your interest is in collaborating with developers or becoming a developer yourself. No matter what your goals are—level up in your current job, start a new career, or even start your own company—*Learn Enough HTML, CSS and Layout* will help get you where you want to go. To get you there as quickly as possible, throughout the tutorial we'll focus on the most important aspects of the subject, grounded in the philosophy that you don't have to learn everything to get started—you just have to learn enough to be *dangerous*.

In addition to teaching you specific skills, this tutorial also helps you develop *technical sophistication*—the seemingly magical ability to solve practically any technical problem. Technical sophistication includes concrete skills like version control and HTML, as well as fuzzier skills like Googling the error message and knowing when to just reboot the darn thing. Throughout *Learn Enough HTML, CSS and Layout*, we'll have abundant opportunities to develop technical sophistication in the context of real-world examples.

Finally, although the individual parts of this tutorial are as self-contained as possible, they are also extensively cross-referenced to show you how all the different pieces fit together. You'll learn how to use CSS to style your HTML elements into a flexible multicolumn layout, use a static site generator to put the same elements on every page without repeating any code, and then deploy your site to the live Web using a custom domain of your choice. The result is an integrated introduction to the foundations of front-end web development that's practically impossible to find anywhere else.

HyperText Markup Language

Part I of *Learn Enough HTML, CSS and Layout to Be Dangerous*, also known as *Learn Enough HTML to Be Dangerous* (https://www.learnenough.com/html), is an introduction to HyperTextMarkup Language, the language of the World Wide Web. It doesn't assume any prior knowledge of web technologies (though readers of *Learn Enough Developer Tools to Be Dangerous* will quickly realize they got a big head start when developing a sample website using version control).

Like all Learn Enough tutorials, *Learn Enough HTML to Be Dangerous* is structured as a technical narrative, with each step carefully motivated by real-world uses. Chapter 1 starts with a "hello, world!" page that you'll immediately deploy to production (!). We'll then fill in the index page with formatted text, links, and images in Chapter 2, expanding it into a multiple-page site with more advanced features like tables and lists in Chapter 3. Finally, we'll add some inline styling in Chapter 4, which will allow us to see the effect of simple style rules on plain HTML elements.

The result of finishing *Learn Enough HTML to Be Dangerous* is a mastery of the core HTML needed for making static websites. It also gives you a big head start on learning how to develop dynamic web applications with technologies like JavaScript (*Learn Enough JavaScript to Be Dangerous* (https://www.learnenough.com/javascript)) or Ruby and Ruby on Rails (*Learn Enough Ruby to Be Dangerous* (https://www.learnenough.com/ruby) and the *Ruby on Rails Tutorial* (https://www.railstutorial.org/)).

Cascading Style Sheets and Page Layout

Building on the simple styling techniques introduced in Chapter 4 of Part I, Part II— also known as *Learn Enough CSS and Layout to Be Dangerous* (https://www .learnenough.com/css-and-layout)—covers both web design with Cascading Style Sheets and front-end web development with a static site generator. We know of no comparable tutorial that brings all this material together in one place, and the result is the ability to make and deploy websites that are attractive, maintainable, and 100% professional-grade.

In Chapter 5, we'll learn the basics of CSS declarations and values by starting with a few super-simple elements on a sample page. We'll end with a first introduction to the essential technique of CSS selectors to target particular page elements for styling. In Chapter 6, we'll discuss aspects of selectors that are important to get right at the beginning of a project, with a focus on managing complexity and maintaining flexibility by choosing good names for things (including an introduction to CSS color conventions).

Chapter 7 introduces two of the most important kinds of CSS values: colors and sizes. These lay an essential foundation for Chapter 8 on the box model, which determines how different elements fit together on the page.

In Chapter 9 and Chapter 10, we'll take the page that we've been working on and factor it into a layout using a static site generator called Jekyll to build professional-grade websites that are easy to maintain and update. In Chapter 11, we'll learn how to make flexible page layouts using flexbox, adding layouts for a photo gallery page (covered in *Learn Enough JavaScript to Be Dangerous*) and a blog with posts.

In Chapter 12, we'll add the blog itself, showing how to use Jekyll to make a professional-grade blog without black-box solutions like WordPress or Tumblr. Because a large and growing amount of web traffic comes from mobile devices, in Chapter 13 we'll cover the basics of using CSS and media queries to make mobile-friendly sites without violating the DRY ("Don't Repeat Yourself") principle.

As a concluding step in developing the main sample application, in Chapter 14 we'll add the kinds of little details that make a site feel complete. The result will be an industrial-strength, nicely styled site deployed to the live Web.

Finally, as a special bonus, in Chapter 15 we'll introduce a more recent and advanced layout technique known as CSS grid. The result is a largely self-contained discussion of how to use grid to accomplish some of the same effects mentioned in previous chapters, as well as some effects you can only accomplish easily with grid.

Custom Domains

In Part III, also known as *Learn Enough Custom Domains to Be Dangerous* (https://www.learnenough.com/custom-domains), you'll learn how to associate your website with a custom domain. This means your site will live at a domain like example.com instead of example.someoneelsesdomain.com—in other words, at a domain you control and that no one can ever take away.

Chapter 16 shows you how to register a custom domain, including guidance on how to pick a good domain name and a discussion of the pros and cons of various top-level domains (TLDs). You'll also learn how to use Cloudflare to configure the DNS settings for your custom domain. As part of this, you'll learn how to use Secure Sockets Layer/Transport Layer Security (SSL/TLS) to make sure your site is secure and how to redirect URLs for a more pleasant user experience.

Chapter 17 shows you how to use custom email addresses with your domain using Google Workspace. The result is the ability to use yourname@example.com instead of yourname152@gmail.com. As a special bonus, you'll learn how to use another Google service, Google Analytics, to monitor traffic to your site and gain insight into how visitors are using it.

Additional Features

In addition to the main tutorial material, *Learn Enough HTML, CSS and Layout to Be Dangerous* includes a large number of exercises to help you test your understanding and to extend the material in the main text. The exercises include frequent hints and often include the expected answers, with community solutions available by separate subscription at www.learnenough.com.

Final Thoughts

Learn Enough HTML, CSS and Layout to Be Dangerous covers everything you need to know to make a website for a personal homepage, hobby, or business—it's basically a one-stop shop for all things "Web." After learning the techniques covered in this tutorial, and especially after developing your technical sophistication, you'll know everything you need to design and deploy professional-grade websites. You'll also be ready for a huge variety of other resources, including books, blog posts, and online documentation. *Learn Enough JavaScript to Be Dangerous*, which builds on this tutorial to make a website with an interactive image gallery, is especially recommended. You can even go on to learn dynamic, database-backed web development with *Learn Enough Ruby to Be Dangerous* and the *Ruby on Rails Tutorial*.

Learn Enough Scholarships

Learn Enough is committed to making a technical education available to as wide a variety of people as possible. As part of this commitment, in 2016 we created the Learn Enough Scholarship program (https://www.learnenough.com/scholarship). Scholarship recipients get free or deeply discounted access to the Learn Enough All Access subscription, which includes all of the Learn Enough online book content, embedded videos, exercises, and community exercise answers.

As noted in a 2019 RailsConf Lightning Talk (https://youtu.be/AI5wmnzzBqc?t=1076), the Learn Enough Scholarship application process is incredibly simple: just fill out a confidential text area telling us a little about your situation. The scholarship criteria are generous and flexible—we understand that there are an enormous number of reasons for wanting a scholarship, from being a student, to being between jobs, to living in a country with an unfavorable exchange rate against the U.S. dollar. Chances are that, if you feel like you've got a good reason, we'll think so, too.

So far, Learn Enough has awarded more than 2,500 scholarships to aspiring developers around the country and around the world. To apply, visit the Learn Enough Scholarship page at www.learnenough.com/scholarship. Maybe the next scholarship recipient could be you!

Register your copy of *Learn Enough HTML, CSS and Layout to Be Dangerous* on the InformIT site for convenient access to updates and/or corrections as they become available. To start the registration process, go to informit.com/register and log in or create an account. Enter the product ISBN (9780137843107) and click Submit. Look on the Registered Products tab for an Access Bonus Content link next to this product, and follow that link to access any available bonus materials. If you would like to be notified of exclusive offers on new editions and updates, please check the box to receive email from us.

About the Authors

Lee Donahoe is Learn Enough cofounder and an entrepreneur, designer, and frontend developer. When he was 16 his father handed him a tutorial on HTML, and for more than 25 years since then he has been creating things for the Web. In addition to doing the design and front-end development for Learn Enough (https://www.learnenough.com/), Softcover (https://www.softcover.io/), and the *Ruby on Rails*™ *Tutorial* (https://www.railstutorial.org/), he is also a cofounder and frontend developer for Coveralls (https://www.coveralls.io/), a leading test coverage analysis service, and also for Buck Mason (https://www.buckmason.com/), a Los Angeles based clothing company that crafts timeless men's and women's clothing. Lee is a graduate of USC, where he studied economics as well as multimedia and creative technologies.

Michael Hartl (https://www.michaelhartl.com/) is the creator of the *Ruby on Rails*™ *Tutorial*, one of the leading introductions to web development, and is cofounder and principal author at Learn Enough. Previously, he was a physics instructor at the California Institute of Technology (Caltech), where he received a Lifetime Achievement Award for Excellence in Teaching. He is a graduate of Harvard College, has a PhD in Physics from Caltech, and is an alumnus of the Y Combinator entrepreneur program.

PART I

Hypertext Markup Language

CHAPTER 1
Basic HTML

Welcome to *Learn Enough HTML, CSS and Layout to Be Dangerous*! This tutorial teaches you how to design modern websites and deploy them to the live Web. It's aimed at anyone who wants to know how to make websites, whether for fun, as a freelance web designer, or as a professional front-end designer and developer. Its only prerequisites are knowledge of the Unix command line, a text editor, and version control with Git, as covered by *Learn Enough Developer Tools to Be Dangerous*.[1]

Learn Enough HTML, CSS and Layout to Be Dangerous consists of three parts, each covering one imporant aspect of web development (and based on the corresponding online course from Learn Enough (https://www.learnenough.com/)):

- Part I: *Learn Enough HTML to Be Dangerous* (https://www.learnenough.com /html) on HyperText Markup Language, the language of the World Wide Web

- Part II: *Learn Enough CSS & Layout to Be Dangerous* (https://www.learnenough .com/css-and-layout) on Cascading Style Sheets (CSS), the design language of the Web, and page layout, including an introduction to *static site generators*

---

1. The contents of *Learn Enough Developer Tools to Be Dangerous* are also available separately online as *Learn Enough Command Line to Be Dangerous* (https://www.learnenough.com/command-line), *Learn Enough Text Editor to Be Dangerous* (https://www.learnenough.com/text-editor), and *Learn Enough Git to Be Dangerous* (https://www.learnenough.com/git). We will occasionally refer to these individual titles, but anything we mention can be found in *Learn Enough Developer Tools to Be Dangerous* as well.

- Part III: *Learn Enough Custom Domains to Be Dangerous* (https://www.learnenough .com/custom-domains) on registering and configuring custom domains[2]

Because of the close association between the parts and the standalone courses, *Learn Enough HTML, CSS, and Layout to Be Dangerous* will use terms like "Part I" and "*Learn Enough HTML to Be Dangerous*" interchangeably.

In this first part of the tutorial, we'll focus on HyperText Markup Language, or *HTML*, which is the universal language of the World Wide Web. Every time you visit a website, the site's web server sends HTML to your browser, which then renders it as the web page you see on your screen. Because this process is universal, anyone who works with web technologies—which these days means virtually all developers, designers, and even many managers—can benefit from knowing the basics of what HTML is and how it works. *Learn Enough HTML to Be Dangerous* is designed to give you this foundation in basic HTML. (If you're already familiar with HTML, you can skip right to Part II and refer back to Part I as necessary.)

Appropriately enough, there are lots of HTML tutorials on the Web, but most of them use toy examples, focusing on HTML syntax in isolation, without showing how HTML is written and deployed in real life. In contrast, *Learn Enough HTML to Be Dangerous* not only shows you how to make real HTML pages; it shows you how to deploy an actual site to the live Web. If you have previously attempted or completed an HTML tutorial, it's likely that *Learn Enough HTML to Be Dangerous* will help you "put everything together" in a way you haven't seen before, including an emphasis on expanding your skillset with *technical sophistication* (Box 1.1).

Box 1.1: Technical Sophistication

If tech is the new literacy, technical sophistication is like being able to read and write, and HTML is like the alphabet of the Web. This includes being able to figure things out on your own (like sounding out words while reading) and look things up when you need them (like consulting a dictionary or thesaurus while writing).

---

2. Because *Learn Enough Custom Domains to Be Dangerous* is intended mainly for reference, it does not have a corresponding interactive course, nor does it have any exercises. Unlike the other tutorials, though, it is available in its entirety, both online and as a downloadable ebook, at https://www.learnenough.com/custom-domains.

In *Learn Enough HTML to Be Dangerous*, we'll constantly be on the lookout for chances to improve our technical sophistication. We'll deploy our website immediately to production (Section 1.3), getting over any bumps along the way. We'll push ourselves to read HTML we don't quite understand, content to get the gist at first before deepening our mastery later. And we'll put all our tools to use, combining the command line, a text editor, and version control to learn how to make HTML websites the Right Way™—professional-grade from the start.

Figure 1.1: The tools of the trade (kitten not included).

Because of our pragmatic approach, the tools we'll be using are all professional-grade (Figure 1.1[3]). They are the same tools covered in *Learn Enough Developer Tools to Be Dangerous* and in the corresponding Learn Enough online courses:

1. *Learn Enough Command Line to Be Dangerous* on the Unix command line
2. *Learn Enough Text Editor to Be Dangerous* on text editors
3. *Learn Enough Git to Be Dangerous* on version control with Git

To get even more out of the sequence, you can join the Learn Enough All Access subscription service (https://www.learnenough.com/all-access), which

---

3. Kitten image courtesy of halfmax.ru/Shutterstock.

includes streaming videos and special enhanced versions of the online tutorials, among other benefits.

If you're just getting started with HTML, the Developer Tools sequence represents a little bit of overhead, but the benefits are enormous. To our knowledge, this combination of software development best practices and deploying to a live website is unique among introductory HTML and CSS tutorials, and gives you a tremendous advantage both when collaborating with others and when taking your skills to the next level by learning to build more complicated sites.

Learn Enough HTML to Be Dangerous focuses on core HTML, starting with a "Hello, world!" page that we'll deploy to production (!) right here in Chapter 1. We'll then fill in the *index page* with formatted text, links, and images in Chapter 2, expanding it into a multiple-page site with more advanced features like tables and lists in Chapter 3. Finally, we'll add some inline styling in Chapter 4, which will allow us to see the effect of simple style rules on plain HTML elements.

The resulting site will be functional, but we'll run into several important limitations imposed by working with raw HTML. This will set the stage for Part II, which creates a fully modern website using *Cascading Style Sheets* (CSS) to separate the design of the site from its HTML structure, while covering site layouts and advanced styling as well.

For the best learning experience, it is generally recommended that you type the code listings in by hand. In case you ever want to copy and paste something, though, all the listings are available online at the following URL:

```
https://github.com/learnenough/learn_enough_html_css_and_layout_code_listings
```

1.1 Introduction

Underneath every website, no matter how simple or complex, you will find HTML. In Part I, by creating and deploying a simple but real website, we'll gain an understanding of the underlying structure that every site uses to organize and display content online.

As a technology standard, HTML has been constantly evolving ever since its introduction in 1993 by Tim Berners-Lee, the original "web developer" (Figure 1.2).[4]

---

4. Image courtesy of dpa picture alliance/Alamy Stock Photo.

Figure 1.2: Sir Tim Berners-Lee, the original web developer.

Nowadays, the specification of what's in HTML and what isn't is managed by the World Wide Web Consortium (W3C). The latest public release, which is what we will be using in this tutorial, is HTML5 (that is, version 5 of HTML). The companies that create web browsers take the specs from the W3C and implement the behaviors that are expected when the browser comes across any of the allowed formatting, such as **making text bold** or changing its color (or even **doing both** at the same time).

Fortunately, we won't need to get into a lot of specifics or worry about what has changed from version to version. Just know that new features are being added regularly to expand browser functionality and modernize the technology. Common elements, including the ones we'll be covering in this tutorial, haven't changed much since the beginning, but that doesn't mean that they will always be safe—the HTML spec is a constantly evolving creature being assembled by a committee (Figure 1.3).[5] We'll discuss some practical effects of this in Section 1.2.

---

5. Image courtesy of Aleksandr Frolov/123RF.

Figure 1.3: HTML in animal form.

1.2 HTML Tags

As the name **H**yper**T**ext **M**arkup **L**anguage indicates, HTML is a *markup* language, which allows a web author to organize and define how content should be displayed. This means HTML can do things like add text formatting; make headings, lists, and tables; and include images and links. You can think of an HTML file as an ordinary written document that has been carefully annotated by the author with instructions on how to display it. Some of these annotations might highlight parts of the text, some might include an image that has been added to the document, and others might tell you where to find additional information.

The "HyperText" part of the HTML initialism refers to the way links on the Web allow you to move from one document to another in a non-linear fashion. For example, if you are reading the Wikipedia article on HTML and see a highlighted link to a related topic like CSS, you can click on that link and be taken immediately to the other article. It also allows a document like this one to link to Wikipedia. (You might notice that external links in this document open in a new browser tab. We'll learn how to do this ourselves in Section 3.3.)

Technologically, hypertext is a great improvement over non-linked documents, as it eliminates the need to flip or scroll through pages of content to find what you are looking for. These days, the ability to link between documents is something that we all take for granted, but when the HTML specification was created it was an innovation important enough to be included in the name of the technology.

HTML source is *plain text*, which makes it ideal for editing with a text editor (as discussed in *Learn Enough Text Editor to Be Dangerous*). Instead of using the convenient but inflexible What You See Is What You Get (WYSIWYG) approach of word processors, HTML indicates formatting using special *tags* which are the text annotations alluded to above.

As we'll see, HTML supports more than one kind of tags, but the most common kind consist of strings (sequences of characters) enclosed in *beginning* and *ending* tags, like this:

```
<strong>make them strong</strong>
```

Figure 1.4 illustrates the detailed anatomy of this typical tag, including the name of the tag (**strong**, in this case), angle brackets, and a forward slash (**/**).

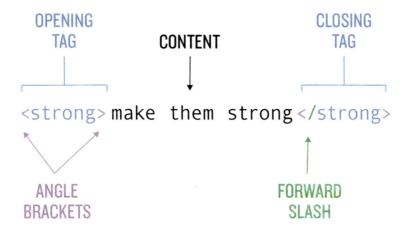

Figure 1.4: The anatomy of a typical HTML tag.

Although HTML tags are not visible to the end-user (i.e., the person viewing your website), they do give the web browser suggestions about how to format the content and how it should be displayed on the page. A simple example using the **strong** tag appears in Listing 1.1.

Listing 1.1: A string with HTML tags in the text.

```
I am a string about things. Some of those things are more important than others, so I
will <strong>make them strong</strong> to stand out among less spectacular neighbors.
```

Most browsers render the **strong** tag as **boldface text**, so in a typical browser Listing 1.1 would appear something like this:

> I am a string about things. Some of those things are more important than others, so I will **make them strong** to stand out among less spectacular neighbors.

If we were to split the contents of the **strong** tag in Listing 1.1 onto two lines by hitting return after "them", the browser would ignore the extra space and format the string as a continuous line of text.

By the way, HTML does support a **b** (bold) tag in addition to **strong**, but over the years HTML has moved away from tag names that specify formatting (i.e., "make the text **bold**") and toward names that focus on *meaning*—or, in fancier terms, *semantics*—leading to an emphasis on so-called *semantic tags* (Box 1.2). For example, the semantic tag **strong** indicates that the enclosed text should be made to look "strong" somehow, letting the browser decide exactly how to do it.

Box 1.2: The Cautionary (Semantic) Tale of <b> and <i>

When HTML was first created, the Internet made funny noises when you connected to it, and you paid for the connection in time or by amount of data sent. Those limitations meant that brevity was an important consideration when deciding on tags, and the whole endeavor was so new that there wasn't as much thought about the meaning the tags conveyed. So short tags were popular, and getting everything to display correctly to people was the end-goal.

As a result of this focus on concision, the original way to make text bold was to use the b tag (<b>...</b>), and to make text italic it was the i tag (<i>...</i>). This worked just fine (in fact, it still works even today), and no one was confused.

What some developers began to notice was that HTML tags were being defined only by how the content inside should be displayed in a browser, rather than by the meaning of the content. That's fine for people looking at content with good ol' eyeballs, but not so good for automated systems that might be rapidly scanning web pages and need to infer what the content wrapped in different HTML tags actually means.

To address this issue, a movement started that pushed for new tags based on semantic meaning instead of on appearance, thereby giving rise to the current preferred method for indicating bold or italicized text with `strong` (`<strong>...</strong>`) and em (`<em>...</em>`, for "emphasized"), respectively. The idea here is that the intent behind making text bold is to make it strongly **stand out** from the rest of the content, and the intent behind italicizing text is to *show emphasis*.

This might seem like a subtle difference, but semantic tags are used for a lot more than just defining strong or emphasized text. Semantic HTML tags will be further discussed in Part II, where we will cover tag conventions and page layout in greater depth.

At this point, we've covered the conceptual core of HTML: HTML consists of text content wrapped in tags, which organize or indicate a change in the display of that content.

But the Devil, as they say, is in the details… and HTML has a whole lot of details.

1.2.1   Exercises

Note: Unlike most other Learn Enough tutorials, the results of some exercises will appear in future screenshots.

1. Identify all the tags in Listing 1.2. Notice that you don't have to know what a tag does to be able to identify it correctly. (This is a good example of technical sophistication (Box 1.1).)

2. Some HTML tags don't contain any content, and instead are known as *void elements*, also called *self-closing tags*. Which tag in Listing 1.2 is a void element?

3. HTML tags can be *nested*, which means that one tag can be put inside another. Which tags in Listing 1.2 are nested? Don't include any self-closing tags.

Listing 1.2: Shall I compare thee to a summer's day?

```html
<p>
  William Shakespeare's <em>Sonnets</em> consists of 154 poems, each fourteen
  lines long (three
  <a href="https://en.wikipedia.org/wiki/Quatrain">quatrains</a>
  followed by a rhyming
  <a href="https://en.wikipedia.org/wiki/Couplet">couplet</a>).
  <strong>Sonnet 18</strong> is perhaps the most famous, and begins like this:
</p>
<blockquote>
  <p>
    Shall I compare thee to a summer's day?<br>
    Thou art more lovely and more temperate.
  </p>
</blockquote>
```

1.3 Starting the Project

Now that we know the basic structure of markup and tags, it's time to get started with the project that will serve as our sample website for learning HTML. The sample project is a mock informational website, whose main page talks a little about this tutorial, the company behind it, and HTML itself. As we develop the homepage and two ancillary pages, we'll see how to use a wide variety of HTML tags, while also showing you how to make the kind of public-facing site that you could use for your own work or as a service to other people. Although some of the information on the site is about Learn Enough to Be Dangerous, ultimately it is about *you*.

We'll begin by following the same steps used in *Learn Enough Git to Be Dangerous*, so this section will also serve as a review of how to use Git. (If you don't have Git proficiency at the level of *Learn Enough Git to Be Dangerous*, we recommend you read that tutorial at this time.) As in the Git tutorial, the result here will be that we can deploy our sample HTML site to the live Web using GitHub Pages (Box 1.3).

Box 1.3: GitHub Pages

Once you have an account at GitHub (and have verified your email address), you can use a free feature called *GitHub Pages* that allows you to host simple HTML sites for free on GitHub's infrastructure.

> This is a major advance compared to the bad old days of the early Web. For example, if this were 1999, you'd not only have to pay money for the hosting, but you'd also be on the hook for the cost of transferring the data to the people visiting your site. For sites with even moderate traffic, the bills could add up fast.
>
> Nowadays, we have many better options, GitHub Pages among them. Not only is GitHub Pages free, but it is incredibly easy to use. By updating a single configuration setting (described below), we can arrange for GitHub Pages to serve our website right from the main branch. As described in Part III, you can even set up your GitHub Pages site to use a custom domain (like www.example.com). The result is an industrial-grade web presence with built-in Git backups, high performance, and zero cost.
>
> That's a combination that's hard to beat!

We'll get started by making a directory and an initial repository for our sample website. First, open a terminal window[6] and make a directory called **sample_website**[7]:

```
$ mkdir -p repos/sample_website
```

Next, **cd** into the directory and **touch** the file for the main page of the site, which should be called **index.html**:

```
$ cd repos/sample_website
$ touch index.html
```

Then initialize the repository:

```
$ git init
$ git add -A
$ git commit -m "Initialize repository"
```

---

6. *Note for Mac users*: Although it shouldn't matter in *Learn Enough HTML to Be Dangerous*, it is recommended that you use the Bourne-again shell (Bash) to complete this tutorial. To switch your shell to Bash, run **chsh -s /bin/bash** at the command line, enter your password, and restart your terminal program. Any resulting alert messages are safe to ignore. See the Learn Enough blog post "Using Z Shell on Macs with the Learn Enough Tutorials" (https://news.learnenough.com/macos-bash-zshell) for more information.

7. The command **mkdir -p** is covered in Section 8.2 of *Learn Enough Developer Tools to Be Dangerous*. Unless otherwise indicated, every command we use in *Learn Enough HTML to Be Dangerous* is covered somewhere in *Learn Enough Developer Tools to Be Dangerous*, so we recommend you look there if you run across any commands that don't look familiar.

The reason we created a file using **touch** is because Git won't let you make a commit in an empty repository.[8] The reason we've called it **index.html** is because that's the default filename for "home" pages on the Web, and most sites will automatically serve up **index.html** when you hit the bare domain. In other words, when you point a browser at example.com, the server will automatically show you example.com/index.html. (Those links work, by the way; amazingly, the HTML standard specifically reserves the site example.com for examples just like this one!)

With the repo initialized, we're now ready to push our (nearly) empty repo up to GitHub. As in *Learn Enough Git to Be Dangerous*, you should go to github.com (https://github.com/), log in if necessary, and then create a new repository using the name **sample_website** and the description "A sample website for Learn Enough HTML to Be Dangerous", as shown in Figure 1.5.[9]

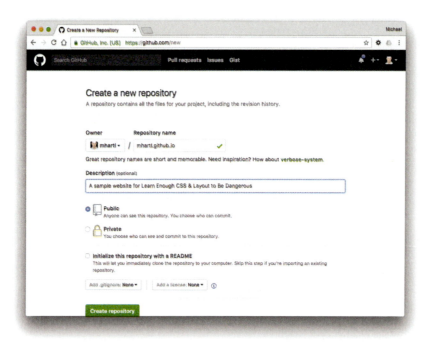

Figure 1.5: Creating a new GitHub repo for our website.

---

8. As mentioned in Chapter 2 of *Learn Enough Developer Tools to Be Dangerous*, the **touch** technique is a personal favorite, but the file doesn't have to be empty; for example, **echo hello > index.html** would also have worked.

9. GitHub is constantly updating its user interface (UI), so in these and other figures you may notice slight differences compared to what you see in your browser. Use your technical sophistication (Box 5.1) to resolve any discrepancies.

After creating the remote repo, you should set the *remote origin* as the URL for the repo, which you can find as shown in Figure 1.6 (or just copy from the section "…or push an existing repository from the command line" on the GitHub setup page). This involves using **git remote** to set the origin URL and then pushing the **main** branch "upstream" using **git push -u**:[10]

```
$ git remote add origin <repo url>
$ git push -u origin main
```

Figure 1.6: Finding the repo URL.

At this point, you will be prompted for your password, which (as noted in *Learn Enough Git to Be Dangerous*) must be a *personal access token* rather than your GitHub password. See the GitHub article "Creating a personal access token" (https://docs.github.com/en/authentication/keeping-your-account-and-data-secure /creating-a-personal-access-token) for more information.[11]

---

10. The screencasts that are available to accompany this book refer to the **master** branch, which was the default branch name for the first 15+ years of Git's existence, but the text has been updated to use **main**, which is the current preferred default. See the Learn Enough blog post "Default Git Branch Name with Learn Enough and the Rails Tutorial" (https://news.learnenough.com/default-git-branch-name-with-learn-enough-and-the-rails-tutorial) for more information.

11. As of this writing, the article is at https://docs.github.com/en/authentication/keeping-your-account-and-data-secure/creating-a-personal-access-token, but Googling "github creating personal access token" is also a good bet.

At this point, you should click on the Settings tab for your new repository and follow the instructions for serving your website from the **main** branch using GitHub Pages, as discussed in Section 11.4 of *Learn Enough Developer Tools to Be Dangerous* and reviewed in Figure 1.7.

Figure 1.7: Serving our website from the **main** branch.

As soon as you click the Save button, the sample website will be live on the Web via GitHub Pages! Its location is given by a github.io URL based on the username and repo name (Listing 1.3).

Listing 1.3: The template for a GitHub Pages URL.

```
https://<username>.github.io/<repo_name>
```

For example, the Learn Enough version of the sample website lives at the URL

https://learnenough.github.io/sample_website_reference_implementation

Incidentally, that means it can be cloned from here for future reference:[12]

https://github.com/learnenough/sample_website_reference_implementation

---

12. Keeping the reference website in sync with the main tutorial is a challenging task, so reports of any discrepancies are gratefully received. You can send such reports to support@learnenough.com.

If you visit your version of this site, it should resolve properly, and it should even automatically serve up the contents of **index.html**. Because those contents are empty, though, all you'll see is a blank white screen. We'll take our first steps toward changing this sad state of affairs in Section 1.4, and then we'll knock it up a notch starting in Chapter 2.

1.3.1 Exercises

1. Add and commit a file called **README.md**, taking care to use at least a few Markdown (https://daringfireball.net/projects/markdown/) tags. What is the result at GitHub?

2. What happens if you visit **<username>.github.io/<repo_name>/README.md** in a browser? What does this imply about including sensitive information in a public website repo?

1.4 The First Tag

In order to initialize the Git repository in Section 1.3, we needed only an empty **index.html** file, but of course our sample site will eventually have much more than that. In this section, we'll begin by adding some content in a single tag—just enough to give us a site to view, commit, and deploy. That's a huge accomplishment, though, and will serve as an essential foundation for what follows.

Now that an empty index page has been created, you should open **index.html** using your favorite editor, which for the purposes of this tutorial we'll assume is Atom. It's possible to open the file directly using **File > Open**, but (as noted in Section 7.4 of *Learn Enough Developer Tools to Be Dangerous*) these days all the cool kids open the full HTML project directly at the command line:

```
$ atom .
```

(As noted in Section 4.3 of *Learn Enough Developer Tools to Be Dangerous*, the . ("dot") refers to the current directory.)

Even though we have only one file for now (and possibly a README (Section 1.3.1)), opening the full project is a good habit to cultivate, since it allows us to easily open and edit multiple files in the same project. We'll put this technique to good use when we start making additional pages in Section 3.1.

At this point, we're ready to fill the index file with some content, which should consist of the phrase "Hello, world!" (Listing 1.4) enclosed in the *paragraph tag* **p**. Note that the **p** tag has exactly the same form as the **strong** tag (Figure 1.4).

Listing 1.4: A short paragraph with the contents "Hello, world!".
index.html

```
<p>Hello, world!</p>
```

We see in Figure 1.8 that Atom automatically highlights the HTML source, which it knows to do because of the **.html** extension on the filename. This *syntax highlighting* is irrelevant to the computer—in fact, it takes place purely in the editor and doesn't have anything to do with **index.html** itself—but it makes it easier for humans to distinguish the difference between tags and content. (This is also why we use syntax highlighting in this tutorial's code listings.)

Figure 1.8: "Hello, world!" in a text editor.

Having made a change to add content to **index.html**, let's view the result in a browser. On macOS, you can do this using the **open** command:

```
$ open index.html      # macOS only
```

On many Linux systems, you can use the similar **xdg-open** command:

```
$ xdg-open index.html    # Linux only
```

A technique that works on almost any system is to view the **sample_website** directory in a graphical file browser and double-click the filename. No matter how you do
it, the result should be to open **index.html** in the default browser on your system,
which should appear something like Figure 1.9.

Figure 1.9: The local index page in a browser.

Note that the "URL" in Figure 1.9 will be a *local* file, like this:

```
file:///Users/mhartl/repos/sample_website/index.html
```

This is because the index page is on our local system and hasn't yet been deployed to
the live Web.

We know how to remedy this, though—commit our changes to the local Git
repository and push up to GitHub Pages:

```
$ git commit -am "Add a short paragraph"
$ git push
```

Upon refreshing the browser pointed at the sample website's GitHub Pages URL
(Listing 1.3), we will see "Hello, world!". (You may have to wait a few moments for
GitHub Pages to load your site. This happens only the first time, and on subsequent
requests the response will be lightning-fast.)

Although the appearance is identical to the local version in Figure 1.9, by inspecting the address bar you should be able to confirm that the URL is at github.io, which
means that the page is now available on the live Web.

Congratulations! You've just published a production website.

1.4.1   Exercises

1. Replace the contents of **index.html** with the markup from Listing 1.2. Can you guess what the **a** tag does?

2. Use your browser's *web inspector* to inspect the source from the previous exercise. (Google for "browser web inspector" to learn how to use your browser's web inspector. Or just right-click on the page.) Does it differ in any way from Listing 1.2?

1.5   An HTML Skeleton

Although modern web browsers are highly fault-tolerant and will render simple HTML like Listing 1.4 just fine, it's dangerous to rely on this behavior. Indeed, we saw in *Learn Enough Git to Be Dangerous* that omitting a single tag resulted in the trademark character ™ not rendering properly (Figure 1.10). This is exactly the sort of thing that

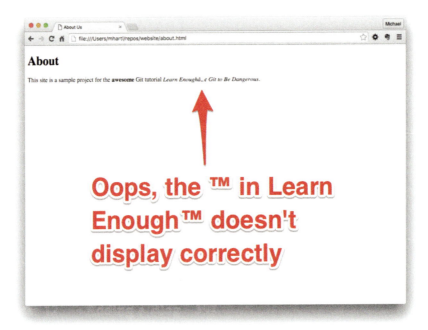

Figure 1.10: The broken About page from *Learn Enough Git to Be Dangerous*.

can go wrong when you don't use a fully valid HTML page. To avoid these sorts of problems, from now on all of our sample web pages will use valid HTML to ensure that they will render properly in the broadest possible range of browsers.

The prototypical HTML skeleton begins with an **html** tag containing two elements, a **head** and a **body**. These latter tags are *nested* inside the **html** tag, as follows:

```
<html><head></head><body></body></html>
```

Because this is hard to read, it's conventional to format the tags using spaces and newlines to make the structure more apparent at a glance:

```
<html>
  <head>
  </head>
  <body>
  </body>
</html>
```

Because HTML generally ignores extra space, it makes no difference in the appearance of the page, but this formatting makes it easier for us to understand the source of the document (Box 1.4).

Box 1.4: Formatting HTML

In order to make HTML easier to read, it's conventional to add extra spaces and newlines to make the document's structure clear at a glance. It might look a little strange at first, but it's a style convention in the development world that helps keep source code readable (and coders sane).

Generally speaking, HTML ignores extra space when displaying in a browser, so

```
<p>Hello, world!</p>
```

will look the same as

```
<p>Hello,
          world!

          </p>
```

It's a good practice to keep your HTML formatting tidy, and it's clear that the former is easier to read.

The readability of the markup can change with time, though, especially after the text grows to more than a couple of sentences, or when there are additional HTML elements nested inside. To keep our content straight and not lose track of tags, in these cases we'll need to format the code more rigorously.

There are no universal rules for formatting markup, but a good rule of thumb is to put new tags on their own line unless they fit easily on one, with lines inside those tags indented one level:

```
<p>Hello, world!</p>

<p>
  Lorem ipsum dolor sit amet, consectetur
  adipisicing elit, sed do eiusmod tempor
  incididunt ut labore et dolore magna aliqua.
  Ut enim ad minim veniam
</p>
```

The main exception to the new-line rule involves tags that modify text in a paragraph. For instance, most people do not add line breaks or indentation for elements that are inside lines of text (referred to as *inline elements*) like the `<strong>make them strong</strong>` example from Listing 1.1. We'll talk more about these types of inline elements, and how they differ from so-called *block elements*, in Section 3.2.

What constitutes an indentation "level" varies by developer, but we prefer the two-space convention shown above. Four spaces are also common, but in our experience this sends the content running off the right side of the page a little too fast. Some developers use tabs instead of spaces, but (at the risk of starting a holy war) we think this should be strenuously avoided. The main issue is that the display of tab characters is device-dependent, so markup that looks great in a text editor could look terrible using `less` at the command line.

It's important to make sure your editor is configured properly to use spaces (sometimes confusingly called *emulated tabs*) instead of genuine tabs. Refer to *Learn Enough Text Editor to Be Dangerous* or use your technical sophistication (Box 1.1) to figure out how.

Finally, it's worth noting that many modern text editors include a way to format HTML automatically. For example, in Atom it's `Edit > Lines > Auto Indent`. This can be a big help when indenting larger HTML files, especially if they come from an outside source and aren't already nicely formatted.

The section of the HTML that is wrapped by **<head>** and **</head>** is a header container that defines *metadata*, a fancy word that just means data about data. This **<head>** section is not displayed to users in their browser window, and therefore gives developers the ability to tell the browser where to find other files (such as CSS and JavaScript) that will be used to properly display the page's content, *without* having that information show up in the actual content of the web page. (We'll cover more things that can be added to the HTML header starting in Part II.)

Meanwhile, the content inside **<body>** and **</body>** is what gets displayed to the browser. Every website you've ever seen consists of content inside an HTML **body** tag. Once we've defined the contents of the **head** tag, most of the modifications we'll make to the site will be inside the **body** tag.

To complete the skeleton, there are only two more elements: one required and one optional but strongly recommended. First, we need to tell browsers what the *document type* is, and inside the **head** tag we need to define a nonempty **title**, as seen in Listing 1.5.

Listing 1.5: A nearly complete HTML skeleton.

```
<!DOCTYPE html>
<html>
    <title>Page Title</title>
  </head>
  <body>
  </body>
</html>
```

Here the **DOCTYPE** is an irregular tag, and you should not spend even a millisecond worrying about its exact form. (Why is there an exclamation point before **DOCTYPE**? We have no idea.) Meanwhile, the **title** tag has exactly the same form as the **p** tag we saw in Section 1.4 (and the **strong** tag before that (Figure 1.4)).

As you can verify by using the W3C HTML validator (https://validator.w3.org/), the page in Listing 1.5 validates as HTML5 (Figure 1.11). (An empty **title** would be invalid, but an empty **body** is fine. Also note that, although there are no *errors* on the page, there is a *warning* regarding the absence of a **lang** (language) attribute; we'll address this detail in Section 3.3.1.)

On the other hand, we learned in *Learn Enough Git to Be Dangerous* (Figure 1.10) that we need one more thing: We need to tell the browser which *character set* to use so

Document checking completed. No errors or warnings to show.

Source

```
1.  <!DOCTYPE html>↵
2.  <html>↵
3.    <head>↵
4.      <title>Page Title</title>↵
5.    </head>↵
6.    <body>↵
7.    </body>↵
8.  </html>
```

Figure 1.11: The HTML in Listing 1.5 is valid but incomplete.

that it can handle the expanded range of characters (called Unicode), which includes symbols like ™ and ©, accented characters (as in *voilà*), etc. We can do this by adding the **meta** tag to the **head**, as shown in Listing 1.6.

Listing 1.6: Adding a **meta** tag to define the character set.

```html
<!DOCTYPE html>
<html>
  <head>
    <title>Page Title</title>
    <meta charset="utf-8">
  </head>
  <body>
  </body>
</html>
```

By the way, the **meta** tag is a special kind of tag called a *void element* and doesn't have a closing tag. Because of this, void elements are also called *self-closing tags*.

With that, the skeleton is complete!

Because of the importance of this HTML skeleton, let's review its elements line by line:

1. The doctype declaration

2. Opening **html** tag

3. Opening **head** tag

4. Opening and closing **title** tags (with the content of the page title)

5. The **meta** tag defining the character set

6. Closing **head** tag

7. Opening **body** tag

8. Closing **body** tag

9. Closing **html** tag

Combining the original paragraph from Listing 1.4 with the skeleton in Listing 1.6 gives us the code for the first valid HTML page in our sample website, as shown in Listing 1.7.

Listing 1.7: A valid "Hello, world!" page.
index.html

```
<!DOCTYPE html>
<html>
  <head>
    <title>Page Title</title>
    <meta charset="utf-8">
  </head>
  <body>
    <p>Hello, world!</p>
  </body>
</html>
```

Note in Listing 1.7 that we've placed the paragraph from Listing 1.4 inside the **body** tag, as required by the HTML standard.

After refreshing the browser, the result of Listing 1.7 is virtually the same as we saw in Figure 1.9. The only visible difference in the body of the page is a small amount of additional space around the paragraph.

A second, browser-dependent difference involves the page title, which some browsers display in the default tab, and others don't show unless you have a second tab in addition to the first (Figure 1.12). In any case, the page title is needed even if it's not displayed, as it's required by the HTML standard, and is important for screen readers and the web spiders used by search engines to index the Web.

Figure 1.12: The page title in Safari.

With that, we're ready to commit our changes and push the results to GitHub Pages:

```
$ git commit -am "Convert index page to fully valid HTML"
$ git push
```

The result appears in Figure 1.13.

Figure 1.13: The valid "Hello, world!" page in production.

1.5.1 Exercises

1. Using the HTML validator, confirm that Listing 1.6 is valid HTML.

2. Remove **</title>** from **index.html** as shown in Listing 1.8 and verify that it breaks the page and that all you see is a blank screen. This underscores the importance of closing your tags! Confirm using the HTML validator that the resulting code fails validation.

3. By pasting the contents of Listing 1.9 into **index.html**, confirm that the browser ignores the extra whitespace (including newlines) in the mailing address.

4. By adding the break tag **
** to the end of each of the first two lines of the address, you can obtain a nicely formatted address.

Listing 1.8: The index page with a missing closing tag.
index.html

```
<!DOCTYPE html>
<html>
  <head>
    <title>Page Title
    <meta charset="utf-8">
  </head>
  <body>
  </body>
</html>
```

Listing 1.9: An unformatted address.

```
<!DOCTYPE html>
<html>
  <head>
    <title>Who am I?</title>
    <meta charset="utf-8">
  </head>
  <body>
    Jean Valjean
    55 Rue Plumet
    Amonate, VA 24601
  </body>
</html>
```

CHAPTER 2
Filling in the Index Page

Now that we've created and deployed a valid HTML page, it's time to start filling in the sample website. We'll begin by scoping out the structure of our index page while adding a more normal-sized paragraph (Section 2.1). We'll then format the resulting text (Section 2.2) while adding links (Section 2.3) and images (Section 2.4). Starting in Chapter 3, we'll add two more pages to go along with our index page, introducing several more important HTML tags along the way.

2.1 Headings

As noted in Section 1.3, our main index page will include some information about Learn Enough to Be Dangerous, so we'll start by updating the **title** tag contents with a new title. Then, we'll replace the paragraph in the HTML **body** with several *headings*, constituting an outline of our document. The results appear in Listing 2.1.

Listing 2.1: Scoping out our index page with headings.
index.html

```
<!DOCTYPE html>
<html>
  <head>
    <title>Learn Enough to Be Dangerous</title>
    <meta charset="utf-8">
  </head>
  <body>

    <h1>The Learn Enough Story</h1>
```

```
    <h2>Background</h2>

    <h2>Founders</h2>

    <h3>Michael Hartl</h3>

    <h3>Lee Donahoe</h3>

    <h3>Nick Merwin</h3>

  </body>
</html>
```

Listing 2.1 shows how to use the HTML header tags **h1**, **h2**, and **h3**, which represent three levels of headings. In this case, the top-level **h1** heading contains the main subject of the page:

```
<h1>The Learn Enough Story</h1>
```

The next two headings indicate additional subjects—in this case, some background on the company and some details about the founders:

```
<h2>Background</h2>

<h2>Founders</h2>
```

Because these subjects are subsidiary to the main story, they use the second-level heading **h2**. Finally, Listing 2.1 uses the third-level heading **h3** to list the three Learn Enough founders:

```
<h3>Michael Hartl</h3>

<h3>Lee Donahoe</h3>

<h3>Nick Merwin</h3>
```

As you might guess, most browsers render the top-level **h1** heading in a large font size, with **h2** and **h3** getting progressively smaller. (Figuring out how many heading sizes HTML supports is left as an exercise (Section 2.1.1).) The result appears in Figure 2.1.

Figure 2.1: The initial headings for the index page.

2.1.1 Exercise

1. Listing 2.1 uses headings **h1** down to **h3**. By experimenting directly in **index.html**, determine how many levels of headings HTML supports.

2.2 Text Formatting

Having added the headings to block out the structure of our document, let's now add an introductory paragraph describing the subject of the page. Unlike our previous one-line paragraph (Listing 1.4), this paragraph will include several lines, as well as requiring some text formatting (this section) and a link (Section 2.3).

The paragraph itself appears in Listing 2.2, where the vertical dots indicate omitted content (just so we don't have to include all the tags in every code listing).

Listing 2.2: Adding a paragraph.
index.html

```
<h1>The Learn Enough Story</h1>

<p>
  Learn Enough to Be Dangerous is a leader in the movement to teach
  technical sophistication, the seemingly magical ability to take
  command of your computer and get it to do your bidding. This includes
  everything from command lines and coding to guessing keyboard shortcuts,
```

```
    Googling error messages, and knowing when to just reboot the darn thing.
    We believe there are at least a billion people who can benefit from
    learning technical sophistication, probably more. To join our
    movement, sign up for our official email list now.
</p>
    .
    .
    .
```

Note that the content is now indented inside the **p** tag. As discussed in Box 1.4, this makes the structure easier to see without affecting the appearance of the page.

It's also worth noting that Listing 2.2 includes newlines at the end of each line, but this is mainly so that the paragraph contents fit within the constraints of a book. As seen in Figure 2.2, these newlines don't have any effect on the display, and in real life it's probably more common to have the content be all on one line, and simply enable word wrap (called "soft wrap" in Atom), as described in Section 6.2 of *Learn Enough Developer Tools to Be Dangerous*. This is what we recommend you do if you type the contents of Listing 2.2 in by hand.

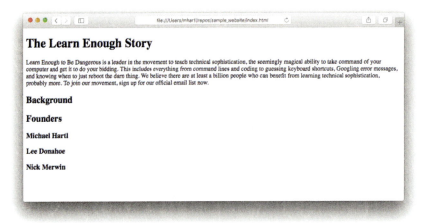

Figure 2.2: Adding a paragraph.

2.2.1 Emphasized Text

The paragraph in Listing 2.2 has the right content, but it also introduces the new term *technical sophistication*, and it's a common typesetting convention to *emphasize*

such terms using italics. As mentioned briefly in Box 1.2, we can accomplish this
using the **em** tag, like this:

```
<em>technical sophistication</em>
```

Applying this idea to Listing 2.2 gives the result shown in Listing 2.3.

Listing 2.3: Emphasized text.
index.html

```
<h1>The Learn Enough Story</h1>

<p>
  Learn Enough to Be Dangerous is a leader in the movement to teach
  <em>technical sophistication</em>, the seemingly magical ability to take
  command of your computer and get it to do your bidding. This includes
  everything from command lines and coding to guessing keyboard shortcuts,
  Googling error messages, and knowing when to just reboot the darn thing.
  We believe there are at least a billion people who can benefit from
  learning technical sophistication, probably more. To join our
  movement, sign up for our official email list now.
</p>
```

We can confirm that this worked by refreshing the browser, which shows that *technical
sophistication* is properly emphasized (Figure 2.3).

Figure 2.3: Emphasized text.

2.2.2 Strong Text

As we saw briefly in Section 1.2, another possibility for drawing attention to particular text is to make it **strong** using the **strong** tag, which most browsers render as boldface text. In this case, we'd like to indicate the strength of our belief that **at least a billion people** can potentially benefit from learning technical sophistication, which we can do like this:

```
<strong>at least a billion people</strong>
```

Applying this idea to Listing 2.3 gives Listing 2.4.

Listing 2.4: Strong text.
index.html

```
<p>
  Learn Enough to Be Dangerous is a leader in the movement to teach
  <em>technical sophistication</em>, the seemingly magical ability to take
  command of your computer and get it to do your bidding. This includes
  everything from command lines and coding to guessing keyboard shortcuts,
  Googling error messages, and knowing when to just reboot the darn thing.
  We believe there are <strong>at least a billion people</strong> who
  can benefit from learning technical sophistication, probably more. To
  join our movement, sign up for our official email list now.
</p>
```

Refreshing the browser confirms that the text is now set in bold (Figure 2.4).

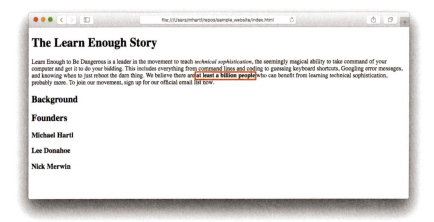

Figure 2.4: Strong text.

2.2.3 Exercises

1. Add the paragraph shown in Listing 2.5 under **founders**, then make the text **at least a billion people** bold.

2. What happens if you nest the **em** and `strong` tags? Is it possible to make something both italic **and** bold?

Listing 2.5: A paragraph with something to be made stronger.
index.html

```
<h2>Founders</h2>

<p>
   Learn Enough to Be Dangerous was founded in 2015 by Michael Hartl, Lee
   Donahoe, and Nick Merwin. We believe that the kind of technical
   sophistication taught by the Learn Enough tutorials can benefit
   at least a billion people, and probably more.
</p>
```

2.3 Links

As mentioned in Section 1.2, much of the point of the Web is hypertext, with hyperlinks that let us move from one page to the next. The way to make such hyperlinks (or *links* for short) is with the HTML anchor tag **a**. (Why isn't it called `link`? We don't know, but at least **a** is short.)

In reading the paragraph from Listing 2.2, you may have noticed that the line

```
sign up for our official email list now
```

is practically begging for a link to a place where people can actually sign up for the email list. The exact text to use for the link is the subject of some debate, with some holding that links should be nouns and others preferring to link a call to action if possible. We take a pragmatic approach, linking based on what seems most natural. In this case, we'll go with linking the text "sign up for our official email list", like this:

```
<a href="https://learnenough.com/email">sign up for our official email list</a>
```

This contains our first example of an *attribute*, which is a bit of text inside an HTML tag that supplies extra information about how to process it. In this case, the attribute is **href**, for "hypertext reference", and the value is the URL for the Learn Enough email list sign-up form.

Adding the email list link to the paragraph from Listing 2.4 gives Listing 2.6. Note how the text of the link breaks across two lines (something we saw before in Listing 1.1). Because HTML is insensitive to whitespace, this is effectively the same as having it all on one line.

Listing 2.6: Adding a link.

```
<p>
  Learn Enough to Be Dangerous is a leader in the movement to teach <em>
  technical sophistication</em>, the seemingly magical ability to take
  command of your computer and get it to do your bidding. This includes
  everything from command lines and coding to guessing keyboard shortcuts,
  Googling error messages, and knowing when to just reboot the darn thing.
  We believe there are <strong>at least a billion people</strong> who
  can benefit from learning technical sophistication, probably more. To
  join our movement, <a href="https://learnenough.com/email">sign
  up for our official email list</a> now.
</p>
```

The result of Listing 2.6 appears in Figure 2.5.

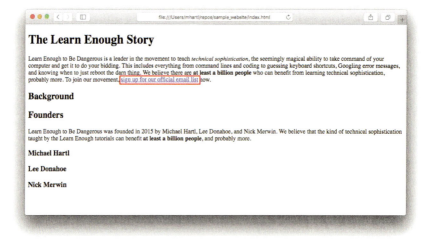

Figure 2.5: The result of adding a link.

Now that we know how to make links, we're ready to add a paragraph on the background of Learn Enough to Be Dangerous, which is rich with links and includes further examples of the text-formatting tags shown in Section 2.2. The resulting paragraph, shown in Listing 2.7, should be placed under the second-level heading from Listing 2.1. Because it contains so many good examples of the tags we've covered so far, we recommend you type it in by hand.

Listing 2.7: Adding a paragraph using several useful tags.

```
<h2>Background</h2>

<p>
  Learn Enough to Be Dangerous is an outgrowth of the
  <a href="https://railstutorial.org/">Ruby on Rails Tutorial</a> and the
  <a href="https://www.softcover.io/">Softcover publishing platform</a>.
  This page is part of the sample site for
  <a href="https://www.learnenough.com/html"><em>Learn Enough HTML to
  Be Dangerous</em></a>, which teaches the basics of
  <strong>H</strong>yper<strong>T</strong>ext <strong>M</strong>arkup
  <strong>L</strong>anguage, the universal language of the World Wide Web.
  Other related tutorials can be found at
  <a href="https://www.learnenough.com/">learnenough.com</a>.
</p>
```

It's worth noting that Listing 2.7 contains an example of tag nesting, in the form of the link to the present tutorial:

```
<a href="..."><em>Learn Enough HTML to Be Dangerous</em></a>
```

As you might expect, this produces a link to emphasized text, as shown in Figure 2.6. You might also note that some of the links in Figure 2.6 are a different color, which is an indication that the links have been followed. (This is the default behavior for link colors, but it can be overridden by CSS, as discussed in *Learn Enough CSS & Layout to Be Dangerous* (https://www.learnenough.com/css-and-layout) and mentioned briefly in Section 4.6.1.)

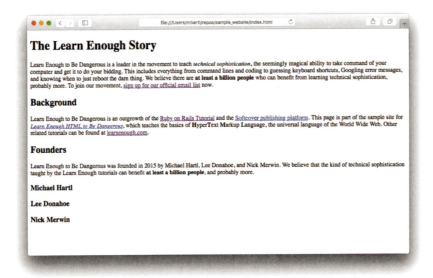

Figure 2.6: Adding a paragraph with formatting and links.

2.3.1 Exercises

1. Using the content shown in Listing 2.8, add short founder bios to the index page.

2. Now add Twitter follow links as shown in Listing 2.9. Does the content appear as shown in Figure 2.7?

3. It's sometimes convenient for external links (like those in the previous exercise) to open in a new browser tab. To do this, add the attribute `target="_blank"` to each of the Twitter links from Listing 2.9. (For technical reasons, it's important to add the rather obscure `rel="noopener"` as well.) Does clicking on one of the links open in a new tab, as shown in Figure 2.7?

Listing 2.8: Adding short founder biographies.
index.html

```
<h3>Michael Hartl</h3>

<p>
  Michael is the creator of the <a href="https://www.railstutorial.org/">
  Ruby on Rails Tutorial</a> and principal author of the
  <a href="https://www.learnenough.com/">Learn Enough to Be Dangerous</a>
  introductory sequence. He is an advanced student of
  <a href="https://www.kravmaga.com/">Krav Maga</a> and has a three-step
  plan for world domination. Rumors that he's secretly a supervillain
  are slightly exaggerated.
</p>

<h3>Lee Donahoe</h3>

<p>
  When he's not literally swimming with sharks or hunting powder stashes
  on his snowboard, you can find Lee in front of his computer designing
  interfaces, doing front-end development, or writing some of the
  interface-related Learn Enough tutorials.
</p>

<h3>Nick Merwin</h3>

<p>
  You may have seen him shredding guitar live with Capital Cities on Jimmy
  Kimmel, Conan, or The Ellen Show, but rest assured Nick is a true nerd
  at heart. He's just as happy shredding well-spec'd lines of code from a
  tour bus as he is from his kitchen table.
</p>
```

Listing 2.9: Adding Twitter links to the bios.
index.html

```
<h3>Michael Hartl</h3>
  .
  .
  .
<p>
  You should follow Michael on Twitter
  <a href="https://twitter.com/mhartl">here</a>.
</p>
```

```
<h3>Lee Donahoe</h3>

.

.

.

<p>
  You should follow Lee on Twitter
  <a href="https://twitter.com/leedonahoe">here</a>.
</p>

<h3>Nick Merwin</h3>

.

.

.

<p>
  You should follow Nick on Twitter
  <a href="https://twitter.com/nickmerwin">here</a>.
</p>
```

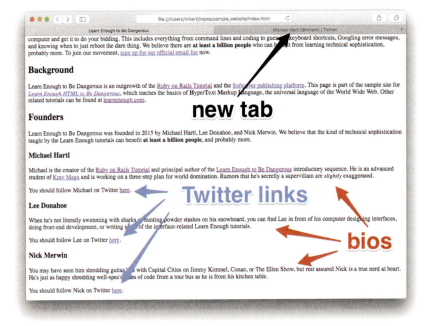

Figure 2.7: The index page after the completion of the exercises.

2.4   Adding Images

At this point, our index page is coming into shape, but it's still missing a critical feature: What would a website be without images (of cats!)? Fortunately, adding images is similar to adding links, although there is an important difference in the structure of the tags. Recall from Section 2.3 that anchor tags take the form

```
<a href="https://example.com/">Example site</a>
```

We can include images in a similar way using the **img** tag, with a source attribute **src** and an alternate attribute **alt**:

```
<img src="images/kitten.jpg" alt="An adorable kitten">
```

Here **src** has a path to the image (either on the filesystem or on the Web), while **alt** lets developers add a bit of alternate text that describes the image in words. On some browsers, this text will display if the user's browser has a problem loading the image, but more importantly, it will be read aloud (or even presented as braille) by screen readers used by the visually impaired and is required by the HTML standard.[1]

The important difference mentioned above is that the **img** tag *doesn't* look like a typical tag, with content inside open and closing tags (Figure 1.4). If it did, it would look like this:

```
<img src="…" alt="…">content</img>
```

Instead, the **img** tag has no content and no closing tag:

```
<img src="…" alt="…">
```

That final **>** is all that's needed to close an **img** tag—like the **meta** tag discussed in Section 1.5, **img** is a void element (self-closing tag). A second variant uses **/>** at the end, like this:

```
<img src="…" alt="…" />
```

---

1. The **alt** attribute is also useful to tell the search engine "spider" programs that crawl the Web which things appear in the image.

Figure 2.8: The likely inspiration for the creation of the World Wide Web.

This syntax is designed to conform to XML, a markup language related to HTML, but using **/>** is not required in HTML5. We mention it mainly because you will still sometimes run across the XML-style syntax in other people's markup, and it's important to know that the two styles are exactly equivalent.

Because the World Wide Web was apparently invented to share pictures of furry felines, we'll add an image of an adorable kitten to our sample index page, as shown in Figure 2.8.[2]

In order to link the kitten image, we could link directly to the source of Figure 2.8 from the live Web, like this:

```
<img src="https://example.com/images/kitten.jpg" alt="An adorable kitten">
```

This practice, called *hotlinking*, is generally considered bad form, for reasons we'll explain in Section 2.4.1. Instead, we'll copy the image to the local computer, which will then be uploaded automatically when we deploy to GitHub Pages.

To do this, first create a directory called **images**:

```
$ mkdir images
```

2. Image courtesy of halfmax.ru/Shutterstock.

Creating a separate **images** directory isn't strictly necessary, but it's useful for keeping our main project directory tidy. Next, download the image to the local disk using **curl**:[3]

```
$ curl -o images/kitten.jpg -L https://cdn.learnenough.com/kitten.jpg
```

Once the image is available on our local disk, we can use its location as the value of the **src** attribute. Because the image is part of the same web project as **index.html**, we can use the *relative path* to the image, like this:

```
<img src="images/kitten.jpg" alt="An adorable kitten">
```

The **src** attribute **images/kitten.jpg** will automatically be interpreted as the correct full path to the file, which locally might be

```
file:///Users/mhartl/repos/sample_website/images/kitten.jpg
```

and on the server will be something like

```
https://learnenough.github.io/sample_website/images/kitten.jpg
```

While we're at it, we'll add a paragraph giving some context about the creation of the World Wide Web (including a correction to the wildly inaccurate claims of its feline origins). The result appears in Listing 2.10.

Listing 2.10: An image, with a paragraph about the original web developer.
index.html

```
<h1>The Learn Enough Story</h1>
  .
  .
  .
<p>
  HTML was created by the original "web developer", computer scientist
  <a href="https://en.wikipedia.org/wiki/Tim_Berners-Lee">Tim
  Berners-Lee</a>. It's not true that Sir Tim invented HTML in order to
  share pictures of his cat, but it would be cool if it were.
</p>

<img src="images/kitten.jpg" alt="An adorable kitten">
```

---

3. The **curl** command is covered in Section 3.1 of *Learn Enough Developer Tools to Be Dangerous.*

```
<h2>Background</h2>
 .
 .
 .
```

After adding the contents of Listing 2.10 to **index.html**, the sample index page should look something like Figure 2.9.

Figure 2.9: An awww-bligatory kitten image.

2.4.1 Hotlinking

We mentioned above that it's possible to link directly to images on the Web, a practice called *hotlinking*. The way to do this is to use a fully qualified URL as the **src** parameter, like this:

```
<img src="https://example.com/images/example.jpg" alt="A nonexistent example">
```

Hotlinking isn't usually a good practice, mainly because the image has to be at that exact spot on that exact site or it will not load, putting you at the mercy of the site's maintainer. The person who runs the site can also be charged for the bandwidth used to serve the image, so hotlinking is considered inconsiderate as well. For these reasons, we generally recommend using local images for most applications.[4]

There are some important exceptions to the hotlinking rule, though, including an application known as *Gravatar*, which stands for "globally recognized avatar". Gravatar allows you to associate standard images with particular email addresses and is used to display profile pictures on a large variety of websites, including GitHub and WordPress.[5] Gravatar images are specifically designed for hotlinking, so in this case the practice is actually encouraged. The image could still change, but here it's not a bug, it's a feature,[6] because it gives the user control over their preferred profile image—if they update their picture, the change will automatically propagate to every site using the right Gravatar URL.

Gravatar URLs include a long string of hexadecimal digits (base 16, meaning 0–9 and a–f), like this:

```
https://gravatar.com/avatar/ffda7d145b83c4b118f982401f962ca6
```

Here **ffda7d145b83c4b118f982401f962ca6** is a unique string based on the email address associated with the Gravatar.[7] Gravatar URLs also support *query parameters*, which are additional pieces of information that come after the main URL, like **?s=150**:

```
https://gravatar.com/avatar/ffda7d145b83c4b118f982401f962ca6?s=150
```

---

4. Here "local" means "local to the site" (which might be a remote server like GitHub Pages), not necessarily local to your development machine.

5. Indeed, Gravatar was originally developed by GitHub cofounder Tom Preston-Werner, and was later acquired by Automattic, the parent company of WordPress.

6. This reference is explained in Box 2.1 of *Learn Enough Developer Tools to Be Dangerous*.

7. It's calculated using something called the MD5 message-digest algorithm, which is covered in the *Ruby on Rails Tutorial*.

Query parameters come after a question mark **?**, in this case **s=150**, which consists of a *key* **s** and a *value* **150**.[8] As you might be able to guess, **s** stands for "size", and in this case the query parameter **s=150** sets the Gravatar size to 150 pixels. (By design, Gravatars are square, so a single parameter specifies the size uniquely.)

Using our newfound Gravatar knowledge, let's add avatar images to our index page under each of the Learn Enough to Be Dangerous founder bios (as added in Listing 2.8 from the exercises in Section 2.3.1). In a typical dynamic web application, such as that developed in the *Ruby on Rails Tutorial* (https://www.railstutorial.org/), these URLs would be calculated on the fly (https://www.railstutorial.org/book/sign_up#sec-a_gravatar_image) based on the users' email addresses, but for convenience we'll supply you with the proper URLs. The result appears in Listing 2.11. (We've removed the leading indentation in Listing 2.11 so that the URLs fit, but in your **index.html** we suggest you keep the indentation as before.)

Listing 2.11: Adding Gravatar hotlinks for the Learn Enough founders.

```
<h3>Michael Hartl</h3>

<img src="https://gravatar.com/avatar/ffda7d145b83c4b118f982401f962ca6?s=150"
    alt="Michael Hartl">
.
.
.

<h3>Lee Donahoe</h3>

<img src="https://gravatar.com/avatar/b65522a6f3a6899705d119d7aa232a6d?s=150"
    alt="Lee Donahoe">
.
.
.

<h3>Nick Merwin</h3>

<img src="https://gravatar.com/avatar/e2d6ce2ba5c1b6d674ae8ff2b3b45d23?s=150"
    alt="Nick Merwin">
.
.
.
```

8. Multiple query parameters are separated by the ampersand symbol **&**, as in **https://example.com?foo=1&bar=2**. If you start looking at the URLs in the address bar of your browser, you'll see these query parameters everywhere.

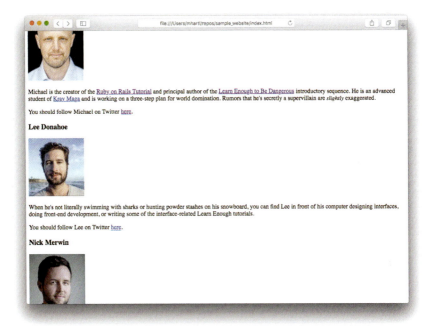

Figure 2.10: Adding Gravatar images.

The result of adding the contents of Listing 2.11 should look something like Figure 2.10, although your page may not match exactly (Section 2.4.2).

With that, our sample website's index page has (nearly) taken its final form, so now is a good time to commit the changes and push to the live server at GitHub Pages:

```
$ git add -A
$ git commit -m "Add content and some images"
$ git push
```

The result should look something like Figure 2.11.

Figure 2.11: The sample index page on the live Web.

2.4.2 Exercises

1. Why might the images shown in Figure 2.10 not match your results exactly? *Hint*: It's not a bug, it's a feature.

2. Under the first paragraph on **index.html**, let's add a link to the Learn Enough Twitter account. First, download the Twitter logo, as shown in Listing 2.12. Then, add a link to both the text and the logo image, as shown in Listing 2.13. Be sure to replace **FILL_IN** with the right path to the image. Note that Listing 2.13 introduces *inline styling*, which is the subject of Chapter 4. *Extra credit*: Follow Learn Enough on Twitter here (https://twitter.com/learnenough).

Listing 2.12: Downloading the Twitter logo.

```
$ curl -o images/small_twitter_logo.png \
>      -L https://cdn.learnenough.com/small_twitter_logo.png
```

Note that the backslash \ should be typed, but your shell will include **>** automatically, so don't just copy and paste the whole thing.

Listing 2.13: Adding links to the Learn Enough Twitter account.
index.html

```
    .
    .
    .
  for our official email list</a> now.
</p>

<p>
  <a href="https://twitter.com/learnenough" target="_blank"
  rel="noopener" style="text-decoration: none;">
    <img src="FILL_IN">
  </a>
  You should follow Learn Enough on Twitter
  <a href="https://twitter.com/learnenough"
     target="_blank" rel="noopener">here</a>.
</p>
```

CHAPTER 3
More Pages, More Tags

Having completed a full index page in Chapter 2 (and having learned a bunch of HTML tags along the way), the time has now come to add a couple more pages to our website. This will give us a chance to learn some more useful HTML tags, while discovering some of the limitations of our purely hand-edited approach.

The first new addition will be a (very meta) page on HTML tags themselves, which will give us a chance to reinforce the preceding material as we build it. The second page includes a lighthearted report on *Moby-Dick* which we will style in Chapter 4.

3.1 An HTML Page About HTML

We'll start by adding a reference page to collect some of the HTML tags we've learned about so far. This means creating a new file, which we can do by creating a new tab (typically with ⌘N) and then saving it as **tags.html**. Another method, and a personal favorite of ours, is to run **touch tags.html** at the command line and then use ⌘P to open it in the editor.

Once you've created **tags.html**, by whatever method, fill it with the contents of Listing 3.1.

Listing 3.1: Adding the beginning of a page on HTML tags.

tags.html

```
<!DOCTYPE html>
<html>
  <head>
    <title>HTML Tags</title>
    <meta charset="utf-8">
  </head>
  <body>

    <h1>Important HTML tags</h1>

    <img src="images/astronaut_tagged.jpg" alt="Tagged Astronaut">

    <p>
      This page is designed as a quick reference for some of the common tags
      covered in <a href="https://learnenough.com/html"><em>Learn
      Enough HTML to Be Dangerous</em></a>. In the process of making it, we'll
      learn how to make HTML <em>tables</em> via <code>table</code> and
      related tags.
    </p>

    <p>
      The tables below don't include all HTML tags, but they do list many of
      the most important ones.
    </p>

  </body>
</html>
```

Note that Listing 3.1 involves repeating the HTML skeleton from Listing 1.6, which is an inconvenient duplication of effort. It also becomes increasingly annoying as the number of pages in a site grows, especially if (as is often the case) we need to make changes to the **head** of the document. We'll deal with this issue the Right Way™ in Part II (using a so-called *templating system*), but for now we'll just live with the annoyance.

Listing 3.1 introduces one new tag, the minor but occasionally useful **code** tag:

```
<code>table</code>
```

Designed to display pieces of markup or source code, the **code** tag is rendered by most browsers in a monospace font, `like this`. (In a monospace font, all letters have the same width, which is especially convenient when lining up formatted code.)

The page defined by Listing 3.1 won't yet render as intended because of the **img** tag, which currently references a nonexistent image. To fix this, download the image to the local disk:

```
$ curl -o images/astronaut_tagged.jpg \
>    -L https://cdn.learnenough.com/astronaut_tagged.jpg
```

Note that the backslash **** should be typed, but your shell will include **>** automatically, so don't just copy and paste the whole thing. The result appears in Figure 3.1[1].

Figure 3.1: The beginning of an HTML tags page.

3.1.1 Exercises

1. Does the HTML in Listing 3.1 validate?

2. Let's practice linking images again. By following the model in Listing 2.12, link the image in Listing 3.1 to NASA's website, https://www.nasa.gov.

---

1. Astronaut image courtesy of svetlichniy_igor/Shutterstock; price tag image courtesy of Pretty Vectors/Shutterstock.

3.2 Tables

Now that we've got a basic page set up, we'll make a list of some of the tags we've learned about so far. Our plan is to indicate the exact HTML code for the tag, its name, and its purpose. The result is a *table* of information, so to display it we'll use the HTML **table** tag. Because HTML tags divide broadly into *inline elements* and *block elements* (Box 3.1), we'll make a separate table for each type of tag.

Box 3.1: Inline vs. Block

All of the elements on a page of HTML either flow with the text around them or interrupt the flow by creating a box of content that is separate from the other content on the page. The first category of tags is known as *inline*; the second category is called *block* (Figure 3.2).

All of the elements that modify text, such as <strong> and <em>, are inline elements, which makes sense since we wouldn't want text to jump to a new line every time we made it bold or italic. Other common inline elements include links and (perhaps surprisingly) images. Inline elements take up only as much width on the page as is necessary to contain the content inside the tags—you can think of inline elements as being shrink-wrapped around the content inside them.

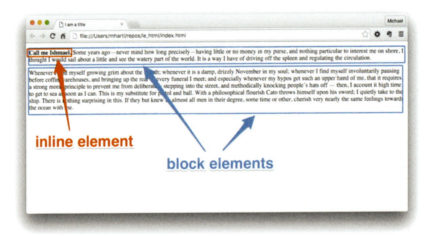

Figure 3.2: Inline vs. block elements.

In contrast, block elements always start on a new line, as if there is a line break in front of them, so one of their main purposes is to divide the page's text into different presentational groups, such as paragraphs or lists. Unlike inline elements, block elements bound the full width of the page, like an inflexible cardboard box.

3.2.1   Block Elements

A table is defined by opening and closing **table** tags, with each *table row* defined by the **tr** tag. Typically, the first row includes labels for the table's columns via *table headers*, defined by the **th** tag, as shown in Listing 3.2.

Listing 3.2: Defining a table with headers.
tags.html

```
<p>
  The tables below don't include all HTML tags, but they do list many of
  the most important ones.
</p>

<h2>Block Elements</h2>

<table>
  <tr>
    <th>Tag</th>
    <th>Name</th>
    <th>Purpose</th>
  </tr>
</table>
```

Because the natural layout inside a file is vertical, whereas the display is horizontal, it can be challenging to mentally map table contents to the visual result, but it gets easier with practice.

After optionally defining the table headers, tables generally consist of a series of *table data* cells defined by the **td** tag. We can get started with the content of the table by adding a row for the heading tags first introduced in Section 2.1. The result (which incidentally solves the exercise from Section 2.1.1) appears in Listing 3.3.

Listing 3.3: Adding a row of data.
tags.html

```
<table>
  <tr>
    <th>Tag</th>
    <th>Name</th>
    <th>Purpose</th>
  </tr>
  <tr>
    <td><code>h1</code>&ndash;<code>h6</code></td>
    <td>headings</td>
    <td>include a heading (levels 1&ndash;6)</td>
  </tr>
</table>
```

Listing 3.3 uses the **code** tag we saw in Listing 3.1, and also introduces **–**, which is a "character entity reference" for an *en dash* (a dash roughly the width of the letter "n", like this: –). Because our HTML document uses the **utf-8** character set (Listing 1.6), we could also use a literal en dash –, but the entity reference is common, and it's good to know how to use both.

This is a lot to handle at once, which makes it good practice for learning to visualize the result of HTML markup. Once you have a guess in your mind's eye, you can refresh your browser to see the result (Figure 3.3).

Figure 3.3: Table headers and a row of table data.

We've now seen the most important table tags, so we're ready to fill in the table with rows for the other block-level tags we've seen so far. These include **p** and the table tags themselves.[2] The result appears in Listing 3.4.[3]

Listing 3.4: A more complete table of HTML block elements.
tags.html

```
<h2>Block Elements</h2>

<table>
  <tr>
    <th>Tag</th>
    <th>Name</th>
    <th>Purpose</th>
  </tr>
  <tr>
    <td><code>h1</code>&ndash;<code>h6</code></td>
    <td>headings</td>
    <td>include a heading (levels 1&ndash;6)</td>
  </tr>
  <tr>
    <td><code>p</code></td>
    <td>paragraph</td>
    <td>include a paragraph of text</td>
  </tr>
  <tr>
    <td><code>table</code></td>
    <td>table</td>
    <td>include a table</td>
  </tr>
  <tr>
    <td><code>tr</code></td>
    <td>table row</td>
    <td>include a row of data</td>
  </tr>
  <tr>
    <td><code>th</code></td>
    <td>table header</td>
    <td>make a table header</td>
  </tr>
  <tr>
    <td><code>td</code></td>
```

---

2. Technically, the **td** tag is more like an "inline block", but this distinction isn't important for our purposes.

3. Some code listings include yellow highlights for important lines, but we'll avoid the "wall of yellow" by omitting the highlights when there are as many new lines as there are in listings like Listing 3.4.

```
      <td>table data</td>
      <td>include a table data cell</td>
   </tr>
</table>
```

There are a lot of new rows in Listing 3.4, so you can copy and paste if you want, but you'll learn more by typing in the tags by hand. (You'll find that it can be quite cumbersome, which is one reason many real-world tables are generated from databases using programming languages like Ruby.) The result appears in Figure 3.4.

Figure 3.4: A table for some HTML block elements.

By the way, you might notice in Figure 3.4 that the spacing around the table data cells isn't ideal. This is exactly the kind of detail that is handled by Cascading Style Sheets (Part II).

3.2.2 Inline Elements

Now that we know how to make a basic table, we're ready to add a new table of inline elements as well. Because inline elements by definition don't start a new line, it's easy to include examples of the tags along with their definitions. For instance, we can include a working example of the **em** tag, as shown in Listing 3.5.

Listing 3.5: A start at a table of inline tags.
tags.html

```
  .
  .
  .

  <h2>Inline Elements</h2>

  <table>
    <tr>
      <th>Tag</th>
      <th>Name</th>
      <th>Purpose</th>
      <th>Example</th>
      <th>Result</th>
    </tr>
    <tr>
      <td><code>em</code></td>
      <td>emphasized</td>
      <td>make emphasized text</td>
      <td><code>&lt;em&gt;technical sophistication&lt;/em&gt;</code></td>
      <td><em>technical sophistication</em></td>
    </tr>
  </table>
```

Listing 3.5 introduces the solution to the tricky problem of displaying literal angle brackets, which arranges for the browser to display, e.g., technical sophistication rather than *technical sophistication*. The way to do it is by "escaping out" < and > with the HTML character entities **<** ("less than") and **>** ("greater than"). The result appears in Figure 3.5.

Some other inline elements we've encountered so far are **strong**, **a**, **img**, and **code**. Adding them to the table in Listing 3.5 is left as an exercise. Either before or

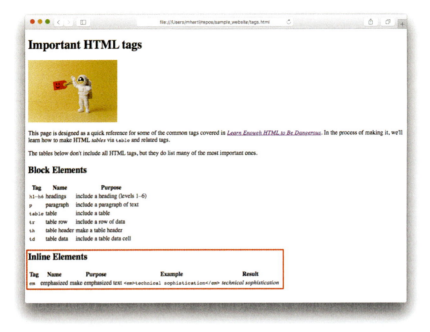

Figure 3.5: A good start at a table of inline elements.

after doing that exercise, we suggest adding and committing the changes and then pushing up to GitHub Pages:

```
$ git add -A
$ git commit -m "Add a tags page"
$ git push
```

3.2.3 Exercises

1. Follow the template in Listing 3.6 to add information on the **strong**, **a**, and **img** tags. Why does the **img** tag example use the Bitly link shortener?

2. Add an additional row for the **code** tag. Does the page validate?

Listing 3.6: Template for adding **strong**, **a**, and **img** tags.
tags.html

```
<h2>Inline Elements</h2>

<table>
  <tr>
    <th>Tag</th>
    <th>Name</th>
    <th>Purpose</th>
    <th>Example</th>
    <th>Result</th>
  </tr>
  <tr>
    <td><code>em</code></td>
    <td>emphasized</td>
    <td>make emphasized text</td>
    <td><code>&lt;em&gt;technical sophistication&lt;/em&gt;</code></td>
    <td><em>technical sophistication</em></td>
  </tr>
  <tr>
    <td><code>strong</code></td>
    <td>strong</td>
    <td>make strong text</td>
    <td>
      <code>&lt;strong&gt;at least a billion people&lt;/strong&gt;</code>
    </td>
    <td>FILL_IN</td>
  </tr>
  <tr>
    <td><code>a</code></td>
    <td>anchor</td>
    <td>make hyperlink</td>
    <td>
      <code>
        &lt;a href="https://learnenough.com/"&gt;Learn Enough&lt;/a&gt;
      </code>
    </td>
    <td>FILL_IN</td>
  </tr>
  <tr>
    <td><code>img</code></td>
    <td>image</td>
    <td>include an image</td>
    <td>
      <code>
        &lt;img src="https://bit.ly/1MZAFuQ" alt="Michael Hartl"&gt;
      </code>
    </td>
    <td>FILL_IN</td>
  </tr>
</table>
```

3.3 Divs and Spans

Having created a new page for our HTML table experiment, we're now ready to make a third page for our sample website. We'll add some initial content while blocking out the structure with three new tags: **header**, **div** (for *division*), and **span**. These tags have little to no impact on the page appearance, but they help us organize the page and its contents into logical units. All three tags, and especially **div**s and **span**s, are heavily used when styling web pages using CSS (Part II). We'll get a preview of this practice when applying inline styles in Chapter 4.

The page itself will take the form of a mock book report on the classic American whaling novel *Moby-Dick* (also styled as *Moby Dick*). As we'll see in Chapter 4, this content will especially lend itself to styling.

The first thing we should do is create a file called **moby_dick.html**. Then, because it's never wrong to include pictures of animals (even non-cats!) on web pages, we'll include a picture of sperm whales (Figure 3.6)[4] to go along with our report, and we'll add an image for the book's cover.

In order to include the images on our web page, we need to download them to the local machine (as we did with the kitten image in Section 2.4):

```
$ curl -o images/sperm_whales.jpg \
>       -L https://cdn.learnenough.com/sperm_whales.jpg
$ curl -o images/moby_dick.png -L https://cdn.learnenough.com/moby_dick.png
```

 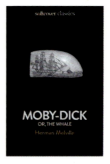

Figure 3.6: A pod of sperm whales, and the cover image for *Moby-Dick*.

---

4. Image courtesy of willyambradberry/123RF.

The initial book report page is fairly long, which makes it an excellent exercise in reading and writing HTML. The result, which highlights a few especially important lines, appears in Listing 3.7. Note especially the use of **target="_blank" rel="noopener"** (introduced briefly in Section 2.3.1), which arranges to open links in a new browser tab.[5] There is also one intentional error in Listing 3.7; catching and fixing it is left as an exercise (Section 3.3.1).

Listing 3.7: The initial *Moby-Dick* book report.
`moby_dick.html`

```html
<!DOCTYPE html>
<html>
  <head>
    <title>Moby Dick</title>
    <meta charset="utf-8">
  </head>
  <body>

    <!-- much here to be styled, will do so in last section -->
    <header>
      <h1>A Softcover Book Report</h1>
      <h2>Moby-Dick (or, The Whale)</h2>
    </header>

    <div>
      <p>
        The <a href="https://www.softcover.io/">Softcover</a> publishing platform
        was designed mainly for ebooks like the
        <a href="https://railstutorial.org/book"><em>Ruby on Rails Tutorial</em></a>
        book</a> and <a href="https://learnenough.com/html"><em>Learn Enough
        HTML to Be Dangerous</em></a>, but it's also good for making more
        traditional books, such as the novel <em>Moby-Dick</em> by Herman
        Melville (sometimes written as <em>Moby Dick</em>). We present below a
        short and affectionately irreverent book report on this classic of
        American literature.
      </p>
    </div>

    <a href="https://commons.wikimedia.org/wiki/File:Sperm_whale_pod.jpg">
      <img src="images/sperm_whales.jpg">
    </a>
```

---

5. Or a new browser window. The exact behavior depends on the user's browser settings.

```
<div>

    <h3>Moby-Dick: A classic tale of the sea</h3>

    <a href="https://www.softcover.io/read/6070fb03/moby-dick"
       target="_blank" rel="noopener">
     <img src="images/moby_dick.png" alt="Moby Dick">
    </a>

    <p>
     <a href="https://www.softcover.io/read/6070fb03/moby-dick"
        target="_blank" rel="noopener">
      <em>Moby-Dick</em></a>
      by Herman Melville begins with these immortal words:
    </p>

    <blockquote>
       <p>
          <span>Call me Ishmael.</span> Some years ago-never mind how long
          precisely-having little or no money in my purse, and nothing
          particular to interest me on shore, I thought I would sail about a
          little and see the watery part of the world. It is a way I have of
          driving off the spleen and regulating the circulation.
        </p>
      </blockquote>

    <p>
      After driving off his spleen (which <em>can't</em> be good for you),
      Ishmael then goes on in much the same vein for approximately one
      jillion pages. The only thing bigger than Moby Dick (who—<em>spoiler
      alert!</em>—is a giant white whale) is the book itself.
    </p>
  </div>
 </body>
</html>
```

In Listing 3.7, the **header** tag contains the **h1** and **h2** tags, and its importance will become apparent only when we add inline styles in Chapter 4. For now, what's important is that it's an abstract semantic tag used to label a part of the page and has no immediate effect on the page's appearance.

Likewise, the **div** tag sets the page divisions apart, but won't have any effect until Chapter 4. We've also wrapped the iconic first line of *Moby-Dick*, "Call me Ishmael.", in a **span** tag in anticipation of styling it in Chapter 4. (The main difference between

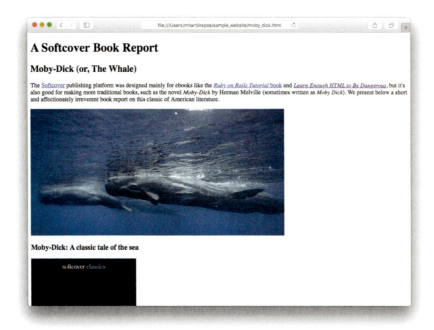

Figure 3.7: The initial Softcover book report on *Moby-Dick*.

the **div** and **span** tags is that **div** is a block element, whereas **span** is an inline element (Box 3.1).) Finally, we've introduced the **blockquote** tag for quoting blocks of text.

In addition to illustrating the **header**, **div**, and **span** tags, Listing 3.7 also shows an HTML *comment*, which appears as follows:[6]

```
<!-- much here to be styled, will do so in last section -->
```

This line, which foreshadows the styling steps in Chapter 4, is ignored by the browser, and is *not* visible on the rendered page, as (not) seen in Figure 3.7.[7]

---

6. In Atom, you can toggle HTML comments using ⌘/ ("Command-slash"), which (as noted in Section 7.2 of *Learn Enough Developer Tools to Be Dangerous*) works for source code as well. Because the text editor infers the file type from the filename extension (or from the "shebang line" **#!**), we can use ⌘/ to comment things out without having to remember the exact syntax for the file type we happen to be editing.

7. The comment is sent over the wire to the browser, though, and is visible to anyone inspecting the HTML source of our page.

3.3.1 Exercises

1. Validate the HTML in Listing 3.7 and confirm that there's one warning and one error. Apply the fixes suggested by the validator and confirm that the new page validates with no warnings.

2. In the previous exercise, you should have found a warning that suggested setting the language of the page to English. Update the site's other pages with the same change. (This repetition of effort is inconvenient and would be handled automatically by a templating system.)

3. Add **header**, **div**, and **span** to the tables in **tags.html**. *Hint*: Like **div**, **header** is a block element.

3.4 Lists

As part of our mini-report on *Moby-Dick*, we'd like to include a couple of lists with some of our observations about the book. As we'll see, HTML lists come in two basic types.

The first list will highlight our top three favorite things about *Moby-Dick*. Because we want these to be in rank-order, we'll use the *ordered list* tag **ol**:

```
<h4>Our top 3 favorite things about Moby Dick</h4>

<ol>
  <li>Vengeful whale</li>
  <li>Salty sailors</li>
  <li>The names "Queequeg" and "Starbuck"</li>
</ol>
```

Here the **li** tag indicates a **l**ist **i**tem (also called a list element), and the result will be numbered in sequence:

```
1. …
2. …
3. …
```

The second list will contain some other miscellaneous musings. Because the order isn't important, we'll use the *unordered list* tag **ul**, together with the same **li** list element tag used for ordered lists:

```
<h4>Other things about Moby Dick</h4>

<ul>
  <li>
    Chapter after chapter (after chapter) of meticulous detail about whaling
  </li>
  <li>
    The story pretty much
    <a href="https://en.wikipedia.org/wiki/Essex_(whaleship)"
       target="_blank" rel="noopener">happened in real life</a>
  </li>
  <li>Mad sea captains are fun</li>
</ul>
```

As we'll see in a moment, unordered list elements are styled as bullet points by default:

- ...
- ...
- ...

They are much more useful than this, though, and in practice unordered lists are used for significantly more than just making bullet points (as we'll see in Part II).

Putting these two lists together and adding them to the end of **moby_dick.html** gives Listing 3.8.

Listing 3.8: Adding lists to our *Moby-Dick* book report.
moby_dick.html

```
<h4>My top 3 favorite things about Moby Dick</h4>

<ol>
  <li>Vengeful whale</li>
  <li>Salty sailors</li>
  <li>The names "Queequeg" and "Starbuck"</li>
</ol>

<h4>Other things about Moby Dick</h4>

<ul>
  <li>
    Chapter after chapter (after chapter) of meticulous detail about
    whaling
  </li>
  <li>
    The story pretty much
```

```
    <a href="https://en.wikipedia.org/wiki/Essex_(whaleship)"
       target="_blank" rel="noopener">happened in real life</a>
    </li>
    <li>Mad sea captains are fun</li>
  </ul>
  </div>
 </body>
</html>
```

The result appears in Figure 3.8, which incidentally also shows the rendered **block-quote** that's not quite visible in Figure 3.7.

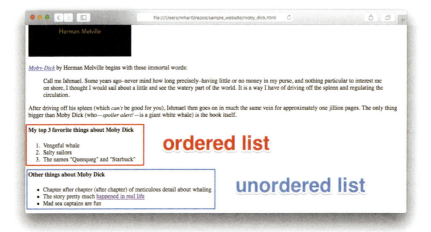

Figure 3.8: Ordered and unordered lists.

3.4.1 Exercise

1. Add **ol**, **ul**, and **li** tags to **tags.html**. Which are block elements and which are inline?

3.5 A Navigation Menu

Before moving on to styling our book report page in Chapter 4, we'll add a component common to most sites on the Web, yet one whose origins are mysterious: a navigation menu with links to all the pages on the site (Box 3.2). In the process, we'll learn how to make links to pages on the current site instead of always linking to external websites. The navigation menu will also give us another chance to see how cumbersome it is to make websites without a templating system.

Box 3.2: Hacked Together with Perl

Having watched the Web evolve from the start, I (Michael) knew how to make web pages from an early date, but I always wondered how it was that so many sites had the same menu on each page. I figured it must be some property of HTML I didn't know about, but even an early book on web design didn't cover it.

I remember thinking, you don't just hard-code the same menu on every page, do you? That seems like an awful lot of duplicated effort. And what if you want to change it?

It turns out that no, well-made sites don't require you to hard-code the menu everywhere. In fact, as I realized much later, most such sites at the time were just "hacked together with Perl" (as the comic strip xkcd once humorously put it), but at the time it was a genuine mystery. (Although Perl is still in use, nowadays it's probably more common to stitch websites together using PHP, Python, JavaScript, or Ruby. The principle, though, remains the same.)

In the present tutorial, we're not in a position to solve this problem the Right Way™, so we *will* have to write everything by hand. But this is a feature, not a bug, because solving the problem by hand helps us appreciate why it should be solved by a computer instead.

We'll reveal the solution to this mystery, called a *templating system*, in Part II, and it's covered thoroughly in the *Ruby on Rails Tutorial* (https://www.railstutorial.org/) as well.

We'll start by adding a **div** containing three links (one for each navigation element) to the index page (Listing 3.9). Note that we've adopted the common convention of referring to the index page as "Home".

Listing 3.9: Adding navigation links.
index.html

```html
<!DOCTYPE html>
<html>
  <head>
    <title>Learn Enough to Be Dangerous</title>
```

```
  <meta charset="utf-8">
</head>
<body>

  <div>
    <a href="index.html">Home</a>
    <a href="moby_dick.html">Moby Dick</a>
    <a href="tags.html">HTML Tags</a>
  </div>

  <h1>The Learn Enough Story</h1>
```

We see from Listing 3.9 that the way to link to a local page simply involves setting the **href** attribute equal to the path to the file, which works exactly the same way as an **img** tag's **src** attribute (Section 2.4):

```
<a href="tags.html">HTML Tags</a>
```

The result appears in Figure 3.9.

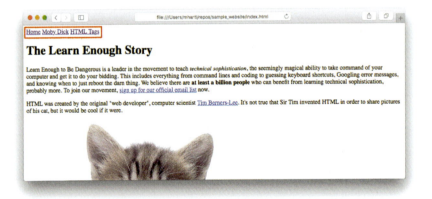

Figure 3.9: The navigation menu on the index page.

We can add the same menu to the HTML tags page with the markup in Listing 3.10. The result appears in Figure 3.10.

Figure 3.10: The navigation menu on the HTML tags page.

Listing 3.10: Adding the navigation menu to the HTML tags page.

tags.html

```
<!DOCTYPE html>
<html>
  <head>
    <title>HTML Tags</title>
    <meta charset="utf-8">
  </head>
  <body>

    <div>
      <a href="index.html">Home</a>
      <a href="moby_dick.html">Moby Dick</a>
      <a href="tags.html">HTML Tags</a>
    </div>

    <h1>Important HTML tags</h1>
```

Adding the menu to the page on *Moby-Dick* is left as an exercise.

By the way, you may have noticed that it would probably be more natural to order the navigation in order of the pages' introduction, i.e., Home, Tags, Moby Dick. Changing this order is also left as an exercise, mainly so that you feel the pain of making the same change on three different pages—a pain that is alleviated by the templating systems covered in Chapter 9. Either before or after doing that exercise, we suggest adding and committing the changes and then pushing up to GitHub Pages:

```
$ git add -A
$ git commit -m "Add a Moby Dick page and a menu"
$ git push
```

3.5.1 Exercises

1. Add the menu links to the Moby Dick page.

2. In the menu links, change the order of the links so that the tags page comes second. How many files do you have to edit?

CHAPTER 4

Inline Styling

Now that we've added the content for our pages and blocked out the basic structure, we're ready to add some styling. Our basic approach involves adding *inline styles*, which means putting styling commands directly inside the site's HTML tags. This approach will allow us to understand exactly what our styling is doing on a per-element basis, giving us immediate results.

Inline styles are generally considered a bad practice, though (Box 4.1). En route to fixing this issue, we'll get just a *tiny* taste of Cascading Style Sheets—the design language of the Web—by converting inline styles for one of our pages to CSS. This in turn will provide an essential foundation for front-end design and development (Part II) and for writing interactive websites using JavaScript (*Learn Enough JavaScript to Be Dangerous* (https://www.learnenough.com/javascript)).

Box 4.1: Separating Style and Content

If adding styles directly to elements gives you the results that you want, why is it considered bad practice to do it?

One reason is that when your styling is kept in a separate file from your content and layout, the HTML files are cleaner and easier to maintain. This doesn't make a huge difference when one developer is working on a single page, but when you have multiple developers all making changes to multiple pages, it quickly becomes a nightmare to make changes efficiently and consistently. Imagine if you decided that you didn't like the size of a font on your site, and had to go around to every place on every page that needed a new style. If this were the only way, no one would ever do it.

Another reason for separating style from content is that it allows for much greater flexibility and efficiency when applying style rules to multiple elements. Instead of having to style each individual tag, we can apply styling to all elements on the entire site, or just to certain elements that we choose.

For instance, it's possible to make a table span the full width of the page using the rule `width: 100%`. If we wanted *every* table on the site to have the same styling, we would have to copy and paste that into every `<table>` tag on every page:

```
<table style="width: 100%;">
```

With CSS, we can tell the browser to style every table with a small bit of code:

```
table {
  width: 100%;
}
```

For an extensive website with lots of different pages, elements, and style rules, this can represent a massive gain in simplicity and efficiency.

Finally, every page on the Internet is sitting on a remote server somewhere sending data to the users visiting the site. Every word or line of code that you add to a page is something extra that needs to be downloaded over the network. Cutting out repetitive elements on a page makes them smaller, and thus helps sites load faster as well.

4.1 Text Styling

As mentioned in Section 3.3, our design efforts will focus on the *Moby-Dick* book report page, which stands to gain the most from changing the default HTML styling. We'll begin by adding a little styling to the quotation from the first paragraph of *Moby-Dick*. Recall from Listing 3.7 that the quotation uses the **blockquote** tag, which is set apart from the surrounding text by extra space and indentation (Figure 4.1).

To make the quotation stand out even more, let's change the font style to *italics* while increasing the font size to 20 pixels (**20px**). The way to do this is with the **style** attribute, which can be added to virtually any HTML tag. In this case, we'll change the **font-style** and the **font-size** as follows:

```
style="font-style: italic; font-size: 20px;"
```

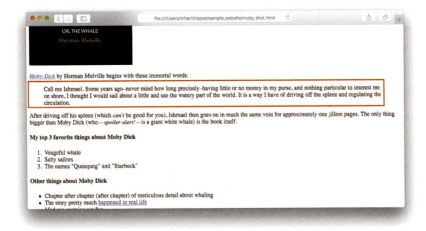

Figure 4.1: The default blockquote styling.

Note that the styling rules after **style=** are a single string of characters, with each individual style separated from the others by a semicolon **;**. (The final semicolon isn't technically necessary, but including it is a good practice since it lets us add additional styles later on without having to remember to add a semicolon.)

Taking this idea and editing **moby_dick.html** leads to the HTML shown in Listing 4.1. The result appears in Figure 4.2.

Listing 4.1: Styling the blockquote.
moby_dick.html

```
<blockquote style="font-style: italic; font-size: 20px;">
```

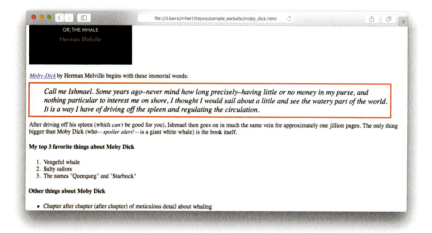

Figure 4.2: A styled blockquote.

Next, we'll add some styling to the famous first line "Call me Ishmael." We'll first revert the font style back to normal (which is how you emphasize text when the surrounding text is already in italics). Then we'll make the font even bigger than the **20px** used for the rest of the quotation, while also making it **bold**. Finally, we'll change the color to an attention-grabbing **red**.

Ordinarily, there would be no way to style just the line "Call me Ishmael." If we had written it as

```
Call me Ishmael. Some years ago…
```

at this point we'd be out of luck. Recall from Listing 3.7, though, that the opening line is wrapped in a **span** tag:

```
<span>Call me Ishmael.</span> Some years ago…
```

The reason for this is that we correctly anticipated wanting to style it later on. (In practice we can't always anticipate such things, but of course we can wrap the relevant text in a **span** tag as needed.)

Although the **span** tag doesn't really do anything by itself, we *can* add styles to it, as follows:

```
<span style="font-style: normal; font-size: 24px; font-weight: bold;
color: #ff0000;">Call me Ishmael.</span>
```

Here we've combined **font-style**, **font-size**, **font-weight**, and **color** to obtain the results outlined above. These are but a few of the many style properties available, which you can learn about at sites like w3schools (https://www.w3schools.com /cssref/). Meanwhile, the color **ff0000** is a hexadecimal code for red, as discussed in Box 4.2.

Box 4.2: HTML and Hexadecimal Color

HTML colors are typically indicated using a system known as *hexadecimal RGB* (for "red, green, blue"), which gives us a flexible way to specify colors with fine-grained precision.

Hexadecimal refers to the use of *base 16*, which uses 16 symbols from 0 to F to specify the decimal numbers 0 through 15:

0	1	2	3	4	5	6	7	8	9	10	11	12	13	14	15
0	1	2	3	4	5	6	7	8	9	A	B	C	D	E	F

Just as base 10 lets us count from 0 to $10^2 - 1 = 99$ using only two digits, hexadecimal lets us count from 0 to $16^2 - 1 = 255$ using 00 = 0 up to FF = 255.

A computer monitor displays colors by combining red, green, and blue pixels together, which represent the three additive primary colors. If all three colors are turned on, which would look like #FFFFFF, the screen will look white. Conversely, if all three colors are turned off, which is #000000, the screen will look black. Intermediate combinations of the three colors combine to produce virtually all the colors you can see:

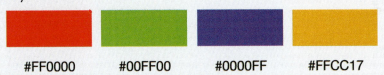

#FF0000   #00FF00   #0000FF   #FFCC17

For convenience, HTML also supports a shorthand that can stand in for the full hex string in some cases. For example, if the numbers are repeated, as in #222222, #bbbbbb, or #aa22ff, you can shorten the whole number to just three digits, like this: #222, #bbb, or #a2f. (Note that we've switched to lowercase letters, which is more common in modern HTML code, but is exactly equivalent to the uppercase versions shown above.) When the browser sees only three digits, it fills in the missing ones automatically.

The hexadecimal color system might seem confusing at first, but you'll find that you quickly come to understand how the three values work together to make different colors (and different shades of those colors). To learn more, we suggest playing around with a color picker to see what kinds of colors you can make.

Figure 4.3: Making the opening line really pop.

Including the styles above in **moby_dick.html** gives us the code in Listing 4.2, with the result shown in Figure 4.3.

Listing 4.2: Adding style to the opening **span**.
moby_dick.html

```
<blockquote style="font-style: italic; font-size: 20px;">
  <p>
    <span style="font-style: normal; font-size: 24px; font-weight: bold;
    color: #ff0000;">Call me Ishmael.</span>
    Some years ago–never mind how long precisely–having little or
    no money in my purse, and nothing particular to interest me on shore,
    I thought I would sail about a little and see the watery part of the
    world. It is a way I have of driving off the spleen and regulating the
    circulation.
  </p>
</blockquote>
```

As a final change, we'll align the text of the book report headers so that it's centered in the page. The way to do this is with the **text-align** property, as shown in Listing 4.3. (Note that Listing 4.3 also removes the comment from Listing 3.7 since it's now obsolete.)

Listing 4.3: Centering the headings.
moby_dick.html

```
<header>
  <h1 style="text-align: center;">A Softcover Book Report</h1>
  <h2 style="text-align: center;">Moby-Dick (or, The Whale)</h2>
</header>
```

The result appears in Figure 4.4.

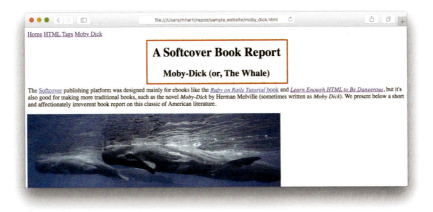

Figure 4.4: Centered headings.

4.1.1   Exercises

1. Verify that **color: red;** has the same effect as **color: #ff0000;**. What are the advantages of each approach?

2. What would you guess the color of **#cccccc** is? Temporarily modify the color of the **span** in Listing 4.2 to check your guess. How does it differ from **#ccc**?

4.2   Floats

Now that we've learned how to move text around, let's look at how to adjust the placement of other elements. We'll start by shrinking the size of the cover image down a little, and then we'll arrange for the text to flow around it as if it were part of the paragraphs and blockquote.

We'll start by adding the **height** attribute to the **img** tag to restrict the height to 200 pixels:

```
<img src="images/moby_dick.png" alt="Moby Dick" height="200px">
```

Several caveats are in order here. First, although inline resizing is still fairly common, using CSS is the best practice. Second, resizing the image this way (whether inline or with CSS) affects only the image *display*, and the entire image still needs to be downloaded from the web server, so this technique should be used only for fairly minor resizings.[1] (If you've ever visited a web page where a seemingly tiny image takes *forever* to load, this is probably the reason why.) Finally, if you go this route you should use *either* **height** *or* **width**, but not both, as the combination forces the browser to attempt to respect both numbers, which can result in weird image-resizing effects (Figure 4.5).

In order to get the text to flow around the image, we need to use a style technique called *floating*. The idea is that when you set an element to "float" to the left or right (there is no center), all the inline content around it will flow around the floated

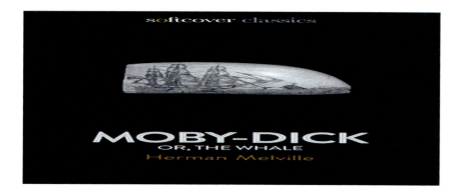

Figure 4.5: Bad image resizing is bad.

---

1. If you need to resize the image itself and don't have access to Photoshop, you can use the free Skitch (https://evernote.com/products/skitch) utility for resizing, cropping, and simple annotation.

element. To see this in action, all we need to do is add **style="float: left;"** to the image attributes:

```
<img src="images/moby_dick.png" alt="Moby Dick" height="200px"
style="float: left;">
```

Inserting this into the book report page gives Listing 4.4, with the result shown in Figure 4.6.

Listing 4.4: Resizing and floating an image.
moby_dick.html

```
<h3>Moby-Dick: A classic tale of the sea</h3>

<a href="https://www.softcover.io/read/6070fb03/moby-dick"
   target="_blank" rel="noopener">
  <img src="images/moby_dick.png" alt="Moby Dick" height="200px"
  style="float: left;">
</a>
```

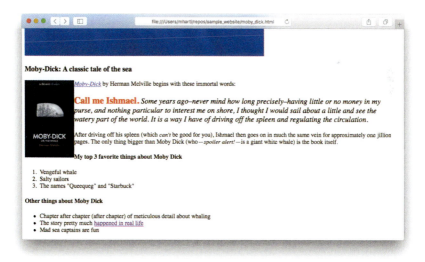

Figure 4.6: A nicely resized & floated image.

In Figure 4.6, the image is effectively treated like text, with the normal text now flowing up and to its side. We'll see in Section 4.5 that the **float** attribute also arranges for the text to flow past the image as well.

4.2.1 Exercise

1. What happens if you change **float: left** to **float: right** in Listing 4.4?

4.3 Applying a Margin

Even though we've floated the image, the page still looks a little weird, with the text smashed up against the book cover. To make it look better, we'll add a *margin* of empty space to the right of the image.

Margins are one of three styles that can be applied to the imaginary boxes that contain HTML content, the others being *padding* (empty space inside the box) and *borders* (a line around the box). We'll talk more about these styles in the context of the *box model* covered in Chapter 8 of Part II, but we can accomplish our immediate goal by applying a margin using inline styling. (We'll see an example of padding in Section 4.5.)

We'll start with the simplest kind of margin declaration, which looks like **margin: 40px;**:

```
<img src="images/moby_dick.png" alt="Moby Dick" height="200px"
style="float: left; margin: 40px;">
```

If we add this to the **img** tag (Listing 4.5), everything surrounding the image moves 40 pixels in each direction, as shown in Figure 4.7.

Listing 4.5: Adding an image margin.
moby_dick.html

```
<h3>Moby-Dick: A classic tale of the sea</h3>

<a href="https://www.softcover.io/read/6070fb03/moby-dick"
   target="_blank" rel="noopener">
  <img src="images/moby_dick.png" alt="Moby Dick" height="200px"
   style="float: left; margin: 40px;">
</a>
```

Figure 4.7: Close, but not quite!

Figure 4.7 shows that we've gotten closer to our goal by putting some space between the text and the image, but the styling still isn't quite what we want. The reason is that writing **margin: 40px;** applies the margin in *all* directions, but we really only want the margin on the right side of the image, to separate it from the text.

The most general way to control where the margin goes is to give the **margin** attribute *four* values, corresponding to the top, right, bottom, and left of the box (Figure 4.8).

For example, to get margins of 40, 30, 20, and 10 pixels going around an image (clockwise from the top), we could use this **style** attribute:

```
<img src="…" style="margin: 40px 30px 20px 10px;">
```

In the present case, we want only a right margin, so we can set the other three sides to **0px** (or just **0** for short):[2]

```
<img src="images/moby_dick.png" alt="Moby Dick" height="200px"
style="float: left; margin: 0 40px 0 0;">
```

---

2. We could use the attribute **style="margin-right: 40px;"** to achieve the same effect, but specifying all four margins is the dominant convention and so is worth learning.

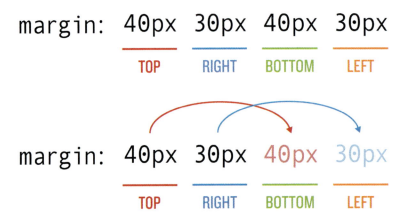

Figure 4.8: Think of the four values as going clockwise from the top.

Applying this to the full source of the book report page gives Listing 4.6.

Listing 4.6: Adding only a right margin.
moby_dick.html

```
<h3>Moby-Dick: A classic tale of the sea</h3>

<a href="https://www.softcover.io/read/6070fb03/moby-dick"
   target="_blank" rel="noopener">
  <img src="images/moby_dick.png" alt="Moby Dick" height="200px"
    style="float: left; margin: 0 40px 0 0;">
</a>
```

The result of Listing 4.6 shows exactly the result we want, with a margin applied only on the right, as seen in Figure 4.9.

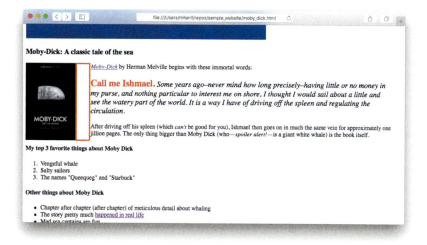

Figure 4.9: Much better!

4.3.1   Exercises

1. How does the margin in Listing 4.6 change if we replace the margin with **margin-right: 40px**?

2. Add the style rule **padding: 10px;** to the **td** elements for the first two block elements in the table in **tags.html**. How annoying would it be to add them to every **td**? How annoying is it to change from **10px** to **20px** everywhere? (This is one reason why in real life you always use CSS.)

4.4   More Margin Tricks

There are a couple more margin tricks worth mentioning, both of which we can immediately put to good use. First, in addition to the shorthand **margin: 40px** (with only one value), it's possible to include only two values:

```
margin: 20px 40px;
```

As illustrated in Figure 4.8, this syntax sets the top and bottom margins to **20px** and the left and right margins to **40px**, so it is equivalent to

```
margin: 20px 40px 20px 40px;
```

This shorthand also works with just three values, like this: `margin: 20px 10px 40px;`. This is missing the last value, which (as seen in Figure 4.8) is the left margin. In this case, it will be filled in automatically from its opposite across the box (in this case, `10px`).

We can apply this to the header for the book report page by adding a bottom margin via `margin: 0 0 80px`, as shown in Listing 4.7.

Listing 4.7: Centering the book report headers.
moby_dick.html

```
<header style="text-align: center; margin: 0 0 80px;">
  <h1>A Softcover Book Report</h1>
  <h2>Moby-Dick (or, The Whale)</h2>
</header>
```

Note that we've also taken this opportunity to hoist the style `text-align: center` into the `header` tag. The result appears in Figure 4.10.

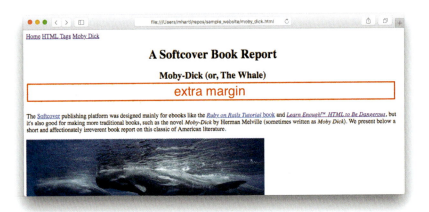

Figure 4.10: Adding a margin under the header.

The second margin trick is the use of **auto**, which inserts a margin with a size that is automatically the same on all relevant sides. Its most common application is probably in the rule

```
margin: 0 auto;
```

which arranges for no top or bottom margin and for automatic margins on the left and right. The result of equal left and right margins is that the element is *centered*, which is especially useful for elements like images that can't be centered using the `text-align: center;` rule we saw in Listing 4.3.

One restriction of `margin: 0 auto;` is that it works only on block elements, but recall from Box 3.1 that the `img` tag is an inline element. We can fix this with the style `display: block;`, which overrides the default. Putting this together with the margin rule leads to Listing 4.8, with the result shown in Figure 4.11.

Listing 4.8: A centered image.
moby_dick.html

```
<a href="https://commons.wikimedia.org/wiki/File:Sperm_whale_pod.jpg">
  <img src="images/sperm_whales.jpg"
  style="display: block; margin: 0 auto;">
</a>
```

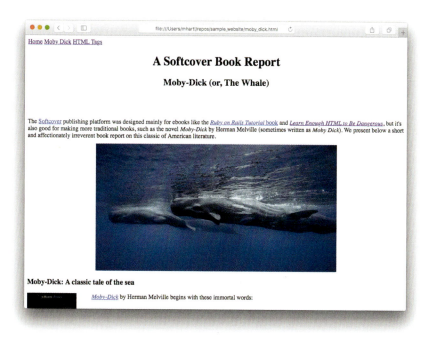

Figure 4.11: A centered image.

4.4.1 Exercise

1. What happens if you use **margin: 0 auto;** for the book cover image (together with **display: block;**) without changing the float rule? What does this tell you about the precedence of the two rules?

4.5 Box Styling

So far, the changes we've made have had a relatively minor impact on the appearance of the book report page. In this section, we'll see how a set of only four style rules can make a surprisingly big difference.

Recall from Listing 3.7 that we wrapped the bulk of the report in a **div** tag, which defines a block element that doesn't get any default styling from the browser, thereby making it perfect to use as a wrapper for styling other content. In this case, we'll use the **width** style to restrict the size of the main report to 500 pixels, and it turns out this lets us use the automatic margin trick from Section 4.4 to center it using **margin: 20px auto;** (thereby also putting a 20-pixel margin on the top and bottom). Finally, we'll combine a **padding** rule with a change in the **background-color** using the hexadecimal color convention covered in Box 4.2. The resulting style rules appear in Listing 4.9.

Listing 4.9: Adding styling to the book report box.
moby_dick.html

```
<div style="width: 500px; margin: 20px auto; padding: 30px;
background-color: #fafafa;">
  <h3>Moby-Dick: A classic tale of the sea</h3>
```

Comparing the before and after (Figure 4.12) shows what a difference a few style rules can make.

As we see in Figure 4.12, the report content has now been set apart from the rest of the page in a styled box.

To recap what happened, we set a width for the box, and because of this we were able to set the left and right margins to **auto**. Then we added padding to the box, which pushed the content inside away from the edges. (Investigating the difference between padding and margins is left as an exercise (Section 4.5.1).) We also added a light gray background color with the hexadecimal code **#fafafa** (Box 4.2). (Don't worry about trying to visualize the color corresponding to a hex code; that's what

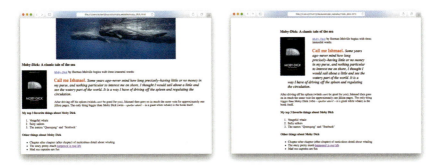

Figure 4.12: The report box before and after adding styling.

color pickers are for.) Finally, because of the narrower width, the text of the *Moby-Dick* quotation now flows around the floated cover image, thereby fulfilling the promise made at the end of Section 4.2.

4.5.1   Exercises

1. Temporarily change **padding** to **margin** in Listing 4.9. What difference does this make in the appearance?

2. Add and style a blockquote with padding and a background color as shown in Listing 4.10. Fill in **TAG** with the right level tag for that location in the document, and replace **FILL_IN** with a reasonable color of your choice. The result for one color choice appears in Figure 4.13.

Listing 4.10: Styling a famous quotation.

index.html

```
<h1>The Learn Enough Story</h1>
.
.
.
<img src="images/kitten.jpg" alt="An adorable kitten">

<TAG>Quotations</TAG>

<p>
  In addition to hosting most of the world's supply of kitten videos, the
  Web is also full of inspiring quotes, perhaps none more so than this one:
</p>
```

```
<blockquote style="padding: 2px 20px; background: #FILL_IN;">
  <p>
    <em>Don't believe every quote you read on the Internet.</em>
    <br>
    —Abraham Lincoln
  </p>
</blockquote>
```

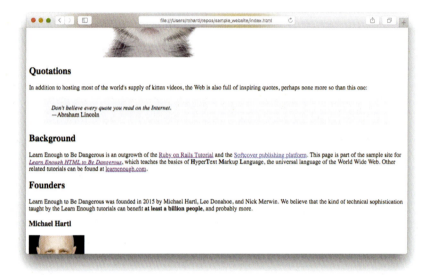

Figure 4.13: Styling a famous quotation from an American president.

4.6 Navigation Styling

As a final change to our sample website, we'll make a change across all three pages by adding styling to the navigation menu added in Section 3.5. In the process, we'll yet again feel the pain of having to make the same change in several places, further preparing us to appreciate the value of the template system developed in Part II.

To style the nav menu, we'll first move it from the top left of the page to the more conventional top right. This will involve adding a style rule to the **div** tag that wraps the whole menu (Listing 3.9). At the same time, we'll add a left margin to the second and third nav links in order to improve the spacing. The changes to the book report page appear in Listing 4.11, and the result appears in Figure 4.14.

Figure 4.14: The styled navigation on the book report page.

Listing 4.11: Styling the navigation menu on the book report page.
moby_dick.html

```
<div style="text-align: right;">
  <a href="index.html">Home</a>
  <a href="tags.html" style="margin: 0 0 0 10px;">HTML Tags</a>
  <a href="moby_dick.html" style="margin: 0 0 0 10px;">Moby Dick</a>
</div>
```

Of course, we're not done yet, as we need to make the same edits to the nav menu on the Home page (Listing 4.12) and HTML Tags page (Listing 4.13).

Listing 4.12: Styling the navigation menu on the Home page.
index.html

```
<div style="text-align: right;">
  <a href="index.html">Home</a>
  <a href="tags.html" style="margin: 0 0 0 10px;">HTML Tags</a>
  <a href="moby_dick.html" style="margin: 0 0 0 10px;">Moby Dick</a>
</div>
```

Listing 4.13: Styling the navigation menu on the HTML Tags page.
`tags.html`

```
<div style="text-align: right;">
  <a href="index.html">Home</a>
  <a href="tags.html" style="margin: 0 0 0 10px;">HTML Tags</a>
  <a href="moby_dick.html" style="margin: 0 0 0 10px;">Moby Dick</a>
</div>
```

The results on the nav menu are exactly the same as shown in Figure 4.14. This is not surprising given that the changes represented by Listing 4.11, Listing 4.12, and Listing 4.13 are *all identical*. This sort of repetition is cumbersome and error-prone—definitely a Bad Thing. As mentioned several times before, we'll solve this problem with a templating system in Part II.

4.6.1 Exercises

1. Change **margin: 0 0 0 10px;** to **margin-left: 10px;** in Listing 4.13. What, if anything, changes in the appearance?

2. It's conventional for navigation links not to change color after being followed, and they also look better if they're not underlined like normal links. Using your Google-fu and the w3schools reference, guess the style rules for making these changes, and apply them to each element in the menu. *Hint*: The property you'll have to modify to remove underlining is **text-decoration**. The result should look something like Figure 4.15.

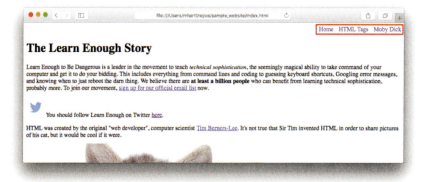

Figure 4.15: Styling the menu links.

3. Add a new table for the "document tags" that define the properties of the document. Include **html**, **head**, **body**, **title**, and **meta**.

4. Add any missing tags to **tags.html**. (By our count there are five, after including the tags from the previous exercise.)

4.7 A Taste of CSS

In this section, we'll get a first taste of Cascading Style Sheets (CSS),[3] using the inline styles from **index.html** as our example. We'll break the transition from inline styles to CSS into two steps: First, we'll move the inline styles into an *internal stylesheet* (Section 4.7.1); second, we'll move the internal style rules into an *external stylesheet* (Section 4.7.2). The result will be a self-contained and centralized location for our page's styling.

4.7.1 Internal Stylesheets

We'll start by *refactoring* the inline styles into an internal stylesheet. Refactoring involves changing the form of code or markup without changing its function. In this case, we'll be moving the style rules on the elements in **index.html** into the **head** of our document, using a special **style** tag designed for exactly this purpose. In preparation for this, we'll add the opening and closing **style** tags with empty space for the style rules, as shown in Listing 4.14.

Listing 4.14: Adding an empty **style** tag (to be filled in in this section).
index.html

```
<!DOCTYPE html>
<html>
  <head>
    <title>Learn Enough to Be Dangerous</title>
    <meta charset="UTF-8">

    <style>

    </style>
  </head>
```

---

3. The words "style" and "sheet" are conventionally written as two words—Style Sheet—only in the context of spelling out the meaning of "CSS". Otherwise, they are generally combined into one word, "stylesheet".

Our first step is to move the navigation styling developed in Section 4.6 (Listing 4.12). Two of the lines contain identical margin styles: **margin: 0 0 0 10px** (which control the spacing between links). To eliminate this repetition, we'll start by replacing each of the inline styles with one of the most important ideas in web design, a CSS *class*, as shown in Listing 4.15.

Listing 4.15: Replacing the inline style with a CSS class.
index.html

```
<div style="text-align: right;">
  <a href="index.html">Home</a>
  <a href="tags.html" class="nav-spacing">HTML Tags</a>
  <a href="moby_dick.html" class="nav-spacing">Moby Dick</a>
</div>
```

A CSS class acts as a named label for the element, and allows us to simultaneously style all elements with the given class. The code for doing this involves the name of the class with a leading dot (**.nav-spacing**) and a list of style rules (in this case, only one) inside curly braces. In order to apply the styling to the page, this code should be placed inside the **style** tag, as shown in Listing 4.16.

Listing 4.16: Moving the inline **margin** rule into an internal stylesheet.
index.html

```
<style>
  .nav-spacing {
    margin: 0 0 0 10px;
  }
</style>
```

Note that the **margin** rule in Listing 4.16 is identical to the one we used inline; this is a general pattern for inline styles and CSS.

Next, we'll replace the inline style for the navigation **div** with another CSS class (Listing 4.17) and a second CSS rule (Listing 4.18).

Listing 4.17: Replacing the inline style with a class.
index.html

```
<div class="nav-menu">
  <a href="index.html">Home</a>
  <a href="tags.html" class="nav-spacing">HTML Tags</a>
  <a href="moby_dick.html" class="nav-spacing">Moby Dick</a>
</div>
```

Listing 4.18: Adding the nav menu rule to the internal stylesheet.
index.html

```
<style>

  .nav-menu {
    text-align: right;
  }
  .nav-spacing {
    margin: 0 0 0 10px;
  }
</style>
```

Here we've placed the **.nav-menu** rule above the **.nav-spacing** rule, but in this case the order doesn't matter. (The order of CSS rules often does matter, though; the details are covered in Part II.)

As a final step, we'll add the counterpart to a CSS class, called a CSS "identifier", or *id* (read as separate letters: "eye-dee"). Adding an id is certainly not necessary, nor is it considered a good practice to use ids for styling (for reasons covered in Part II); we include it here mainly for purposes of illustration. But ids can be quite useful for *deep linking* (discussed in Section 4.7.3), and they are essential for many JavaScript applications (as covered in *Learn Enough JavaScript to Be Dangerous*).

In this case, we'll call the id **main-nav** (to indicate the main navigational element) and add it to the main navigational **div**, as shown in Listing 4.19. This has no effect on the page's appearance but serves to illustrate the syntax. Note that, unlike classes, which can be used multiple times on a page, a given CSS id can be used only once.

Listing 4.19: Adding a CSS id.
index.html

```
<div id="main-nav" class="nav-menu">
  <a href="index.html">Home</a>
  <a href="tags.html" class="nav-spacing">HTML Tags</a>
  <a href="moby_dick.html" class="nav-spacing">Moby Dick</a>
</div>
```

At this point, if you've done everything right, the styles should be exactly the same as before, so upon refreshing the browser the appearance of the page should also be the same as it was before we started.

4.7.2 External Stylesheets

Now that we've refactored the inline styles into an internal stylesheet, putting them in an *external* stylesheet is easy. All we need to do is create a CSS file (which we'll call **main.css**), move the styles there, and then link to the file in the **head** of our document.

By convention, CSS files are usually located in a directory called **css** or **stylesheets**; we'll pick the former for brevity:

```
$ mkdir css
$ touch css/main.css
```

All that's needed now is to cut the CSS rules from **index.html** (don't include the **<style>** tags though) and paste them into **main.css** (Listing 4.20).

Listing 4.20: The style rules in an external stylesheet.
css/main.css

```
.nav-menu {
  text-align: right;
}
.nav-spacing {
  margin: 0 0 0 10px;
}
```

Finally, we'll delete the **<style></style>** tags and replace them with a **link** tag that includes the stylesheet into the page, as shown in Listing 4.21. (The **rel** in Listing 4.21 stands for "relationship"; in our experience, it has never been important to know this.)

Listing 4.21: Including the external stylesheet.
index.html

```
<!DOCTYPE html>
<html>
  <head>
    <title>Learn Enough to Be Dangerous</title>
    <meta charset="UTF-8">
    <link rel="stylesheet" href="css/main.css">
  </head>
```

Putting styles in an external stylesheet is the technique that is generally used in real websites.

As before, moving the CSS into an external stylesheet should have changed nothing about the rules being applied, so the resulting page should look exactly the same as before!

The final step is to make a Git commit (taking care to run **git add** since we've added a new file and directory):

```
$ git add -A
$ git commit -m "Refactor inline styles into a stylesheet"
```

With that, we're done with our brief overview of CSS. This background is (barely) sufficient to skip to a beginning programming tutorial like *Learn Enough JavaScript to Be Dangerous*, although we recommend solidifying your knowledge by following Part II of this book, which also covers how to use a professional-grade static site generator with a proper templating system to prevent repeated use of code.

4.7.3 Exercises

1. If you followed the exercises in Section 2.4.2, there is an image link to the Learn Enough Twitter account that has an inline style to remove underlining, as shown in Listing 2.14. Add a sensible class to this element (such as **"image-link"**)

and move the corresponding style rule into **main.css**. Does the page remain unchanged as required?

2. The updated menu shown in Listing 4.17 appears only on the Home page; to fix this, propagate the changes to the other two pages. (Appreciate once again how cumbersome this is and how nice it would be to have a proper templating system.)

3. Move the style rules for the HTML Tags page and the Moby Dick page into **main.css** and confirm that the appearance of the pages stays the same.

4. One of the simplest and most useful applications of CSS ids is for creating links to arbitrary HTML elements using a convenient hash symbol (#) syntax. By adding the id **founders** to the "Founders" **h2** tag (Listing 4.22), show that you can visit that section of the page directly by pasting the URL sample_website/index.html#founders into your browser's address bar.

Listing 4.22: Adding a CSS id for deep linking.
index.html

```
<h2 id="founders">Founders</h2>
```

4.8 Conclusion

Congratulations! You now know enough HTML to be *dangerous*. All that's left is to commit (in case you've made changes in Section 4.7.3) and deploy the final sample website:

```
$ git commit -am "Finish the sample website"
$ git push
```

The result is a full website running in a production environment (Figure 4.16).

For reference, summary tables of all the block-level tags and inline tags appear in Table 4.1 and Table 4.2, respectively.

At this point, you've got a solid foundation in the basics of HTML. This means you have the perfect preparation for learning how to make a professional-grade website with attractive styling and fancy page layouts. In other words, you're now ready for Part II!

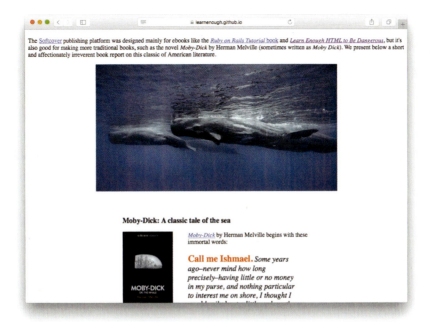

Figure 4.16: Our website available on the live Internet.

Table 4.1: The block-level tags covered in this tutorial.

Tag	Name	Purpose
h1–h6	Headings	Include a heading (levels 1–6)
p	Paragraph	Include a paragraph of text
table	Table	Include a table
tr	Table row	Include a row of data
th	Table header	Make a table header
td	Table data	Include a table data cell
div	Division	Define block-level section in document
header	Header	Label the page header
ol	Ordered list	List elements in numerical order
ul	Unordered list	List elements whose order doesn't matter
li	List item	Include a list item (ordered or unordered)
blockquote	Block quotation	Show formatted quotation
br	Break	Enter line break

Table 4.2: The inline tags covered in this tutorial.

Tag	Name	Purpose	Example	Result
em	Emphasized	Make emphasized text	`<em>technical sophistication</em>`	*technical sophistication*
strong	Strong	Make strong text	`<strong>at least a billion people </strong>`	**at least a billion people**
a	Anchor	Make hyperlink	`<a href="#"> Learn Enough</a>`	Learn Enough
img	Image	Include an image	`<img src="mhartl .jpg" alt= "Michael Hartl">`	
code	Code	Format as source code	`<code>table</code>`	`table`
span	Span	Define inline section in document	`<span>Call me Ishmael.</span>`	Call me Ishmael.

PART II

Cascading Style Sheets and Page Layout

CHAPTER 5

Introduction to CSS

In Part I, we learned how to make a simple website using HTML. In Part II, also known as *Learn Enough CSS & Layout to Be Dangerous* (https://www.learnenough .com/css-and-layout), we'll learn how to build a more complex website and style it using CSS.

CSS—short for *Cascading Style Sheets*—is the design language of the World Wide Web. CSS lets developers and designers define what a web page looks like and how it behaves, including how elements are positioned in the browser. Every website that you visit (with some incredibly rare exceptions) uses CSS to make the user experience and interface look inviting, which means that learning the basics of CSS is an essential part of becoming a web developer or designer. It's also useful for anyone who *interacts* with developers and designers, which these days seems like practically everyone.

Most CSS tutorials teach the subject in isolation, showing you how to make individual changes to things like text color or font size, without showing you how to put everything together as an integrated whole. This approach is a lot like trying to teach a foreign language by having students read the dictionary. You might learn lots of words, but you would end up with little to no context or ability to have a real conversation (Figure 5.1).[1]

---

1. Image courtesy of irantzuarbaizagoitia/123RF.

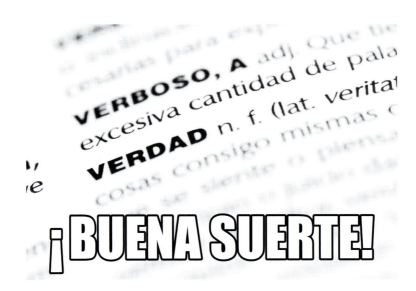

Figure 5.1: You're not going to learn Spanish from the dictionary alone.

In contrast, *Learn Enough CSS & Layout to Be Dangerous* is specifically designed to show you how CSS works in the context of a real website.

It's especially hard to find tutorials that cover how to develop the *layout* of the page—that is, how one positions elements on the page and determines what content goes where. It's because this subject is so important—and yet so neglected—that we called this tutorial *Learn Enough CSS & Layout to Be Dangerous*, rather than simply *Learn Enough CSS to Be Dangerous*.

Why is layout so often ignored? It's partially because the layout aspects of CSS can be rather complicated, but it's also because doing layout well calls for more than plain HTML and CSS. Making a real, industrial-grade website requires using a *templating system* to assemble the various parts—there are simply too many repeated and custom elements (such as headers, footers, dynamically generated names and dates, etc.) to build such sites by hand (Figure 5.2).

As a result, even learning enough CSS to be *dangerous*—that is, enough to accomplish your goals without taking the time to become a complete expert—is far more extensive than most people realize. You need to learn not only the basic CSS rules, but also more advanced rules governing page layout, together with a tool to assemble all the parts into a combined whole.

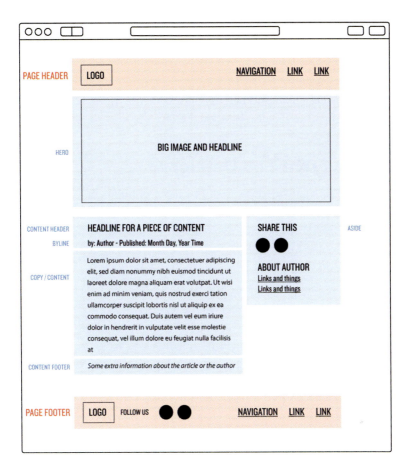

Figure 5.2: Most modern websites have many repeated and custom elements.

Learn Enough CSS & Layout to Be Dangerous is designed to fill this need. It fits into the Learn Enough introductory sequence (https://www.learnenough.com/) immediately after *Learn Enough HTML to Be Dangerous* (https://www.learnenough .com/html) (equivalent to Part I of this tutorial), but it's also suitable for more experienced developers who want to strengthen their knowledge of web design.[2] Among other things, this means that *Learn Enough CSS & Layout to Be Dangerous* is both a possible prerequisite and also an excellent follow-on to the *Ruby on Rails Tutorial* (https://www.railstutorial.org/book).

---

2. Such as, for example, this guy (https://www.michaelhartl.com/).

Because Part II builds on Part I and the material covered in *Learn Enough Developer Tools to Be Dangerous*, this tutorial is also unusual in that it allows you to deploy the main sample website to the live Web right from the start while following professional-grade development practices throughout. Because of this integrated approach, *Learn Enough CSS & Layout to Be Dangerous* puts everything together in a way you probably haven't seen before, even if you've previously studied CSS.

5.1 You're a Front-End Developer

CSS isn't the kind of language that's useful to learn in little half-steps—the part that people find difficult is dealing with handling styling when they are deep into creating an honest-to-goodness website with many levels of complexity. The real skill comes in knowing how to plan for a multipage site that uses a bunch of different snippets of code[3] placed into a flexible layout that organizes content and data in a useful way.

There are already many sites (like the Mozilla Developer Network CSS Reference) that exhaustively document every CSS property, so going over each and every option from the specification would just be a duplication of effort. Instead, *Learn Enough CSS & Layout to Be Dangerous* is designed to complement such reference works by showing you how CSS applies to the design of a real website. The resulting narrative explanation gives you the context necessary to understand and apply CSS documentation—especially when combined with a little technical sophistication (Box 5.1).

Box 5.1: Technical Sophistication

As noted in Part I, one of the principal themes of the Learn Enough tutorials is the development of *technical sophistication* (Box 1.1), which is the ability to figure out and solve technical problems.

Because of the relative complexity of CSS compared to HTML, Part II includes even more opportunities than Part I to learn and apply technical sophistication. For example, many of the code listings require you to orient yourself in a CSS file and figure out where to put the new style rules introduced by the listing. Another important technique is learning to *comment out* CSS rules and then refreshing the

---

3. Technically, HTML and CSS are *markup* and not *code*, but we'll sometimes use the latter term as a catchall, especially when discussing principles from coding (such as avoiding repetition) that apply as much to HTML and CSS as they do to programming languages like JavaScript or Ruby.

browser to see what they do. We'll also occasionally add CSS rules that are purely for demonstration purposes; technical sophistication is the skill you need to figure out that such demo code can safely be deleted, especially if a future listing omits it.

Later chapters, particularly after Chapter 9, also require that you successfully configure a *development environment* and run a templating system to build a professional-grade website. A huge number of things can go wrong when getting these to work; if you get stuck, there's no substitute for Googling around and determination—both of which are key aspects of technical sophistication.

The important thing at this point in your progress as a developer is to start learning how styling and layout concepts work together, how HTML and CSS combine to make a layout that is actually useful, and how to use some sort of system that allows you to avoid repeating sections of the site or styling on multiple pages (Box 5.2). Doing otherwise would make you an expert at changing text color and size, but you'd have no chance of applying the knowledge you've gained to a real-world scenario. In fact, by learning CSS in a holistic way, you'll not just be getting an introduction to styling—this tutorial is also going to be your first introduction to the world of front-end development.

Box 5.2: Staying DRY

If you've been poking around the Internet in places where developers talk shop, you might have noticed someone mention staying *DRY*, with "dry" in all caps. They aren't talking about relative moisture levels. What they are talking about is a core principle in programming: *Don't Repeat Yourself.*

The idea behind DRY is that good coding should include as few instances of unnecessary repetition as humanly possible, simply because if you have the same code in a bunch of places, then every time you want to make a change you'll have to update all the different spots in the application where that code is repeated. For example, if you wanted to change a link to the navigation bar of a hand-built site, you'd have to make the same change on *every* page. On a two-page site this wouldn't be a big deal, but for a bigger website it would be a nightmare.

Programmers are a special sort of lazy—especially when it comes to doing something repetitive that could be done more efficiently with a little bit of extra programming. To make it easier to be lazy, enterprising programmers spend countless hours creating systems that allow other developers not to have to repeat themselves. We all benefit from developers who at some point decided they were going to work really hard *now* so they could work less hard in the future.

Templating software, like the system we will be using starting in Chapter 9, allows us not to repeat ourselves by collecting repeated code into individual files, and then including these code snippets on any page where they're needed.

The result is that we can write something like the navigation menu for a site *once*, put it in its own little file, and then include that file every place where the navigation needs to appear. If we want to change the navigation later on, we need to edit only that single file, and the changes will automatically be applied to every page that includes it. We'll learn how to do this in Section 9.6.

5.1.1 So, What Is Front-End Development?

When someone says that they are a front-end developer, that means that they work on the parts of a site that people see and interact with. That includes things like HTML, CSS, and JavaScript. You'll also hear people talk about user interface (UI) design (the way things look) and user experience (UX) design (the way that the interface and different pages function to move users through the site to a goal).

The complement to front-end development is back-end development, which involves the architecture of data, how it is stored, and how it is delivered. Later Learn Enough tutorials (starting with *Learn Enough Ruby to Be Dangerous* (https://www.learnenough.com/ruby)) cover the basics of back-end development, culminating in the *Ruby on Rails Tutorial* (https://www.railstutorial.org/), which teaches how to develop a full web application with a database, users, login and authentication, and more.

So, how do we turn an HTML caterpillar into a front-end developer butterfly?

The Plan

We'll start by building on the styling introduced in Chapter 4. In the final sections of that tutorial, we showed how to add styling directly to elements on a page, while also briefly covering how to factor that styling into a stylesheet. In this tutorial, we'll expand greatly on this theme.

Throughout the rest of this chapter, we'll learn the basics of CSS declarations and values by starting with a few super-simple elements on a sample page, with a particular focus on applying the DRY principle (Box 5.2). We'll end with a first introduction to the essential technique of *CSS selectors* to target particular page elements for styling.

In Chapter 6, we'll discuss aspects of selectors that are important to get right at the beginning of a project, with a focus on managing complexity and maintaining flexibility by choosing good names for things (including an introduction to CSS color conventions).

Chapter 7 introduces two of the most important kinds of CSS values: colors and sizes. These lay an essential foundation for Chapter 8 on the *box model*, which determines how different elements fit together on the page.

In Chapter 9 and Chapter 10, we'll take the page that we've been working on and factor it into a layout using a *static site generator* (which includes a templating system) called *Jekyll* to build professional-grade websites that are easy to maintain and update.

In Chapter 11, we'll learn how to make flexible page layouts using *flexbox*, adding layouts for a photo gallery page (to be filled in in *Learn Enough JavaScript to Be Dangerous* (https://www.learnenough.com/javascript)) and a blog with posts. In Chapter 12, we'll add the blog itself, showing how to use Jekyll to make a professional-grade blog without black-box solutions like WordPress or Tumblr.

Because a large and growing amount of web traffic comes from mobile devices, in Chapter 13 we'll cover the basics of using CSS and *media queries* to make mobile-friendly sites without violating the DRY principle (Box 5.2).

As a concluding step in developing the main sample application, in Chapter 14 we'll add the kinds of little details (like custom fonts and `meta` tags) that make a site feel complete. The result will be an industrial-strength, nicely styled site deployed to the live Web.

Finally, as a special bonus, we'll introduce a more recent and advanced layout technique known as *CSS grid* in Chapter 16. The result is a largely self-contained discussion of how to use grid to accomplish some of the same effects mentioned in previous chapters, as well as some effects specific to grid.

Let's go!

5.2 CSS Overview and History

CSS takes the form of plain-text declarations inserted into an HTML or CSS file using a text editor (https://www.learnenough.com/text-editor). A typical series of CSS declarations might look like Listing 5.1. (You are not expected to understand these styles at this point.)

Listing 5.1: Typical CSS declarations.

```css
body {
  color: black;
}

p {
  font-size: 1em;
}

p.highlighted {
  font-size: 1.5em;
  background: yellow;
}
```

The "Cascading" part of Cascading Style Sheets refers to the way the defined styles flow, or "cascade", down from element to element on a page based on a few factors like which declaration came first, whether an element is the child of a parent element that has styles applied to it, or the strength of the declaration (more on this in Section 6.3). This inheritance of style (from the top levels to elements below) happens so that we as developers can avoid having to define how every single element should look. For example, if we changed the **color** in the **body** tag in Listing 5.1, that change would cascade down and change the **color** attribute on every interior element as well.

The "Style Sheet" part of the name (sometimes written as the single word *stylesheet*) refers to how CSS allows developers to collect all the style declarations in a separate section of the page (called an *internal stylesheet*), or place them into an external file (called, you guessed it, an *external stylesheet*). External stylesheets are loaded onto the page as a link in the **head** section of the HTML. (We'll learn how to do this ourselves in Chapter 9.) The result is that we end up separating the code that defines how something looks (or is positioned) from the actual content—all of which makes for simpler and more maintainable code.

5.2.1   CSS Is Always Changing

One important thing to note about CSS is that, like HTML, it's constantly evolving to better serve the needs of web designers and developers. In fact, in many ways CSS is evolving even faster than HTML.

Even though future additions are added to the official CSS specification all the time, they aren't evenly distributed—when new additions to CSS are proposed, the adoption of those new concepts happens on a browser-by-browser basis. A style that might work in Google Chrome might be totally unsupported by Mozilla Firefox or Microsoft Internet Explorer (or IE's latest incarnation, Microsoft Edge). Or it's possible that a given style might be supported, but only if you use a special temporary name to declare the style, a feature that lets developers target only the browsers that support the style they want to use (Box 5.3).

Box 5.3: Vendor Prefixing

Because it takes a while for an addition to the language to go from a suggested new specification (or *spec*) to an officially included part of CSS, new features aren't accepted by all browsers at the same time. Most browser makers aren't interested in waiting around for the spec to be officially updated, though—they want their software to push the envelope and do really cool stuff. So vendors take these CSS spec proposals and implement their own versions of the spec.

To get around the potential confusion that could happen if things work differently from browser to browser, the browser vendors typically add a prefix to the experimental styles, such as -webkit-, -moz-, and -ms- (respectively for WebKit, Mozilla, and Microsoft browsers). This allows the applied style to target specific browsers in case the support differs.

For instance, the CSS transition declaration (covered in Section 11.4) was implemented in most browsers before it was a part of the official spec, and to use it you would have needed to declare the styling like the following examples with vendor prefixes:

```
-webkit-transition: all 0.1s linear;
-moz-transition: all 0.1s linear;
-ms-transition: all 0.1s linear;
transition: all 0.1s linear;
```

The first rule here specifically targets browsers that use the WebKit layout engine (which includes Safari and Chrome), while the second targets browsers using Mozilla's Gecko engine (principally Firefox), and the third targets Microsoft browsers (Internet Explorer and Edge). Finally, the fourth rule is an unprefixed declaration—in this case, just transition by itself—which is included so that when support becomes official we won't have to go back into our code and add it in. (The transition style is supported by all major browsers today, so if you see the prefixed versions in code that you are working on, you can safely delete them.)

Luckily, at this point the most common styling definitions are essentially the same across different browsers,[4] and we aren't going to cover anything in this tutorial that has questionable browser support. At some point, though, you'll probably find yourself wanting to use a more cutting-edge style, and when that happens we recommend using a tool like CanIUse to figure out how well-supported the style is. Don't ever feel self-conscious about using reference sites like that—the fast-changing nature of the language and the spotty browser support make it a necessary tool even for people who have been doing this for years.

5.2.2 How Did CSS Develop?

In the beginning, content on the Internet was simply plain text. Then, as methods for organizing content started to come into existence (such as HTML around 1990), a number of methods sprang up to affect the appearance and layout of the data.

At first, many styling solutions that affected how the page looked would be set by individual users' browser preferences rather than by the creator of the page. As the complexity of the web increased, it became increasingly obvious that there should be a way for the *owner* of a site to at least suggest how a page should look, rather than leaving the appearance up to each individual browser.

Lots of interesting suggestions were put forward that never got widely adopted, usually because the proposed styling was overly complicated or used a totally non-intuitive structure:

- Robert Raisch developed RRP, which used arcane two-character style declarations and was fairly unreadable.

- Pei-Yuan Wei created the ViolaWWW browser and a styling system called PWP, which introduced nesting styles and external stylesheets, but it was only released for Unix operating systems and never really caught on.

- FOSI was created for an HTML precursor called SGML, and it worked by adding complicated tags on the page around content (not good).

---

4. Anyone who's spent much time in the world of front-end development can tell you horror stories about when that wasn't the case (*cough* IE6 *cough*).

- DSSSL allowed for complex declarations and was more of a programming language with styling attached, but it had a complicated syntax that made it overly complex for styling.

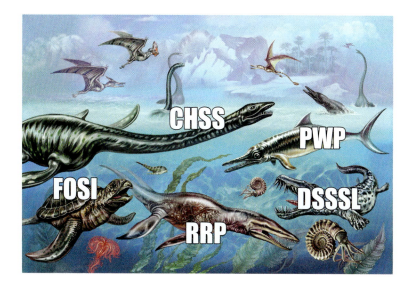

Figure 5.3: There were a lot of precursors to CSS... not all of them successful.

In short, there was a real Cambrian explosion of proposed standards to make the web pretty, and while some of these systems ended up contributing elements to what became CSS, none of them are direct ancestors (Figure 5.3).[5]

About five years after the introduction of HTML, Håkon Lie (working with Bert Bos) put forward a styling system proposal in December of 1996 called CHSS (Cascading HTML Style Sheets). As you might expect, the original proposal has some details that are no longer present in the language, but in his doctoral thesis Håkon Lie simplified the specification into something that more closely resembles modern CSS. Eventually, the concept was adopted by the World Wide Web Consortium (W3C) as the system for styling web content.

Although it represented a big step forward, creating a specification is only half the battle—browsers have to support the standard for it to be of any use to the end-user.

---

5. Image courtesy of Liliya Butenko/Shutterstock.

Figure 5.4: You can't fully understand hate until you try to design for IE6.

No browser even partially supported CSS until 1997, and there wasn't full support of the standard in any one browser until March of 2000—partially because browser makers still had their own ideas for how to accomplish styling, and partially because many browsers supported non-standard HTML tags (we're looking at you, Internet Explorer…).

Each browser handled CSS in its own idiosyncratic way for a long time, and anyone who has been working in front-end development for a while can tell you how maddeningly difficult it was to style a website so that it looked the same across browsers. Microsoft's Internet Explorer was *by far* the biggest problem (Figure 5.4), and we can only imagine the number of people who gave up on the world of web design and development thanks to horrific CSS support in early versions of IE.[6]

The differences between implementations of CSS in different browsers remained significant until just a few years ago, with the rise to dominance of the WebKit browsers (Google Chrome and Apple Safari) and Gecko-powered Mozilla Firefox.

---

6. If you are ever asked to develop something that can work in Internet Explorer 6 or 7, just laugh and walk away. Trying to make a site work on those browsers just isn't worth it, and thankfully they are finally disappearing from the world.

So when reading this tutorial, just keep in mind that styling the Web was a complete and utter mess until *very* recently—about 15 years after the initial release of the CSS spec in 1997.

5.2.3 The Bog of Eternal Subjectivity

One last bit of meta-information before we jump in and start styling: deciding how to actually implement CSS on a given page can be a confusing mess. Whereas Part I was a little more prescriptive in nature, with many cases where there was only one right way to do things, we are now going to be venturing into places where there is often no right answer. When designing websites with CSS, many solutions to a problem typically exist, which means subjective judgment is the rule rather than the exception (Figure 5.5).[7]

Figure 5.5: Smell baaaad!

---

7. Image courtesy of Historic Collection/Alamy Stock Photo.

Helping you navigate this mess is where we come in.

Oh, and to make this all a little more fun, you may recall from Box 5.3 that every browser implements some parts of the CSS standard in its own slightly different manner, so you can never be absolutely certain that something will look the same to different users if they are using different browsers… to say nothing of how something will look on different screen sizes and resolutions for different operating systems (Chapter 13).

You have to get used to the idea that no site is going to be exactly the same when viewed by different people. You'll learn to design (or implement other people's designs) in a way that allows room for CSS's inherent ambiguity. Unlike the tightly constrained world of print design, getting things to look exactly the same in every browser and on every operating system is just something you have to give up worrying about.

Additionally, when talking about which CSS rules to use when styling a site or creating a layout, best practices tend to move in fads, or are influenced by the subjective opinion of the developers who worked on a project before you. For example, as discussed in Section 5.5, elements on the page frequently need to be assigned classes or ids, and the way that names are picked is entirely up to the person writing the code. As you might guess (if you know many developers or designers), people have *lots* of strong opinions on how you should be naming things—a classic holy war situation.[8]

The most important thing is to be *consistent*. If you start a project and do things one way, make sure to keep following the same conventions for the life of the project. Or, if you decide to make a drastic change, spend the next couple of days updating all your old code, for the sake of future developers (including yourself). Keep an eye out in this tutorial for "Style Note" boxes that have tips on what the current best practices are for different uses of CSS.

5.3 Sample Site Setup

Now that we've got an overview of the purpose and origins of CSS, it's time to start looking at some concrete examples. The initial styling rules will necessarily be simple, so it's important to have patience while we lay this crucial foundation for the working website (with layout) that we'll be developing starting in Chapter 9.

---

8. The notion of a technological "holy war" is discussed in Box 5.4 of *Learn Enough Developer Tools to Be Dangerous*.

We'll start by creating a new project in the **repos** folder using the same basic **mkdir** command covered in Section 1.3 (Listing 5.2).[9]

Listing 5.2: Adding the folder for our sample project.

```
$ cd                               # cd to the home directory
$ mkdir -p repos/<username>.github.io   # Make site directory
$ cd repos/<username>.github.io      # cd into new directory
```

Note that we've used a special directory name that corresponds to the main GitHub Pages site for your account:

```
<username>.github.io
```

In Listing 5.2, **<username>** should be replaced with your GitHub username, so the full URL should look something like **learnenough.github.io**.

GitHub Pages actually supports serving sites out of subdirectories, like **learnenough.github.io/sample_css**, but unfortunately this solution fails if you have additional subdirectories in your site, such as **learnenough.github.io/sample_css/gallery**. The reason is that if you include files and images in one subdirectory (e.g., **sample_css**), there's no natural way to include the same files and images in further subdirectories (e.g., **sample_css/gallery**). Since our sample site will eventually have exactly this kind of structure (Section 10.4), we've opted to use the root Pages domain. An even better solution is to use a *custom domain*, which lets you host your GitHub Pages site at a URL like www.example.com; this is the subject of Part III.

To get our site started, we'll also create an **index.html** file using the **touch** command (as discussed in Section 1.3), as shown in Listing 5.3.

Listing 5.3: Adding a blank **index.html**.

```
$ touch index.html       # Create an empty index file
```

---

9. *Note for Mac users:* Although it shouldn't matter in *Learn Enough CSS & Layout to Be Dangerous*, it is recommended that you use the Bourne-again shell (Bash) rather than the default Z shell to complete this tutorial. To switch your shell to Bash, run **chsh -s /bin/bash** at the command line, enter your password, and restart your terminal program. Any resulting alert messages are safe to ignore. See the Learn Enough blog post "Using Z Shell on Macs with the Learn Enough Tutorials" (https://news.learnenough.com/macos-bash-zshell) for more information.

Inside the new folder, use your favorite text editor to open the newly created **index.html** file and paste in the markup shown in Listing 5.4. For convenience, the contents of Listing 5.4 and all other code listings in this tutorial are available online at the following URL:

```
https://github.com/learnenough/learn_enough_html_css_and_layout_code_listings
```

Listing 5.4: The initial HTML for our site.
index.html

```html
<!DOCTYPE html>
<html>
  <head>
    <title>Test Page: Don't Panic</title>
    <meta charset="utf-8">
    <style>

    </style>
  </head>
  <body>
    <h1>I'm an h1</h1>
    <ul>
      <li>
        <a href="https://example.com/" style="color: red;">Link</a>
      </li>
      <li>
        <a href="https://example.com/" style="color: red;">Link</a>
      </li>
      <li>
        <a href="https://example.com/" style="color: red;">Link</a>
      </li>
    </ul>
    <h2>I'm an h2</h2>
    <div style="border: 1px solid black;">
      <a href="https://example.com/" style="color: green;">I'm a link</a>
    </div>
    <div style="border: 1px solid black;">
      <a href="https://example.com/" style="color: green;">I'm a link</a>
    </div>
    <div style="border: 1px solid black;">
      <a href="https://example.com/" style="color: green;">I'm a link</a>
    </div>
    <div style="border: 1px solid black;">
      <a href="https://example.com/" style="color: green;">I'm a link</a>
    </div>
  </body>
</html>
```

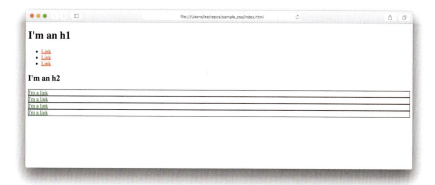

Figure 5.6: This is the beginning of something great, unassuming though it may seem.

When you open that HTML document in your browser (if you aren't sure how to do that, refer back to Section 1.4), you'll see a series of three red links, some headers, and a series of green links in boxes (Figure 5.6). This will be our initial test page.

Note: Due to various slight differences between browsers, browser window sizes, etc., your results may not always match the screenshots exactly, so small discrepancies are not a cause for concern. As we'll emphasize throughout this tutorial, it's important to focus on achieving good-enough results without chasing the unreachable goal of pixel-perfection.

As in Chapter 1, we'll deploy our new website immediately to production, which is a good habit to cultivate. First, you'll need to create a new project at GitHub, using the steps shown in Section 1.3, which in this case looks like Figure 5.7.

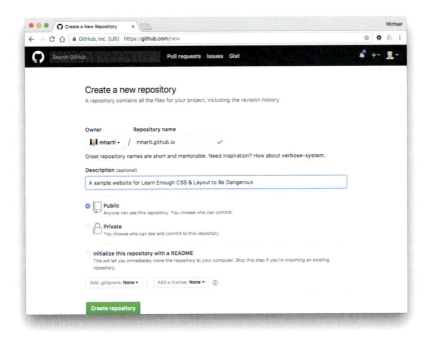

Figure 5.7: Creating a new GitHub repo.

Once you've finished the steps needed to create the repository, initialize and deploy it using the commands shown in Listing 5.5.

Listing 5.5: Deploying the initial site to GitHub Pages.

```
$ git init
$ git add -A
$ git commit -m "Initialize repo"
$ git remote add origin <repo url>
$ git push -u origin main
```

If you find the sequence of commands in Listing 5.5 challenging instead of familiar, it's probably a good idea to review *Learn Enough Git to Be Dangerous* (https://www.learnenough.com/git) and Section 1.3. (Confirming that the deployment succeeded is left as an exercise (Section 5.3.1).) Finally, although we'll add in the occasional Git commit/deployment in this tutorial, ultimately these will be up to you, and now is a good time to practice making such decisions on your own (Box 5.1).

5.3.1 Exercise

1. By visiting the URL <username>.github.io/index.html, confirm that the deployment to GitHub Pages succeeded. Is it necessary to include index.html in the URL?

5.4 Start Stylin'

As discussed in Section 5.2, CSS is a way of defining how elements on an HTML page look and are positioned, with styling that flows ("cascades") down from element to element based on factors like which declaration came first, whether an element is the child of a parent element that has styles applied to it, or the specificity of the declaration.

So what do "parent", "children", and "specificity" mean in the context of a web page and how it gets styled? The idea is that every element on the page is contained inside another element, which in turn can contain other elements—like Russian nesting dolls.

We can visualize the parent and child structure of the elements on a typical page using the diagram in Figure 5.8.

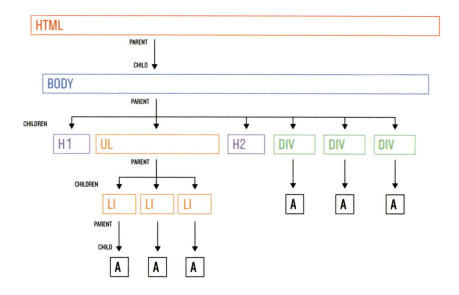

Figure 5.8: Relationships always cascade down.

The hierarchical tag structure shown in Figure 5.8 is known as the *Document Object Model*, or DOM for short.[10] Each new level in the DOM is a child of the level above it. In other words, the **html** tag is the parent of the entire page, the **body** tag is a child of the **html** tag, and so on. The **body** tag then has its own children, which are the **h1** and **h2** elements, the unordered list **ul**, and the **div** elements. In CSS, styling rules flow down from parents to children unless another style interrupts and takes priority.

Our first application of these ideas will be to the repetitive inline styles that exist in our current example page. Now that you know about the DRY principle (Box 5.2), all that redundant styling should be causing a mild case of programmer's itch, and the only cure is to eliminate the duplication.

If you are reading this after recently finishing Section 4.7, this sort of *refactoring* should be familiar, though this time through we are going to go a little more into details that weren't covered before. If literally none of this is familiar, please refer back to Section 4.7.1 and then come back.

Let's first look at cleaning up the **div** elements that share identical inline border styling, as seen in Listing 5.6.

Listing 5.6: Repeated inline styles violate the DRY principle.
index.html

```
<div style="border: 1px solid black;">
<div style="border: 1px solid black;">
<div style="border: 1px solid black;">
```

To make the example code cleaner, we are going to use the **style** block that has already been added to our new initial HTML in Listing 5.4 (the best practice is actually to put the CSS rules in a separate file, a task we'll undertake in Section 9.6).

Now let's get rid of the repetition in Listing 5.6 by adding in our first CSS declaration, as shown in Listing 5.7.[11]

---

10. "DOM" is usually pronounced as a word, so "DOM" rhymes with "Mom".

11. For simplicity, partial code listings like Listing 5.7 won't necessarily show the full indentation level, but (as discussed in Box 1.4) you should strive to use the proper indentation level in order to keep your markup tidy.

Listing 5.7: Adding our first CSS style.
index.html

```
<style>
  div {
    border: 1px solid black;
  }
</style>
```

Figure 5.9 shows the anatomy of the CSS rule from Listing 5.7: the **div** part of the statement, which is outside the curly braces, is called the CSS *selector* (in this case targeting only **div** HTML elements). Then there is a *declaration* made up of a property (**border**) and a *value* (**1px solid black**) separated from the property by a colon. Finally, there is a semicolon at the end of the line that ends the style. (Just a warning: a lot of these terms get mixed up in regular usage. For example, people will sometimes refer to the whole thing, including the selector, as the declaration.)

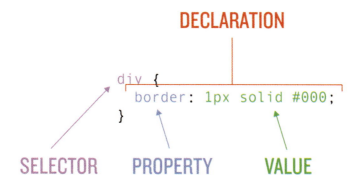

Figure 5.9: What's in a name?

Although the spacing shown in Listing 5.7 is typical, CSS is similar to HTML in that whitespace is ignored by the browser. For the sake of any humans viewing your markup, though, it's a good idea to follow certain formatting conventions (Box 5.4).

Box 5.4: Style Note: Formatting Styles

The styling statement from Listing 5.7 can also be written with everything on one line, like this:

```
div {border: 1px solid black}
```

While that might look nice and tidy at first, you should probably avoid writing CSS that way, as it would make for unreadable code as you start to add more styles. It is far easier to read a list of style declarations like this:

```
button {
    background-color: gray;
    border: 1px solid black;
    color: white;
    cursor: pointer;
    display: inline-block;
    font-family: "proxima-nova", "Proxima Nova",
                 sans-serif;
    font-size: 12px;
    font-weight: bold;
    letter-spacing: 0.15em;
    padding: 10px 15px;
    text-decoration: none;
    text-transform: uppercase;
    transition: all 0.1s linear;
}
```

than it is to read this:

```
button { background-color: gray; border: 1px solid
black; color: white; cursor: pointer; display:
inline-block; font-family: "proxima-nova",
"Proxima Nova",
sans-serif; font-size: 12px; font-weight: bold;
letter-spacing: 0.15em; padding: 10px 15px;
text-decoration: none; text-transform: uppercase;
transition: all 0.1s linear}
```

Now just imagine trying to find specific properties on a page with hundreds of styles where every declaration looks like that... "Nightmare" wouldn't even begin to describe your development experience.

A second point about formatting is that you'll notice that the style properties are all in alphabetical order. It might seem annoying to keep your properties alphabetized, but if you do you'll find that over time you will find things much faster than if the ordering is haphazard. Fortunately, your text editor of choice likely has an alphabetize feature. For example, in Sublime Text you can select multiple lines and hit a function key (F5 on Mac, F9 on Windows) to automatically rearrange things in alphabetical order! Other editors frequently have packages that do the same.

After adding the CSS in Listing 5.7, delete all the **style="border: 1px solid black;"** attributes from the four **div** tags (Listing 5.8).

Listing 5.8: How the entire page should now look.
index.html

```
    <h2>I'm an h2</h2>
    <div>
      <a href="https://example.com/" style="color: green;">I'm a link</a>
    </div>
    <div>
      <a href="https://example.com/" style="color: green;">I'm a link</a>
    </div>
    <div>
      <a href="https://example.com/" style="color: green;">I'm a link</a>
    </div>
    <div>
      <a href="https://example.com/" style="color: green;">I'm a link</a>
    </div>
  </body>
</html>
```

Save the changes, refresh the page in your browser… and BAM! Everything should look the same. (If not, double-check your work to see if you can get your results to match.)

So what happened here? The declaration that we added in Listing 5.7 is a CSS statement that tells the browser it needs to apply a 1-pixel wide solid black border to all of the **div**s in the **body** of the **html**. (We'll learn more about pixels in Section 7.3.) The result is a simplification of the code without any change in the page's appearance.

Now that we've seen how to consolidate a bunch of inline styles into a single CSS declaration, let's do the same thing for the links that are colored red via inline styles inside the **li**s. First add the new style, as shown in Listing 5.9.

Listing 5.9: Add the new CSS.
index.html

```
<style>
  a {
    color: red;
  }
```

And then remove the inline styles from the links:

```html
<li>
  <a href="https://example.com/">Link</a>
</li>
<li>
  <a href="https://example.com/">Link</a>
</li>
<li>
  <a href="https://example.com/">Link</a>
</li>
```

As before, the appearance shouldn't change after refreshing the browser.

At this point, we've definitely made progress in the fight against inline style redundancy, but what about those links that are colored green at the bottom using inline styling? One way to clean up the inline styles would be to use *CSS classes*, which we'll start covering in Section 5.5, but for now let's see if we can do it with just generic CSS selectors.

Because the links in question are contained inside **div**s, and the other links on the page are not, we can use the nesting inheritance of CSS to define a style that changes *only* the color of links inside **div**s. We can accomplish this by adding a declaration to the style block, and then removing the inline styles from the links on the page. Your entire test page should now look like Listing 5.10.

Listing 5.10: Whole page with new styling to target links inside **div**s.
index.html

```html
<!DOCTYPE html>
<html>
  <head>
    <title>Test Page: Don't Panic</title>
    <meta charset="utf-8">
    <style>
      a {
        color: red;
      }
      div {
        border: 1px solid black;
      }
      div a {
        color: green;
      }
```

```
    </style>
  </head>
  <body>
    <h1>I'm an h1</h1>
    <ul>
      <li>
        <a href="https://example.com/">Link</a>
      </li>
      <li>
        <a href="https://example.com/">Link</a>
      </li>
      <li>
        <a href="https://example.com/">Link</a>
      </li>
    </ul>
    <h2>I'm an h2</h2>
    <div>
      <a href="https://example.com/">I'm a link</a>
    </div>
    <div>
      <a href="https://example.com/">I'm a link</a>
    </div>
    <div>
      <a href="https://example.com/">I'm a link</a>
    </div>
    <div>
      <a href="https://example.com/">I'm a link</a>
    </div>
  </body>
</html>
```

The page is a lot cleaner now, isn't it? Separating the styling from the content makes the page's code much easier to read, but maybe you can already see the problem with the way that we've targeted the styles…

The problem is: if we were to add new **div**s anywhere on the page, and they happened to have links inside them, those links would be green even if that isn't what we want. The reason why is that the selector we used in that declaration is way too generic. In Section 5.5, we'll take a look at how to add styling with far greater specificity using CSS ids and classes.

5.4.1   Exercises

1. Using what we learned about targeting links inside other objects, change the color of the links inside the **li**s.

2. Add a border around the **li**s using the same styling as we used to add the borders around the **div**s.

5.5   CSS Selectors

Between Part I and the beginning of Part II, we have so far used only rudimentary targeting techniques for styles. In Part I, we learned how to add styles directly to elements, but this approach is brittle and inefficient. In this tutorial, so far we've used CSS that is separated from the content, but we have used only generic selectors like **div** or **a**. The problem with generic element selectors is that they apply to *all* the elements on the page. So, how can we apply styling to *specific* elements rather than to every single one?

There are two methods, one that targets only one element per page—the *id* (or "identification") selector[12]—and one able to target multiple elements—the *class* selector. Let's edit our example HTML to add this kind of targeting to our page.

Ids and classes are always applied only to the opening tag of an element, and they always have the same format. We'll use the **div** tag for concreteness:

```
<div id="foo" class="bar">
  .
  .
  .
</div>
```

We see here that both ids and classes consist of key-value pairs, where each value is a string that serves as a label for the id or class. In this case, the key **id** has value **"foo"** and the key **class** has value **"bar"**.

Although CSS offers a great deal of flexibility in choosing id and class names, there are a few restrictions and usage suggestions:

---

12. The traditional contraction for "identification" is the uppercase "ID", but in computer contexts the lowercase "id" has become a common alternative (despite the possible confusion with the psychoanalytic word *id*). This is due in large part to the convention of using lowercase tags (e.g., **div** instead of **DIV**) in modern HTML markup.

- Use only one id per element.

- No numbers are allowed at the beginning of the name (e.g., **name1** is valid, but **1name** isn't).

- Dashes (**-**), underscores **_**, and CamelCase can be used to join multiple words (so **foo-bar-baz**, **foo_bar_baz**, and **FooBarBaz** are all valid names).

- Spaces are invalid in id names, and are used to separate multiple names in the case of classes (so **id="foo bar"** is illegal, while **class="foo bar baz"** places three separate classes on an element).

- Be consistent (e.g., if using dashes as separators, use them everywhere—don't mix them with underscores unless you have a good reason—see Box 6.1).

To see how this works in practice, let's add some ids and classes to our sample page. On the first opening **div** tag that comes right after the **h2**, add **id="exec-bio"**, and then add **class="bio-box"** to all of the **div**s in that section, as shown in Listing 5.11.

Listing 5.11: Adding CSS classes and an id to the sample page.
index.html

```html
<h2>I'm an h2</h2>
<div id="exec-bio" class="bio-box">
  <a href="https://example.com/">I'm a link</a>
</div>
<div class="bio-box">
  <a href="https://example.com/">I'm a link</a>
</div>
<div class="bio-box">
  <a href="https://example.com/">I'm a link</a>
</div>
<div class="bio-box">
  <a href="https://example.com/">I'm a link</a>
</div>
</body>
</html>
```

(This use of a class is a good CSS practice, but we generally don't recommend using an id in this context; we include it here mainly for demonstration purposes. We'll discuss this issue in more detail in Section 6.2.)

Next, let's update our CSS block to target these new selectors. To target an id in CSS, you put a **#** (usually read "hash") in front of the name, and to target a class you add a **.** (usually read "dot"). For example, to change the background color of the **#exec-bio** id, we can use the following CSS rule:

```css
#exec-bio {
  background-color: lightgray;
}
```

(Here **lightgray** represents (surprise!) a light gray,[13] which is an example of a *CSS color name*. We'll cover the details of color naming in Section 7.1.) Similarly, to apply a rule to the **.bio-box** class,[14] we can use the following CSS:

```css
.bio-box {
  border: 1px solid black;
}
```

As we'll see in a moment, this rule keeps the thin black border added in Listing 5.8, but in such a way that it doesn't apply to *all* the divs on the site.

Finally, we can target the anchor tags inside the bio boxes using the combination of the class name and the tag name, like this:

```css
.bio-box a {
  color: green;
}
```

This turns the **a** tags green, but only if they're inside an element with class **"bio-box"**. This class-based approach gives us much finer-grained control than the method used in Listing 5.10.

Adding these three rules to the **style** block (while removing the rules we no longer need) leads to the markup shown in Listing 5.12.

---

13. CSS supports both the American spelling *gray* ("a" for "American") and the English spelling *grey* ("e" for "English").

14. We'll often refer to elements with applied classes using the corresponding CSS notation. In other words, **.bio-box** refers to an element with the rule **class="bio-box"**.

Listing 5.12: Adding CSS rules to target the classes and id.
index.html

```
a {
  color: red;
}
#exec-bio {
  background-color: lightgray;
}
.bio-box {
  border: 1px solid black;
}
.bio-box a {
  color: green;
}
```

After saving your changes and refreshing the browser, you should see that the boxes at the bottom have the same border as before, but now the one with the CSS id has a light gray background (Figure 5.10).

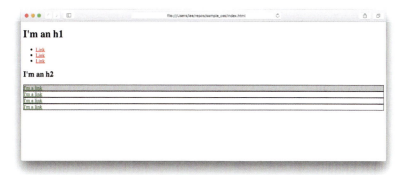

Figure 5.10: Elements targeted with classes and ids.

Congrats! You've just used ids and classes to target styles at specific elements, and have leveled up your CSS knowledge. Now that you've learned how to make declarations, and how to use ids and classes, we can start getting into the nitty-gritty of how CSS works.

5.5.1 Exercises

1. Try adding a new CSS id to the style section (you pick the name) that sets the background color of an element to **orange**, and then add that id to one of the links on the page.

2. Add a new class to the style section (you pick the name again) that changes the background color to **azure**, and add that class name as a second class on the **.bio-box**es. You'll notice that one box is different from the rest, something that we'll discuss in Section 6.3.

3. Commit your changes from this chapter and deploy the result to GitHub Pages. Confirm that the deployed site renders correctly. (It may take a minute or two for the cache to clear, so keep refreshing until the result is what you expect.)

CHAPTER 6
The Style of Style

We can think of CSS as operating at two main levels: the browser and the text editor. From the browser's perspective, the exact choices for CSS classes and ids are irrelevant; indeed, as far as the browser is concerned, there is hardly any difference between beautiful self-contained CSS with perfectly comprehensible class names and horrible inline styles on every element.[1]

At the level of the text editor, though, these concerns matter a lot to the people writing the HTML and CSS for the site—in this case, us. The browser might not care much about the repetition and complexity from inline styles and poorly named classes, but we sure do.

Moreover, bad styling choices can haunt us throughout a project, so it's important to do our best to get them right from the start (bearing in mind that we might have to make some changes down the line).

In this chapter, we'll focus on developing an understanding of the "style of style"—how to make good choices in naming and structuring the various parts of our site—as early as possible. The result will be a codebase that is flexible and maintainable, both for us and for any other developers who need to modify the site later on.

---

1. There might be slight differences in download and processing times, but on most modern systems these differences would hardly be detectable to the user.

6.1 Naming Things

As computer scientist Phil Karlton once remarked, "There are only two hard things in Computer Science: cache invalidation and naming things."[2] This latter "hard thing" applies to front-end development as well.

When coming up with names for classes and ids, it's often helpful to think in terms of how something functions or what its intent is, and it's usually best to be specific. For example, making a class called **"box1"** is a bad idea because the name is so generic; on a big project, you might not remember what **"box1"** refers to when you come back to the code at some point in the future. Better to introduce a class like **"bio-box"**, which makes reference to a specific kind of element on the page (in this case, a box for short biographies).

One important thing to avoid is naming classes or ids after how the element looks on the page. For example, suppose that for some reason the last **.bio-box** on the test page has information that we want a user to be alerted to, which we want to indicate by setting the background color of the box to red. We could add a class of **"red"** to the last box (as in Listing 6.1), making sure it is separated from the other class by a space, and then style it in the CSS like in Listing 6.2.

Listing 6.1: Adding the class **.red** to a **.bio-box**.

index.html

```html
<div class="bio-box">
  <a href="https://example.com/">I'm a link</a>
</div>
<div class="bio-box red">
  <a href="https://example.com/">I'm a link</a>
</div>
```

Listing 6.2: Creating the **.red** class styling.

index.html

```css
  .bio-box a {
    color: green;
  }
  .red {
    background: red;
  }
</style>
```

2. An anonymous jokester once quipped that "There are only two hard things in Computer Science: cache invalidation, naming things, and off-by-one errors."

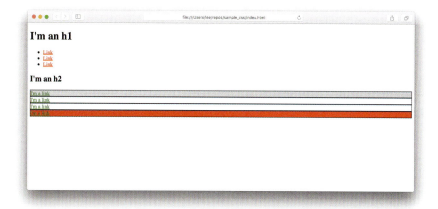

Figure 6.1: Sure, this worked. But is it a good idea?

When you save your work and refresh the browser, you'll see that the background of the box has changed (Figure 6.1).

But let's say that at some point in the future we decide that red isn't our favorite color for alerts anymore, and now we want to use purple. So we open up our project file, and in the CSS we change the **background** property to **purple**, as in Listing 6.3.

Listing 6.3: The problem when you name classes based on appearance.
index.html

```
.bio-box a {
  color: green;
}
.red {
  background: purple;
}
</style>
```

Now the class name and the effect it has on the page not only don't match up; they are downright confusing.

This might seem like no big deal on our simple test page, but imagine if that class were used on elements all over a project. We'd have two choices: go through and change all the class names on all the elements, or just live with the class and its effect being confusing.

Instead, if we use a naming convention where the class names are based on what the intended purpose is of the element on the page, and therefore used a more descriptive name like **"alert"**, then we can change the text color without needing to worry about contradictory or confusing names (Listing 6.4).

Listing 6.4: A more appropriately named class based on the intention.
index.html

```
.alert {
  background: purple;
}
</style>
```

Then we can update the class name on the HTML element:

```
<div class="bio-box alert">
```

With the convention shown in Listing 6.4, if we later decide that alerts should be purple instead of red, there's nothing confusing in the code. Some other examples: instead of calling something **"small"**, choose a class name like **"collapsed"** if that is the functionality; or use **"disabled"** instead of **"gray"** for grayed out elements that a user isn't allowed to interact with.

Of course, there are exceptions, and ultimately the naming system is totally up to you, but as a rule of thumb, it's a good idea to stick with functional naming (Box 6.1).

Box 6.1: Style Note: Naming Conventions

Strict prescriptive class naming systems have become popular recently, and with good reason: there were a lot of projects out there with naming conventions that were completely arbitrary—projects that had more in common with a Dr. Seuss story than a coherent development project. These sorts of strict naming systems are frequently used when there is no limit to the number of developers who might work on a project over its lifetime (think of web applications developed and managed at large corporations).

We aren't going to get into any of these in this tutorial, but we thought it would be a good idea to at least mention that they exist. If you get more into front-end development, it might not be a bad idea to look into some of the conventions other developers are using:

- Block Element Modifier (BEM) (https://csswizardry.com/2013/01/mindbemding -getting-your-head-round-bem-syntax/)
- Object Oriented CSS (OOCSS) (https://www.smashingmagazine.com/2011/12 /an-introduction-to-object-oriented-css-oocss/)
- Scalable and Modular Architecture for CSS (SMACSS) (http://smacss.com/)

Whether you find these systems useful or not, the most important thing is to strive for some semblance of consistency.

6.2 When and Why

One of the other decisions we have to make is to decide when we should use ids and when we should use classes. As noted in Section 5.5, ids are intended to target only one element on the page, while classes can target multiple things. To enforce this design, HTML elements will accept multiple class names on a single object (separated by spaces) but allow for only one id per element (anything after the first is ignored). But that isn't the whole story, because browsers treat ids and classes differently, and here is the first place where we're going to run the risk of starting a holy war…

Our view is as follows:

You should strive to use ids only when you absolutely have to (for example, if you are using JavaScript, and then use them *only* for JavaScript).

Yes, in Section 5.5 we added an id to the first **div** and targeted styles at it, but that was just for demonstration purposes, and in general it's a practice that should be avoided. The reason is that when you use an id to apply styles, it is nearly impossible to change that styling with another declaration without making your code full of ugly hacks.

To see why, add our new **.alert** class onto that first **div** (the one that also has the id **#exec-bio**), while also changing the alert color back to **red**:

```
<div id="exec-bio" class="bio-box alert">
```

```
.alert {
  background: red;
}
```

Save and refresh, and you'll notice that nothing changed; even though you'd expect the background to be red, it isn't, and instead looks just like Figure 6.1.

The problem is that ids are considered by the browser to have a higher *specificity*, and that means that any styles declared in the more specific statement will take precedence over less specific styles. You can think of classes like a machine gun spraying out lots of little projectiles, and ids like a rocket launcher. The style that gets launched by an id just has more power.

One way to make the `.alert` style apply would be to increase the specificity of our declaration by adding a new declaration that targets any element that has both the id **#exec-bio** and the class **.alert**, as shown in Listing 6.5.

Listing 6.5: Overcoming the strength of an id style by combining the id and a class. *index.html*

```
  .alert {
    background: red;
  }
  #exec-bio.alert {
    background: red;
  }
</style>
```

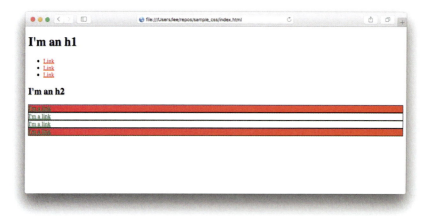

Figure 6.2: Combining the id and class makes for an unusually specific style.

The CSS in Listing 6.5 chains together the rules for an id and a class using **#exec-bio.alert**, and its effect in this case is to force a red background to be added to the div (Figure 6.2).

Using a combined style selector like that will change the background color, but it will apply the style only in the specific situation where both that id and class are present. If your site relies on styles targeted at ids, then over time you'll find yourself adding more and more of these hyper-specific declarations. That isn't the most effective way to use CSS.

It's better in the long run to use a system that's modular, so that designing and developing the front-end of a site is like snapping together LEGOs. This way, you can add a class to an element and be confident that the styles from that class will be applied correctly.

In case you were wondering, the browser merges together all the different declarations and then sorts out conflicts property by property. This means that stronger declarations don't override *all* styles on an object, only the properties that are included in that stronger declaration. In the case of the **.bio-box** that we've been messing around with, all the properties in Listing 6.6 are being simultaneously applied.

Listing 6.6: All the styles that are affecting the one **.bio-box**.

```css
#exec-bio {
  background-color: lightgray;
}
.bio-box {
  border: 1px solid black;
}
.alert {
  background: red;
}
#exec-bio.alert {
  background: red;
}
```

Through the magic of the browser, all those rules are merged, and conflicts are automatically resolved. In the case of Listing 6.6, the merged styling would look something like Listing 6.7 (which indicates unused rules with CSS *comments*, which are discussed further in Section 6.4).

Listing 6.7: The merged styles with the superseded ones commented out.

```
{
  /* background: red; */
  /* background-color: lightgray; */
  background: red;
  border: 1px solid black;
}
```

Because of the specificity of the combined **#exec-bio.alert** class, the **background: red;** rule overrides both the general **background: red;** and the more specific **background-color: lightgray;** rules.[3]

Let's take a closer look at how the browser determines which rules take precedence.

6.3 Priority and Specificity

CSS was designed to allow for multiple stylesheets from multiple locations to influence the appearance of a single document without catastrophically crashing. The result is a system of priority and specificity rules devised to resolve contradictory style declarations like the ones we were playing with in Section 6.2.

To make this clearer, let's take a look at the simplified example shown in Listing 6.8, which uses a **width** set to a particular *percentage*. (We'll learn more about percentages in Section 7.4.)

Listing 6.8: Different rules targeting the same class.
index.html

```
  .bio-box {
    width: 75%;
  }
  .bio-box {
    width: 50%;
  }
</style>
```

---

3. The **background** declaration combines a bunch of different background rules, as seen in the Stack Overflow answer to the question "What is the difference between background and background-color" (https://stackoverflow.com/questions/10205464/what-is-the-difference-between-background-and-background-color).

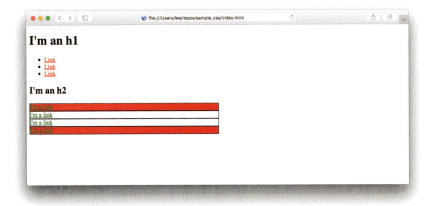

Figure 6.3: A 50%-width box showing how the final CSS rule gets applied.

If you update the style section of your test page with the styling above, you'll notice that the boxes end up being half the width (50%) of the page—i.e., the second rule in Listing 6.8 is the one that gets applied (Figure 6.3). This is part of a general pattern: in the case of conflicting CSS rules, the final one gets applied.

The full list of CSS priority rules appears in Table 6.1. You don't need to memorize this table—over time you'll get a feel for how the priority works. Also, of all these rules, only numbers 3 and 5–8 are priorities that you'll have to understand, and you should *strenuously* try and avoid using numbers 1 (Box 6.2) and 2 (makes for difficult-to-maintain code). Numbers 4 and 9 are out of your control.

Now you might be asking, "OK, but now what happens when we apply two styles that have the same priority?" In this case, we need to consider *specificity* as well as priority, which is used to resolve any situation where multiple styles with the same priority level are applied (#5 in Table 6.1).

At the most basic level, specificity just means that the more specific you are when you target an element, the greater the strength the browser will give to the styles in that declaration. For example, suppose we wanted to make all **a** elements gray by declaring a style as in Listing 6.9.

Listing 6.9: A not-very-specific style.

```
a {
  color: gray;
}
```

Table 6.1: CSS priority rules.

Priority	Name	How it functions
1	Importance	Adding **!important** (e.g., "**width: 100% !important**") to a value overrides all other similar styles (but never use **!important** (Box 6.2).
2	Inline	A declaration that is put on an element using **style=**.
3	Media type	When a style is applied through a media query (more in Chapter 13).
4	User defined	Most browsers have the accessibility feature: a user defined CSS.
5	Selector specificity	Styling applied via a class or id overwrites generic styling.
6	Rule order	The last style written has priority.
7	Parent inheritance	If there is no style specified, then children inherit styles from their parent.
8	CSS	CSS rules from a stylesheet or **style** block that are applied to generic elements.
9	Browser defaults	Lowest priority, these are the default styles that browsers ship with.

Without even needing classes or ids, we could override this style by being a little more specific. So if we had links that were inside of **h1** headers, we could make all **a**s that are inside of those **h1** elements green using a declaration like the one in Listing 6.10.

Listing 6.10: A more specific style.

```
h1 a {
  color: green;
}
```

That slightly more specific declaration overrides the initial styling that made the **a** text gray, and instead the text would be green. (This is the technique we used in Listing 5.10.)

Table 6.2 has a more detailed listing of the values that different selectors are assigned by the browser. The styles get more specific as you go down the table, meaning that lower ones would override the styles above.

You'll notice that there isn't a simple numbering system for Table 6.2 like there is for the priority list in Table 6.1. That's because the specificity uses a separate system

Table 6.2: The confusingly complex rules of specificity.

Type	Example	Specificity
Simple HTML selector	`em {color: #fff;}`	1
HTML selector targeting element inside another element	`h1 em {color: #00ff00;}`	2
CSS class name	`.alert {color: #ff0000;}`	1,0
HTML element with a class name	`p.safe {color: #0000ff;}`	1,1
CSS id	`#thing {color: #823706;}`	1,0,0
CSS id with a class name	`#thing .property {color: #823706;}`	1,1,0
Inline style	`style="color: transparent;"`	1,0,0,0

that has different levels noted by adding new numbers with a comma—it's confusing and we've never actually heard of a developer work through a specificity problem using the number system, but we've included it for the sake of completeness.

This all seems really complicated, right?

Well, most developers don't actually know all these rules by heart. Instead, what we all use are systems of simple conventions like trying to keep declarations simple and general, with exceptions targeted via a class, not using ids to target styles, not using `!important` (Box 6.2), etc. Over time you'll build up a gut feeling for the specificity.

Box 6.2: Style Note: Never Use `!important`

There's another bad way of getting a style to apply, and that is to use the `!important` flag to the declaration, which automatically overrides any conflicting styles (Table 6.1). You should think about `!important` (read "important"; the "!" is silent) like this: if you've had to use `!important`, then you've failed at styling something.

The problem with using `!important` is that once you start using it, there's a tendency to use it more and more over time, since the only way to overcome a style that was applied with `!important` is to use another `!important`. Such proliferating `!important` rules are the tribbles of CSS.

It is always better to rethink how you are styling something than to use
`!important`. Now that you know about `!important`, erase it from your memory.

One way to avoid getting caught in situations where overlapping layers of complexity keep your styles from being applied is to try to keep your selectors as simple as possible (Listing 6.11), rather than using an ugly and complicated set of selectors (Listing 6.12).

Listing 6.11: Good, clean CSS.

```css
.bio-box a {
  color: green;
}
.alert {
  background: red;
}
```

Listing 6.12: Ugly and complicated CSS.

```
body div#exec-bio.bio-box a {
  color: orange;
}
```

Often, simplicity is the best solution.

6.3.1 Exercises

1. Use the **!important** flag to force the background color of the **.alert** class to be red (make sure to remove **#exec-bio** from the style).

2. Remove what you did in Exercise #1 and promise never to use **!important** again (Box 6.2).

3. Try changing the color of the **.bio-box a** links not by changing the **color** property on the existing style, but instead by adding a new identical selector below the existing one and a new **color** declaration that changes the link color to **pink**.

6.4 How to Be a Good Styling Citizen

So, how should you be a good developer and use CSS selectors in a reasonable way that takes advantage of the intricate priority and specificity rules… without requiring a lot of mental overhead? Start with the concept we mentioned in Section 6.2: that classes should be combined like LEGOs to get the result we are looking for. Make design choices that are modular so that your styles only affect things inside modules instead of leaking out to affect elements site-wide.

If you need to have a module do slightly different things depending on placement or status, multiple classes on an element are a valid usage of the class selector, but at the same time don't take that to mean that you need to give every single element on the page a class or (even worse) multiple classes. It's a fine balancing act between under- and over-classing your markup.

Looking at the styling we've done, you might have wondered why we didn't give the links in the **.bio-box**es classes of their own. We definitely could have, and there would have been nothing wrong with that, but this is another one of those subjective areas in styling. One good practice is to divide the styling into two different categories: global styles that will apply in many different places in order to create greater

consistency, and individual sections that are self-contained modules of functionality
or content.

As an example, let's assume that the **.bio-box**es are going to be located in a part
of the site that always has one link in each box—they are going to be repeating and
regular modules. In this case, we can just skip classing the individual links and apply a
more general style for an **a** tag within the **.bio-box**, without needing to drill down
and add new styles. But if we need to add another link, then we'd have to consider
whether or not we want the two links to look the same. If not, it would be necessary
to come up with a different way to target the elements.

Let's add some content to make these ideas more concrete. Replace the dummy
.bio-boxes with the markup shown in Listing 6.13, which includes the entire page
to help you sync up. Note that, among other things, we've eliminated the **exec-bio**
id, which (as mentioned in Section 6.2) we recommend using only when absolutely
necessary, and we've also slimmed down the CSS rules.

Listing 6.13: Using more realistic example HTML.
index.html

```html
<!DOCTYPE html>
<html>
  <head>
    <title>Test Page: Don't Panic</title>
    <meta charset="utf-8">
    <style>
      a {
        color: red;
      }
      .bio-box {
        border: 1px solid black;
      }
      .bio-box a {
        color: green;
      }
    </style>
  </head>
  <body>
    <h1>I'm an h1</h1>
    <ul>
      <li>
        <a href="https://example.com/">Link</a>
      </li>
      <li>
        <a href="https://example.com/">Link</a>
      </li>
      <li>
```

```
      <a href="https://example.com/">Link</a>
    </li>
  </ul>
  <h2>I'm an h2</h2>
  <div class="bio-box">
    <h3>Michael Hartl</h3>
    <a href="https://twitter.com/mhartl">here</a>
    <p>
      Known for his dazzling charm, rapier wit, and unrivaled humility,
      Michael is the creator of the
      <a href="https://www.railstutorial.org/">Ruby on Rails
      Tutorial</a> and principal author of the
      <a href="https://learnenough.com/">
      Learn Enough to Be Dangerous</a> introductory sequence. Michael
      is also notorious as the founder of
      <a href="http://tauday.com/">Tau Day</a> and author of
      <a href="http://tauday.com/tau-manifesto"><em>The Tau
      Manifesto</em></a>, but rumors that he's secretly a supervillain
      are slightly exaggerated.
    </p>
  </div>
  <div class="bio-box">
    <h3>Lee Donahoe</h3>
    <a href="https://twitter.com/leedonahoe">here</a>
    <p>
      When he's not literally swimming with sharks or hunting powder stashes on
      his snowboard, you can find Lee in front of his computer designing
      interfaces, doing front-end development, or writing some of the
      interface-related Learn Enough tutorials.
    </p>
  </div>
  <div class="bio-box">
    <h3>Nick Merwin</h3>
    <a href="https://twitter.com/nickmerwin">here</a>
    <p>
      You may have seen him shredding guitar live with Capital Cities on Jimmy
      Kimmel, Conan, or The Ellen Show, but rest assured Nick is a true nerd at
      heart. He's just as happy shredding well-spec'd lines of code from a tour
      bus as he is from his kitchen table.
    </p>
  </div>
  <div class="bio-box">
    <h3>??</h3>
    <p>
      The Future
    </p>
  </div>
  </body>
</html>
```

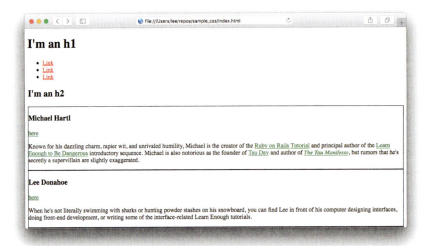

Figure 6.4: All-green links.

If you save and refresh the page, you'll find that all of the links in the boxes look the same, i.e., they're green (Figure 6.4).

Looking back at Listing 6.13, we see that each bio contains a link to the corresponding person's Twitter account, and it would be nice to distinguish these visually from the others. We'll continue to improve these links throughout the tutorial, but for now we'll just make them blue, while keeping the others green.

One way to do this would be to retarget the style that makes the links green by making the style only apply to links that are *inside* paragraph **p** tags, as shown in Listing 6.14.

Listing 6.14: Styling link color inside the paragraphs.
index.html

```
.bio-box p a {
  color: green;
}
```

This would change the Twitter links to red (the color specified by the generic rule for anchor tags in Listing 5.9), reserving green for links inside paragraph tags, but it would also start bumping up against a suggested *three-selector limit* rule of thumb, as discussed in Box 6.3.

Box 6.3: Style Note: Selector Depth

In general, and for a couple of reasons, it's a good idea to keep the number of selectors in a declaration under three (i.e., to three or fewer). This might seem easy right now with our super-simple test page, but on a complicated site things can get very messy. One obvious reason you want your selectors to be as short as possible is for readability. It's just easier to find what you are looking for in a big section of CSS if the selectors are short.

The other reason is that CSS selectors are read by the browser from right to left, so the more selectors there are, and the more general they are, the more work the browser has to do to render your page. It's a little counter-intuitive, since you'd think that the browser would start on the left and narrow down the scope of the styling by moving right… but for technical reasons it doesn't. So if you declared a style using `#first-table tr td h1`, the browser would first identify all `h1`s, then all `td`s, then all `tr`s, and finally restrict everything to just the elements that are in something with an id of `#first-table`.

If you have lots of elements on a page, this kind of inefficiency can really slow down rendering times, so keeping the number of selectors down is good both for us (the developers) and for our users.

Using the rule shown in Listing 6.14 would be fine—we'd just have to pay attention and avoid making it more complicated in future changes—but let's instead use a more robust practice by applying the specificity rules to get what we want while still adhering to Box 6.3's three-selector limit. We can accomplish this by changing the style selector back to just **.bio-box a** while adding a class of **social-link** to all the Twitter links (Listing 6.15).

Listing 6.15: Adding a class to the social media links.
index.html

```
<a href="https://twitter.com/mhartl" class="social-link">here</a>
   .
   .
   .
<a href="https://twitter.com/leedonahoe" class="social-link">here</a>
   .
```

.
.
.

```
<a href="https://twitter.com/nickmerwin" class="social-link">here</a>
```

Then we can style the links by adding the new class declaration in the CSS, as in Listing 6.16. (Put this new declaration somewhere below the **.bio-box a** declaration.)

Listing 6.16: Adding a style declaration for our social links.
index.html

```
.bio-box a {
  color: green;
}
a.social-link {
  color: blue;
}
```

Now, any links that are inside paragraphs will be green, while the social links will be a nice blue (Figure 6.5).

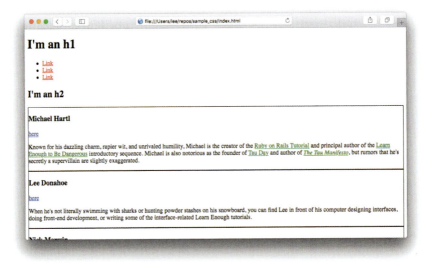

Figure 6.5: The class combined with **a** allows the styling to apply.

When combined, the class and element selectors have higher specificity than **.bio-box a**. So, if you were to remove the **a** from **.social-link** in the selector, the link would turn green again.

So what's the point of this seemingly simple exercise?

It wouldn't seem like choosing a link color is all that important, but little mistakes in how you deal with specificity at the beginning of a project can cause problems down the road. Even in this simplified example, there are a bunch of decisions that have to be made that could affect the future development of the page. Choosing poorly could require us to have to go back to the code and rewrite it if our original styling was too generic or restrictive.

For example, suppose we kept the green link styling targeted using **.bio-box p a**. If we then later wanted to put images into the links—along with styles that target the images—we would have to add classes to all the images to cleanly target them (because **.bio-box p a img** is too many selectors deep). On the other hand, while classes for the images might be a good option if there are only a few, if there are a whole lot of images it could be a hassle to add in class names on each and every one.

You could get around both of these problems by adding a class to the **p** tag, which would let you cut out a level in the declaration, but then what happens if you want multiple paragraphs in a bio? Now each **p** would need a class… and you are back into the mess of having to add class names to a large number of elements. An easy solution would be to wrap that whole text section in a new **div** with a class like **.bio-copy**, and then target the links inside with **.bio-copy a** and images in links with **.bio-copy img**.

Let's look at an example of what it looks like to wrap the text content in an element with its own class to allow for more precise targeting. This involves adding **.bio-copy** wrappers around each biography's copy,[4] as shown in Listing 6.17, which we'll put to use in a moment.

Listing 6.17: Wrapping each of the bios in a **div** to better target the text.
index.html

```
<div class="bio-box">
  <h3>Michael Hartl</h3>
  <a href="https://twitter.com/mhartl" class="social-link">here</a>
  <div class="bio-copy">
```

---

4. Here "copy" refers to "the text to be typeset", i.e., the kind of thing a copy editor edits.

```
        .
        .
        .
    </<div>
</div>

<div class="bio-box">
    <h3>Lee Donahoe</h3>
    <a href="https://twitter.com/leedonahoe" class="social-link">here</a>
    <div class="bio-copy">
        .
        .
        .
    </<div>
</div>

<div class="bio-box">
    <h3>Nick Merwin</h3>
    <a href="https://twitter.com/nickmerwin" class="social-link">here</a>
    <div class="bio-copy">
        .
        .
        .
    </<div>
</div>
```

Now let's look at another styling wrinkle. If you were to stick with the style declaration **a.social-link** from Listing 6.16 as the way to target all **.social-link**s, then you'd have to ask yourself, "Could there be a situation where I want the styling of a **.social-link** on an element that isn't actually a link?" It sounds a little weird to ask the question, since it would seem that if you call something a link, you'd expect it always to be a link, but you'll often have styling for links that you need to apply to something that isn't an **a**.

An example of this would be if you have a navigational menu where you have a bunch of links to pages. Often, you want to have a menu item for the current page a user is looking at, and you don't want users to be able to click a link for the page they are already on (that would refresh the page), but you *do* want this type of menu item to look like the rest of the navigational links. In that case, the menu item that isn't a link would need to inherit all the same styling that the links got, and in our example that would be difficult if the selector was a combined HTML element and class name: **a.social-link**.

To allow the `.social-link` class to change the styling of the link without combining the HTML element and the class name, we should retarget the generic declarations in favor of the more specific method using the `.bio-copy` class name from Listing 6.17. The result is a change from the current `.bio-box` rule from Listing 6.11 to the more targeted style, which affects only links that are in the `.bio-copy` section of the boxes:

```
.bio-copy a {
  color: green;
}
```

At this point, we can also change `a.social-link` to just `.social-link`:

```
.social-link {
  color: blue;
}
```

Because the CSS changes we've just made were a refactoring, the appearance should be the same as before (Figure 6.5).

As a final step, we'll add some descriptive *CSS comments* while rearranging our CSS rules so that they are grouped thematically, according to whether they're global, apply only to social links, or apply to the page biographies. This practice makes it easier to navigate, read, and edit the CSS rules later on (Box 6.4). The result appears in Listing 6.18, which shows the full page in case you need to sync up.

Listing 6.18: The final form of our page for this chapter.
index.html

```
<!DOCTYPE html>
<html>
  <head>
    <title>Test Page: Don't Panic</title>
    <meta charset="utf-8">
    <style>
      /* GLOBAL STYLES */
      a {
        color: red;
      }

      /* SOCIAL STYLES */
      .social-link {
        color: blue;
```

```
    }

    /* BIO STYLES */
    .bio-box {
      border: 1px solid black;
    }
    .bio-copy a {
      color: green;
    }
  </style>
</head>
<body>
  <h1>I'm an h1</h1>
  <ul>
    <li>
      <a href="https://example.com/">Link</a>
    </li>
    <li>
      <a href="https://example.com/">Link</a>
    </li>
    <li>
      <a href="https://example.com/">Link</a>
    </li>
  </ul>
  <h2>I'm an h2</h2>
  <div class="bio-box">
    <h3>Michael Hartl</h3>
    <a href="https://twitter.com/mhartl" class="social-link">here</a>
    <div class="bio-copy">
      <p>
        Known for his dazzling charm, rapier wit, and unrivaled humility,
        Michael is the creator of the
        <a href="https://www.railstutorial.org/">Ruby on Rails
        Tutorial</a> and principal author of the
        <a href="https://learnenough.com/">
        Learn Enough to Be Dangerous</a> introductory sequence. Michael
        is also notorious as the founder of
        <a href="http://tauday.com/">Tau Day</a> and author of
        <a href="http://tauday.com/tau-manifesto"><em>The Tau
        Manifesto</em></a>, but rumors that he's secretly a supervillain
        are slightly exaggerated.
      </p>
    </div>
  </div>
  <div class="bio-box">
    <h3>Lee Donahoe</h3>
    <a href="https://twitter.com/leedonahoe" class="social-link">here</a>
    <div class="bio-copy">
      <p>
        When he's not literally swimming with sharks or hunting powder
```

```
          stashes on his snowboard, you can find Lee in front of his computer
          designing interfaces, doing front-end development, or writing some of
          the interface-related Learn Enough tutorials.
        </p>
      </div>
    </div>
    <div class="bio-box">
      <h3>Nick Merwin</h3>
      <a href="https://twitter.com/nickmerwin" class="social-link">here</a>
      <div class="bio-copy">
        <p>
          You may have seen him shredding guitar live with Capital Cities on
          Jimmy Kimmel, Conan, or The Ellen Show, but rest assured Nick is a
          true nerd at heart. He's just as happy shredding well-spec'd lines
          of code from a tour bus as he is from his kitchen table.
        </p>
      </div>
    </div>
    <div class="bio-box">
      <h3>??</h3>
      <p>
        The Future
      </p>
    </div>
  </body>
</html>
```

Box 6.4: Style Note: Group Your Styles and Add Comments!

It might seem obvious, but if you have any concern for other human beings who might ever look at your code, for the love of $DEITY, please group all styles that relate to the same part of the site in the same place, and to be extra helpful, add in a comment or two that explain what the styles are for!

CSS comments are any text that is between the asterisks /* */, which looks like this in practice:

```
/* HOMEPAGE STYLES */
```

Comments don't affect how the code is displayed to users, but you should know that they can be seen by anyone who browses the site source code... so don't put anything into the comments you'd be embarrassed to say out loud in a crowded place.

From this point on, when we add new styles we'll usually include a comment name for the section, like the /* HOMEPAGE STYLES */ above. If the styles should be grouped into an existing section, we'll indicate that using this convention:

```
/* HOMEPAGE STYLES */
.
.
.
.some-style {
}
```

That means that you should put the new styles somewhere after the existing styles in that section (represented by the vertical ellipsis). The only time that we won't include the section name when adding styles is when we are already working and making changes in that section.

6.4.1 Exercises

1. Add a new style that sets generic **div**s to have a border style of **border: 1px solid green**. Save and refresh, and all **div**s other than the **.bio-box**es should have a green border. Change the selector to **div.bio-box**, and then save and refresh.

2. Add the **.social-link** class onto the **h1**. Even though it isn't a link, the color should change.

3. Add your own comment to the style section, and inside add **html{background: red;}**. Save and refresh. Then delete the first **/*** and then save and refresh. Your page should look very different—always remember to balance your comment tags.

CHAPTER 7
CSS Values: Color and Sizing

Now that we've learned how to make our site's skeleton, it's time to start fleshing it out with some more CSS values. In this chapter, we'll learn about two of the most important kinds of values that CSS can apply to HTML elements: color and sizing. These will allow us to go from putting elements on a page (Chapter 6) to controlling the color of the elements and how big they are.

Values in a CSS declaration (Figure 5.9) can take a lot of different forms, from numbers, to dimensions, to idiosyncratic options, to colors, etc. On top of all that, there are shorthand methods that let you write multiple style properties and values on a single line. Most CSS declarations are self-explanatory—not too many people are going to be confused by **text-align: left**—but there are quite a few that have extra complications, weird exceptions, or just odd ways of defining a value.

The next few sections are going to recap some style values that you might have seen before, but we'll also dive into some of the less obvious use cases.

7.1 CSS Color

So far in this tutorial we've defined colors with descriptive words like **red**, **green**, and **lightgray**. CSS supports a large number of such *color names*, and there are online references that list all the color names supported by all browsers. It's not the most flexible or even the most common system of defining CSS colors, though, and in this section we'll discuss other, more powerful ways of applying colors in CSS.

7.1.1 Hexadecimal Colors

As discussed previously in Box 4.2, one common method for defining colors is *hexadecimal RGB* (red-green-blue). While this name might sound complicated, in practice the concept is fairly simple.

A quick way to show how hexadecimal color works is to change the color of the red link text on our sample page to its equivalent hexadecimal RGB color. Change the word **red** in the **color** property to the one shown in Listing 7.1.

Listing 7.1: Switching from a color name to a specific color value.
index.html

```
/* GLOBAL STYLES */
a {
  color: #ff0000;
}
```

Now when you save and refresh your browser, the link text will still be the same bright red (and if something is different, check your work!).

The reason the color system is called *hexadecimal* RGB is that it uses base-16 numbers instead of the usual base 10 ("hexadecimal" is a mishmash of Greek and Latin meaning "six" (hex) and "tenth" (decimal)). In hexadecimal, or *hex* for short, **0** is equal to 0 and **f** is equal to 15—letting you count 16 values in a single numeral (Table 7.1).

Table 7.1: Counting in hex.

0	1	2	3	4	5	6	7	8	9	10	11	12	13	14	15
0	1	2	3	4	5	6	7	8	9	a	b	c	d	e	f

In base 10, we can count from 0 to 99 with two digits, where $99 = 10^2 - 1$. Similarly, hex lets us count from 0 to $ff = 16^2 - 1 = 255$. In other words, putting two hex numbers next to each other lets us count from 0 to 255 using just two characters, with **00** = 0 and **FF** or **ff** = 255. (CSS hex is case-insensitive, so it doesn't matter if you use upper- or lowercase letters.)

A computer monitor consists of picture elements, or *pixels*, and displays colors by combining the light from red, green, and blue elements of a pixel (Figure 7.1). Hexadecimal RGB puts three sets of two hex numbers next to each other to define

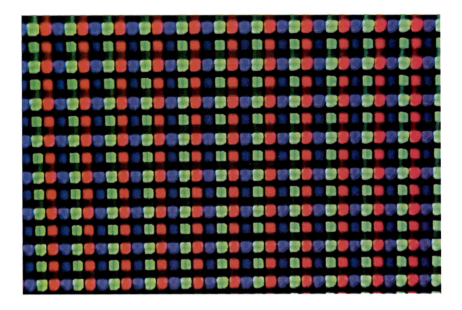

Figure 7.1: The elements in a single pixel of a computer screen's display.

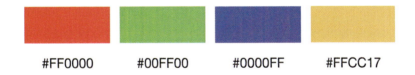

#FF0000   #00FF00   #0000FF   #FFCC17

Figure 7.2: Some hexadecimal color examples.

the red, green, and blue values that make up a single color, so **#ff0000** can also be read as **red=ff, green=00, blue=00** or **red=255, green=0, blue=0**. As we mentioned in Listing 7.1, this is the same as the color word **red**.

If all three colors are turned on (each is set to **ff**, or **#ffffff**), the pixel will look white; if they are all off (each is set to **00**, or **#000000**), it will look black. Combinations of the three colors can be used to create all the colors you see (Figure 7.2).

CSS also supports a useful shorthand in the common case that some of the hex numerals are the same. If the digits are the same, as in **#222222**, **#cccccc**, or **#aa22ff**, we can shorten the whole number to just three digits, like this: **#222**, **#ccc**, or **#a2f**. When the browser sees only three digits, it fills in the missing ones.

Thus, using **#f00** in place of **#ff0000** (Listing 7.1) should lead to the same color red (Section 7.1.3). The result of making this change on our sample site is shown in Listing 7.2.

Listing 7.2: Using the more compact hex notation.
index.html

```
/* GLOBAL STYLES */
a {
  color: #f00;
}
```

The RGB color system might seem confusing at first, but with practice you'll quickly come to understand how the three values work together to make different colors and different shades of those colors. For making more complicated colors, we suggest using a *color picker*, but there are some common cases that you should know off the top of your head.

For instance, the grayscale spectrum from black to white always has all three hex numbers the same: all **00** (or **#000000**) is black, all **ff** (or **#ffffff**) is white, and numbers in the middle, like **#979797**, are some shade of gray (Figure 7.3).[1]

In practice, most web developers and designers use common hex values interchangeably with their color-word equivalents, so it's important to know that **#000** and **#000000** are both **black**, **#fff** and **#ffffff** are both **white**, **#00f** and **#0000ff** are both **blue**, etc.

#000   #979797   #fff

Figure 7.3: Hexadecimal grayscale.

---

1. There are 255 colors that match the pattern **#979797**, but two of them are **#000000** (black) and **#ffffff** (white), leaving 253 shades of gray (which is way more than 50).

7.1.2 Setting Color and Transparency via `rgb()` and `rgba()`

In addition to using RGB hex, you can also use RGB directly using `rgb()`, which allows you to use decimal numbers in place of hex. In other words, `rgb(255, 255, 255)` is the same as `#ffffff`, etc. But the main reason to use RGB directly is to set *transparency* via the `rgba()` command.

In `rgba()`, the **a** stands for *alpha*, because the conventional name for transparency level in image processing is the *alpha level*. The alpha level is indicated using a number between 0 and 1, where 0 is transparent, 1 is opaque, and decimals in between define all the levels of partial transparency (50% is 0.5, 25% is 0.25, etc.).

For example, let's make the social link's background a transparent gray using `rgba()`. We'll select a fairly dark gray, corresponding to RGB values of 150 each (out of 255), and initially set an opacity of **1** (Listing 7.3).

Listing 7.3: Using the `rgba()` property to set an opaque background color.
index.html

```
.social-link {
  background: rgba(150, 150, 150, 1);
  color: blue;
}
```

The result appears in Figure 7.4.

Now let's switch to 50% opacity (which is the same as 50% transparency), as shown in Listing 7.4.

Listing 7.4: Using the `rgba()` property to set a partially transparent background color.
index.html

```
.social-link {
  background: rgba(150, 150, 150, 0.5);
  color: blue;
}
```

As you can see by comparing Figure 7.4 with Figure 7.5, the social links now have a partially transparent gray background. (We'll see another, more practical example of transparency in Section 9.7.1.)

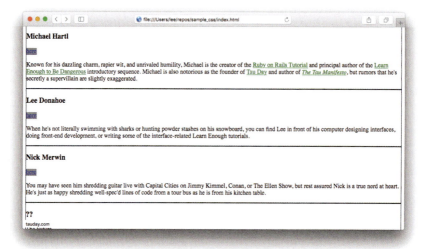

Figure 7.4: Social links with an opaque gray background.

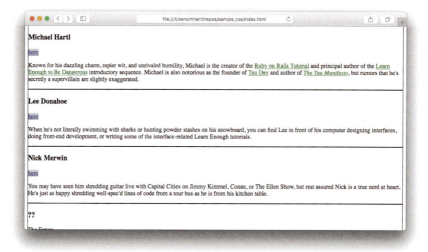

Figure 7.5: Blue text and 50% transparent gray background.

Amazingly, there are still more ways to set colors in CSS (HSL and HSLa), but we aren't going to go into them, as you are far less likely to encounter them in practice.

7.1.3 Exercises

1. Using a color picker, change the color of the links on the page (the **a** declaration) to a light purple color using a hex value.

2. Convert the remaining color words to their hex equivalents, using the more compact notation if possible.

3. Use the **rgba** color system to fade the links by making their opacity 20%.

4. Set the links that are inside the **li**s at the top of the page to have a class of **.social-link**.

7.2 Introduction to Sizing

In this tutorial, we frequently use *pixel* measurements to set the sizes of things like fonts, margins, and padding (Chapter 8), but there are actually a confusingly wide variety of different ways to define the size of elements. As a result of having to reliably display multiple generations of HTML across many different computers and devices, web browsers are an unimaginably complicated kluge of different standards. No one sat down and planned out how the Web would work in one go—features and support aggregated over time like a snowball rolling downhill, as various people suggested new methods of styling. Dimensional units are one area that has seen many such additions over time.

You might think it would be easiest for us to do what we've been doing and almost always specify sizes using pixels (**px**)—after all, isn't a screen just a big grid of pixels?

Sizing an element this way would work great if everyone in the world had exactly the same screen size and resolution, but they don't, and some screens combine many physical pixels into a smaller number of virtual pixels. That means that when you size something to look good on your screen, someone using a lower-resolution screen might find the element size to be unusably large, or if they are using a high-resolution screen (like a Retina display on an iPhone or iMac) it would look really small (Figure 7.6).[2]

---

2. DPI stands for "dots per square inch"; in this context, "dot" is a synonym for pixel.

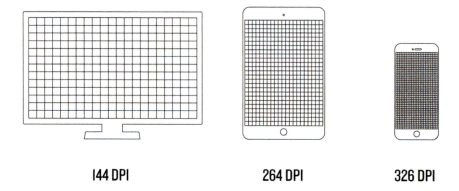

144 DPI   **264 DPI**   **326 DPI**

Figure 7.6: Different-sized displays have wildly different pixel densities.

The good news is that modern browsers can zoom in and out to make things easier, but that can cause page layouts that use absolute sizes to break. Also, modern devices can scale their output to make something that has an incredibly high pixel density work as though it were a normal lower-density screen.

For most of the last few years, the agreed-upon modern best practice has been to mostly use *relative* sizes, which style element sizes based on the size of other elements, or even to the size of the screen. For example, for a header you might say (in CSSese), "I want my header text to be four times as big as the default text size," and the browser would figure out the rest.

This type of relative sizing helps deal with the different screen scale issues, and also allows for easy resizing of the contents of a page. If you really want to, though, you can use absolute sizes pretty much anywhere, as a lot of issues with browsers have been worked out, but it's still a lot easier to stick with the convention and use relative sizes in most cases.

The rest of this chapter takes a closer look at some of the most common units, their uses, and some of their caveats.

7.3   Pixels (and Their Less-Used Cousin, the Point)

The pixel (px) and point (pt) units in CSS are absolute measurements that are defined as 1/96 of an inch for a pixel and 1/72 of an inch for a point. From this point on we're going to ignore the point because no one really uses it for web sizing (it's a holdover from the world of print design), and because it work justs like the pixel (just with a different base size). Pixels, on the other hand, are most definitely useful (Box 7.1).

Box 7.1: Style Note: Anti-Pixel Fundamentalists

As you keep progressing in your understanding of web development, you will inevitably come across people who are on an anti-pixel crusade. They believe that you should never use absolute sizes and should do everything relatively. The truth is that there is a time and a place for everything, even absolute units like the pixel.

Some measurements just *feel* better or make more sense in pixels (hooray for subjectivity!), such as margins and padding (Chapter 8). Sure, you could define those using some of the relative measures we'll learn about below, and define all padding and margins based on the size of the size around it, but sometimes it is nice to know that whatever zoom level a user goes to, there will be exactly 40 pixels of padding or margin around an element.

The real determining factor is how what you are designing is going to be used. If that pixel unit makes your job easier, and it is used in a place where it will never cause the layout to break, then go ahead and use it. Just know that if you get complaints from users that the site is breaking, you'll probably have to redo the sizing to be relative!

Using an absolutely defined unit is great if you want to define the size of an element in a way that isn't dependent on the size of the browser or screen resolution, or anything else on the page, but it can lead to situations where the size of elements is completely inappropriate for a user's device. This type of unit isn't an inherently good or bad thing; you just need to be aware that anything sized using an absolute measurement is not going to be resized relative to anything else on the page—many sites have a mix of absolutely sized and relatively sized elements. The trick comes in knowing when to use the different units.

YOU KNOW, THESE KIND OF ADS

Figure 7.7: You've seen this sort of ad in a million places.

For instance, if you have banner ad images on your site, you are selling that advertising space based on the size of the element (one of the most common ads is the

728 × 90 leaderboard ad, as in Figure 7.7). In that situation, you want the ads to be defined with absolute dimensions and not be relative (after all, when you think about it, you are selling screen real estate, and you want to make sure the size of the ad is what they paid for).

Images are also always sized by the browser, so that 1 pixel of the image equals 1 pixel on the browser. It's possible to have the browser resize images and use relative sizes, but the underlying default size of the image is 1 pixel to 1 pixel. This also is why you should never scale an image up from its default size in a browser—resizing should only be done to make an image smaller than it really is; otherwise, the browser has to spread pixels from the image over multiple pixels on the screen, and the image will look terrible (Figure 7.8).

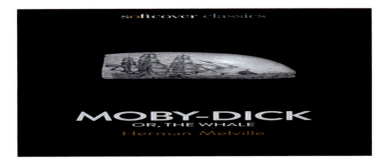

Figure 7.8: You've seen this before... it was bad then and it still is bad!

So, that all still sounds reasonable, right? Why can't we just use **px** measurements for everything if 96 pixels equals an inch? Well, not so fast. It turns out that a "screen inch" made up of 96 pixels isn't actually always the same as a real-world inch—for that measurement to be accurate, every screen's pixel density would have to be 96 pixels per inch.

Unfortunately, as mentioned at the beginning of this chapter, this is not the case. Modern smartphones and high-end displays have pixel densities of 400 pixels per inch and up, and the operating systems that run on them are often scalable, meaning that what you see on the screen can be resized in a way that isn't dependent on the phys-ical number of pixels in the display—a bunch of smaller physical pixels are packaged together into a bigger "virtual" pixel. The point is, pixels at the software level no longer are directly related to physical pixels. As a result, the exact length of a 96px line is difficult to guarantee in a way that is universal for all users and screens.

One place where you will often see pixel sizes used online is in the definition of *font sizes*, which determine the size of text on the page. (This is also a place where you will find the most-heated "pixel vs. non-pixel" holy wars.) Part of the reason for the prevalence of absolute sizing in fonts is that it's a holdover from the days when pixel sizing was the only way to define font sizes on computers, and part of it is because there were people who were used to the conventions of print design where there were design requirements that said "this font should be exactly 24 pixels." When transitioning from print to screen, people familiar with absolute print sizing just brought their habits over to the Web. So if a design in Photoshop had a font that was 24px, they'd make the design on the site 24px.

Absolute sizes were fine for the period when pretty much all screens had the same characteristics (and there were no other options), but over time screen sizes, resolution, and densities proliferated, and the inflexibility of absolute font sizes made relative sizing the preferred method.

There is another caveat that should make you not want to use pixels for fonts: If you set font sizes using pixels and then want to change some sizes later (either for a mobile-specific view or just because you didn't like the way it looked), you will have to go through and change every place where you defined a font size. If you had used relative values for those fonts, you could make changes in only one place, and everything else would inherit the new styling while still displaying in proportion. Making all text on a page bigger, or smaller, could be as easy as changing a single value.

So, with all those warnings about how you shouldn't use pixel sizes for fonts... let's use pixel sizes for fonts, and for element sizing, in a quick little pixel exercise! We'll make the **.bio-box**es have a width of **200px**, and set the font size of the **h2** element to be **30px**, as shown in Listing 7.5. (We'll undo this font sizing in Section 7.6.)

Listing 7.5: Styling elements with pixel values.
index.html

```
/* GLOBAL STYLES */
.
.
.
h2 {
  font-size: 30px;
}
```

```
/* BIO STYLES */
.
.
.
.bio-box {
  border: 1px solid black;
  width: 200px;
}
```

After saving and refreshing, your page should look like Figure 7.9.

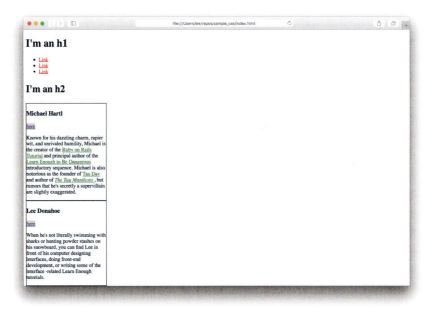

Figure 7.9: Hey, look, resized elements. Woo.

7.3.1 Exercise

1. You can (and should) use pixels to set the width of borders. Try changing the
   width of the `.bio-box` borders to `10px`.

7.4 **Percentages**

We've already sized elements using percentages earlier in the tutorial (Section 6.3), and from that you might be able to guess how useful this measurement can be when you are trying to use relative sizes to force an element to fill a space. There are a few catches, though:

- Percentage sizing is based on the parent container that an element is wrapped by—it isn't determined by the size of the browser or the page as a whole.

- Percentage heights are a little weird because they require a set height on the parent element—they can't just assume a height the way that they assume a width.

Let's take a look at how percentages work, and you'll see what we are talking about. Add a new **div** that wraps the four **.bio-box**es, and set the class of that **div** to **bio-wrapper** (Listing 7.6).

Listing 7.6: Adding a wrapper around the **bio-box**es and giving it a class.
index.html

```
<div class="bio-wrapper">
  <div class="bio-box">
    <h3>Michael Hartl</h3>
    <a href="https://twitter.com/mhartl" class="social-link">
      here
    </a>
    .
    .
    .
    <div class="bio-copy">
      <p>
        The Future
      </p>
    </div>
  </div>
</div>
```

This wrapper is going to be the parent container that determines the size of the children **.bio-box**es for which we'll set a percentage width. Add a style declaration that sets the width of this new class to be **500px**, and also change the width of the **.bio-box**es from the rather squished **200px** in Listing 7.5 to **50%**, as seen in Listing 7.7.

Listing 7.7: Changing the width of the parent element.
index.html

```
.bio-wrapper {
  width: 500px;
}
.bio-box {
  border: 1px solid black;
  width: 50%;
}
```

Still pretty squished, right (Figure 7.10)?

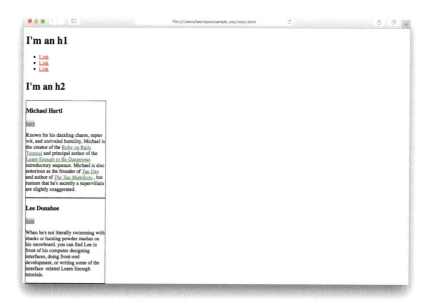

Figure 7.10: Still not a lot of room for those boxes.

Those boxes are small because they are each taking their width setting as 250px (50% of the 500px-wide parent). In order to get them to stretch all the way across the page, we need to make their parent stretch all the way across the page too. One way to do that is to remove the width from `.bio-wrapper` and then save and refresh. Your browser will assume that the percentage width for the `.bio-box`es should be based on the width of the browser (Listing 7.8).

Listing 7.8: Style declarations can be empty.
index.html

```
.bio-wrapper {
}
```

Now that the parent goes all the way across the window, the child boxes definitely look bigger (Figure 7.11)!

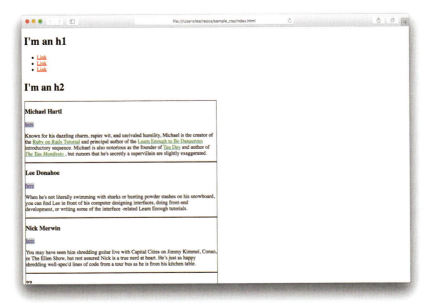

Figure 7.11: The boxes are now taking up 50% of the width of the browser window.

Like we said above, percentage units work well for dimensions like width, but they behave a little strangely for height, and they don't work at all for thickness—meaning you can't use percentages for borders. In order for a percentage height to have an effect, the parent needs a set height (and even then things can get weird).

So, what if you wanted a box that was the height of the browser window? You'd think that setting a style to make it **height: 100%** would do the trick, but it won't work. To see what we mean, add the code from Listing 7.9 at the top of your page, above the **h1**.

Listing 7.9: Adding a test element for a quick and dirty example.
index.html

```
<div style="border:1px solid #000;width: 50%;height:100%;">I'm a percent test</div>
<h1>I'm an h1</h1>
.
.
.
```

That will give you a box that is half the width of the page, but surprisingly only the height of the content that is inside the **div** (Figure 7.12).

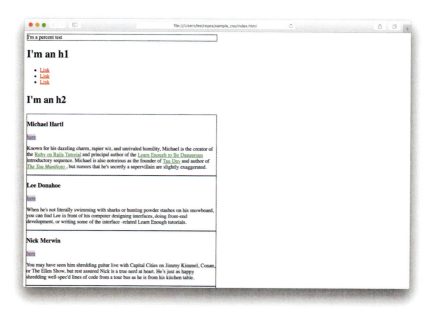

Figure 7.12: Not quite what you'd expect for **height: 100%**.

Figure 7.13: A more effective `height: 100%`.

Let's see what happens if instead we add a style that sets the height of the **body** element of the page, as shown in Listing 7.10. When you save and refresh, you'll find that your "percent test" box has grown to be really tall (Figure 7.13).

Listing 7.10: Adding an absolute height to the parent.
index.html

```
/* GLOBAL STYLES */
body {
  height: 800px;
}
```

What happened there? When you specify a height in percent, the parent container has to have some sort of defined height set in order for the child percent height to be applied. Otherwise, the browser just makes the element the height needed to contain the content within.

Even though we made the percent height work, at times it will act differently from how you expect, as it is dependent on the end height of the parent container. If the parent ends up being tall, you might end up with the percent height child displaying on-screen far larger than you wanted. Or, if you inadvertently add a style that removes the set height from the parent, the child element with a percent height would suddenly return to being the height only of the content it contains (like in Figure 7.12).

Don't worry if this sounds confusing—we'll look at some other solutions for getting elements to take up a proportion of a space later in the tutorial, both when we cover ways to make elements the size of the browser with the **vh** and **vw** units in Section 7.7, and then when we arrange to take up the full height of arbitrarily sized parents using the *flexbox* method in Chapter 11.

In the meantime, you should delete the "percent test" **div** from Listing 7.9, and make sure also to delete the style from Listing 7.10.

7.4.1 Percentage Fonts

You *can* use percentages to set text sizes, but there is a consideration that you will have to keep in mind. If you use a percentage for a text size, the resulting size of the font is based not on the pixel dimensions of the container, but rather on whatever **font-size** style that container has inherited. So the box itself could be **1000px** tall, but if it inherited a font size of **16px**, and you set the font size of a child element to 50%, you are going to get only an **8px**-tall font (50% of **16px**), not a **500px**-tall font like you might think.

The fact that percentage sizing uses different sources for sizing the height and width of boxes (based on the actual pixel dimensions of an element) versus sizing text (based on inherited font size) is why it is only infrequently used for text sizing. Most people find it easier to think of percentages as a way of determining the size of box-shaped things, and use other relative sizing methods for fonts.

Once again, if that all sounds confusing, don't worry—Section 7.5 will explain it in greater detail using the **em** unit, whose behavior is similar to percentage. However, unlike percentage measurement, **em**s are regularly used for sizing text and less used for sizing boxes. (*Warning*: This is a potential holy-war statement to make.)

7.4.2 Exercises

1. Try setting a 10% margin on the **.bio-box**. This will push each box away from its neighbors by 10% of the width of the parent container, even the vertical margins. (Sharp-eyed readers might notice something weird with the vertical margins that we'll discuss in Section 8.6.)

2. To see the way that percentage font sizes can be cumulative, set the `.bio-box` font size to 150%, and then also set the `.bio-copy` font size to 150%. The end result will be 150% of 150% of 16px (the page base font size), or in pixels…

7.5   em

The **em** unit is a relative size unit that is commonly used for sizing text (most would say it is the preferred method). The name comes from the approximate width of the letter m; in CSS, one em represents a number of pixels equal to the current font size of any given element's parent container. If there is no font size that is inherited, then the default page font size is used.

For plain text (that is, not something like an **h1** header), the default size is **16px**, so the default size of an em is also **16px**. Fractions of an em then represent fractions of the full font size; for example, if the font size is **16px**, a unit of **0.5em** would be 50% of 16, or **8px**, and **2.25em** would be 225% of 16, or **36px**.

One of the things that makes ems useful, in comparison to something like pixel sizing, is that they automatically change value based on the font size that is inherited by the parent object that they are contained in. This means that if you used em sizing throughout your site, you can modify the entire site's text simply by changing a single base font size, and all the fonts in all the child containers will resize in correct proportion based on this new declared font size. If you used pixels for everything, you'd have to change every declared font size by hand.

As an example, let's say we set the font size of **.bio-copy** to **0.5em**, as shown in Listing 7.11. Because the default base font size of the entire page is **16px**, the result in the browser is tiny **8px** text, as shown in Figure 7.14.

Listing 7.11: Changing the bio copy font size.

index.html

```
/* BIO STYLES*/
.
.
.
.bio-copy {
  font-size: 0.5em;
}
```

Figure 7.14: The bio copy text after shrinking down to **0.5em**.

Now let's see the effect of changing the font size of the parent element. In Listing 7.6 we added a **.bio-wrapper** div to wrap the bio boxes, so we can redefine the base font size by adding a CSS rule as shown in Listing 7.12. The new rule in Listing 7.12 changes the font size from the default **16px** to **24px**, so the **.bio-box** font size of **0.5em** is now 50% of 24, or **12px**.

Listing 7.12: Setting a new base font size.
index.html

```
.bio-wrapper {
  font-size: 24px;
}
```

To determine what the actual font size should be, the browser crawls up the parent–child tree until it finds a parent with a font size set with an absolute value, and then it calculates back down the tree to set the font sizes. As noted above, if there is no such absolute value, the page default is **16px**, but by changing the parent div to **24px** we've managed to change the default for all child elements.

As a result, the font size of **0.5em** is no longer 50% of 16, but rather is 50% of 24, for a total of **12px**. The font size of the bio boxes automatically increases from the **8px** shown in Figure 7.14 to **12px**, as shown in Figure 7.15.

Figure 7.15: The bio copy in the `.bio-box`es has automatically increased.

One important property of **em** units is that they are *cumulative*: If an element that has its font size set to **0.5em** appears inside an element whose font size is also **0.5em**, then the resulting font size for that bottom child element is $0.5 \times 0.5 = $ **0.25em**. In real numbers, if the base size is **24px**, this means that the most deeply nested element is 25% of 24, or **6px**. This cumulative effect can be helpful, or it can cause unintentional display errors—you just have to be careful.

Schematically, our current page consists of nested divs, with **.bio-copy** inside **.bio-box** inside **.bio-wrapper**. We already changed the font size of **.bio-copy** to **0.5em** (Listing 7.11); if we change the **.bio-box** font size to **0.5em** as well (Listing 7.13), the result will be 50% of 50% of 24, or **6px**.

Listing 7.13: Adding a relative font size to the **.bio-box**.
index.html

```
.bio-box {
  border: 1px solid black;
  font-size: 0.5em;
  width: 50%;
}
.bio-copy {
  font-size: 0.5em;
}
```

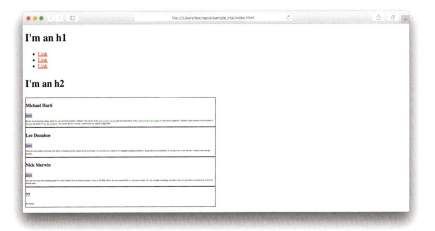

Figure 7.16: Now the font size is unreadably tiny!

Look at the resulting teeny tiny font (Figure 7.16)!

As outlined above, this happened because starting from the `.bio-copy`, the browser goes up one level to the parent and sees that there is a font size set, so it says, "OK, the font should be half the size of this parent size, but the `.bio-box` size is relative too, so let's go up again until we find an absolute font size." Going up one more level, the browser finds that the `.bio-wrapper` declaration sets the font to **24px**, so now it can work back down and set the `.bio-box` to **12px**, and then the content inside the `.bio-copy` to **6px**.

This works the other way too. If we set both the `.bio-box` and `.bio-copy a` font sizes to **1.5em** we'll end up with a giant font that is the equivalent of **54px** (24 × 1.5 × 1.5 = **54px**), as shown in Figure 7.17.

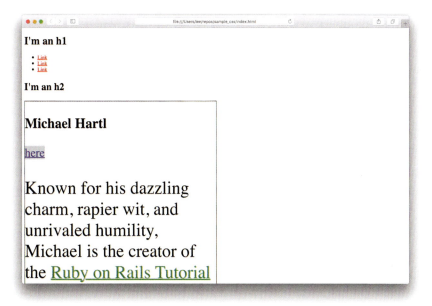

Figure 7.17: Now the font is just ridiculously huge.

Now that we've seen some really wacky values, let's change the bio box to use a more sensible font size of **1em** (Listing 7.14).

Listing 7.14: A sensible font size for the bio box.
index.html

```
.bio-box {
  border: 1px solid black;
  font-size: 1em;
  width: 50%;
}
.bio-copy {
  font-size: 1em;
}
```

So far we've used ems only for fonts, but the **em** unit *can* be used for things like margin, padding, and width (Chapter 8). In those cases, you have to remember that the size of an **em** is based on the local font size, so if you set a width for an object in

em it will size the object based on the font size inside that element. For example, if the calculated font size in an element ends up being **16px**, and you set the padding to **1.5em**, then the padding will end up getting set to $1.5 \times 16 = $ **24px**.

Sound confusing? Figure 7.18 shows a quick diagram to explain.

Figure 7.18: Dimensions inside the box get calculated based on the font size.

The argument for doing your sizing using ems is that all your elements, and their attributes like padding or margin, will be sized relative to the size of the text. But just because we want to increase the size of fonts on a page doesn't necessarily mean that we also want to change something like margin or padding. Sometimes you want the boxes that hold the content to stay the same and only the stuff inside to change, so styling every dimension of a container based on the text it contains can be inconvenient. As a result, in this tutorial we'll use the **em** unit primarily for fonts, but will also use it in margins or padding where it is helpful to have the sizing be responsive.

Warning: As is often the case with such subjective judgments, this is holy-war territory (Figure 7.19).[3]

---

3. Image courtesy of melnyk58/123RF.

Figure 7.19: Well… that's just, like, your opinion, man.

7.5.1 Exercises

1. Give the `.bio-box` class a padding of `2.5em`, and see how at small sizes the padding seems reasonable.

2. Set the `.bio-box` font size to `48px`, and see how now your boxes' padding is a significant percentage of the entire browser width.

3. Set the `.bio-box` padding to a pixel size of `20px` to see how that can make the space sizing independent from the content sizing.

7.6 **rem** Isn't Just for Dreaming

The cumulative effect of the **em** unit (Section 7.5) can at times make designing layouts difficult since it makes it harder to drop sections of a page into other sections and be confident that you aren't going to end up with some weird cumulative sizing issue. (Recall the goal from Section 6.4 to make our markup as modular and LEGO-like as possible.) In the years since the original release of CSS, browsers have implemented a new relative unit that allows for us to create modular sections that can be placed on the page without sizing uncertainties, the *root em*, or **rem**.

This **rem** unit works similarly to **em**, in that it is a percentage of an absolute font size, but instead of being cumulatively sized based on the whole parent–child tree, the **rem** unit *always* refers back to the font size of the **html** tag—in other words, it always refers to the most basic font size for the whole page. (As noted in Section 7.5, this default size is **16px**.)

In effect, the **rem** unit works like a document-wide setting, so you can set the size of elements like boxes, or font sizes, and have them all tie back to a single value: the font size of the **html** element. If you want to make everything a little bigger, or smaller, you can change just this one font size and everything on the page adapts in a controlled manner.

rem is especially useful in combination with **em** units in developing modules. The best practice is to set a font size for the module's wrapper using a **rem** unit, and then style the fonts inside using **em** units. Because **rem** values are absolute (in relation to the page font size), you don't need to worry that the cumulative nature of **em** will keep going up the parent tree and make everything in the box tiny or huge (Section 7.5). This kind of styling allows you to create modules that can be safely dropped into any part of a page, while keeping the advantages of using relative font sizes.

To see this in action, let's set the size of the **.bio-box** to **1rem** and then add in a new declaration to set the header **h3**s to be **1.5em** and the **.bio-copy** to be **1em**.

Listing 7.15 has the entire CSS block at this point—copy and paste if you aren't synced up.[4] (Note that Listing 7.15 removes the **h2** rule from Listing 7.5.)

Listing 7.15: The CSS section up to now, with new font sizes.
index.html

```
<style>
  /* GLOBAL STYLES */
  a {
    color: #f00;
  }

  /* SOCIAL STYLES */
  .social-link {
    background: rgba(150, 150, 150, 0.5);
    color: blue;
  }

  /* BIO STYLES */
```

---

4. Recall that the code listings are available at https://github.com/learnenough/learn_enough_html_css_and _layout_code_listings.

```
.bio-wrapper {
  font-size: 24px;
}
.bio-box {
  border: 1px solid black;
  font-size: 1rem;
  width: 50%;
}
.bio-box h3 {
  font-size: 1.5em;
}
.bio-copy {
  font-size: 1em;
}
.bio-copy a {
  color: green;
}
</style>
```

Now the whole page will be set to be the same size as the **html** default font size of **16px**, and the header in the bio box will always be one and a half times that size even though the **.bio-wrapper** is set to a very large **24px**. Meanwhile, the bio copy will remain at the default size for the page. If we decide that all the copy on the site should be bigger, we can easily reset the default size with a rule like

```
html {
  font-size: 18px;
}
```

With the change in Listing 7.15, all the copy in the boxes will resize but will stay in proportion without any cumulative effects (Figure 7.20). All of those benefits become important the moment you need to design a site that looks good on different devices, such as a desktop computer and a mobile phone. We'll discuss this important issue further in Chapter 13. (If you added the 18px font size styling to the **html** element, go ahead and delete it now.)

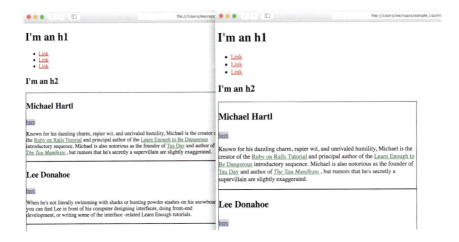

Figure 7.20: The 16px base font size is on the left; the 18px size is on the right, with everything scaled proportionally.

7.6.1 Exercises

1. Copy the entire first `.bio-box` and paste it inside the **h1**. You should see that **rem** sizing allowed for the whole section to be modular and retain the set styling.

2. In the CSS, change the font size for `.bio-box` from **1rem** to **1em** and notice the effect.

7.7   vh, vw: The New(er) Kids on the Block

Speaking of mobile-friendly units, we arrive now at two newer dimensional units that are also incredibly useful for responsive (mobile) layouts: the viewport height, **vh**, and viewport width, **vw**. These units allow us to size elements on the page based on the actual size of the browser window or mobile device screen. Each **vh** or **vw** is 1% of the corresponding screen dimension, so **3vh** would equal 3% of the height of the screen and **100vw** would be 100% of the width.

Neither **vh** nor **vw** is affected by parent elements, and neither has any weird cumulative inheritance issues—everything is determined by the size of the browser window or device screen. Up until relatively recently these units weren't reliably supported by all browers, but as long as a good percentage of your users aren't using really old browsers you can safely use **vh** and **vw** to do some fun things, like design sections that fill the browser window no matter what the size of that window is.

We'll apply the viewport units as part of adding a *hero section* to our site, a design pattern that involves having an attention-grabbing area at the top of the page containing a dramatic image, a call to action, etc. We'll start by wrapping the top section of our test page in a new **div** with two classes, **.full-hero** and **.hero-home** (Listing 7.16). (We'll use **.full-hero** starting in Section 8.3 and **.hero-home** starting in Chapter 10.)

Listing 7.16: Adding a wrapper around the content, and giving it class names.
index.html

```
<div class="full-hero hero-home">
  <h1>I'm an h1</h1>
  <ul>
    <li>
      <a href="https://example.com/" class="social-link">Link</a>
    </li>
    <li>
      <a href="https://example.com/" class="social-link">Link</a>
    </li>
    <li>
      <a href="https://example.com/" class="social-link">Link</a>
    </li>
  </ul>
</div>
```

Note that Listing 7.16 also includes the results of the exercise in Section 7.1.3 that added the **.social-link** class to the link inside each **li**.

With the classes defined in Listing 7.16, we're in a position to start giving the hero section some styles. We'll start by adding a background color and a height equal to 50% of the viewport using **50vh**, as shown in Listing 7.17.

Listing 7.17: Adding a height based on browser size.
index.html

```
/* HERO STYLES */
.full-hero {
  background-color: #c7dbfc;
  height: 50vh;
}
```

Note that the box isn't all the way to the top, and that there's extra space on the top, right, and left (Figure 7.21).

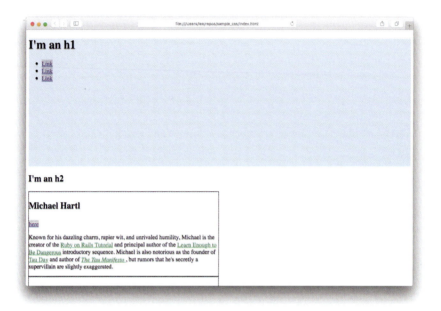

Figure 7.21: The box is now 100% of the page width and 50% of the height.

The extra space in Figure 7.21 is due to the browser's default *margin* on the **html** and **body** tags, a kind of spacing that we mentioned briefly in Section 4.3 and will cover more in Chapter 8. There is also an issue with the spacing around the **h1**, whose separate default margin is bleeding through the boundaries of the **.full-hero** parent due to something called *margin collapsing* (to be further explained in Section 8.2.1).

The solution is to *reset* the default styles using CSS. We'll implement a full CSS reset in Section 9.6, but for now let's apply a quick fix by adding the styles in Listing 7.18.

Listing 7.18: Resetting the default margin and padding.
index.html

```
/* GLOBAL STYLES */
.
.
```

```
html, body {
  margin: 0;
  padding: 0;
}
h1 {
  margin-top: 0;
}
```

Now the hero area takes up the whole top section of the site (Figure 7.22)!

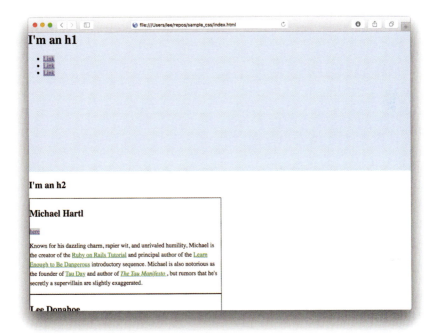

Figure 7.22: Everything looks a lot nicer without the margins around the page.

If you've ever been to a site that has a big image that fills the top of the page, this is likely how they did it.

As with all the other values, viewport dimensions work for fonts too. For example, we can arrange for the **h1** to have a font size equal to 7% of the width of the browser window using **7vw** (Listing 7.19).

Listing 7.19: Defining a font size relative to the browser width.
index.html

```
h1 {
  font-size: 7vw;
  margin-top: 0;
}
```

One possible result appears in Figure 7.23, but if you resize the browser you'll notice that the font size changes.

Figure 7.23: Nice to see no margin around the edges and some big type.

This sort of dynamically resizing font may seem simple, but it was practically impossible for most of the history of the Web, so in reality it's pretty mind-blowing (Figure 7.24[5]).

---

5. Image courtesy of photoschmidt/123RF.

Figure 7.24: Fonts that resize based on viewport size = MIND. BLOWN.

As useful as the viewport dimensions are, if we used them for everything our site would look bad on either mobile or desktop (depending on which platform you were using when you designed the page). Desktop windows are just so much bigger than mobile that elements designed to fit a mobile screen would look giant, and elements designed for desktop would look impossibly tiny on mobile.

The solution is to use a *media query*, which allows us to set different styles for elements based on the size of the user's browser window. We'll cover this important technique in Chapter 13.

7.7.1   Exercises

1. We used the **vw** unit only on a font, but of course it works for element widths too. Using the **vw** unit, set the **.full-hero** class to take up 75% of the viewport width.

2. Guess what? We're going to blow your mind again… you can use **vw** to set a height, and **vh** to set a width! This is actually really useful when you want to make something responsively sized, but square in shape (so you need the height

and width to be the same). To try it out, set both the height and the width of `.full-hero` to `50vw`.

7.8 Just Make It Look Nice

We'll end our discussion of CSS sizing with some notes on choosing good styles for text (e.g., font size).

When choosing font sizes, the goal should always be to have readable text on the page. Nicely laid-out copy should be the equivalent of somewhere between 14px and 18px in height.

The default size of 16px is right in the middle of this 14–18px range, but having a base unit of `1em` equaling `16px` can make the math a little difficult if you start using fractional sizes like `1.33em`. If for some reason you care about exact pixel sizes, there is a hack that you can use to combine em with pixel-precision—set a `font-size` on the `body` of `62.5%`, which makes `1em` elsewhere on the page equal `10px` (62.5% of 16). In web design circles, this is sometimes known as the "62.5% trick."

Although you are welcome to use the 62.5% trick, we think it's better to stop thinking in terms of absolute pixels when it comes to fonts—there's just no reason that you need to be exact on the sizing since there can be differences between browsers when displaying the same element. Also, even though the 62.5% trick gives you exact em sizing, you are also setting the default size of everything to a really small font size—for most people, `10px` is basically unreadable.

To sum up our recommendations: Use relative units for text, don't use the 62.5% trick, and simply pick random numbers that set the font sizes somewhat close to what your design calls for (seriously).

What matters ultimately is how the end product looks and the relationship between different elements. Trying to achieve pixel-perfection is simply not a reasonable goal on the Web, and pixel sizing is really just an artifact from the bad old days of doing designs in Photoshop where elements' heights and widths were set in pixels.

Just embrace the imprecision (Figure 7.25).

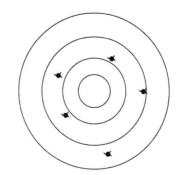

EH, CLOSE ENOUGH

Figure 7.25: Just make sure that your imprecision is at least consistently around the target.

7.8.1   Exercises

1. Let's try the 62.5% trick. Set the **body** of your test page to have a font size of **62.5%**. Notice that most of the text got smaller, with the exception of the **.bio-box**es which are still being sized off of the **html** font size thanks to the **rem** unit.

2. Change the font size of the **h1** to **20px**, and then, after seeing what it looks like, change it to **2em**. There should be no change.

3. Delete the font size that is on the **.bio-wrapper** class, and then set the font size of the **.bio-box** to **1em** so that you can see what the new default size looks like.

CHAPTER 8
The Box Model

In Chapter 7, we saw how to set sizing parameters; in this chapter, we'll apply such sizing to one of the most important concepts in web design: the *box model*.

You may recall from Section 4.3 that, when rendering HTML, the browser considers a page to be a collection of different boxes that contain content. Along with height and width, boxes can be styled to have *borders* (a line around the box), *margins* (the distance away from other boxes), and *padding* (empty space inside the box separating content from the border).

The CSS *box model* is the name for all the rules that determine how height, width, margin, padding, and borders are applied to elements (Figure 8.1). Some aspects of the box model can be quite confusing. There are weird interactions between elements, counter-intuitive applications of styles, and ways of writing style values that can look strange at first glance. In this chapter, we'll take a tour through these different idiosyncrasies, learn a couple of methods for getting boxes to sit next to each other, and lay the necessary foundation for applying the box model to our full website starting in Chapter 9.

8.1 Inline vs. Block

We'll begin our introduction to the box model by discussing the different effects of spacing and borders on *inline* vs. *block* elements. These two types of elements, which we discussed in Box 3.1, behave differently in the context of the box model, so it's important to clarify the differences at the beginning.

Elements that are considered *inline elements*, like **span** or **a**, are only allowed to have margins and padding applied to the left and right (not top or bottom), and they

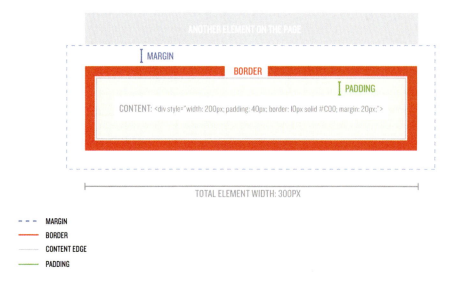

Figure 8.1: The default HTML box model.

won't accept a width or height set by CSS. None of these restrictions apply to block elements.

Confusingly, some styles can cause an inline element to switch to be a block element. You already saw an example when we *floated* the linked cover image in Section 4.2. Floated elements become block elements and can suddenly have top and bottom margins or padding, plus active dimensions like height and width that were previously ignored. Changing an element's position on the page can also switch it from inline to block (as discussed further in Section 9.8).

You don't have to rely on these quirks to change elements from inline to block, though—you can also directly force an element to change using CSS. There are actually a bunch of display property values that affect the way elements are drawn, with more being added all the time. In this tutorial, though, we are only going to consider five of the most important ones. Let's take a look!

8.1.1 `display: none`

The `display: none` style prevents the element from displaying on the page. For example, try updating the `.social-link` class rules to include `display:none`, as shown in Listing 8.1.

Listing 8.1: Removing elements from the page.
index.html

```
.social-link {
  background: rgba(150, 150, 150, 0.5);
  color: blue;
  display: none;
}
```

When you save and refresh, you'll see that all those social links are now gone. This style is commonly used for hiding elements in interactive websites, especially when combined with JavaScript (*Learn Enough JavaScript to Be Dangerous* (https://www.learnenough.com/javascript)). (Setting **display: none** here is just for demo purposes, so you should undo Listing 8.1 before proceeding.)

To restore the display of an element that has been hidden, all you need to do is set the **display** property to anything other than **none**, such as **initial** or **block**. (In *Learn Enough JavaScript to Be Dangerous*, we'll use this technique to make hidden elements appear with the click of the mouse.)

8.1.2 `display: block`

display: block forces an element to be a block element regardless of what it was before. If you don't set dimensions after changing an element to **display: block**, it will behave like any normal block element by taking up the entire width of its parent element.

As mentioned briefly above, inline elements (such as links and spans) can't have a width or height, but once you change the display property the dimensional styles get applied. To see how this works, let's first add a height to **.social-link** (Listing 8.2).

Listing 8.2: Adding dimensions to an inline element won't have an effect.
index.html

```
.social-link {
  background: rgba(150, 150, 150, 0.5);
  color: blue;
  height: 36px;
}
```

When you save and refresh, you'll notice nothing changed—that's because the **.social-link**s are inline elements. Now add in the magical **display: block** (Listing 8.3) and save.

Listing 8.3: Changing the display property allows the dimensional styles to apply.
index.html

```
.social-link {
  background: rgba(150, 150, 150, 0.5);
  color: blue;
  display: block;
  height: 36px;
}
```

Refresh your browser and you'll see that your social links are now 36px-tall block elements that stretch all the way across their parent elements (Figure 8.2).

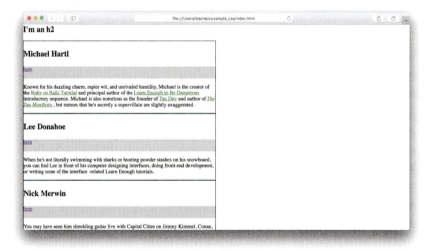

Figure 8.2: Look at those beautiful big gray rectangles.

8.1.3 display: inline

display: inline turns a block element into an inline element (essentially the opposite of the **display: block** property). Any styles that don't apply to inline elements (such as width and height, top margins, and padding) will no longer be applied. In addition, the element will no longer be on its own line, but rather will flow with text like any other inline element.

8.1.4 `display: inline-block`

The `display: inline-block` property, which is a hybrid of `inline` and `block`, is a useful display setting, as it allows styling that normally works only on block elements—such as width and height, top margins, and padding—to be applied to a particular element. At the same time, it also lets the element as a whole act like an inline element. This means that text will still flow around it, and it will only take up as much horizontal space as it needs to contain the content (as opposed to the way that block elements stretch all the way across the page unless you give them a set width).

To see how this works, set the `.social-link`s to display as `inline-block` on your index page (Listing 8.4).

Listing 8.4: Setting the display of social links to `inline-block`.
index.html

```
.social-link {
  background: rgba(150, 150, 150, 0.5);
  color: blue;
  display: inline-block;
  height: 36px;
}
```

Figure 8.3: The links are now a combination of inline and block, stretching only as wide as the content.

When you save and refresh, you'll see that the links have the height style applied, but they are only as wide as the content (Figure 8.3).

Eventually, in Section 14.1.1, we are going to add in icons for the different social media websites, and we'll want these links to all have the same dimensions regardless of the content that is inside. To make sure that they are all exactly the same size, let's also add a width property to the social links (Listing 8.5).

Listing 8.5: The `inline-block` display lets you add a width to an inline element.
index.html

```
.social-link {
  background: rgba(150, 150, 150, 0.5);
  color: blue;
  display: inline-block;
  height: 36px;
  width: 36px;
}
```

Your social links will now be nice little gray squares, like in Figure 8.4.

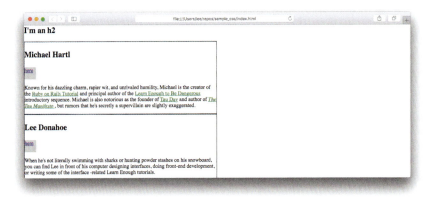

Figure 8.4: The links now have the same width and height.

So, where do sites use this CSS style? The `inline-block` declaration is especially helpful when making site navigation, and when styling a group of elements so that they are side by side. We'll discuss this aspect of `inline-block` further in Section 8.5, and then again when we make page navigation in Section 9.6.2.

8.1.5 `display: flex`

`display: flex` is a powerful display property that forces all child elements to fill the entire parent element, and is highly customizable to allow for incredibly useful layout possibilities. The `flex` property is something that solves some of the most difficult long-running problems in page layouts.

We aren't going to play around with `display: flex` here because it really needs a whole chapter of its own to properly understand—a task we'll undertake in Chapter 11.

8.1.6 Exercises

1. After the `social-link` class, add to your CSS a new class called `show` and give it a display value of `block`. Set the `.social-link` display property to `none` again. When you save and refresh the page, all the links should be gone. Now pick one of them and add `show` as a second class. What happens?

2. Set the `.social-link` display property to `inline-block` again. Now let's try changing a block element to an inline element. Use CSS to target the `li`s that are inside the `.full-hero`, and set their display property to `inline`.

8.2 Margins, Padding, and Borders

One of the most common places where developers interact with the box model is when adding *margins*, *padding*, and *borders* to elements on the page—the `margin` and `padding` properties control the space around or inside the elements, while the `border` property specifies the appearance of the boundary of the box. In this section, we'll take a first look at how these styles affect the box model (which includes some surprises), and then in Section 8.6 we'll look in detail at how margin, padding, and border styles are used in practice.

We'll begin by investigating padding and borders, which are different from margins in a key respect. In particular, if you specify the width of a block element, like a `div` or a `p`, and then apply a border or padding to it, the additional border or padding will go *outside* the content. That means you can end up with an element that is bigger than the dimensions you specified. You'd think that if you said something should be 200px wide, it would always be 200px wide… but no, in the default state, CSS assumes that when you set a size for an element you are only talking about *the content part* of the element (Figure 8.5). This tends to generate a lot of confusion for people learning CSS, as they automatically assume that elements and their content are the same thing. Let's look at an example.

Suppose that you make a **div** and apply the following style:

```
width: 200px;
padding: 40px;
border: 10px solid #c00;
```

In this case, the entire element will end up being 300px wide on the page: 200px for the content, 40px each for the left and right padding, and 10px each for the left and right borders ($200 + 40 \times 2 + 10 \times 2 = \textbf{300px}$). This is the scenario illustrated in the original diagram for the box model (Figure 8.1), reproduced in Figure 8.5.

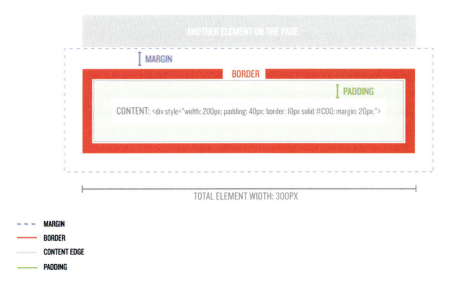

Figure 8.5: The default HTML box model again.

It is also possible to fix the total width of the content box, and force the border and padding to fit inside. The way to do this is with the **box-sizing** declaration. To see how this works, let's add some throwaway elements and styles to the page (which you can delete after seeing how this works).

We'll start with the HTML shown in Listing 8.6, which you can paste under the **h2** on the test page.[1]

Listing 8.6: Adding some test elements to the page to demonstrate box model properties.
index.html

```
<h2>I'm an h2</h2>

<div class="test-box">
  200px wide
</div>
<div class="test-box test-box-nosizing">
  200px wide + border + padding = 300px
</div>
<div class="test-box test-box-nosizing test-box-sizing">
  200px wide + border + padding + box-sizing: border-box = 200px
</div>
```

Then add the styles in Listing 8.7 to the bottom of your style block (we'll be deleting these too).

Listing 8.7: Adding classes and styles for the test elements.
index.html

```
  .test-box {
    background: #9db6dd;
    width: 200px;
  }
  .test-box-nosizing {
    border: 10px solid #000;
    padding: 40px;
  }
  .test-box-sizing {
    box-sizing: border-box;
  }
</style>
```

---

1. Recall that the code listings are available at https://github.com/learnenough/learn_enough_html_css_and _layout_code_listings.

When you save your work and refresh the browser, you'll see an assortment of boxes of different widths (Figure 8.6). Note how the `.test-box-sizing` class forces the div to be 200px wide in total. The **border-box** property caused the browser to draw the borders and padding *inside* the defined width.

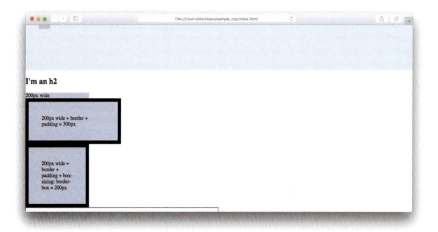

Figure 8.6: Different results even though all elements are set to 200px wide.

8.2.1 Margin Weirdness

So, we've talked about how the box model can behave unexpectedly when it comes to borders and padding, but what about margins? Well, you would expect that when two elements that both have margins are on the page next to each other, their margins would always apply. For example, if two elements both have **20px** of margin, you might expect that the elements would always end up being **20 + 20 = 40px** apart—but that isn't necessarily how it works.

A wise man (though not wise enough to exercise caution on the Ides of March) once said "experience is the teacher of all things," and in that spirit we will make changes to the page that let you see both examples shown in Figure 8.7.

We'll start by creating a situation where margins *do* behave in the intuitively expected manner. We'll do this by changing the test boxes introduced in Listing 8.6 to take the form shown in Listing 8.8.

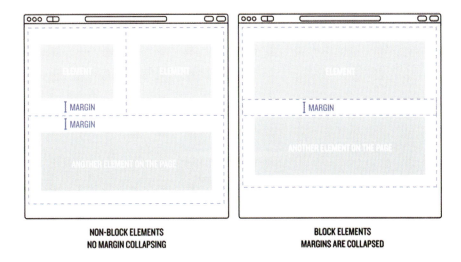

Figure 8.7: How the box model deals with margins between block and non-block elements.

Listing 8.8: Changing our test boxes to show expected margin behavior.

index.html

```
.test-box {
  background: #9db6dd;
  display: inline-block;
  margin: 50px;
  width: 200px;
}
.test-box-nosizing {
  border: 10px solid #000;
  padding: 40px;
}
.test-box-sizing {
  box-sizing: border-box;
  display: block;
  width: auto;
}
```

When you save and refresh the browser, you'll see the boxes from Figure 8.6 all separated from each other by 50px (Figure 8.8).

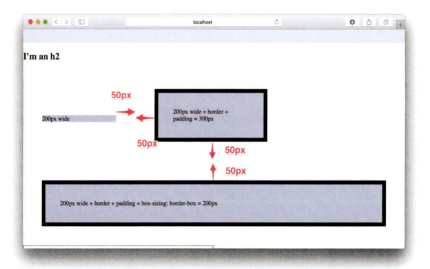

Figure 8.8: Trust us, they are all separated by the same distance.

Now we'll remove the **display** properties, so that each of the **div**s introduced in Listing 8.6 is reduced to its default (block) styling, while also removing the width styles, as shown in Listing 8.9.

Listing 8.9: Collapsing the margins.

index.html

```
.test-box {
  background: #9db6dd;
  margin: 50px;
}
.test-box-nosizing {
  border: 10px solid #000;
  padding: 40px;
}
.test-box-sizing {
  box-sizing: border-box;
}
```

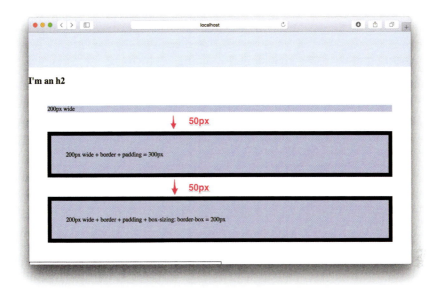

Figure 8.9: Less space now that the margins have collapsed.

The result is to magically collapse the margins: Now all the boxes are vertically separated by only 50px of margin, as shown in Figure 8.9.

The reason the first example worked as expected is that the first two elements weren't block elements, so the browser fully respected their set margins. Once they became block elements, though, the browser allowed for only one of the margins to apply.

The reason this exists goes all the way back to the bad old early days of HTML (Section 5.2.2), when most websites used browser defaults for all elements (because there was no CSS). Some block elements (like paragraph **p**s) have default top and bottom margins to keep text away from other elements to enhance readability, and if there were no margin collapsing, then whenever you put two of these elements next to each other there would be too much space between them. So at some point early on it was decided that when two block elements with margins follow each other, one of the top or bottom margins is canceled out.

In the next few sections, starting with Section 8.3, we'll be looking at how to put boxes side by side. If you are going to do the exercises, save the test blocks and styles; otherwise, you can delete the HTML and CSS styles from this section.

8.2.2 Exercises

1. Let's see if the width of the elements matters to margin collapsing. Change the size of the first two block elements by adding a style to set the width of `.test-box` to `200px`, and set the width for `.test-box-sizing` to `auto` to unset the previously set width value.

2. How does the browser determine which margin value to use? Try adding a style that sets a top margin of `100px` on the `.test-box-sizing` class.

8.3 Floats

Now that we've seen some of the things to watch out for in the box model, let's start using it to style our sample site. When you are designing a site you will often need different elements to sit next to each other on the page, and new developers often run into problems with how the box model affects their attempts to accomplish this. Perhaps unsurprisingly, there are a bunch of different ways to do this using CSS, and all have different positives and negatives. No single technique can be used across an entire site, so let's get started by learning about floating elements.

In Section 4.2, we used a property value called a **float** to move an image to the left side of a block of text. The idea is that when you set an element to float to the left or right (there is no **float: center**), all the inline content around it will flow around the floated element like water. Floated elements will always sit next to other floated elements on the same line, as long as there is horizontal room. If the elements are too wide, they will drop down to the next line.

Let's see this in action. We'll add **float: left** to the **.bio-box** class, and we'll also give the boxes some padding and a new (narrower) width. Listing 8.10 has the new styles. (Reminder: If you haven't done it already, remove the HTML and CSS from Section 8.2.)

Listing 8.10: The entire **index** page up to this point.
index.html

```css
.bio-box {
  border: 1px solid black;
  float: left;
  font-size: 1rem;
  padding: 2%;
  width: 25%;
}
```

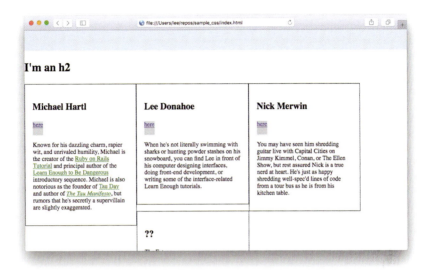

Figure 8.10: The boxes are next to each other, but they don't fit.

After you save your work and refresh the browser, the result should appear as in Figure 8.10.

Now all the boxes are in a row, but why is the last one spilling over to the next line?

It's because of the box model sizing issue from Section 8.2! The left and right borders, and the left and right padding got added onto the width of each **div**, making each one **25% + 1px border-left + 1px border-right + 2% padding-left + 2% padding-right**, for a total size of **29% + 2px** of the page for each. Multiplied by 4, this gives **116% + 8px**, which is greater than 100%.

Let's fix this by adding the **box-sizing: border-box** style to the **div** to force the borders and padding inside the set-width **div** (Listing 8.11).

Listing 8.11: Adding **border-box** to the bio boxes.
index.html

```
.bio-box {
  border: 1px solid black;
  box-sizing: border-box;
```

```
  float: left;
  font-size: 1rem;
  padding: 2%;
  width: 25%;
}
```

Now when you save and refresh you'll have four boxes in a row that fill the page (Figure 8.11)!

Figure 8.11: Box sizing saves the day, and now our floated boxes fit.

8.3.1 Clearing Floats

So, why might a developer not want to always use floating to get elements to line up side by side?

For one, there are only two options, **float: left** and **float: right**, but no **float: center**. That's annoying, but manageable. The bigger problem is that the browser doesn't always know where to end the float. When you float elements, you are telling the browser that you'd like the element to show up on the page in the place it would naturally "float" to, but after that starting position you want the rest of the page content to flow around the floated element. This can disrupt the orderly box-like arrangement of elements and create some odd-looking layouts.

To see what we mean, add the paragraphs from Listing 8.12 onto your test page below the closing **</div>** tag of the **.bio-wrapper**.

Listing 8.12: Adding text to the page below the bios.
index.html

```
<div class="bio-wrapper">
  .
  .
  .
</div>
<p>
  Learn Enough to Be Dangerous is a leader in the movement to teach the
  world <em>technical sophistication</em>, which includes both "hard
  skills" like coding, command lines, and version control, and "soft
   skills" like guessing keyboard shortcuts, Googling error messages, and
  knowing when to just reboot the darn thing.
</p>
<p>
  We believe there are <strong>at least a billion people</strong> who can
  benefit from learning technical sophistication, probably more. To join
  our movement,
  <a href="https://learnenough.com/#email_list">sign up for our official
  email list</a> now.
</p>
<h3>Background</h3>
<p>
  Learn Enough to Be Dangerous is an outgrowth of the
  <a href="https://www.railstutorial.org/">Ruby on Rails Tutorial</a> and the
  <a href="https://www.softcover.io/">Softcover publishing platform</a>.
  This page is part of the sample site for
  <a href="https://learnenough.com/css-tutorial"><em>Learn Enough CSS and
  Layout to Be Dangerous</em></a>, which teaches the basics of
  <strong>C</strong>ascading <strong>S</strong>tyle
  <strong>S</strong>heets, the language that allows web pages to be styled.
  Other related tutorials can be found at
  <a href="https://learnenough.com/">learnenough.com</a>.
</p>
```

When you save your work and refresh the page, you'll see that the floated elements have caused the text we just added to start under the rightmost float instead of starting on a new line (Figure 8.12).

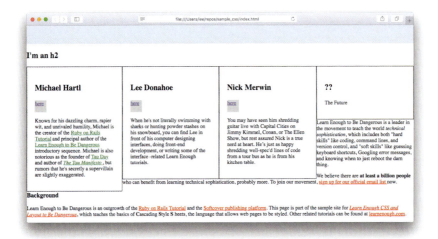

Figure 8.12: This is not what the doctor ordered.

In an ideal world, those paragraphs should stretch across the entire page since they are block elements. One way to get things back to the expected result would be to use the CSS **clear** rule, which is used to let the browser know to end floats. In this case, we could add **clear: left** to the first paragraph.

You can try it by adding an inline style (Listing 8.13).

Listing 8.13: A simple inline style to clear the float.
index.html

```
<p style="clear: left;">
  Learn Enough to Be Dangerous is a leader in the movement to teach the
```

This will force the paragraph onto a new line below the floated elements, and it will prevent any other element below it on the page from being altered by the float (Figure 8.13).

If the floating elements had been floated to the right using **float: right**, you would need to clear their float status with **clear: right**, or (if you just want to be extra careful) you can clear both types of floats using **clear: both**.

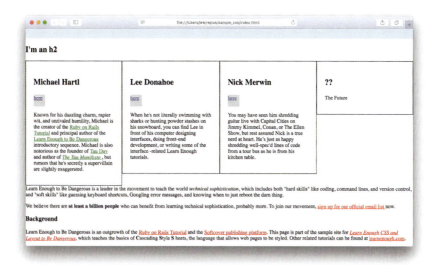

Figure 8.13: This works, but you don't want to have to manage clearing things on potentially every element.

If you tried clearing the float with an inline style on your test page, you should remove the style from the **p** tag—just the mere sight of an inline style should make you feel queasy at this point (but they are handy at times for quickly testing styles).

Having to add a **clear** style directly onto any element (either inline or in the stylesheet) after floated elements is kind of a pain—especially on a dynamic site that might pull in snippets of code to build a page. You don't always know which elements will be following floats.

A better way to clear floats is to apply a rule to clear everything inside a wrapper, such as the **.bio-wrapper** added in Listing 7.6. The idea is to arrange for the **.bio-wrapper** element, and everything in it, to act like a LEGO block that can safely be moved around without needing to worry about uncleared floats messing up a layout.

There are two methods to clear floats inside a wrapper: the **overflow** method and the **:after** "clearfix" method. We'll look at both of these methods here, and give more extensive coverage to the **overflow** property in Section 8.4 and the **:after** declaration in Section 10.3.1.

To see the **overflow** method in action, add the style from Listing 8.14 to **.bio-wrapper**.

Listing 8.14: When `overflow` is set to `hidden`, floats are cleared.

index.html

```
/* BIO STYLES */
.bio-wrapper {
  font-size: 24px;
  overflow: hidden;
}
```

When you save and refresh, the paragraph of text will be safely below the floated elements with no inline styles and no use of the **clear** property (Figure 8.14).

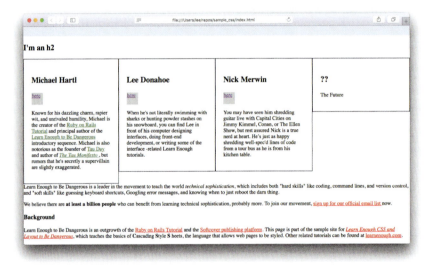

Figure 8.14: Same result, but self-contained instead of needing inline styling.

The problem with this method is that if you also need to set a height or width on the element that has **overflow: hidden** set, the content inside can get cut off. This happens most often with poorly built *dropdown menus* in a site navigation with floats that are cleared using the **overflow** method but where the header also had a set height. For example, Figure 8.15 shows what Amazon.com's homepage dropdown menu would look like if they had mistakenly also set **overflow: hidden**.[2]

---

2. Tricks like changing the live Amazon homepage can be accomplished by using a web inspector to edit a site's CSS dynamically in-browser, and then taking a screenshot of the result.

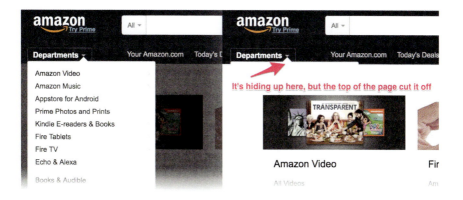

Figure 8.15: Changing the overflow on an element can hide parts that were supposed to stick out.

So, if you need to clear floats but also are worried about content being cut off because you absolutely, positively *have* to set a height on the wrapper element, you can use the **:after** method.

Let's see how it works. Remove **overflow: hidden** from the **.bio-wrapper** class, and add in the entire new declaration from Listing 8.15.

Listing 8.15: The more complicated **:after** method.
index.html

```
.bio-wrapper {
  font-size: 24px;
}
.bio-wrapper:after {
  visibility: hidden;
  display: block;
  font-size: 0;
  content: " ";
  clear: both;
  height: 0;
}
```

There's a lot of new stuff in there, but don't worry about it for now. We'll discuss **:after** in more detail in Section 10.3.1. The important thing for now is that **:after** creates a kind of imaginary element that comes at the end of the **bio-wrapper**—an imaginary element that we can add styles to! Setting **clear: both** on that element clears the floats and allows the content below to appear as intended. If you save the changes and refresh your browser, the text will still be cleared below the floated elements, as in Figure 8.13 and Figure 8.14.

8.3.2 Exercises

1. Let's try floating something to the other side to see how floats can change the order of content. Change the float property on **.bio-box** to float to the right. Notice which box is now on the left. (After viewing the change in your browser, change the float property back to **left**.)

2. Change the clear property in the **:after** style to clear to the right. You should see that the content in the wrapper no longer is being cleared. You need to make sure to either match floats to clears or use **clear: both**!

8.4 A Little More About the overflow Style

In Section 8.3, we used the **overflow** method to clear floats, but you may be wondering exactly why this method works… and also, what does **overflow** do in the first place?

The CSS **overflow** property tells the browser how to handle content inside a wrapper, if that wrapper has a set height or width. If the content in the wrapper doesn't fill the box, then **overflow** does nothing, but when there is more content than room to display that content, **overflow** comes into play. Because this property can be used to clear floats and control how content is displayed, it is worth exploring in detail.

The **overflow** style can be set to **visible**, which shows everything; **hidden**, which cuts content off at the boundaries of the wrapper; or **scroll**, which adds scrollbars to let you scroll up and down or left and right to see all the available content.[3] You've seen this before if you've ever scrolled inside a box on a website without scrolling the entire page (Figure 8.16).

---

3. The Mozilla Developer Network page on the CSS overflow property (https://developer.mozilla.org/en-US/docs/Web/CSS/overflow) includes a list of all the possible values.

Figure 8.16: Scrolling within a box on a page without scrolling the page.

overflow: hidden works for clearing floats because it makes the browser want to keep content contained entirely within the wrapper. If there is no set dimension on the wrapper, the browser just expands the boundaries of the wrapper to reach the end of the floated elements, and then lets the elements that follow display on the page normally.

Figure 8.17 shows diagrams of some of the different possible overflow situations when containing floated elements, and why you have to be careful when adding a height to an element with **overflow** set to **hidden**.

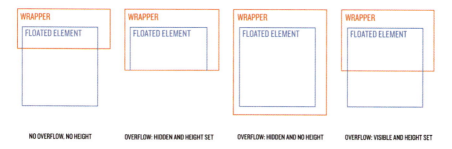

Figure 8.17: Some examples of overflow and containers.

To see what happens with the different settings in practice, let's start with **overflow: hidden**, and also give the **.bio-wrapper** a background color and a height (Listing 8.16).

Listing 8.16: **overflow** set to **hidden** with a height set on the container.
index.html

```
.bio-wrapper {
  background-color: #c0e0c3;
  font-size: 24px;
  height: 300px;
  overflow: hidden;
}
```

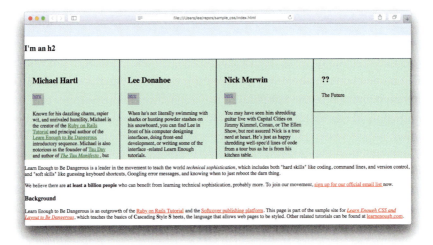

Figure 8.18: Setting **overflow** to **hidden** and adding a height cuts off the content.

You can see in Figure 8.18 that any content that is taller than the wrapper gets cut off. Now let's try **overflow: visible** (Listing 8.17).

Listing 8.17: **overflow** set to **visible** with a height set on the container.
index.html

```
.bio-wrapper {
  background-color: #c0e0c3;
  font-size: 24px;
  height: 300px;
  overflow: visible;
}
```

You can see the content extending past the boundary of the **.bio-wrapper** (Figure 8.19).

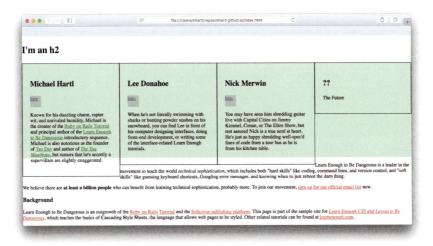

Figure 8.19: The content extends out of the green box due to **overflow: visible**.

Finally, let's try setting the value to **scroll** (Listing 8.18). An **overflow** set to **scroll** with a height set on the container will keep all the content inside the container, but you can scroll to see it.

Listing 8.18: Setting the **overflow** to **scroll**.
index.html

```
.bio-wrapper {
  background-color: #c0e0c3;
```

```
    font-size: 24px;
    height: 300px;
    overflow: scroll;
}
```

Now the content is cut off, but if you put your cursor in the green box and scroll up or down with your mouse or trackpad, you'll be able to see the hidden content (Figure 8.20).

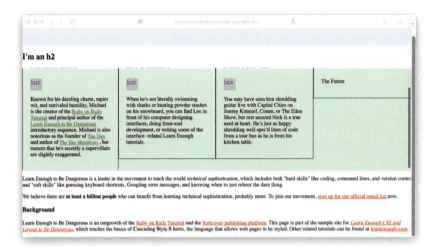

Figure 8.20: A scrollbar appears on the right just for the green box.

If you tried out these styles on your test page, set the `.bio-wrapper` back to the styles in Listing 8.19.

Listing 8.19: Returning the `.bio-wrapper` to `overflow: hidden`.
index.html

```
.bio-wrapper {
    font-size: 24px;
    overflow: hidden;
}
```

8.5 Inline Block

The second way to get things next to other things is to set the elements to **display: inline-block** (Section 8.1.4). This allows them to keep their block-style formatting (so they can have height and top/bottom margins and padding), while also letting us do things like control an element's position on a line of text by setting the style **text-align** on a wrapper to make everything align left, right, or center.

For this example, we are going to style the **li**s that contain the **.social-link**s inside the **.full-hero** at the top of the test page. Let's first give the unordered list tag **ul** a class called **.social-list** (Listing 8.20).

Listing 8.20: Adding a class name to the unordered list.
index.html

```
<ul class="social-list">
  <li>
    <a href="https://example.com/"
       class="social-link">Link</a>
  </li>
  <li>
    <a href="https://example.com/"
       class="social-link">Link</a>
  </li>
  <li>
    <a href="https://example.com/"
       class="social-link">Link</a>
  </li>
</ul>
```

By default, the **li** tag produces block elements that each start on their own new line; list elements that are part of an unordered list also include a bullet point before each element's content.[4] Why would we want to use such a list to display a person's social links?

The answer is that we can unstyle the list (removing the bullet points, making it inline instead of block, etc.) and use it however we want! It has become a common practice to use the **ul** tag to contain sets of links for things like navigation, menus, etc.,

---

4. Recall from Section 3.4 that the result of an **li** tag depends on the parent list type. In particular, when wrapped inside the ordered list tag **ol**, the list elements get numbers instead of bullet points.

because it's the logical HTML element for grouping lists of things, which as designers gives us a nice structure to work with.

So, first let's unstyle that list, and then add a second declaration that targets the **li**s inside **.social-list** and switches them to **display: inline-block** (Listing 8.21). By the way, the right angle bracket **>** on Line 12 in Listing 8.21 is a more advanced selector called the *child selector*, discussed briefly in Box 8.1 (following this section) and covered in more depth in Section 9.7.3.

Listing 8.21: Unstyling the list and making the **li**s **inline-block**.
index.html

```
/* SOCIAL LINKS */
.
.
.
.social-list {
  list-style: none;
  padding: 0;
}
.social-list > li {
  display: inline-block;
}
```

Hey, look at those elements all in a row (Figure 8.21)!

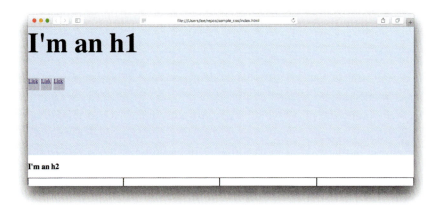

Figure 8.21: Our **li**s are now in a row and have no bullet points.

Notice that there are little spaces between the elements in Figure 8.21. This is an annoyance that comes with using this technique, and it stems from the way that browsers treat **inline-block** elements as though they are just funky-shaped words in a sentence. There are ways to get rid of that space, but we aren't going to get into those weeds here; instead, we are just going to ignore them since in our case it is nice to have a bit of space between elements. (For the record, when you use a float to get elements next to each other, there is no space between them at all.)

Box 8.1: Intro to Advanced Selectors

If you thought things weren't going to get any more complicated with selectors... you were wrong. We've barely scratched the surface! We are going to cover them more later in the tutorial (Section 9.7.3), but for now we want to explain the child selector.

Take a look again at the style we declared in Listing 8.21:

```
.social-list > li {
    display: inline-block;
}
```

What this says is "select only lis that are direct children of the .social-list parent, and make them inline-block." Remember that one of the goals when you are styling pages is to style only the things that need styling, without accidentally styling elements that will later need to be unstyled (Section 6.4). When you use advanced selectors, you can better target your declaration.

For example, suppose we had a second nested unordered list in one of those lis, like this:

```
<ul class="social-list">
  <li>
    <a href="https://example.com/"
       class="social-link">Link</a>
  </li>
  <li>
    <a href="https://example.com/"
       class="social-link">Link</a>
    <ul>
      <li>Item 1</li>
      <li>Item 2</li>
    </ul>
  </li>
  <li>
    <a href="https://example.com/"
       class="social-link">Link</a>
```

```
    </li>
  </ul>
```

In this case, the `li`s in the nested list would remain as block elements. This is because they are children of a plain `ul` element, and the CSS rule targets only children of a parent element with class `social-list`. If you like, you can try out that example on your test page (and then delete it when you're done).

Now let's center the links (Listing 8.22).

Listing 8.22: Centering the `inline-block` elements.

index.html

```
.social-list {
  list-style: none;
  padding: 0;
  text-align: center;
}
```

Figure 8.22: A simple `text-align: center` puts the boxes right in the middle.

You have no idea how hard what we did in Figure 8.22 used to be before this **inline-block** technique was available. In the bad old early days of the Web, when we had to use tables for everything, it used to be a giant pain to get things to work right, but now it is as easy as we just saw. We can play around with aligning the links left or right, and everything will be nicely contained inside the **ul** without any need to clear floats.

8.5.1 Exercises

1. Add a number to the end of the link text in the hero so that they now read as "Link1", "Link2", etc. Now, align the `.social-link`s to the right by changing the text alignment property for `.social-list` to `right`. Notice that, unlike when we floated elements to the right, the order doesn't change.

2. Test out the child selector by creating a new style declaration that changes only links that are the direct children of the `.bio-box`es to `#c68bf9`. You'll see that this declaration has a high specificity and will override the color set in the `.social-link` class.

8.6 Margins for Boxes

Now that we have a handle on arranging our boxes, let's look in detail at margin, padding, and borders. These styles allow developers to control the spacing between boxes (with `margin` in this section), the spacing inside boxes (with `padding` in Section 8.7), and the size and look of the edges of boxes (with `border` in Section 8.8).

We'll start with the simplest kind of margin declaration, which we'll add to the `.bio-box`es at the bottom of the page, as shown in Listing 8.23.

Listing 8.23: Adding a margin declaration.
index.html

```
.bio-box {
  border: 1px solid black;
  box-sizing: border-box;
  float: left;
  font-size: 1rem;
  margin: 20px;
  padding: 2%;
  width: 25%;
}
```

When you refresh the test page, you'll see that each one of the containers has moved away from everything else by **20px** in all directions (Figure 8.23).

The next question that you might be asking is, "Why are the boxes on two lines again? I thought we took care of that with **box-sizing: border-box** (Listing 8.11)?"

The answer is that in the box model, margins always apply *outside* an element. So even though we've set the **box-sizing** style to **border-box**, the four **div**s at the bottom are now taking up 100% *plus* 8 × 20px, which is wider than 100%.

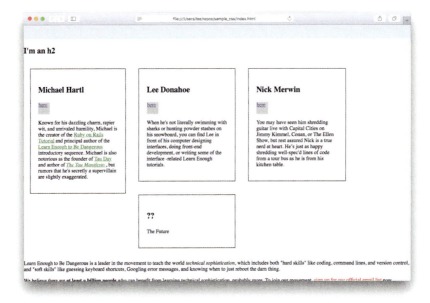

Figure 8.23: The boxes got some extra space, but broke onto two lines again.

So, how do we get everything to fit again? First, to make this easier we are going to switch to using the same units for each measurement (all percentages), and we are going to have to do a little bit of math.

Let's first set the margins to be percentages, as shown in Listing 8.24

Listing 8.24: Changing the margin from pixels to percent.
index.html

```
.bio-box {
  border: 1px solid black;
  box-sizing: border-box;
  float: left;
  font-size: 1rem;
  margin: 3%;
  padding: 2%;
  width: 25%;
}
```

Based on the result (Figure 8.24), this looks like a reasonable amount of spacing.

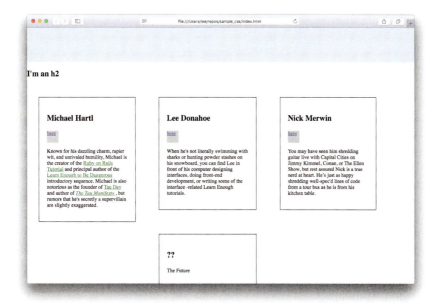

Figure 8.24: Pretty good margin size.

Now let's do the math. If we have a left and right margin of 3%, that means we need to reduce the size of each of the containers by $3\% + 3\% = 6\%$ to get everything to fit. Because the original width was 25%, this means the new width should be $25\% - 6\% = 19\%$, as shown in Listing 8.25.

Listing 8.25: Changing the width to accommodate the margins.
index.html

```
.bio-box {
  border: 1px solid black;
  box-sizing: border-box;
  float: left;
  font-size: 1rem;
  margin: 3%;
  padding: 2%;
  width: 19%;
}
```

It fits again (Figure 8.25)!

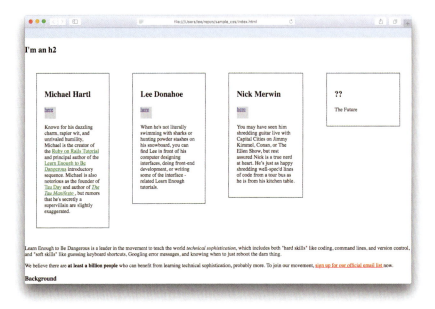

Figure 8.25: Everything is happy again.

Now let's take a look at the actual style declaration to dig a little deeper into how it works. When we write **margin: 3%**, we are applying the margin in *all* directions around the box, which is the equivalent of applying these four styles all at once:

```
margin-top: 3%;
margin-right: 3%;
margin-bottom: 3%;
margin-left: 3%;
```

The simple **margin** declaration that we used is a shorthand version that combines all the directions of the margin onto one line, and **margin: 3%** is the equivalent of writing this:

```
margin: 3% 3% 3% 3%;
```

As you may recall from Section 4.3, the order here is top, right, bottom, left, as illustrated in Figure 8.26.

Figure 8.26: Think of the four values as going clockwise from the top.

What if you really only want the margin on certain sides of the **div**? For example, to set the top margin to **40px** and the left margin to **30px**, we could use the more specific declarations shown in Listing 8.26.

Listing 8.26: Changing the width to accommodate the margins.
index.html

```
.bio-box {
  border: 1px solid black;
  box-sizing: border-box;
  float: left;
  font-size: 1rem;
  margin-top: 40px;
  margin-left: 30px;
  padding: 2%;
  width: 19%;
}
```

That will work just fine, but our code will start getting cluttered if we have to define every direction for every declaration that has a direction option. A better way to control where the margin goes is to use the single **margin** attribute and leverage the shorthand from Figure 8.26. To get margins of 40, 30, 40, and 30 pixels going around the **div** (clockwise from the top), we could style the **margin** like this:

```
margin: 40px 30px 40px 30px;
```

But guess what? As Figure 8.26 shows, in addition to the shorthand **margin: 40px** (using a single number), it's possible to include only two values if your top and bottom values are the same, and your left and right values are also the same (but different from the top and bottom):

```
margin: 40px 30px;
```

This shorthand also works with just three values, like **margin: 20px 10px 40px**. This is missing the final value, which (as seen in Figure 8.26) is the left margin, and will be filled in automatically from its opposite across the box (in this case, **10px**).

For our test page, let's set only a top margin of **40px** and a right and left margin of **1%**, and also increase the size of each container back to **23%** so that the entire row fills the available space (Listing 8.27).

Listing 8.27: Adding the margin declaration.
index.html

```
.bio-box {
  border: 1px solid black;
  box-sizing: border-box;
  float: left;
  font-size: 1rem;
  margin: 40px 1% 0;
  padding: 2%;
  width: 23%;
}
```

After saving your work and refreshing the browser, you'll see that the **div** with the link has now moved down **40px** from the content above and 1% from the sides of the browser and from the other containers (Figure 8.27).

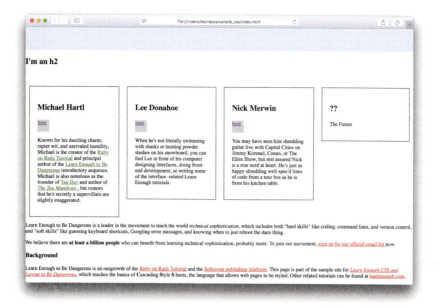

Figure 8.27: Much nicer spacing.

Looks great!

If you noticed that the margin between the boxes is different from the ends, that's because it's being doubled (due to the same margin on the left and right). We'll tackle this sort of issue with an advanced selector solution later in Section 9.7.3.

8.6.1   An Exception: `margin: auto`

You might be getting used to this by now, but of course there is another oddity that you should be aware of: `margin: auto`.

If you have a block element, like a `div`, `p`, or `ul`, that has a width set by a style, you can make the browser center that element horizontally within its parent container by setting the left and right margins to `auto`.[5]

---

5. The `margin: auto` trick does nothing for the top and bottom margins, though. Vertical centering is a much tougher nut to crack. We'll take a look at it starting in Section 9.8, and we'll introduce an even more powerful method called *flexbox* in Section 11.2.

To see **margin: auto** in action, let's change the styling (Listing 8.28) for the
.bio-wrapper to give it a **max-width**, and then set the margin to **auto**. **max-width**
is a CSS style that lets an element adapt its width to fit a space (up to a specified value);
there's also a **min-width** that does the opposite. Both are helpful when designing sites
that are intended to look good on both mobile and desktop platforms, since on the
smaller screen you want content to fill the browser, but on a big screen that could
look sloppy.

Listing 8.28: Applying **margin: auto**.
index.html

```
.bio-wrapper {
  font-size: 24px;
  margin: auto;
  max-width: 960px;
  overflow: hidden;
}
```

Save and refresh, and watch the box magically center (Figure 8.28).

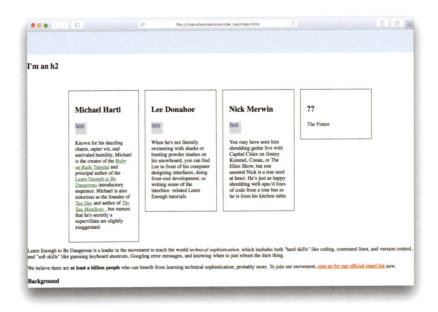

Figure 8.28: It's boxes… in the middle of the page!

8.6.2   Yet Another Exception: Negative Margins

Guess what? You can also make margins *negative* for elements. This draws the element up and out of the normal place it occupies on the page and overlays it on content that normally it wouldn't be able to affect.

To see this in action, let's first add some images (you can grab photos from the always fun placekitten (https://placekitten.com/) website) to the **.bio-box**es. Place an image above the **h3**s in each **.bio-box**, as shown in Listing 8.29.

Listing 8.29: Adding an image to each **.bio-box**.
index.html

```
<div class="bio-box">
  <img src="https://placekitten.com/g/400/400">
  <h3>Michael Hartl</h3>
  .
  .
  .
</div>
<div class="bio-box">
  <img src="https://placekitten.com/g/400/400">
  <h3>Lee Donahoe</h3>
  .
  .
  .
</div>
<div class="bio-box">
  <img src="https://placekitten.com/g/400/400">
  <h3>Nick Merwin</h3>
  .
  .
  .
</div>
<div class="bio-box">
  <img src="https://placekitten.com/g/400/400">
  <h3>??</h3>
  .
  .
  .
</div>
```

And then add a little bit of CSS to resize the images (Listing 8.30).

Listing 8.30: A style to control the size of the images that we added.
index.html

```
/* BIO STYLES */
.
.
.
.bio-box img {
  width: 100%;
}
.
.
.
```

With that, the images nicely fill up the space (Figure 8.29).

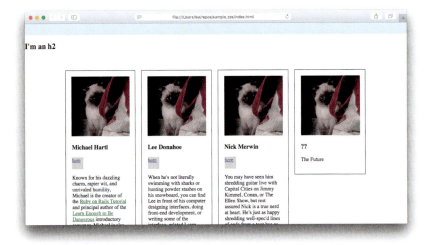

Figure 8.29: Your `.bio-boxes` should now look a little fluffier.

Now we'll add a negative top margin to the `.bio-box` `h3`s (changing from `margin-top` to the three-value `margin` shorthand mentioned in Section 8.6), as well as some extra styling for the text (Listing 8.31).

Listing 8.31: A negative margin moves an element out of its natural position.
index.html

```
.bio-box h3 {
  color: #fff;
  font-size: 1.5em;
  margin: -40px 0 1em;
  text-align: center;
}
```

Our new styles have pulled the header text out of its normal place and instead have drawn it on top of the images (Figure 8.30).

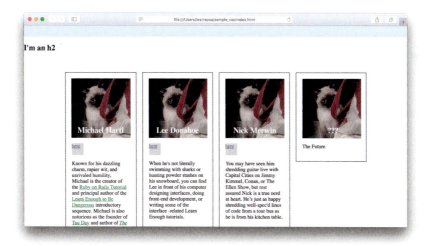

Figure 8.30: Negative margins move elements outside their natural position on the page.

Negative margins might seem like an odd property to allow, but they are actually useful from time to time. Negative margins also allow us to extend some content up and out of a box and overlap that content into a space where it normally wouldn't be able to be positioned, all while maintaining its properties as a normal block–level element.

8.6.3 Exercises

1. Use what we've learned about the margin shorthand to add in some space below the bottom of the **.bio-wrapper**, while using the CSS shorthand to keep the margin set to zero on top, and auto for the left and right.

2. Try to center the **.social-link**s that are inside the **.bio-box**es using a margin set to **auto**. Why doesn't this work, even though the elements have set widths?

8.7 Padding… Not Just for Chairs

As we saw at the beginning of Section 8.2, padding is similar to margins, except instead of pushing away things that are *outside* the element, it pushes the content *inside* an element away from the edges of the element. This is ideal when you want to have a box containing text have a background color or a border but you don't want the text ending up smashed against the edge of the container.

Padding values are declared using the same syntax as for margins, including the shorthand from Figure 8.26. Let's try it out and remove only the top padding from our **.bio-box**es by changing the styling to match Listing 8.32.

Listing 8.32: The padding value shorthand works just like the margin shorthand.
index.html

```
.bio-box {
  border: 1px solid black;
  box-sizing: border-box;
  float: left;
  font-size: 1rem;
  margin: 40px 1% 0;
  padding: 0 2% 2%;
  width: 23%;
}
```

The result of Listing 8.32 appears in Figure 8.31. (We'll revert this style choice in Section 8.8.)

Padding is one of the easier CSS properties to understand, as it doesn't have a whole lot of weird exceptions.

Figure 8.31: Hey, look, no top padding.

8.7.1   Exercise

1. Add a padding of **20px** to the links that are inside the **.bio-copy** sections. You'll see how top and bottom padding can't be applied to an inline element like a default link element, but the left and right padding will still be added.

8.8   Fun with Borders

You might have wondered about the **border: 1px solid black** style that has been on the **div**s this whole time. As you might have guessed, this style declaration is also a shorthand similar to margin and padding, but slightly different in that it is three totally different style declarations condensed into one (instead of just different directions, as with margin and padding).[6] The most common usage is to apply a border to all sides of an element, like this:

```
border: 1px solid black;
```

---

6. I did not guess this. —Michael

This is actually a condensed version of the following rules:

```css
border-width: 1px;
border-style: solid;
border-color: black;
```

All of those styles behave like the margin and padding in that they are directional shorthand that applies styling to the top, right, bottom, and left, like this:

```css
border-width: 1px 1px 1px 1px;
border-style: solid solid solid solid;
border-color: black black black black;
```

Note that the **border-style** declaration isn't a number, but rather can take on the following values: **none**, **hidden**, **dotted**, **dashed**, **solid**, **double**, **groove**, **ridge**, **inset**, and **outset**.

You might ask, "Well, that is all well and good, but what if I don't want all sides of a border to be the same?" The shorthand doesn't seem to cover that. What would the most efficient way be to make a 1px border that is colored black on three sides, but is red on one side (let's say the bottom side)? One way to achieve this look would be to separately declare all the different sub-declarations of the shorthand, like this:

```css
border-width: 1px;
border-style: solid;
border-color: black black red;
```

Or you could do it in a more condensed way and take advantage of the fact that rules that come after a similar declaration take precedence (Section 6.3), as in Listing 8.33.

Listing 8.33: Styling a border to have different colors on different sides.
index.html

```css
.bio-box {
  border: 1px solid black;
  border-color: black black red;
  box-sizing: border-box;
  float: left;
  font-size: 1rem;
  margin: 40px 1% 0;
  padding: 0 2% 2%;
  width: 23%;
}
```

Listing 8.33 sets a border around the entire element and then changes the color of one of the sides. The second declaration doesn't overwrite the entire border declaration; instead, it has an effect only on the part that pertains to border color. So by starting with a more generic style and then adding another style that changes some specific element, you can often accomplish a lot of work in just a couple lines of CSS (Figure 8.32).

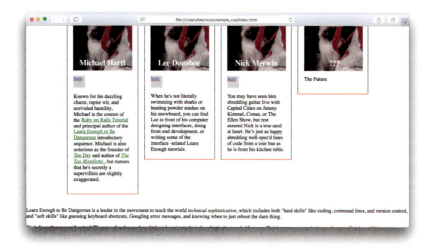

Figure 8.32: Now the bottom border is red.

Before moving on, let's remove the red border and revert the padding change from Listing 8.32. The result should look like Listing 8.34.

Listing 8.34: Reverting a couple of `.bio-box` styles.
index.html

```
.bio-box {
  border: 1px solid black;
  box-sizing: border-box;
  float: left;
  font-size: 1rem;
  margin: 40px 1% 0;
  padding: 2%;
  width: 23%;
}
```

8.8.1 Border Radius

The border can also have a *radius* set, which creates a box with rounded corners. To see how this works, add the CSS in Listing 8.35 to the styles targeting the social links on the test page.

Listing 8.35: Adding a **border-radius** to an object to make rounded corners.
index.html

```
.social-link {
  background: rgba(150, 150, 150, 0.5);
  border-radius: 10px;
  color: blue;
  display: inline-block;
  height: 36px;
  width: 36px;
}
```

The box should now have nicely rounded corners (Figure 8.33)!

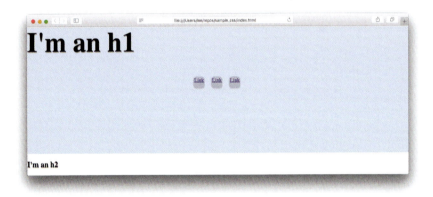

Figure 8.33: Rounded corners on the social links.

8.8.2 Making Circles

Want to see how to make circles using just HTML and CSS? The trick is to give the elements a set width and height, and then make the **border-radius** big enough to make the border larger than the width of the element, while also making sure the height and width of the element are equal (so that the "box" is a perfect square). Let's bump up the **border-radius** from Listing 8.33, and also give the **li**s in the **.social-list** a little margin (Listing 8.36).

Listing 8.36: A very large value for **border-radius** makes a circle.
index.html

```
/* SOCIAL STYLES */
.social-link {
  background: rgba(150, 150, 150, 0.5);
  border-radius: 99px;
    .
    .
    .
}
.social-list {
  list-style: none;
  padding: 0;
  text-align: center;
}
.social-list > li {
  display: inline-block;
  margin: 0 0.5em;
}
```

Look at those circles (Figure 8.34)!

Figure 8.34: Rounded boxes have become circles!

The links look a little weird with all that text, though, so let's change the text in the links in the hero and in the **.bio-box**es to the more compact values "Fb", "Tw", and "Gh" (for Facebook, Twitter, and GitHub, respectively). (We'll replace these with nice icons in Chapter 14.) The result appears in Listing 8.37.

Listing 8.37: Making the text a little shorter for the social links.
index.html

```
<ul class="social-list">
  <li>
    <a href="https://example.com/" class="social-link">Fb</a>
  </li>
  <li>
    <a href="https://example.com/" class="social-link">Tw</a>
  </li>
  <li>
    <a href="https://example.com/" class="social-link">Gh</a>
  </li>
</ul>
  .
  .
  .
<a href="https://twitter.com/mhartl" class="social-link">Tw</a>
  .
  .
  .
<a href="https://twitter.com/leedonahoe" class="social-link">Tw</a>
  .
  .
  .
<a href="https://twitter.com/nickmerwin" class="social-link">Tw</a>
```

Save and refresh, and your links should look like Figure 8.35.

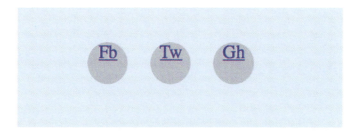

Figure 8.35: A little better.

Hmm… it still looks a little odd with the text up at the top, and down at the bottom of the page the text isn't even centered in the circle (in the `.full-hero` container it is inheriting a **text-align: center** style). Let's clean up the look and make sure that it stays the same regardless of usage.

We are going to add padding, and you may recall from Section 8.2 that we'll need to add in a **box-sizing: border-box** so that we make sure the padding doesn't change the dimensions of the element:

```
box-sizing: border-box;
padding-top: 0.85em;
```

Let's also change the color of the text, change the font, make it bold, align it to the center, and remove the underline with a new style called **text-decoration** (set to **none** to remove the default underline for links):

```
color: #fff;
font-family: helvetica, arial, sans;
font-weight: bold;
text-align: center;
text-decoration: none;
```

Finally, we'll set the font size using an **em** value (so that its size makes sense in the local context), add equal height and width, and set the *line height*, which we'll talk about more in a moment (Section 8.8.3):

```
font-size: 1em;
height: 2.5em;
line-height: 1;
width: 2.5em;
```

The equal height and width make the element a square, so that it will be a circle when **border-radius** is applied.

All together, those changes (plus a few more) are shown in (Listing 8.38). (To figure out the effect of the additional rules for yourself, apply the comment-out trick mentioned in Box 5.1.)

Listing 8.38: Changes to almost all the properties of the social links.

index.html

```
.social-link {
  background: rgba(150, 150, 150, 0.5);
  border-radius: 99px;
  box-sizing: border-box;
  color: #fff;
  display: inline-block;
  font-family: helvetica, arial, sans;
  font-size: 1rem;
  font-weight: bold;
  height: 2.5em;
  line-height: 1;
  padding-top: 0.85em;
  text-align: center;
  text-decoration: none;
  vertical-align: middle;
  width: 2.5em;
}
```

Those fully rounded and styled links look pretty great (Figure 8.36)!

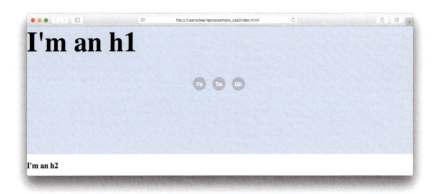

Figure 8.36: Muuuuch better.

Of all the new styles that we used, the most potentially confusing ones are probably **font-family** and **vertical-align**.

Looking back at Listing 8.38, you might think that **vertical-align** is something that can position elements in the middle of other elements, but in reality it has an effect only on objects that are inline, or inline block, and it centers them only in relation to the line of text that they appear on. We'll be covering vertical alignment a couple of times later in the tutorial—using positioning in Section 9.8, and using a more modern method called *flexbox* in Chapter 11.

The **font-family** change in Listing 8.38 involves defining what is called a *font stack*, which is just a list of font options that the browser should try to use:

```
font-family: helvetica, arial, sans;
```

Sometimes fonts can't be loaded from the Internet, or aren't available on a user's computer, so you start with the specific font you want as the first font, and then add the names of alternate fonts (separated by commas). Different computers have different fonts installed by default, and users can also add their own.

For instance, Apple computers have a classic font called Helvetica (by "classic" we mean that it was designed in 1957 and there's even a documentary about it). Windows has a knockoff of Helvetica called Arial (and designers hate it). To see what the two look like in comparison, check out Figure 8.37.[7]

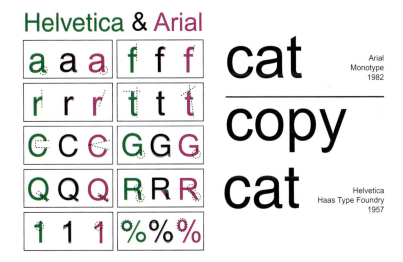

Figure 8.37: Arial is considered a cheap knockoff of Helvetica, and you probably shouldn't use it.

7. Font comparison chart from "Arial vs. Helvetica, Can You Spot the Difference?"

To find out which common fonts are available on which operating systems, you should consult a resource like CSS Font Stack (https://www.cssfontstack.com/). It is also possible to load your own custom fonts onto a user's computer, which is a great way to add to the unique visual branding of your site. We'll be covering such custom font loading in Section 14.1.

8.8.3 Line Height

As seen briefly in Listing 8.38, another aspect of text design is the *line height*, which defines the space above and below text and other inline elements. Any text on your site that is multiline should have the line height increased to make reading easier. An ideal amount would be around 140% to 170%, depending on the font.

The **line-height** property works like **em** in that **1** equals **100%**, but there's no associated unit as with **em**, **px**, etc. For example, to arrange for the **.bio-copy** to have a line height equal to 150% of the base font size, we can set the **line-height** to **1.5**, as shown in Listing 8.39.

Listing 8.39: Changing the line height for the **.bio-copy**.
index.html

```
.bio-copy {
  font-size: 1em;
  line-height: 1.5;
}
```

Figure 8.38: The result of increasing the line height.

The spacing between lines is now increased, which in some contexts can make the copy easier to read (Figure 8.38).

8.8.4 Syncing Up

Before moving on to Chapter 9, you can sync up your index page using the code in Listing 8.40.

Listing 8.40: The current index page.

index.html

```html
<!DOCTYPE html>
<html>
  <head>
    <title>Test Page: Don't Panic</title>
    <meta charset="utf-8">
    <style>
      /* GLOBAL STYLES */
      html, body {
        margin: 0;
        padding: 0;
      }
      h1 {
        font-size: 7vw;
        margin-top: 0;
      }
      a {
        color: #f00;
      }

      /* HERO STYLES */
      .full-hero {
        background-color: #c7dbfc;
        height: 50vh;
      }

      /* SOCIAL STYLES */
      .social-link {
        background: rgba(150, 150, 150, 0.5);
        border-radius: 99px;
        box-sizing: border-box;
        color: #fff;
        display: inline-block;
        font-family: helvetica, arial, sans;
        font-size: 1rem;
        font-weight: bold;
```

```css
  height: 2.5em;
  line-height: 1;
  padding-top: 0.85em;
  text-align: center;
  text-decoration: none;
  vertical-align: middle;
  width: 2.5em;
}
.social-list {
  list-style: none;
  padding: 0;
  text-align: center;
}
.social-list > li {
  display: inline-block;
  margin: 0 0.5em;
}

/* BIO STYLES */
.bio-wrapper {
  font-size: 24px;
  margin: auto;
  max-width: 960px;
  overflow: hidden;
}
.bio-box {
  border: 1px solid black;
  border-color: black black red;
  box-sizing: border-box;
  float: left;
  font-size: 1rem;
  margin: 40px 1% 0;
  padding: 0 2% 2%;
  width: 23%;
}
.bio-box h3 {
  color: #fff;
  font-size: 1.5em;
  margin: -40px 0 1em;
  text-align: center;
}
.bio-box img {
  width: 100%;
}
.bio-copy {
  font-size: 1em;
  line-height: 1.5;
}
.bio-copy a {
  color: green;
```

```
      }
    </style>
  </head>
<body>
  <div class="full-hero hero-home">
    <h1>I'm an h1</h1>
    <ul class="social-list">
      <li>
        <a href="https://example.com/" class="social-link">Fb</a>
      </li>
      <li>
        <a href="https://example.com/" class="social-link">Tw</a>
      </li>
      <li>
        <a href="https://example.com/" class="social-link">Gh</a>
      </li>
    </ul>
  </div>
  <h2>I'm an h2</h2>
  <div class="bio-wrapper">
    <div class="bio-box">
      <img src="https://placekitten.com/g/400/400">
      <h3>Michael Hartl</h3>
      <a href="https://twitter.com/mhartl" class="social-link">Tw</a>
      <div class="bio-copy">
        <p>
          Known for his dazzling charm, rapier wit, and unrivaled humility,
          Michael is the creator of the
          <a href="https://www.railstutorial.org/">Ruby on Rails
          Tutorial</a> and principal author of the
          <a href="https://learnenough.com/">
          Learn Enough to Be Dangerous</a> introductory sequence.
        </p>

        <p>
          Michael is also notorious as the founder of
          <a href="http://tauday.com/">Tau Day</a> and author of
          <a href="http://tauday.com/tau-manifesto"><em>The Tau
          Manifesto</em></a>, but rumors that he's secretly a supervillain
          are slightly exaggerated.
        </p>
      </div>
    </div>
    <div class="bio-box">
      <img src="https://placekitten.com/g/400/400">
      <h3>Lee Donahoe</h3>
      <a href="https://twitter.com/leedonahoe" class="social-link">Tw</a>
      <div class="bio-copy">
        <p>
          When he's not literally swimming with sharks or hunting powder
```

```
          stashes on his snowboard, you can find Lee in front of his computer
          designing interfaces, doing front-end development, or writing some of
          the interface-related Learn Enough tutorials.
        </p>
      </div>
    </div>
    <div class="bio-box">
      <img src="https://placekitten.com/g/400/400">
      <h3>Nick Merwin</h3>
      <a href="https://twitter.com/nickmerwin" class="social-link">Tw</a>
      <div class="bio-copy">
        <p>
          You may have seen him shredding guitar live with Capital Cities on
          Jimmy Kimmel, Conan, or The Ellen Show, but rest assured Nick is a
          true nerd at heart. He's just as happy shredding well-spec'd lines
          of code from a tour bus as he is from his kitchen table.
        </p>
      </div>
    </div>
    <div class="bio-box">
      <img src="https://placekitten.com/g/400/400">
      <h3>??</h3>
      <p>
        The Future
      </p>
    </div>
  </div>
  <p>
    Learn Enough to Be Dangerous is a leader in the movement to teach the
    world <em>technical sophistication</em>, which includes both "hard
    skills" like coding, command lines, and version control, and "soft
     skills" like guessing keyboard shortcuts, Googling error messages, and
    knowing when to just reboot the darn thing.
  </p>
  <p>
    We believe there are <strong>at least a billion people</strong> who can
    benefit from learning technical sophistication, probably more. To join
    our movement,
    <a href="https://learnenough.com/#email_list">sign up for our official
    email list</a> now.
  </p>
  <h3>Background</h3>
  <p>
    Learn Enough to Be Dangerous is an outgrowth of the
    <a href="https://www.railstutorial.org/">Ruby on Rails Tutorial</a> and the
    <a href="https://www.softcover.io/">Softcover publishing platform</a>.
    This page is part of the sample site for
    <a href="https://learnenough.com/css-tutorial"><em>Learn Enough CSS and
    Layout to Be Dangerous</em></a>, which teaches the basics of
    <strong>C</strong>ascading <strong>S</strong>tyle
```

```
      <strong>S</strong>heets, the language that allows web pages to be styled.
      Other related tutorials can be found at
      <a href="https://learnenough.com/">learnenough.com</a>.
    </p>
  </body>
</html>
```

8.8.5 Exercises

1. Change the border style of the **.bio-box**es from **solid** to **dashed**, then change it to **dotted**.

2. Use the **border-color** property, and shorthand values, to set the top and left of the **.bio-box**es to be invisible using either **transparent** or **rgba(0, 0, 0, 0)**, and the right and bottom sides to be black.

Laying It All Out

Now that we've got a good base of CSS knowledge, it's time to learn how to put everything together into a real website. This chapter and the next is where we really kick things into high gear, with material you're unlikely to see in any other CSS tutorial. To get started, our first step will be to transform our previous work into a more manageable set of *templates* and *page layouts* that can be easily reused and updated (in accordance with the DRY principle (Box 5.2)).

Along the way, we'll add more styling as a way to learn more complex aspects of CSS, while refining our design to be more suitable for use as a personal or business website. Combined with Chapter 10, the result will be a professional-grade example that shows a variety of aspects of modern site design.

9.1 Layout Basics

There are an infinite number of ways that you can design content layouts for the Web, but over the years certain conventions have become common to many sites, as shown in Figure 9.1. These may include elements like a header that contains site navigation and a logo (which typically links to the homepage); a hero section (Section 7.7); paragraph-style content with optional asides; and a page footer containing repetition of some elements from the header, as well as things like links to About or Contact pages, privacy policy, etc. These commonalities are the result of years of trial and error, and by incorporating such familiar elements into our site, we help new visitors orient themselves and find what they're looking for.

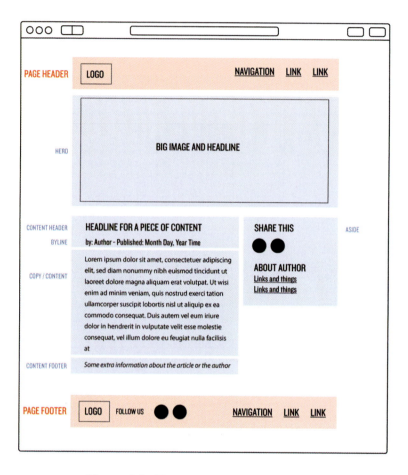

Figure 9.1: Elements of a typical web page.

One thing you may notice from Figure 9.1 is that many elements, such as the header and footer, are the same (or nearly the same) on every page of our site. If we made each page by hand, that would make our markup ridiculously repetitive—if we wanted to make a change, updating all those pages would be a nightmare.

This is an issue we faced repeatedly in Part I, where we simply copied and pasted common elements like navigation links onto every individual page. Such repetition is a violation of the DRY principle (Box 5.2), and in Box 3.2 we promised to teach you how to use a *templating system* to solve this problem. In this section, we'll fulfill this promise by installing and using the *Jekyll* static site generator to eliminate duplication in our layout.

Figure 9.2: Not Jekyll and Hyde… rather, Jekyll the static site generator!

9.2 Jekyll

When building a professional-grade website, it's essential to use a system capable of supporting templates to eliminate duplication. To accomplish this, we'll be using *Jekyll* (https://jekyllrb.com/) (Figure 9.2[1]), a free and open-source program for generating static websites (that is, sites that don't change from visit to visit).[2]

By learning Jekyll, you'll cultivate the skills needed to develop and deploy a real website—skills that are transferable to other static site generators (such as Middleman and Hugo) and to full-blown web frameworks (like Ruby on Rails (https://www.railstutorial.org/)). Learning the template language used by Jekyll (called *Liquid*) is also a valuable skill in itself, as Liquid is widely used in systems like the Shopify ecommerce platform.[3]

---

1. Poster image courtesy of BFA/Alamy Stock Photo.

2. Making *dynamic* sites that allow user registration, login, input, etc. requires using a full web application framework. In future Learn Enough tutorials, we'll cover two such frameworks, Sinatra and Rails (in *Learn Enough Ruby to Be Dangerous* (https://www.learnenough.com/ruby) and the *Ruby on Rails Tutorial*, respectively).

3. Indeed, as noted in Section 9.3, Liquid was originally developed by Shopify cofounder Tobi Lütke for exactly this purpose.

In addition to supporting templates, Jekyll also includes a bunch of other useful features:

- Write content in Markdown (the lightweight markup format we first discussed in Chapter 6 of *Learn Enough Developer Tools to Be Dangerous*) in your text editor of choice.

- Write and preview your content on your site locally in your dev environment.

- Publish changes via Git (which also gives you an automatic off-site backup).

- Host your site for free on GitHub Pages.

- No database management.

Originally developed by GitHub cofounder Tom Preston-Werner, Jekyll is used by millions of people around the world and is an industrial-strength tool for creating static websites. For example, the fundraising platform for U.S. President Barack Obama's 2012 reelection campaign, which handled 81,548,259 pageviews and raised over $250 million, was built using Jekyll:

> *By using Jekyll, we managed to avoid the complexity that comes with most CMSes (databases, server configuration) and instead were able to focus on things like optimizing the UI and providing a better user experience. To work in this environment, the most a front-end engineer had to learn was the Liquid template language that Jekyll uses, and boy is that simple.*[4]

9.2.1 Installing and Running Jekyll

Jekyll is written in the Ruby programming language, and is distributed as a Ruby *gem*, or self-contained package of Ruby code. As a result, installing Jekyll is easy once you have a properly configured Ruby development environment.

If your system is not already configured as a dev environment, you should consult *Learn Enough Dev Environment to Be Dangerous* (https://www.learnenough.com/dev-environment) at this time. This step might prove challenging, especially if you decide to configure your native system, but in the long run the effort is well worth the reward.

---

4. Originally published at http://kylerush.net/blog/meet-the-Obama-campaigns-250-million-fundraising-platform/ (since removed). Quoted selection has been lightly annotated and copyedited.

Once you've got a working dev environment, you can install Jekyll using *Bundler*, a manager for Ruby gems. We can install Bundler using the **gem** command, which comes with Ruby:

```
$ gem install bundler -v 2.3.14
```

Next, we need to create a so-called **Gemfile** to specify the Jekyll gem:

```
$ touch Gemfile
```

Then use a text editor to fill the **Gemfile** with the contents shown in Listing 9.1.

Listing 9.1: Adding the Jekyll gem.
Gemfile

```
source 'https://rubygems.org'

gem 'jekyll', '4.2.2'
gem 'webrick', '1.7.0'
```

If you run into any trouble, check the **Gemfile** at https://github.com/mhartl/mhartl .github.io to see if it has been updated.

Finally, we can install the jekyll gem using **bundle install** (with a little extra code to ensure that we're using the right version of Bundler):

```
$ bundle _2.3.14_ install
```

Although Jekyll is designed to work with a system of templates (Section 9.3), in fact it can work with a single file, such as our current **index.html**. To see how it works, we can run the Jekyll server in our project directory (using **bundle exec** to ensure that the right version of Jekyll gets run):

```
$ bundle _2.3.14_ exec jekyll serve
```

If you're working on a native system or a virtual machine (as opposed to a cloud IDE), at this point the Jekyll app should be available at the URL http://localhost:4000, where localhost is the address of the local computer and 4000 is the *port number* (Box 9.1). The result should look something like Figure 9.3.

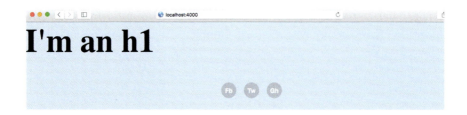

Figure 9.3: No more URL pointing to a file—you're running on a server now!

Box 9.1: Server Ports

If you look at the URL for the Jekyll site, you'll notice that it ends in ":4000". That is the *server port*. If you end a URL with a colon followed by a number, you are telling the browser to connect to that port on the server… so what does that mean?

You can think of server ports as being like individual phone numbers for different services that run on a computer. The default port number for the World Wide Web is port 80, so http://www.learnenough.com:80 is the same thing as http://www.learnenough.com, while the default port for a secure connection is 443, so https://learnenough.com:443 is the same thing as https://learnenough.com (with `https` in place of `http`). Other common port numbers include 21 (`ftp`), 22 (`ssh`), and 23 (`telnet`).

In the context of developing applications on a development machine, using port numbers allows us to solve the important problem of being able to run two or more apps simultaneously. Suppose, for example, that we wanted to run two different Jekyll websites on our development server. By default, both of them would be located at localhost:4000, but this would cause a conflict because the browser would have no way of knowing which site to serve when visiting that address. The solution is to add an extra piece of information, the port number, which allows the computer to distinguish between, say, app #1 running on localhost:4000 and app #2 running on localhost:4001.

As noted above, Jekyll's default server port is 4000, but we can set a different port number using the `--port` command-line option as follows:

```
$ bundle _2.3.14_ exec jekyll serve --port 4001
```

To connect to this second server, we would then type localhost:4001 into our browser's address bar.

Figure 9.4: Sharing the URL on the cloud IDE.

If you're using the cloud IDE (https://www.learnenough.com/dev-environment-tutorial#sec-cloud_ide) suggested in *Learn Enough Dev Environment to Be Dangerous*, you'll have to pass options for the port number (Box 9.1) and host IP number when running the **jekyll** command:

```
$ bundle _2.3.14_ exec jekyll serve --port $PORT --host $IP
```

Here **$PORT** and **$IP** should be typed in literally; they are *environment variables* provided by the cloud IDE to make the development site accessible on an external URL. Once the server is running, you can visit it by selecting Share and then clicking on the server URL, as shown in Figure 9.4. The result, apart from the browser URL, should be the same as for the local system shown in Figure 9.3. (For simplicity, in what follows we sometimes refer to localhost:4000, but users of the cloud IDE should use their personal URL instead. *Mutatis mutandis.*)

After starting the Jekyll server, you should find a new folder in your project called **_site** (with a leading underscore):

```
$ ls
_site       index.html
```

This folder contains the output from the Jekyll server as it builds your site from the source files (currently just **index.html**).

The **_site** directory and all its contents are generated by Jekyll every time a file is saved, and if you were to make any changes in the **_site** folder, they will be automatically overwritten. As a result, you should never make changes in any of the

Figure 9.5: TFW changes accidentally made in generated files get overwritten.

`_site` files themselves—they would only be overwritten by Jekyll. There's nothing more frustrating than accidentally working on updates in an automatically generated folder, only to have your changes overwritten by an uncaring static site generator (Figure 9.5).[5]

Because all its content is generated by Jekyll, it's a good idea to ignore the `_site` directory by adding it to your `.gitignore` file, and there's a Bundler configuration directory called `.bundle` that should also be ignored:

```
$ echo _site/ >> .gitignore
$ echo .bundle >> .gitignore
$ git add .gitignore
$ git commit -m "Ignore the generated site and Bundler directories"
```

You should also add the **Gemfile** (and the associated auto-generated **Gemfile.lock** file) to the repository:

```
$ git add -A
$ git commit -m "Add a Gemfile"
```

---

5. Image courtesy of mangostar/123RF.

9.2.2 Exercises

1. Try starting Jekyll on a non-standard port like **1234**.

9.3 Layouts, Includes, and Pages (Oh My!)

One of the most powerful features of Jekyll is its ability to factor different parts of a website into reusable pieces. To accomplish this, Jekyll uses a system of folders and conventional names for files, along with a mini-language called *Liquid*. Originally developed by Tobi Lütke, cofounder of online store powerhouse Shopify,[6] Liquid is a system for adding content to a site using what are in effect simple computer programs.

Files inside a Jekyll project can be static, meaning that they do not get processed by the Jekyll engine, or they can be dynamic and get constructed with Jekyll magic. (The *site* is still static because it consists of static files on the server, even if those files are generated dynamically by Jekyll. In other words, the files don't change once they've been generated by Jekyll, so the results are the same for every visitor of the site.)

There are four main types of magic objects/files that the Jekyll engine can use in an automated way to build your site:

- Layouts/layout templates
- Includes
- Pages/page templates
- Posts

We'll discuss each of these in abstract terms for reference, but their exact uses won't become clear until we see some concrete examples starting in Section 9.4.

9.3.1 Layouts/Layout Templates

Anything in the special **_layouts** directory (which we'll create in Section 9.4) can have Jekyll magic, meaning those files get read by the engine looking for Liquid tags and other Jekyll formatting.

---

6. Tobi is also an alumnus of the Rails core team.

One of the key parts of many Jekyll pages is *frontmatter*, which is *metadata* at the top of an HTML file (in YAML format) that identifies the kind of layout to be used, a page-specific title, etc. A fairly complicated example might look like this, where the frontmatter is everything between the two triple-dashes `---`:

```
---
layout: post
title: This is the title of the post
postHero: images/shark.jpg
author: Me, Myself, and I
authorTwitter: https://twitter.com/mhartl
gravatar: https://gravatar.com/avatar/ffda7d145b83c4b118f982401f962ca6?s=150
postFooter: Additional information, and maybe a <a href="#">link or two</a>
---

<div>
  <p>Lorem ipsum dolor sit paragraph.</p>
<div>
```

In a simpler but still common example, the frontmatter identifies only the page layout template to be used when rendering the page:

```
---
layout: default
---

<div>
  <p>Lorem ipsum dolor sit paragraph.</p>
<div>
```

We'll see the effects of this sort of code starting in Section 9.4.

If there is no frontmatter in a layout file, then it is a true layout, and it needs to have a full HTML page structure. If there *is* frontmatter, then the file is a layout template that can be built into other layouts, and it doesn't need to have a full HTML page structure.

Layouts are often the most base-level objects, defining a standard page with a **DOCTYPE**, **html**/**head**/**body** tags, **meta** tags, stylesheet links, JavaScript, etc., and they usually pull in snippets like a site header or site footer. You often need only one default layout for a site, but you can also use layout templates for things like blogs (Section 12.3).

Layouts have the special ability to load content, like posts, using a generic Liquid tag that looks like this: **`{{ content }}`**. We'll see a short example of this in an exercise (Section 9.6.3), and we'll apply it to our full site in Chapter 10.

9.3.2 Includes

Files in the **`_includes`** folder can have Jekyll magic even though they don't need frontmatter, and these files are always intended to be built into something else. Includes tend to be little snippets of a site that get repeated on many pages, such as the header and footer (Figure 9.1) or a standard set of social media links. Includes will be covered in Section 9.6.

9.3.3 Pages/Page Templates

Any other HTML file in the project directory is a *page*. If there is no frontmatter in the file it is a *static page*, and Jekyll magic will not work (Liquid tags go unprocessed). If a page has frontmatter, though, it will need to specify a layout, and then all the Jekyll magic will be available. We'll cover pages more in Chapter 10.

9.3.4 Posts, and Post-Type Files

Posts are self-contained pieces of content, such as blog posts or product details, that are saved as files in the **`_posts`** directory. Some forms of content (like blog posts) are typically organized by date, while others (like product descriptions) are organized based on other attributes into *collections*. We'll discuss posts further in Chapter 12; collections are beyond the scope of this tutorial, but you can read about them in the Jekyll documentation on collections (https://jekyllrb.com/docs/collections/).

9.4 The Layout File

Let's start playing around with a Jekyll layout by adapting our site into the framework. The end result of this section will be a page that looks exactly like the current **`index.html`**, but which is created in a way that will give us greater power and flexibility down the road. This includes getting a first taste of templates and frontmatter (which we'll cover in greater depth in Chapter 10).

This isn't how you would normally go about creating a site if you were starting from scratch. Layout files are usually pretty bare-bones (as we'll see in Section 10.1), and a more common development process is to create a spartan layout using the command **jekyll new** and then start doing the real work in the pages and includes. In our case, though, we've already done a lot of work in our single **index.html** file; using it as our initial layout means that, as we learn about different aspects of Jekyll, we can pull the parts we need out of the layout, thereby showing how a whole site can be sliced up and reassembled.

As we explained in Section 9.3, the Jekyll convention for layouts is to place these files in a directory called **_layouts** (with a leading underscore), which you should create in the root directory of your application (**repos/<username>.github.io**):

```
$ mkdir _layouts
```

Any HTML file in the **_layouts** directory can serve as a layout, so to get started we'll copy the existing **index.html** into the layouts directory to create a default layout:

```
$ cp index.html _layouts/default.html
```

At this point, your project files should look something like Figure 9.6.

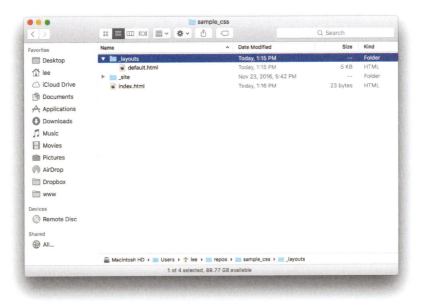

Figure 9.6: Your files and directories should look like this.

To get our site back up and visible, replace the entire contents of **index.html** with the code shown in Listing 9.2.

Listing 9.2: The site index with Jekyll frontmatter.
index.html

```
---
layout: default
---
```

As mentioned in Section 9.3, the content in Listing 9.2 is known as the Jekyll *front-matter*, and by adding it to the **index.html** file we've turned a static page into a Jekyll *page template*.

The frontmatter is the secret sauce that lets Jekyll know that it needs to read through an HTML page to see if it should process any of the content. By specifying **layout: default**, we've arranged for Jekyll to use **default.html** as the page layout. Because **default.html** is currently a fully self-contained page, the result of visiting http://localhost:4000 is to render our entire test page (Figure 9.3). In other words, Jekyll just takes the contents of **default.html** and inserts it into **index.html**.

As mentioned in Section 5.4, this sort of transformation, where we change the underlying code without changing the result, is known as *refactoring*. It may seem like we've done nothing, but we'll see in Section 9.6 how this new structure lets us slice and dice our website into reusable pieces.

9.4.1 Exercises

1. To see the way frontmatter affects how pages are built, delete the frontmatter in **index.html**, and write "Hello world." Save the file and refresh the page.

2. Revert your changes from Exercise 1, and change the layout to one called **test**. Then create a new file in the **_layouts** directory called **test.html**, and add in some text like "Hello again, world."

3. In the root directory of your project, create a new file called **tested.html** and add in some text in it like "For the third time, hello world!" Now, in your browser go to http://localhost:4000/tested.html to see what happens.

9.5   CSS File and Reset

Now that we've refactored our test page into a layout (**default.html**) and a page template (**index.html**), we're going to start the process of breaking our monolithic HTML/CSS file into its component parts. The first step is to create a standalone CSS file with a *reset* that eliminates troublesome browser defaults for margins, padding, etc. (Listing 7.18). Then we'll pull all the CSS out of the test site's **style** block and put it into the same external file.

To get started, create a new folder in the project directory called **css**, and then create a new file in that directory called **main.css**, either using the terminal like in Listing 9.3, or by just adding the folders and files in your text editor.

Listing 9.3: Creating a new CSS folder and blank document in the terminal.

```
$ mkdir css
$ touch css/main.css
```

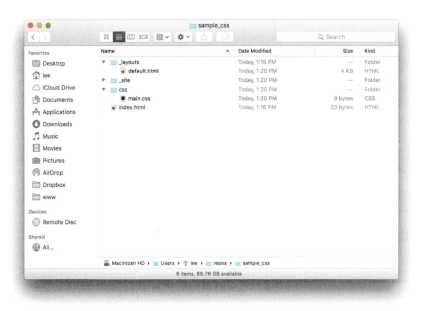

Figure 9.7: The new **css** folder and **main.css** file.

You have to name your directory exactly **css**, because Jekyll automatically looks for CSS files in that location, but you can use whatever filename makes you happy for the actual CSS file.

After you've created the folder and file as in Listing 9.3, your project directory should look something like Figure 9.7.

Recall from the discussions in Section 7.5 and Section 7.7 that browsers have built-in default styling for many common elements. Those browser defaults can differ from browser to browser, and if we were to allow them to remain it would mean that many elements on the page would start with styles we didn't pick. No self-respecting and properly perfectionist developer wants to leave the appearance of important elements up to the browser makers, so we'll apply a full *CSS reset* to create a blank slate for our designs.

Recall that we created a mini-version of a CSS reset in Listing 7.18, where we reset the margin and padding for **html** and **body** tags. Now it's time to upgrade our site to use an industrial-strength reset. The resulting CSS may look intimidating, but don't worry—we're putting it in Listing 9.4 precisely so that you can copy and paste it without having to understand the details.[7]

Listing 9.4: A standard CSS reset.
`css/main.css`

```
html, body, div, span, applet, object, iframe,
h1, h2, h3, h4, h5, h6, p, blockquote, pre,
a, abbr, acronym, address, big, cite, code,
del, dfn, em, img, ins, kbd, q, s, samp,
small, strike, strong, sub, sup, tt, var,
b, u, i, center, dl, dt, dd, ol, ul, li,
fieldset, form, label, legend, table, caption,
tbody, tfoot, thead, tr, th, td, article, aside,
canvas, details, embed, figure, figcaption, footer,
header, hgroup, menu, nav, output, ruby, section,
summary, time, mark, audio, video {
  margin: 0;
  padding: 0;
  border: 0;
  font: inherit;
  vertical-align: baseline;
}
/* HTML5 display-role reset for older browsers */
```

---

7. Recall that the code listings are available at https://github.com/learnenough/learn_enough_html_css_and_layout_code_listings.

```css
article, aside, details, figcaption, figure,
footer, header, hgroup, menu, nav, section {
  display: block;
}
body {
  line-height: 1;
}
blockquote, q {
  quotes: none;
}
blockquote:before, blockquote:after,
q:before, q:after {
  content: '';
  content: none;
}
table {
  border-collapse: collapse;
  border-spacing: 0;
}
strong, b {
  font-weight: bold;
}
em, i {
  font-style: italic;
}
a img {
  border: none;
}
/* END RESET*/
```

Note that the CSS in Listing 9.4 doesn't need to be wrapped with the **style** tags the way the styles in the HTML file did; as we'll see in Listing 9.7, the browser understands from the link that everything inside the file is CSS.

We see in Listing 9.4 that most of the standard HTML elements get some sort of styling applied to them. The big block of selectors at the top is pretty much every HTML element in the spec forced to have margin and padding set to zero, a border of zero, and told to inherit font styles. This might seem a little extreme to target every element, but when we are making a custom website there is no reason to leave browser defaults for things like margin, padding, and border in place—otherwise, we could end up having to *undo* styling all over our stylesheet. It's better to undo a lot of stuff right off the bat, and then only add positive styling later on.

Also, don't think that the above reset styling is something set in stone (Figure 9.8[8]). If later in your development career you find yourself adding the same styling to every

8. Etching image courtesy of World Archive/Alamy Stock Photo; tablet graphic courtesy of Oleksiy Mark/Shutterstock.

Figure 9.8: Reset rules aren't set in stone... or any other kind of tablet.

(say) **table** tag on every site you design, it's probably best just to add that to your reset. As usual, the DRY principle applies (Box 5.2).

With the reset added, we're now in a position to move the custom CSS style developed so far in the tutorial into **main.css**. This involves first opening **default.html** and cutting all the CSS inside the **style** tag, leaving the tag empty (Listing 9.5).

Listing 9.5: The default layout with CSS cut out.
_layouts/default.html

```
<!DOCTYPE html>
<html>
  <head>
    <title>Test Page: Don't Panic</title>
    <meta charset="utf-8">
    <style>
```

```
    </style>
  </head>
  <body>
    .
    .
    .
  </body>
</html>
```

Next, paste the CSS into **main.css** (possibly using something like Shift-Command-V, which pastes at the proper indentation level), and then delete the mini-reset targeting only **html, body** that we added before since it is now redundant. The full resulting code is shown in Listing 9.6.

Listing 9.6: The entire CSS file up to this point.

css/main.css

```css
html, body, div, span, applet, object, iframe,
h1, h2, h3, h4, h5, h6, p, blockquote, pre,
a, abbr, acronym, address, big, cite, code,
del, dfn, em, img, ins, kbd, q, s, samp,
small, strike, strong, sub, sup, tt, var,
b, u, i, center, dl, dt, dd, ol, ul, li,
fieldset, form, label, legend, table, caption,
tbody, tfoot, thead, tr, th, td, article, aside,
canvas, details, embed, figure, figcaption, footer,
header, hgroup, menu, nav, output, ruby, section,
summary, time, mark, audio, video {
  margin: 0;
  padding: 0;
  border: 0;
  font: inherit;
  vertical-align: baseline;
}
/* HTML5 display-role reset for older browsers */
article, aside, details, figcaption, figure,
footer, header, hgroup, menu, nav, section {
  display: block;
}
body {
  line-height: 1;
}
blockquote, q {
  quotes: none;
}
blockquote:before, blockquote:after,
```

```css
q:before, q:after {
  content: '';
  content: none;
}
table {
  border-collapse: collapse;
  border-spacing: 0;
}
strong, b {
  font-weight: bold;
}
em, i {
  font-style: italic;
}
a img {
  border: none;
}
/* END RESET*/

/* GLOBAL STYLES */
h1 {
  font-size: 7vw;
  margin-top: 0;
}
a {
  color: #f00;
}

/* HERO STYLES */
.full-hero {
  background-color: #c7dbfc;
  height: 50vh;
}

/* SOCIAL STYLES */
.social-link {
  background: rgba(150, 150, 150, 0.5);
  border-radius: 99px;
  box-sizing: border-box;
  color: #fff;
  display: inline-block;
  font-family: helvetica, arial, sans;
  font-size: 1rem;
  font-weight: bold;
  height: 2.5em;
  line-height: 1;
  padding-top: 0.85em;
  text-align: center;
  text-decoration: none;
  vertical-align: middle;
```

```css
    width: 2.5em;
}
.social-list {
  list-style: none;
  padding: 0;
  text-align: center;
}
.social-list > li {
  display: inline-block;
  margin: 0 0.5em;
}

/* BIO STYLES */
.bio-wrapper {
  font-size: 24px;
  margin: auto;
  max-width: 960px;
  overflow: hidden;
}
.bio-box {
  border: 1px solid black;
  box-sizing: border-box;
  float: left;
  font-size: 1rem;
  margin: 40px 1% 0;
  padding: 2%;
  width: 23%;
}
.bio-box h3 {
  color: #fff;
  font-size: 1.5em;
  margin: -40px 0 1em;
  text-align: center;
}
.bio-box img {
  width: 100%;
}
.bio-copy {
  font-size: 1em;
  line-height: 1.5;
}
.bio-copy a {
  color: green;
}
```

As you can verify by refreshing the browser, the page is now completely unstyled (Figure 9.9).

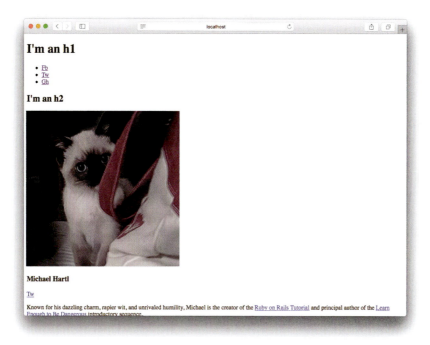

Figure 9.9: It's been a long time since our site was this naked and unstyled.

To restore the styling, all we need to do is tell the layout page about **main.css**. The way to do this is to replace the **style** tags in the **head** section with a link to our stylesheet, as shown in Listing 9.7.

Listing 9.7: Using a **link** tag to load **main.css**.
_layouts/default.html

```
<!DOCTYPE html>
<html>
  <head>
    <title>Test Page: Don't panic</title>
    <meta charset="utf-8">
    <link rel="stylesheet" href="/css/main.css">
  </head>
  .
  .
  .
```

The **link** tag in Listing 9.7 tells the browser that it will be loading a stylesheet (**rel** is short for "relationship"), and then specifies a URL (in this case an absolute one that looks at the site's root directory by starting the URL with a forward slash)[9] that leads to the file.

It's important to understand that using the **link** tag to load an external stylesheet has nothing to do with Jekyll; this general technique works even on hand-built websites that don't use any site builder. The stylesheet doesn't actually need to be local, either—theoretically, it can be anywhere on the Internet—but for our purposes, we want to use a local file so that it's easy to make changes.

Now when you refresh the browser the styles should be properly applied, and the page will pretty much look how it did before our refactoring, although there will be some places where things don't look right because of the CSS reset (Figure 9.10).

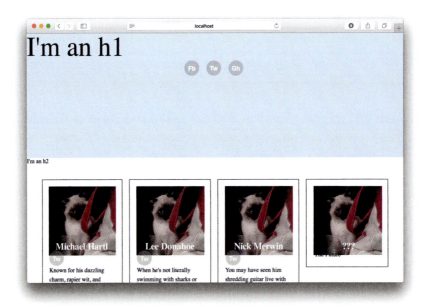

Figure 9.10: Same old page, with some minor oddities.

---

9. Recall from Section 2.4 that paths can be either relative (local to the computer serving the file) or absolute (accessed by a full URL). For example, the path **css/main.css** is relative, while **/css/main.css** is absolute.

Before moving on, let's make a few minor changes to prove that we know how to update styles via the CSS file. Ever since we started with this page, the fonts have looked a little... old-school. Let's add in a general style to the page **body** that will cascade down to every element on the page and change all body text to a nice, clean, sans-serif font (Listing 9.8).

Listing 9.8: A good spot for this would be in the "Global Styles" section of the CSS file.
`css/main.css`

```
/* GLOBAL STYLES */
body {
  font-family: helvetica, arial, sans;
}
```

When you save your work and refresh the browser, everything should still look the way it did before, but with all-new fonts across the page (Figure 9.11).

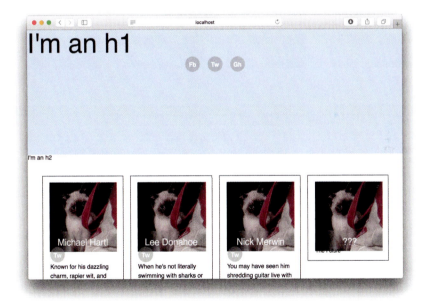

Figure 9.11: Same old page, all-new fonts.

Finally, in order to avoid the overlap between the bio box and social links, we'll change the CSS for the latter to be **display: block** with a margin, as shown in Listing 9.9.

Listing 9.9: Fixing up the social link spacing.
index.html

```
.bio-box img {
  width: 100%;
}
.bio-box .social-link {
  display: block;
  margin: 2em 0 1em;
}
.bio-copy {
  font-size: 1em;
}
```

The result appears in Figure 9.12.

Figure 9.12: Better spacing for the social links.

9.5.1 Exercises

1. Create a second CSS file in the **css** folder, and add a second link to this new CSS file in the head of the document (making sure that this second link comes after the original CSS link). In your new CSS file, add a style that changes the **.full-hero** background color to a color of your choice. This shows that the order in which stylesheets load affects which styles take priority.

2. Rename the new CSS to **reset.css**, and move the stylesheet link above the link to **main.css**. Now cut and paste the entire reset section from **main.css** into the new CSS file (overriding the style added in Exercise 1). Save everything and make

sure that your test page looks the same in your browser. You've made your reset portable!

9.6 Includes Intro: Head and Header

Now that we've factored the CSS into a separate file (and added a CSS reset), it's time to start slicing up the default page into reusable pieces. As discussed in Section 9.3, Jekyll provides *includes* to help us with this important task. (*Note*: In this context, the word "include" is used as a *noun*, which is not standard English but is standard in the world of static site generators. This usage also changes the pronunciation; the verb form is "in-CLUDE", but the noun form is "IN-clude".)[10]

Includes are supposed to be the smallest/most reusable snippets of site code. They are usually loaded into either layouts or templates, but in fact can be used anywhere on a site—you can even have includes call other includes (Figure 9.13).[11] Since these snippets of code are intended to get dropped into the site almost anywhere, you should

Figure 9.13: You can put includes in includes, so your includes have includes.

---

10. This distinction exists in many other English words, such as AT-tri-bute (noun)/at-TRI-bute (verb) and CON-flict (noun)/con-FLICT (verb).

11. Image courtesy of vividpixels/123RF.

always try to make sure that any includes you create have code that is portable and self–contained.

Jekyll includes are located in a dedicated folder called **_includes** (as with **_layouts**, the underscore is important). Go ahead and create that folder now, together with a new file called **head.html** (Listing 9.10).

Listing 9.10: Creating the includes folder and adding in a new file.

```
$ mkdir _includes
$ touch _includes/head.html
```

At this point, your project folder should look something like Figure 9.14.

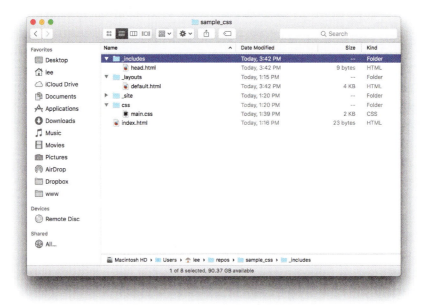

Figure 9.14: The project directory with added includes.

As you might have guessed, we're going to use **head.html** to hold the **head** tag and its contents. The way to do this is first to cut that content out of **default.html**, and then paste it into **head.html** (possibly using Shift-Command-V to paste with the proper indentation), as shown in Listing 9.11.

Listing 9.11: Moving **head** to its own file.
_includes/head.html

```
<head>
  <title>Test Page: Don't Panic</title>
  <meta charset="utf-8">
  <link rel="stylesheet" href="/css/main.css">
</head>
```

To include the contents of **head.html** back into the **default.html** layout, we'll use our first example of the Liquid language mentioned in Section 9.3, which looks like this:

```
{% include head.html %}
```

Here **include** is a Liquid command to include the file in question (in this case, **head.html**). The special syntax **{% ... %}** tells Jekyll to replace the contents of that line with the result of evaluating the code inside. Because Jekyll automatically knows to look in the **_includes** directory, the result will be to insert the contents of **head.html**.

Replacing the original **head** section with the corresponding Liquid snippet gives the code shown in Listing 9.12.

Listing 9.12: Including the site head using Liquid.
_layouts/default.html

```
<!DOCTYPE html>
<html>
  {% include head.html %}
  <body>
```

After making these changes, you should refresh your browser to confirm that the page still works.

9.6.1   Page Header: Up Top!

At the top of a typical web page, you will usually find some sort of site-level *navigation* that takes users from page to page on the site, and also includes site branding.

This section is often referred to as the *site header* (Figure 9.15) (not to be confused with the **head** tag, which is the HTML header). Implementing such a header site-wide is a perfect application of Jekyll includes.

Figure 9.15: Some site headers from popular websites.

To get started, let's add a new Liquid tag to **header.html** (which we'll create in a moment) at the top of the **default.html** file, as shown in Listing 9.13.

Listing 9.13: Including the header HTML.
_layouts/default.html

```
<!DOCTYPE html>
<html>
  {% include head.html %}
  <body>
    {% include header.html %}
    <div class="full-hero hero-home">
      <h1>I'm an h1</h1>
      <ul class="social-list">
```

Next, create a new blank document in the **_includes** folder called **header.html**:[12]

```
$ touch _includes/header.html
```

The header itself will use two *semantic elements* (i.e., elements that have meaning): **header** to contain the header and **nav** for the navigation links, which (as with the

---

12. You can of course use your text editor to create the file rather than using **touch**.

social links in Section 8.5) are organized as an unordered list **ul**. We'll also use the classes **"header"** and **"header-nav"** to make it easier to apply styles across a range of browsers (Box 9.2). The resulting code appears in Listing 9.14.

Listing 9.14: The basic structure of our site header.
_includes/header.html

```
<header class="header">
  <nav>
    <ul class="header-nav">
      <li><a href="/">Home</a></li>
      <li><a href="#">Nav 1</a></li>
      <li><a href="#">Nav 2</a></li>
      <li><a href="#">Nav 3</a></li>
    </ul>
  </nav>
  <a href="/" class="header-logo">Logo</a>
</header>
```

Save and refresh your browser and now you'll see your new site header (Figure 9.16). (We'll explain the placement of the logo in Section 9.6.2.)

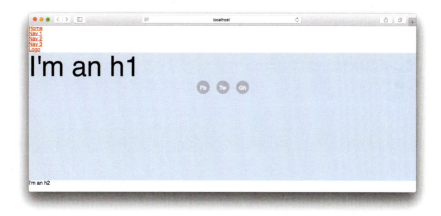

Figure 9.16: Our not-very-attractive header.

Box 9.2: Style Note: Style HTML5 Elements with Classes

To ensure maximum backward compatibility, it's not a good idea to target the newer HTML5 semantic elements like header and nav directly. There are inevitably going to be some users who visit your site on an old browser that doesn't support them—though luckily there are fewer such cases with each passing year.

When an old browser encounters new HTML tags, it sees them as regular divs, and any styles targeting those tags are ignored. To avoid this situation, it's better to give such elements classes, and then target your styles at the classes.

For example, we want to avoid styling header directly:

```
header {
    background: #000;
}
```

Instead, we'll give the header tag a class "header" (like in Listing 9.14), and then target that class (note the leading dot):

```
.header {
    background: #000;
}
```

This way, our styles will work even in older browsers.

9.6.2 Navigation and Children

Now, let's style that ugly header!

The end goal for our design is to create a traditional sort of header, with a logo on the left-hand side that will send users back to the homepage, and site navigation at the top right. As a final step, we'll change the position of the header so that it will sit on top of content below it.

The first thing that we are going to do is move the navigation to the right and put the **li**s into a horizontal row by changing their display property to **inline-block**. The result, which we suggest inserting immediately after the global styles, appears in Listing 9.15.

Listing 9.15: Adding header styles.

css/main.css

```
/* HEADER STYLES */
.header-nav {
  float: right;
}
.header-nav > li {
  display: inline-block;
}
```

Note in Listing 9.15 that we've used the more advanced child selector **>** to target the **li**s (as discussed before in Box 8.1). That is to make sure that if we wanted to put a second level of links into the menu, only the direct children would be **inline-block** (which we will in fact do in Section 13.4).

After saving and refreshing, you'll see that the menu has moved (Figure 9.17).

Figure 9.17: Navigation moved to the right and all in a line.

You might have wondered why the logo is *below* the navigational list in Listing 9.14 even though it comes first when viewing the header from left to right. The reason is that we knew all along that we were going to float the navigation to the right side of the screen, and if the logo appeared before the navigation in the HTML order then the menu would start at the *bottom* of the logo. This is because even a floating element respects the line height and position of normal block or inline elements that come before it, which in this case would lead to unwanted space around the logo. You can

Figure 9.18: Switching the logo to come first adds unwanted space.

check this yourself by switching the positions of the logo and nav links; you'll see that the menu starts lower as a result (Figure 9.18).

Now let's add in some padding on the list items and make those links a little more stylish. We are going to add some padding to move the navigation away from the edges of the page:

```
padding: 5.5vh 60px 0 0;
```

We are also going to give each `li` in the navigation a bit of left margin so that it isn't bumping right up against its neighbor:

```
margin-left: 1em;
```

For the links themselves, we'll change the color and the size, make the font bold so that it is easier to read, get rid of the default link underlines (as is done in about 99% of site headers), and also automatically transform the text to be uppercase:

```
color: #000;
font-size: 0.8rem;
font-weight: bold;
text-decoration: none;
text-transform: uppercase;
```

Here we've used **#000** instead of **black**; as noted in Section 7.1.1, it's important to learn how to use these two interchangeably.

After adding the appropriate selectors, the styling changes look like Listing 9.16.

Listing 9.16: Styling the navigational links.
css/main.css

```
.header-nav {
  float: right;
  padding: 5.5vh 60px 0 0;
}
.header-nav > li {
  display: inline-block;
  margin-left: 1em;
}
.header-nav a {
  color: #000;
  font-size: 0.8rem;
  font-weight: bold;
  text-decoration: none;
  text-transform: uppercase;
}
```

Your page navigation should now look like Figure 9.19.

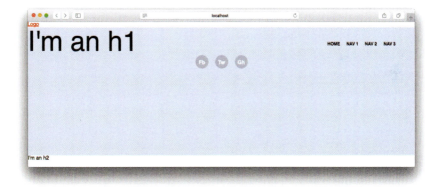

Figure 9.19: Navigational links are now a bit more stylish.

So how did we come up with those exact styles? The values came from just adding a couple of styling rules, and then tweaking the numbers until things looked good. Design isn't always a systematic process—often you just need to make changes and then play around with the numbers until you get something you like. When designing websites, there tends to be an extended period of experimentation, so don't worry if it takes you time to get things right when you work on your own!

9.6.3 Exercise

1. You can load dynamic text into includes. To try this, add the extra code `{{ include.content }}` somewhere in your `header.html` include, and then in the layout change the include tag to `{% include header.html content="This is my sample note." %}`.

9.7 Advanced Selectors

In order to add an extra bit of polish to the site header, we are going to introduce a few more advanced CSS selectors, and then we'll continue to add in more styling for the rest of our page. These advanced selectors include *pseudo-classes*, *first-child/last-child*, and *siblings*.

9.7.1 Pseudo-Classes

It's always nice to have links do something when a user rolls over them, especially since we removed the underlines from the links in Listing 9.16. Those underlines on links are called *design affordances*, and they are there to give users the suggestion that something will happen if they move the cursor to the link and click.

Some people may argue that all links on a site should have some affordance that clearly marks them as something clickable, either with underlines or by making them look like buttons (HOLY WAR!!!). At this point in time, though, the design convention of putting plain-text links that don't have underlines (or some other special style) in a header is something that most Internet users are now accustomed to. You just know that the things at the top of the page are clickable.

Without underlines or other immediately visible affordances, though, it is important to show users a response to rolling over the link with their cursor (including on mobile (Box 9.3)). You really want people to know that they are interacting with an element that does something after they perform an action.

Box 9.3: Style Note: Mobile Hover Consideration

Mobile users don't see rollover states, so you always need to be sure that the things you are designing will make sense to both mobile and desktop users. One way to do this is to make sure that you also style things so that there is a change when the link is actively clicked.

You might think that this would be something that happens automatically no matter what, but if you make any styling changes that alter links from their browser default, you will actually need to use the `:active` pseudo-class to define how you want a link to appear when someone interacts with it.

If you do end up removing all hints that something is clickable for your site on desktop, you might want to consider using a mobile media query to add in some hints specifically for mobile users. We'll be discussing this further in the context of *media queries* in Chapter 13.

All HTML links have a set of what are called *pseudo-classes* that allow developers to style different interactions with the link:

- **`:hover`**: Styles what happens when a user rolls over the link (applies to any element, not just links)

- **`:active`**: Styles what happens when a user clicks the link

- **`:visited`**: Styles what the link should look like if a user has already visited the linked page

The way to add a pseudo-class to a style declaration is by combining the element or class name with the pseudo-class, like this:

```
.header-nav a:hover {
  color: #ed6e2f;
}
```

This use of the **`:hover`** pseudo-class arranges to change the color of the link when the user's mouse hovers over it. (For now we've just picked a random orange color that will stand out nicely against the blue background.)

We'll add a second change as well, which is to make the logo partially transparent on hover using the **opacity** property. The combined result appears in Listing 9.17.

Listing 9.17: Adding hover states to the navigational links.
css/main.css

```
.header-nav a:hover,
.header-nav a:active {
  color: #ed6e2f;
}
.header-logo:hover,
.header-logo:active {
  opacity: 0.5;
}
```

Note that we've added the same styling to the `:active` pseudo-class in order to give mobile users feedback as well (as discussed in Box 9.3).

Save your styles and refresh, and now the nav links will turn orange on rollover, and the logo will turn 50% transparent (the opacity style works like a decimal percentage), as shown in Figure 9.20.

Figure 9.20: Muuuuch better.

There are a bunch of other very useful pseudo-classes that are regularly used in designing layouts. We'll talk about some of these throughout the rest of this section, and we'll see further examples in Section 13.5.

9.7.2 Exercises

1. Now that you've seen how to style rollovers, try styling the `.social-link`s to have rollover states where the background color changes.

2. As stated in this section, psuedo-classes like **:hover** don't just apply to links. Try adding a hover state that changes the background color of the **.full-hero** element.

9.7.3 `first-child`

In order to indicate that the Home link in the navigation menu is particularly important, let's arrange for it always to be a different color from the others. We could do this with a separate class, but since Home is always going to be the first link in the menu we can target it using what is called the **first-child** pseudo-class. This pseudo-class applies the corresponding styles only to the first child of the parent element. (There's also a **last-child** pseudo-class, which we'll use in Section 13.4, and many others that are beyond the scope of this tutorial.)

Let's make the Home link work the *opposite* of the styling for the other links, so that it's orange by default and black on rollover. To use the **first-child** pseudo-class, we need to make sure that whatever we're targeting is contained in a wrapper, and that there is nothing else in the wrapper. That just means that when you are using the child pseudo-classes, you need the elements to be inside some other HTML element.

If there is anything like text, or an HTML element of a different type, between the top of the parent and the element you are trying to target, the first and last child pseudo-classes won't work, but in this case we *are* going to target the first **li** in **.header-nav** (Listing 9.18). The **ul** with the class **.header-nav** is our wrapper, and the **li**s are all children that can be targeted.

Listing 9.18: Changing the appearance of just the first link.
`css/main.css`

```css
.header-logo:hover,
.header-logo:active {
  opacity: 0.5;
}
.header-nav > li:first-child a {
  color: #ed6e2f;
}
.header-nav > li:first-child a:hover {
  color: #000;
}
```

Note how specific we are in Listing 9.18: We're using the child selector to target only **li**s that are direct children of the **.header-nav** class. You don't technically need this level of precision, but later on we will add in a dropdown menu in the header (Section 13.4), and if we target styles too generally then we'll make styling the dropdown difficult.

Now when you save and refresh the first link should look different (Figure 9.21).

Figure 9.21: Making the first nav link orange.

9.7.4 Exercise

1. We mentioned that there are other child selector types. Try out **:last-child** by changing the color of the link that is in the last **li** in the page header.

9.7.5 Siblings

Let's look at two additional advanced selectors, and then after seeing how they work, we'll use one to add another little style detail to our site navigation. CSS supports two sibling selectors, both of which are written like the child selector **>** when making a declaration:

- The *adjacent sibling* **+**: Selects a single element only if it is right next to the primary element in the declaration. For example, **h2 + p** selects a **p** tag only if it is immediately preceded by an **h2** tag.

- The *general sibling* ~: Selects all elements of the type in the declaration if they follow the primary element. For example, **h2 ~ p** applies to *all* **p** tags preceded by an **h2** tag.

Let's hop out of working on the header for a second to create an example to use with the sibling selectors. In your **default.html** file, replace the **h2** tag with the HTML from Listing 9.19.

Listing 9.19: Replacing the **h2** and adding some text.
_layouts/default.html

```
<h2>THE FOUNDERS</h2>
<p>
  Learn Enough to Be Dangerous was founded in 2015 by Michael Hartl, Lee Donahoe,
  and Nick Merwin. We believe that the kind of technical sophistication taught by
  the Learn Enough tutorials can benefit at least a billion people, and probably
  more.
</p>
<p>Test paragraph</p>
```

We can target the paragraph that directly follows the **h2** with the style shown in Listing 9.20.

Listing 9.20: Adding an adjacent sibling selector.
css/main.css

```
h2 + p {
  font-size: 0.8em;
  font-style: italic;
  margin: 1em auto 0;
  max-width: 70%;
  text-align: center;
}
```

Notice that only the first paragraph is styled (Figure 9.22).

Figure 9.22: Only the **p** immediately after the **h2** is styled.

Now if we change to the general sibling selector ~ as in Listing 9.21, both paragraphs will get styled (Figure 9.23).

Listing 9.21: The general selector targets all elements that come after a specified element.
css/main.css

```
h2 ~ p {
  font-size: 0.8em;
  font-style: italic;
  margin: 1em auto 0;
  max-width: 70%;
  text-align: center;
}
```

Figure 9.23: All **p** tags after the **h2** are now styled the same.

You may also have noticed from Figure 9.23 that the **p**s in the **.bio-box**es below aren't styled. That is because the sibling selectors don't pass styles to elements that are wrapped inside any other elements. They only work on elements inside the same parent.

Looking back to the header, we can use a sibling selector in the site header navigation to target all the **li**s after the first **li**, and add in a little extra styling to help visually separate the links using the styles in Listing 9.22. You might have seen something like this online: a little vertical line between navigational links to help separate them from other links in a list. Let's use a *sibling selector* to add some divider lines.

Listing 9.22: Using the general sibling selector to add styling to the header navigation.
css/main.css

```
.header-nav > li {
  display: inline-block;
  margin-left: 1em;
}
```

```
.header-nav > li ~ li {
  border-left: 1px solid rgba(0, 0, 0, 0.3);
  padding-left: 1em;
}
```

The rule **.header-nav > li ~ li** in Listing 9.22 says to apply the subsequent rules to all **li** elements next to an initial **li** inside an element with class **".header-nav"**— in other words, every **li** in the menu after the first one. This way, the divider lines appear before every menu item except the first (Figure 9.24).

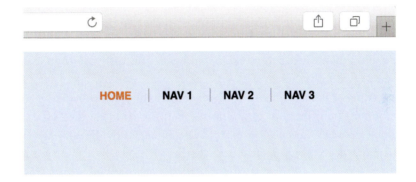

Figure 9.24: Menu divider lines.

Now that the navigation is fairly spiffy, let's turn our attention to the logo, which will give us a chance to learn a little bit about CSS positioning.

9.7.6 Exercise

1. What if you didn't use the ~ in Listing 9.22, but rather the adjacent sibling selector? Would the divider line appear before every menu item?

9.8 Positioning

In this section, we are going to take a look at how positioning works in CSS, focusing on the site logo, and then we'll finish off the header design. CSS positioning can be a little tricky, and honestly there are people who work with CSS all the time who regularly get confused trying to get positioning to work right. So if this section seems long and loaded with examples, just bear with us and work through it all—you'll find that understanding CSS positioning is an essential skill.

When you style an element's position, there are two basic possibilities:

1. Have the browser draw the element in its natural position in the normal flow of content on the page.
2. Remove the target from the flow of content and display it in a different place using directional styles—left, right, top, and bottom—and an additional dimension, the so-called **z-index**.

When an element is moved around out of its natural position with directional styles, it doesn't affect other elements in the document—it either covers them up or is hidden behind them. It becomes like a ship cast adrift, torn free from its mooring on the page.

While it might be self-explanatory to move something left or right, or to change its top or bottom position, you might not be familiar with the idea of a **z-index**. The **z-index** property (usually a nonnegative number, 0 by default—negatives put elements behind everything) determines whether an element is displayed above or below other elements, as in farther "into" the screen or farther "out" toward the viewer. It's an element's 3D position.

You can think of this like looking down at a big stack of papers—the higher the **z-index** number is, the higher up the stack toward you the element is. A **z-index** of **0** would be the bottommost piece of paper. We'll see a concrete example of the **z-index** in Section 9.9.

In order to change those directional styles, we first need to alter an element's **position** property. The **position** style in CSS can be given five different values (though one of them isn't really used). We'll start with one of the most common one, *static*.

- **position: static** (Figure 9.25)
  - This is the default positioning of elements in the flow of content.
  - An element that has no position style set, or has **position: static**, will ignore directional styles like left, right, top, and bottom.

Figure 9.25: How `position: static` affects elements.

- `position: absolute` (Figure 9.26)
  - Positions the element at a specific place by taking it out of the document flow, either within a parent wrapper that has a **position:** value other than **static**, or (if there is no parent) a specific place in the browser window. It is still a part of the page content, which means when you scroll the page, it moves with the content.
  - Also lets you define a **z-index** property.
  - Because the element is removed from the document flow, the width or height is determined either by shrinking to the content inside or by setting dimensions in CSS. It behaves kind of like an element set to **inline-block**.
  - Causes any float that is set on the object to be ignored, so if you have both styles on an element you might as well delete the float.

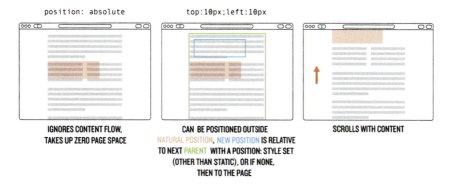

Figure 9.26: How `position: absolute` affects elements.

- **position: relative** (Figure 9.27)
    - This is like static in that it respects the element's starting position in the flow of content, but it also allows directional styles to be applied that nudge the element away from the boundary with other elements.
    - It allows absolutely positioned items to be contained within, as though the relatively positioned element were a separate canvas. In other words, if an absolutely positioned element is inside a relatively positioned element, a style of **top: 0** would cause the absolutely positioned element to be drawn at the top of the relatively positioned element rather than at the top of the page.
    - Also allows you to change the **z-index** of the element.

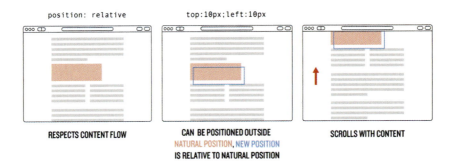

Figure 9.27: How **position: relative** affects elements.

- **position: fixed** (Figure 9.28)
    - Positions the element at a specific place within the browser window totally separate from the page content. When you scroll the page, it won't move.
    - Lets you set **z-index**.
    - Has the same need to have dimensions set as **position: absolute**; otherwise, it will be the size of the content inside.
    - Also causes floats to be ignored.

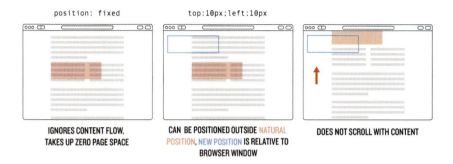

IGNORES CONTENT FLOW, TAKES UP ZERO PAGE SPACE   CAN BE POSITIONED OUTSIDE NATURAL POSITION, NEW POSITION IS RELATIVE TO BROWSER WINDOW   DOES NOT SCROLL WITH CONTENT

Figure 9.28: How **position: fixed** affects elements.

- **position: inherit**
  - This is not very common, so we aren't going to discuss it other than to say it makes the element inherit the position from its parent.

Let's play around with some examples. First, let's add in some styles for the header to better see the boundaries and to give it dimensions (Listing 9.23).

Listing 9.23: Added styles for the **.header** class.
css/main.css

```
/* HEADER STYLES */
.header {
  background-color: #aaa;
  height: 300px;
  width: 100%;
}
```

Let's now absolutely position the **.header-logo** and set it to **50px** from the bottom (Listing 9.24).

Listing 9.24: Adding an initial **position: absolute** to the logo.
css/main.css

```
.header-nav > li:first-child a:hover {
  color: #fff;
}
.header-logo {
  bottom: 50px;
  position: absolute;
}
```

Now save and refresh... where did the logo go (Figure 9.29)?

Figure 9.29: The parent container has no position style set.

The logo link ended up way at the bottom because the parent element that wraps the `.header-logo` doesn't have any **position** style applied. Also, if you scroll the page up and down you'll notice that the `.header-logo` still moves with the page. Let's constrain the logo to stay within the header by adding a position property, as shown in Listing 9.25.

Listing 9.25: Setting a position other than static on the wrapper.
css/main.css

```
.header {
  background-color: #aaa;
  height: 300px;
  position: relative;
  width: 100%;
}
```

With the **position** rule in Listing 9.25, the **.header-logo** will now be **50px** from the bottom of the gray header box, and any positions that we give to **.header-logo** will be determined based on the boundaries of the **.header** container (Figure 9.30). The way that the position is based off of the boundaries of the parent is what we meant when we said that setting a parent wrapper to **position: relative** made it like a separate canvas—everything inside that is absolutely positioned takes its place based on the dimensions of the parent.

Figure 9.30: The absolutely positioned .header-logo.

Note here that when an element is absolutely positioned, the directional styles don't add or subtract distance—setting **bottom: 50px** doesn't move it *toward* the bottom, but rather sets the position **50px** *from* the bottom. So **right: 50px** puts the element **50px** from the right edge.

Negative positions work as well, and as long as the overflow of the parent wrapper isn't set to **hidden**, the absolutely positioned element will get placed outside the boundaries of the parent (Listing 9.26).

Listing 9.26: Trying out negative positioning on our object.
css/main.css

```
.header-logo {
  bottom: -50px;
  position: absolute;
  right: 50px;
}
```

After adding that style and refreshing your browser, the logo should be in a position similar to what is shown in Figure 9.31.

Figure 9.31: Positioning the logo on the right-hand side.

You might be asking, "Well, what happens if I set both a top *and* bottom, or a left *and* right?" The answer is that, for whatever reasons, the top and left properties will take priority and the bottom and right will be ignored.

Another thing to consider is when you set a position property, you are manipulating elements and messing around with the natural page flow, which means that it is possible to cause misalignments. So if you add **left: 200px** to the **.header**, the width of the element (which is 100%) isn't recalculated. Instead, the entire **.header** box is pushed over by 200px, and your browser window will have horizontal scrollbars and look broken (Figure 9.32).

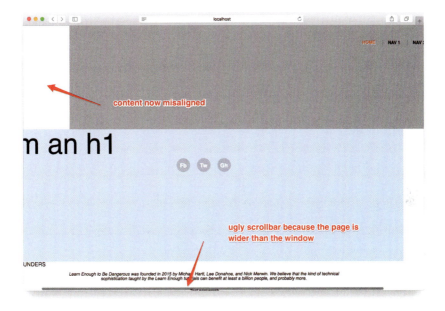

Figure 9.32: This sort of thing looks sloppy.

You have to be careful!

While we are still just playing around in the positioning sandbox, we should take a look at ways to deal with a situation that comes up anytime positioning in CSS is discussed: How do you center an absolutely positioned object horizontally and vertically in a way that allows the object to be any size… and allows the wrapper to be any size?

Let's first look at an old method where the object that we are centering has a set height and width—centering this is easy. Give the logo a width and height, remove the old positioning, and change the background to better see the object (Listing 9.27).

Listing 9.27: Adding height and width dimensions to the logo.
css/main.css

```
.header-logo {
  background-color: #000;
  height: 110px;
  position: absolute;
  width: 110px;
}
```

Now let's center it.

You might think that centering the element would be as simple as giving the `.header-logo` class a style of `left: 50%` and `top: 50%`—that should put it in the middle, both horizontally and vertically, right (Listing 9.28)?

Listing 9.28: Positioning the `.header-logo` in the center?
css/main.css

```
.header-logo {
  background-color: #000;
  height: 110px;
  left: 50%;
  position: absolute;
  top: 50%;
  width: 110px;
}
```

Well, no, the reason this didn't work is that when the browser positions an object, it calculates the distance using the same-named edge—so when you apply `top: 50%`, it moves the top edge (not the center point) of `.header-logo` 50% away from the top of `.header`; similarly, applying `left: 50%` tells the browser to move the left edge 50% away from the left of `.header`. The result is that the object we are trying to position is off-center by half of its width and height (Figure 9.33).

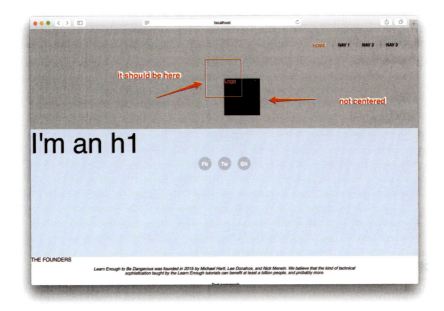

Figure 9.33: The red box in the expected position if centered vertically and horizontally.

How do we solve this and get our object in the actual center? The older method mentioned above was to use a negative margin (Section 8.6.2) to move the object up and left. This only works if you know the size of the object, though, since trying to use something like a percentage would move the object based on the size of the parent (recall from Section 7.4 that percentage values are based on the size of the parent object). Since the height and width of the box are **110px**, half of that is **55px** (Listing 9.29).

Listing 9.29: Adding in the negative margins to position the black box in the right spot.
css/main.css

```css
.header-logo {
  background-color: #000;
  height: 110px;
  left: 50%;
  margin: -55px 0 0 -55px;
  position: absolute;
  top: 50%;
  width: 110px;
}
```

That works just fine, but you'd always be limiting yourself to centering only objects with fixed dimensions (Figure 9.34).

Figure 9.34: Negative margins worked!

If you wanted to make a slightly bigger (or smaller) centered object, you'd have to recalculate sizes and margins, and then make changes to your CSS. That's too much work, and it wouldn't work at all with dynamically sized elements. Thankfully there is a better, relatively new CSS style called **transform** that can help. The **transform** property allows developers to do all sorts of amazing things like move objects around, rotate them, and simulate three-dimensional movement.

The upside for centering objects is that this new style calculates all these movements based on the object itself. So if we move it 50% to the left using **transform**, the browser looks at the object's width, and then moves it to the left 50% of its own width, not the width of the parent.

The actual style declaration looks like this: **transform: translate(x, y)**—where **x** is replaced by the distance along the x-axis (left is negative, right is positive), and the same for the y-axis (up is negative, down is positive). So, to move our object left and up half its width and height, we'd add the **transform** style like you see in Listing 9.30 (make sure to remove the margin styling that we added in Listing 9.29).

Listing 9.30: Moving an object using `transform`.
css/main.css

```
.header-logo {
  background-color: #000;
  height: 110px;
  left: 50%;
  position: absolute;
  top: 50%;
  transform: translate(-50%, -50%);
  width: 110px;
}
```

Now when you save your work and refresh the browser you'll have a black box in the center of the gray header. It doesn't matter what dimensions you give for either the `.header-logo` or `.header`—you'll always have a vertically and horizontally centered object. To try it out, delete the height and width that we gave the `.header-logo`.

When you save and refresh your browser, the now-smaller box will still be centered vertically and horizontally (Figure 9.35).

Figure 9.35: No matter what size the object is, it stays right in the center.

9.8.1   A Real Logo

All right, enough positioning playtime. Let's get back to making this site look good by putting an actual logo in that **.header-logo**. In your project directory, add a new folder called **images** (Figure 9.36):

```
$ mkdir images
```

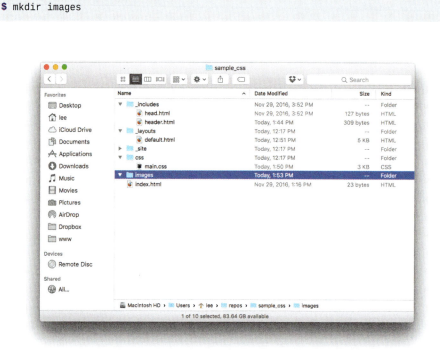

Figure 9.36: New images folder in your project directory.

Then use this **curl** command to grab the logo image off the Learn Enough servers:

```
$ curl -o images/logo.png -L https://cdn.learnenough.com/le-css/logo.png
```

Now let's put the image into the **header.html** (Listing 9.31). The result appears in Figure 9.37.

Listing 9.31: Replacing the word *logo* with a logo image.
_includes/header.html

```
<header class="header">
  <nav>
    <ul class="header-nav">
      <li><a href="/">Home</a></li>
      <li><a href="#">Nav 1</a></li>
      <li><a href="#">Nav 2</a></li>
      <li><a href="#">Nav 3</a></li>
    </ul>
  </nav>
  <a href="/" class="header-logo">
    <img src="/images/logo.png" alt="Learn Enough">
  </a>
</header>
```

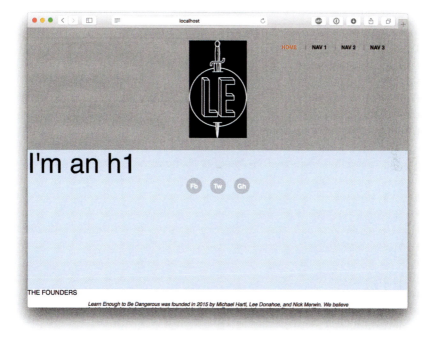

Figure 9.37: The initial (sub-optimal) logo placed on the page.

Now we are going to make a whole lot of changes to whip this part of the site into shape. As in Section 9.6.2, we aren't going to go through and give a reason why each value is the exact number we chose. Styling a section of a site is a non-linear process at times, and you'll likely need to experiment a lot if you are doing this on your own starting from a blank slate.

First, we are going to make the header background color black and any text in the header white as follows:

```
.header {
  background-color: #000;
  color: #fff;
}
```

That's also going to require that we change the color of the links, as well as the rollover color for the first-child link in the navigation:

```
.header-nav > li:first-child a:hover {
  color: #fff;
}
```

We'll also need to change the background color of our little divider lines so that it is partially transparent white instead of partially transparent black:

```
border-left: 1px solid rgba(255, 255, 255, 0.3);
```

Then we are going to move the **.header-logo** into the top left, and shrink the image a bit:

```
.header-logo {
  background-color: #000;
  box-sizing: border-box;
  display: block;
  height: 10vh;
  padding-top: 10px;
  position: relative;
  text-align: center;
  width: 10vh;
}
.header-logo img {
  width: 4.3vh;
}
```

We chose **10vh** for the size of the link, and for the image we set the width to be 4.3% of the height of the container (**4.3vh**). We got those values after playing around with different numbers and settling on this size for a balance of readability while not taking up too much space.

You'll notice that most of the sizing styles are on the link that wraps the image and not on the image itself. The reason we did that was so that if there is a problem downloading the image, or a delay, there is still a nice, big clickable link in the header.

Putting everything together gives us Listing 9.32, which includes all the styling for the site header so far.

Listing 9.32: Changing up the styling for the header and logo.
css/main.css

```css
/* HEADER STYLES */
.header {
  background-color: #000;
  color: #fff;
}
.header-logo {
  background-color: #000;
  box-sizing: border-box;
  display: block;
  height: 10vh;
  padding-top: 10px;
  position: relative;
  text-align: center;
  width: 10vh;
}
.header-logo:hover,
.header-logo:active {
  background-color: #ed6e2f;
}
.header-logo img {
  width: 4.3vh;
}
.header-nav {
  float: right;
  padding: 5.5vh 60px 0 0;
}
.header-nav > li {
  display: inline-block;
  margin-left: 1em;
}
.header-nav > li ~ li {
  border-left: 1px solid rgba(255, 255, 255, 0.3);
  padding-left: 1em;
}
```

```css
.header-nav a {
  color: #fff;
  font-size: 0.8rem;
  font-weight: bold;
  text-decoration: none;
  text-transform: uppercase;
}
.header-nav a:hover,
.header-nav a:active {
  color: #ed6e2f;
}
.header-nav > li:first-child a {
  color: #ed6e2f;
}
.header-nav > li:first-child a:hover {
  color: #fff;
}
```

Save and refresh, and your header should look like Figure 9.38. That logo's lookin' sharp!

Figure 9.38: The header, now styled.

9.8.2 Exercise

1. Try moving the **ul** that contains the social links to the bottom–left corner of the **.full-hero** using the positioning rules you've learned. What changes are you going to need to make to **.full-hero** to allow the social links to remain inside?

2. To see why we gave dimensional styling and an **alt** tag to our image, try removing the image source link to simulate the browser not finding the file.

9.9 Fixed Header

You may have noticed the recent design trend where the header sticks to the top of the screen as you scroll down the page. This is called a *fixed header*—the header is styled to use **position: fixed** to take the header entirely out of the page content and stick it to the top of the user's browser. If your site has a bunch of different sections that your users need to navigate to, a fixed header can be a good solution to keep them from getting annoyed that they always have to scroll to the top to do something new.

The way to implement a fixed header is to change the positioning of the header to **fixed** while specifying a **z-index** for the header. Recall from the beginning of Section 9.8 that the **z-index** determines whether an element is drawn in front of or behind other elements. We'll want to give our header a large value for **z-index**, which will force the browser to draw the element above other elements (i.e., closer to the user using our stack-of-paper analogy).

The styles to change the positioning value and set a **z-index** are shown in Listing 9.33.

Listing 9.33: Fixing the header's position means that content will now scroll under it.
css/main.css

```
.header {
  background-color: #000;
  color: #fff;
  position: fixed;
  width: 100%;
  z-index: 20;
}
```

When you check the work in your browser, you'll find that the header is now pinned to the top of the screen, and when you scroll, all the content will scroll underneath.

The resulting black bar at the top looks cool, but what if we were to put a border around the entire page? It could look interesting to have a dark area around the whole site to frame the content. We can arrange for this with the styling shown in Listing 9.34.

Listing 9.34: Just for fun, let's put a border around the entire site.
css/main.css

```
/* GLOBAL STYLES */
html {
  box-shadow: 0 0 0 30px #000 inset;
  padding: 0 30px;
}
```

Listing 9.34 introduces the **box-shadow** style, which is a relatively new CSS style that lets you add drop shadows to HTML elements, and the declaration that we added is a shorthand for **box-shadow: x-axis y-axis blur size color inset**. We aren't going to go any deeper into it, but if you want to play around with box shadows there are a number of sites that let you fiddle with the settings, such as CSSmatic box shadow (https://www.cssmatic.com/box–shadow).

After applying the code in Listing 9.34, your page should look like Figure 9.39.

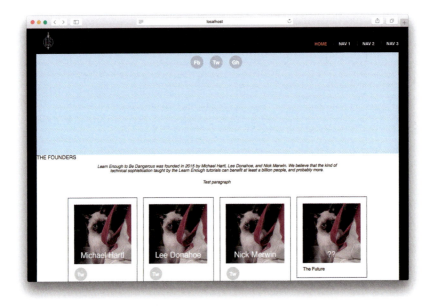

Figure 9.39: Box shadow inset around the entire page. Nifty.

After saving and refreshing, you might have noticed that the logo in the header now looks a little off since it isn't right up in the corner anymore. This is because we increased the padding on the entire site by **30px** for the black border. Let's use a negative value (**-30px**) on the positioning to get it back in place, as shown in Listing 9.35.

Listing 9.35: Using a negative value to move the logo back into place.

css/main.css

```css
.header-logo {
  background-color: #000;
  box-sizing: border-box;
  display: block;
  height: 10vh;
  left: -30px;
  padding-top: 10px;
  position: relative;
  text-align: center;
  width: 10vh;
}
```

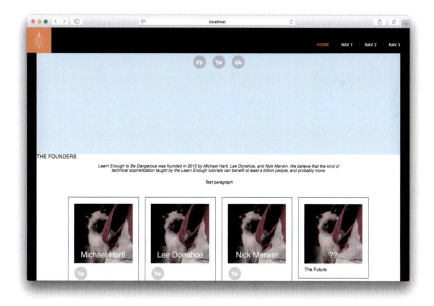

Figure 9.40: A completed page header.

The fixed final header should now look like Figure 9.40 (shown as it should appear with the mouse cursor on the logo, making it orange).

One thing you might have noticed is that after adding fixed positioning to the header, the big **h1** text in the hero is covered. We'll tackle this issue in Section 10.2.

Now that we've got the header squared away, let's turn our attention to the other end of the site.

9.9.1 Exercise

1. To see why it is important to define the **z-index** of the header, try setting the value to **1**, and then add styles to the **.social-list** class to set **position: relative** and **z-index: 40**. Then scroll the page.

9.10 A Footer, and Includes in Includes

After creating and styling a site header, a natural next step is to style the page footer. This is the navigational/informational section that can be found at the bottom of a site (Figure 9.41).

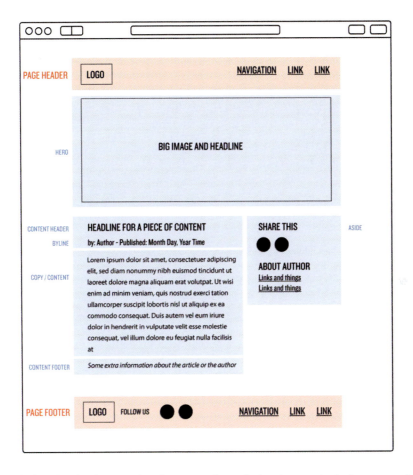

Figure 9.41: A refresher on the elements of a typical web page, including a page footer.

Often, the footer is a partial replication of the navigational elements from the header (just styled in a slightly different way), but many sites add to that a bunch of other content—everything from store locations and hours to additional content links.

Since the footer is found at the end of the page and contains ancillary information, you don't really need to worry about space (there's plenty of room at the bottom!). What we mean by that is that you can think of the footer as extra space, where users aren't *required* to see everything there. Many sites, such as Amazon, have a lot of content in a giant footer at the bottom of the page (Figure 9.42).

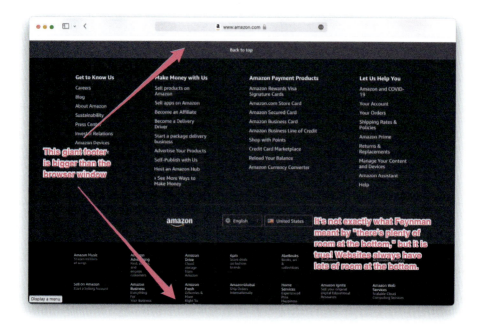

Figure 9.42: A giant footer.

We'll start by creating a new **footer.html** file inside the **_includes** folder:

```
$ touch _includes/footer.html
```

Next, we'll add some HTML. We're going to wrap the footer in another HTML5 semantic tag, the **footer** tag. As with the **header** tag, this is a semantic element that works just like a standard **div**, but gives automated site readers (such as web spiders and screen readers for the visually impaired) a better idea of what the purpose is of the content inside. We are also going to add in a logo link similar to the one in the header. The result appears in Listing 9.36.

Listing 9.36: Adding in the basic footer structure.
_includes/footer.html

```
<footer class="footer">
  <a class="footer-logo" href="/">
    <img src="/images/logo.png" alt="Learn Enough"/>
  </a>
```

```
<h3>Learn Enough <span>to Be Dangerous</span></h3>
</footer>
```

To include the footer in the default layout, we'll follow the model from Listing 9.12 and use Liquid to insert the contents of **footer.html** just before the closing **body** tag in **default.html** (Listing 9.37).

Listing 9.37: Add in the Liquid tag to the default layout.
_layouts/default.html

```
      .
      .
      .
    </p>
    {% include footer.html %}
  </body>
</html>
```

Now let's add some styling as well. We'll give the footer a black background, like the header, and we'll give it some padding. We'll make sure that the content inside is easy to read by using **vh** units, which causes our padding to take up a large portion of the screen:

```
background-color: #000;
padding: 10vh 0 15vh;
```

We'll also constrain the size of the logo so that it isn't a giant image, and style the **h3** and the span that is inside it (just to add a little design detail to give some of the text a different color). All together the footer styling looks like Listing 9.38.

Listing 9.38: The initial styles for the footer.
css/main.css

```
/* FOOTER STYLES */
.footer {
  background-color: #000;
  padding: 10vh 0 15vh;
  text-align: center;
}
.footer-logo img {
```

```
  width: 50px;
}
.footer h3 {
  color: #fff;
  padding-top: 1.5em;
  text-transform: uppercase;
}
.footer h3 span {
  color: #aaa;
}

/* HERO STYLES */
```

Save and refresh, and the result should appear as in Figure 9.43.

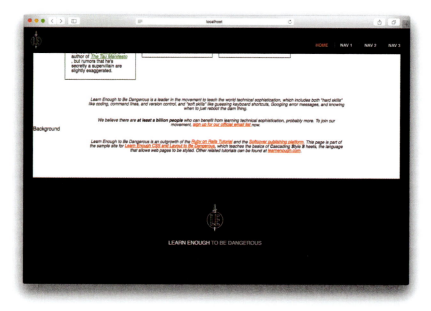

Figure 9.43: The first stab at the footer is looking pretty good.

And it looks... not too bad!

But let's make it a little more useful and also add in the navigational links from the header. You could just copy and paste the HTML from the header, but if you added a new page you'd have to edit your navigation in two spots... we hope the mere suggestion of that is making your programmer's itch flare up again. Since those nav links are always going to be the same in both the header and the footer, we can create a new include to include in includes (thereby fulfilling the promise from Figure 9.13—it wasn't (just) a joke!).

We don't want to take the outer **ul** from Listing 9.14 since it has a **header-nav** class applied to it (well, you *could* add that in the include, then unstyle all the header styles, and then restyle to fit the footer—but that would be a lot of unnecessary work). So the content of our new include will just be the **li**s and the links—in other words, the content that definitely needs to be repeated.

To eliminate repetition in the links, let's create a new file in the **_includes** directory and name it **nav-links.html**:

```
$ touch _includes/nav-links.html
```

Then cut the **li**s and links out of the **.header-nav** and paste them into the new include, as shown in Listing 9.39.

Listing 9.39: We've cut and pasted in the **li**s and links.
_includes/nav-links.html

```
<li><a href="/">Home</a></li>
<li><a href="">Nav 1</a></li>
<li><a href="">Nav 2</a></li>
<li><a href="">Nav 3</a></li>
```

With the code in Listing 9.39, we can replace the links in the header file with a Liquid tag, as shown in Listing 9.40.

Listing 9.40: Updating the header with an include and a second class.
_includes/header.html

```
<ul class="header-nav nav-links">
  {% include nav-links.html %}
</ul>
```

Note that we've also added a **.nav-links** class in Listing 9.40 so we can add styling to the links that will be shared between the header and footer. Before, we were targeting and styling the links using the class **.header-nav** (introduced in

Listing 9.14), but now that the links are going to be in multiple places, that isn't a good name to use to target the styling common to both the header and the footer.

Now that we've factored the nav links into a separate include, let's add them to the navigation section in the footer. In order to allow footer-specific styling, we'll also add a **footer-nav** class (in analogy with the header's **header-nav** class), as well as the general **nav-links** class added in Listing 9.40. The result appears in Listing 9.41.

Listing 9.41: The new Liquid tag to load the links in the footer.
_includes/footer.html

```
<footer class="footer">
  <a class="footer-logo" href="/">
    <img src="/images/logo.png" alt="Learn Enough"/>
  </a>
  <nav>
    <ul class="footer-nav nav-links">
      {% include nav-links.html %}
    </ul>
  </nav>
  <h3>Learn Enough <span>to Be Dangerous</span></h3>
</footer>
```

Now let's add some styling. First, we should move some of the styles that before were defined on **.header-nav a** over to **.nav-links a**, and change the class that is targeting the **:hover** and **:active** states from **.header-nav** to **.nav-link**, as in Listing 9.42.

Listing 9.42: Moving link styling into a new **.nav-links** class.
css/main.css

```
.header-nav a {
  color: #fff;
}
.nav-links a {
  font-size: 0.8rem;
  font-weight: bold;
  text-decoration: none;
  text-transform: uppercase;
}
.nav-links a:hover,
.nav-links a:active {
  color: #ed6e2f;
}
```

Again, the idea is that we want navigational links to look similar between the header and footer, and then for any changes that are specific to one location or the other by targeting the links using either the **.header-nav** or the **.footer-nav** class.

Finally, we'll add footer-specific styles, as shown in Listing 9.43.

Listing 9.43: New styling for footer navigation and links.
`css/main.css`

```css
.footer-nav li {
  display: inline-block;
  margin: 2em 1em 0;
}
.footer-nav a {
  color: #ccc;
}
```

When you save and refresh, you'll have a nice header and footer, both pulling their navigational links from the same place (Figure 9.44).

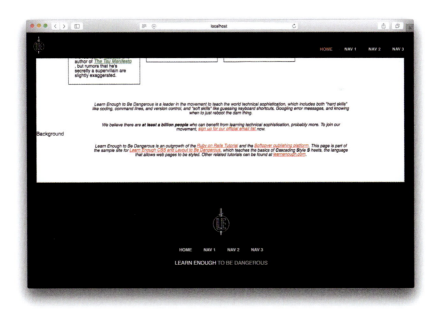

Figure 9.44: Styled header and footer with nav links from an include.

If you want to double-check and sync up all your styles, Listing 9.44 has the current state of the CSS declarations for the site.

Listing 9.44: The full header and footer styles.

css/main.css

```css
html, body, div, span, applet, object, iframe,
h1, h2, h3, h4, h5, h6, p, blockquote, pre,
a, abbr, acronym, address, big, cite, code,
del, dfn, em, img, ins, kbd, q, s, samp,
small, strike, strong, sub, sup, tt, var,
b, u, i, center, dl, dt, dd, ol, ul, li,
fieldset, form, label, legend, table, caption,
tbody, tfoot, thead, tr, th, td, article, aside,
canvas, details, embed, figure, figcaption, footer,
header, hgroup, menu, nav, output, ruby, section,
summary, time, mark, audio, video {
  margin: 0;
  padding: 0;
  border: 0;
  font: inherit;
  vertical-align: baseline;
}
/* HTML5 display-role reset for older browsers */
article, aside, details, figcaption, figure,
footer, header, hgroup, menu, nav, section {
  display: block;
}
body {
  line-height: 1;
}
blockquote, q {
  quotes: none;
}
blockquote:before, blockquote:after,
q:before, q:after {
  content: '';
  content: none;
}
table {
  border-collapse: collapse;
  border-spacing: 0;
}
strong, b {
  font-weight: bold;
}
em, i {
  font-style: italic;
```

```css
}
a img {
  border: none;
}
/* END RESET*/

/* GLOBAL STYLES */
html {
  box-shadow: 0 0 0 30px #000 inset;
  padding: 0 30px;
}
body {
  font-family: helvetica, arial, sans;
}
h1 {
  font-size: 7vw;
  margin-top: 0;
}
a {
  color: #f00;
}
h2 ~ p {
  font-size: 0.8em;
  font-style: italic;
  margin: 1em auto 0;
  max-width: 70%;
  text-align: center;
}

/* HEADER STYLES */
.header {
  background-color: #000;
  color: #fff;
  position: fixed;
  width: 100%;
  z-index: 20;
}
.header-logo {
  background-color: #000;
  box-sizing: border-box;
  display: block;
  height: 10vh;
  left: -30px;
  padding-top: 10px;
  position: relative;
  text-align: center;
  width: 10vh;
}
.header-logo:hover,
.header-logo:active {
```

```css
    background-color: #ed6e2f;
}
.header-logo img {
  width: 4.3vh;
}
.header-nav {
  float: right;
  padding: 5.5vh 60px 0 0;
}
.header-nav > li {
  display: inline-block;
  margin-left: 1em;
}
.header-nav > li ~ li {
  border-left: 1px solid rgba(255, 255, 255, 0.3);
  padding-left: 1em;
}
.header-nav a {
  color: #fff;
}
.nav-links a {
  font-size: 0.8rem;
  font-weight: bold;
  text-decoration: none;
  text-transform: uppercase;
}
.nav-links a:hover,
.nav-links a:active  {
  color: #ed6e2f;
}
.header-nav > li:first-child a {
  color: #ed6e2f;
}
.header-nav > li:first-child a:hover {
  color: #fff;
}

/* FOOTER STYLES */
.footer {
  background-color: #000;
  padding: 10vh 0 15vh;
  text-align: center;
}
.footer-logo img {
  width: 50px;
}
.footer h3 {
  color: #fff;
  padding-top: 1.5em;
  text-transform: uppercase;
```

```
}
.footer h3 span {
  color: #aaa;
}
.footer-nav li {
  display: inline-block;
  margin: 2em 1em 0;
}
.footer-nav a {
  color: #ccc;
}

/* HERO STYLES */
.full-hero {
  background-color: #c7dbfc;
  height: 50vh;
}

/* SOCIAL STYLES */
.social-list {
  list-style: none;
  padding: 0;
  text-align: center;
}
.social-link {
  background: rgba(150, 150, 150, 0.5);
  border-radius: 99px;
  box-sizing: border-box;
  color: #fff;
  display: inline-block;
  font-family: helvetica, arial, sans;
  font-size: 1rem;
  font-weight: bold;
  height: 2.5em;
  line-height: 1;
  padding-top: 0.85em;
  text-align: center;
  text-decoration: none;
  vertical-align: middle;
  width: 2.5em;
}
.social-list > li {
  display: inline-block;
  margin: 0 0.5em;
}

/* BIO STYLES */
.bio-wrapper {
  font-size: 24px;
  margin: auto;
```

```css
  max-width: 960px;
  overflow: hidden;
}
.bio-box {
  border: 1px solid black;
  box-sizing: border-box;
  float: left;
  font-size: 1rem;
  margin: 40px 1% 0;
  padding: 2%;
  width: 23%;
}
.bio-box h3 {
  color: #fff;
  font-size: 1.5em;
  margin: -40px 0 1em;
  text-align: center;
}
.bio-box img {
  width: 100%;
}
.bio-box .social-link {
  display: block;
  margin: 2em 0 1em;
}
.bio-copy {
  font-size: 1em;
}
.bio-copy a {
  color: green;
}
```

Finally, in case you haven't been doing your own Git commits and deploys, now would be a good time to do one:

```
$ git add -A
$ git commit -m "Finish initial layout"
```

You'll discover that GitHub Pages is fully Jekyll-aware, and automatically generates and displays the site based on the contents of the repository—free static site hosting!

9.10.1 Exercise

1. **(challenging)** In the same manner that we just made the header links modular, first create a new include that makes the social links in the hero into an include that can be inserted into other places on the site. Then use the correct include tag to put it back where it originally was, and also a second include that builds the social links into a new **ul** in the footer.

CHAPTER 10

Page Templates and Frontmatter

You might have noticed that we finished Chapter 9 with a big loose end: The default "layout" `default.html` contains all the content from our main index page—this makes it effectively useless as a layout because it can't show content for other pages. In this chapter, we'll tie up this loose end by learning how to insert content dynamically, thereby making our layout a truly reusable template.

Site-wide elements like the header and footer will be the same on every page, while the content in between (the part shown in blue in Figure 9.41) will vary. We will use Jekyll page templates to do this and simplify our site's structure, with a focus on developing unique content for each page. Along the way, we'll learn a new Liquid command for inserting content (Section 10.1), style the hero section (Section 10.2), learn some more advanced selectors (Section 10.3), and add pages other than the default index (Section 10.4).

10.1 Template Content

As mentioned in Section 9.4, the current state of `default.html` doesn't represent the standard way of using a Jekyll layout. The reason is that layouts should be *templates*, providing instructions for assembling the full page, rather than containing the full page content itself. Currently, the content in `default.html` is in fact only the content for `index.html`. If we want to use `default.html` as a template for additional pages, we need some way to insert the content specific to those pages.

The way to do this in Jekyll is to replace the content in the template with a special Liquid tag that inserts the content dynamically, so that it can be different for each page. The tag itself looks like this:

```
{{ content }}
```

This tag tells Jekyll to insert into the layout file whatever content is on the page that a user is loading (such as the homepage **index.html**). With this new tag in place, we can make as many additional pages as we want, and each will have its own content that will get built into a final page. All those new pages will have the same header, footer, and any other structure (thereby adhering to the DRY principle (Box 5.2)) that we want all pages to have.

To get this to work, we'll start by refactoring the index page, moving the index-specific content from **default.html** to **index.html**, and then dynamically inserting that content in the default template. The first step is to use your text editor to cut the content in **default.html** between the header and footer includes and replace it with the Liquid tag from above. The result should appear as in shown in Listing 10.1.

Listing 10.1: Replacing the content with a Liquid tag.
_layouts/default.html

```
<!DOCTYPE html>
<html>
  {% include head.html %}
  <body>
    {% include header.html %}

    {{ content }}

    {% include footer.html %}
  </body>
</html>
```

The second step is to paste the content you just cut out of **default.html** into **index.html** (while preserving the Jekyll frontmatter from Listing 9.2). Because this was a refactoring, when you refresh the page the content should appear unchanged. If you think that you might have done it incorrectly, don't worry, there's a code listing of the full file coming up in Listing 10.2.

The way this works is that Jekyll automatically collects the content in **`index.html`** (i.e., everything other than the frontmatter) into a special variable (Box 10.1) called **`content`**, which then gets inserted by the Liquid command in Listing 10.1 into the template specified by **`layout: default`**.

Figure 10.1: A concrete manifestation of computer variables.

Box 10.1: What Is a Variable?

If you've never programmed a computer before, you may be unfamiliar with the term *variable*, which is an essential idea in computer science. You can think of a variable as a named box that can hold different (or "variable") content.

As a concrete analogy, consider the labeled boxes that many elementary schools provide for students to store clothing, books, backpacks, etc. (Figure 10.1[1]).

---

1. Image courtesy of Africa Studio/Shutterstock.

> In the context of a Jekyll template, the content on the page (such as `index.html`) is automatically collected into a variable called `content`, which can be inserted into the template using the special command `{{ content }}` as described above (Listing 10.1).

Note that `{{ content }}` is a generic instruction to Jekyll to insert the value of the `content` variable, which in this context is the content from whatever page the user has visited (e.g., `index.html`). It's kind of a wildcard, as opposed to Liquid tags like `{% include footer.html %}` (Section 9.6), which include only a specific file's contents. We'll be talking about variables more in Section 12.1.

We'll put our new fully flexible layout template to good use in Section 10.4, and again in Section 12.1. First, though, we should probably make our homepage look a little less boring.

10.1.1 Exercises

1. Make a new file called `test.html` in your root directory, specify the default layout in the frontmatter, and for content add something like "For the fourth, and I hope final time, hello world." Visit http://localhost:4000/test.html in your browser to verify that it worked.

2. Create a new file in your `_layouts` directory, and add in only a `{{ content }}` tag. Then change the `index.html` frontmatter to use that new layout to build the page. Visit http://localhost:4000/ in your browser to see the result.

10.2 There's No Place Like Home

We'll start our homepage styling right at the top with the hero section that we created all the way back in Section 7.7. As we mentioned there, you've likely seen a lot of sites with nice big images at the top of the page, and these sections are called a variety of different names—hero sections, billboards, splashes, etc.—but, whatever the name, the goal is the same: to add a big attractive graphical element to the page to set the tone and grab the reader's attention. But our current plain blue hero is a bit of a zero… so we should change that.

As preparation for the hero improvements, we're going to update the markup on our index page a bit. The new `index.html` appears in Listing 10.2. Notice that we've taken the text that was at the bottom of the page and wrapped it inside new divs with new classes (everything inside the **div** with the class of **.home-callout**), and we've moved it to the top of the page. We've also eliminated the final **.bio-box** with the question marks.

You may find it easier to copy and paste from Listing 10.2 rather than rewrite it all yourself,[2] but if you feel like getting your hands dirty feel free to adapt the content on your page so that it matches. The result should look something like Figure 10.2.

Listing 10.2: Updating the HTML on the homepage.
index.html

```
---
layout: default
---

<div class="full-hero hero-home">
  <h1>I'm an h1</h1>
  <ul class="social-list">
    <li>
      <a href="https://example.com/" class="social-link">Fb</a>
    </li>
    <li>
      <a href="https://example.com/" class="social-link">Tw</a>
    </li>
    <li>
      <a href="https://example.com/" class="social-link">Gh</a>
    </li>
  </ul>
</div>

<div class="home-callout">
  <h1 class="callout-title">The Learn Enough Story</h1>
  <div class="callout-copy">
    <p>
      Learn Enough to Be Dangerous is a leader in the movement to teach the world
      <em>technical sophistication</em>, which includes both "hard skills" like
      coding, command lines, and version control, and "soft skills" like guessing
      keyboard shortcuts, Googling error messages, and knowing when to just
      reboot the darn thing.
    </p>
    <p>
      We believe there are <strong>at least a billion people</strong> who can
      benefit from learning technical sophistication, probably more. To join our
```

---

2. Recall that the code listings are available at https://github.com/learnenough/learn_enough_html_css_and _layout_code_listings.

```
      movement, <a href="https://learnenough.com/#email_list">sign up for our
      official email list</a> now.
    </p>
    <h3>Background</h3>
    <p>
      Learn Enough to Be Dangerous is an outgrowth of the
      <a href="https://www.railstutorial.org/">Ruby on Rails Tutorial</a> and the
      <a href="https://www.softcover.io/">Softcover publishing platform</a>. This
      page is part of the sample site for <a
      href="https://learnenough.com/css-tutorial"><em>Learn Enough CSS and Layout
      to Be Dangerous</em></a>, which teaches the basicics of
      <strong>C</strong>ascading <strong>S</strong>tyle
      <strong>S</strong>heets, the language that
      allows web pages to be styled. Other related tutorials can be found at
      <a href="https://learnenough.com/">learnenough.com</a>.
    </p>
  </div>
</div>

<div class="home-section">
  <h2>THE FOUNDERS</h2>
  <p>
    Learn Enough to Be Dangerous was founded in 2015 by Michael Hartl, Lee
    Donahoe, and Nick Merwin. We believe that the kind of technical
    sophistication taught by the Learn Enough tutorials can benefit at least a
    billion people, and probably more.
  </p>

  <div class="bio-wrapper">
    <div class="bio-box">
      <img src="https://placekitten.com/g/400/400">
      <h3>Michael Hartl</h3>
      <a href="https://twitter.com/mhartl" class="social-link">
        Tw
      </a>
      <div class="bio-copy">
        <p>
          Known for his dazzling charm, rapier wit, and unrivaled humility,
          Michael is the creator of the
          <a href="https://www.railstutorial.org/">Ruby on Rails
          Tutorial</a> and principal author of the
          <a href="https://learnenough.com/"> Learn Enough to Be Dangerous</a>
          introductory sequence.
        </p>
        <p>
          Michael is also notorious as the founder of
          <a href="http://tauday.com/">Tau Day</a> and author of
          <a href="http://tauday.com/tau-manifesto"><em>The Tau
          Manifesto</em></a>, but rumors that he's secretly a supervillain are
          slightly exaggerated.
```

```
      </p>
    </div>
  </div>
  <div class="bio-box">
    <img src="https://placekitten.com/g/400/400">
    <h3>Lee Donahoe</h3>
    <a href="https://twitter.com/leedonahoe" class="social-link">
      Tw
    </a>
    <div class="bio-copy">
      <p>
        When he's not literally swimming with sharks or hunting powder stashes
        on his snowboard, you can find Lee in front of his computer designing
        interfaces, doing front-end development, or writing some of the
        interface-related Learn Enough tutorials.
      </p>
    </div>
  </div>
  <div class="bio-box">
    <img src="https://placekitten.com/g/400/400">
    <h3>Nick Merwin</h3>
    <a href="https://twitter.com/nickmerwin" class="social-link">
      Tw
    </a>
    <div class="bio-copy">
      <p>
        You may have seen him shredding guitar live with Capital Cities on
        Jimmy Kimmel, Conan, or The Ellen Show, but rest assured Nick is a true
        nerd at heart. He's just as happy shredding well-spec'd lines of code
        from a tour bus as he is from his kitchen table.
      </p>
    </div>
  </div>
</div>
</div>
```

Figure 10.2: An updated index page.

To get started on the hero update, let's first increase the size of the `.full-hero` class that we styled in Section 7.7 to make it the size of the entire browser window. To do this, we'll set the `height` to 100% of the viewport height using `height: 100vh` (Section 7.7):

```
.full-hero {
  height: 100vh;
}
```

We'll also add in a background image (an extremely *dangerous* shark) using the `background-image` attribute, which takes an absolute path (with a leading slash `/` in `/images/shark.jpg`) as follows:

```
.hero-home {
  background-image: url(/images/shark.jpg);
}
```

(We'll download `shark.jpg` in a moment.)

Putting these elements together, and adding a few extra rules for the `.full-hero` class, gives us Listing 10.3.

Listing 10.3: New styles for the hero section.
css/main.css

```css
/* HERO STYLES */
.full-hero {
  background-color: #c7dbfc;
  box-sizing: border-box;
  height: 100vh;
  padding-top: 10vh;
}
.hero-home {
  background-image: url(/images/shark.jpg);
}
```

Note in Listing 10.3 the placement of the hero styles below site-wide styles like those for the header and footer. The reasoning is that the header and footer sections of CSS tend to stay relatively unchanged through updates, whereas you often find yourself making additions to the CSS that deal with the site content, so it makes sense to us to have things that change less often at the top of a file and add new stuff to the bottom.

Note also that we've added in a **border-box** style to make sure that the padding we'll add doesn't affect the overall element height (Section 8.2), and we've added padding to the top so that content isn't covered up by the fixed-position header.

To get the hero image, use **curl** to download **shark.jpg** to your local disk:[3]

```
$ curl -o images/shark.jpg -L https://cdn.learnenough.com/le-css/shark.jpg
```

Save and refresh and… hmm… Figure 10.3 doesn't look quite right.

---

3. Great White Shark photograph copyright © 2015 by Lee Donahoe. (What did you think Lee's bio meant by "literally swimming with sharks"?)

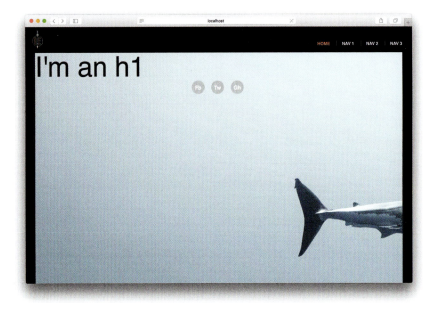

Figure 10.3: Our hero image is looking a little less than heroic.

What happened? Well, when the browser loads an image as a background, it isn't any different from when you put an image on a page using an HTML **img** tag—the image is displayed at its full dimensions. We've changed the size of images in this tutorial by giving a width or height to the **img** element in CSS (e.g., Listing 9.32), but the **height** and **width** properties don't work for background styles. To resize a background image to fit a container, we need to use the **background-size** style, as shown in Listing 10.4.

Listing 10.4: Adding the style to resize the background image.
css/main.css

```
.full-hero {
  background-color: #c7dbfc;
  background-size: cover;
  box-sizing: border-box;
  height: 100vh;
  padding-top: 10vh;
}
```

```
.hero-home {
  background-image: url(/images/shark.jpg);
}
```

Setting the **background-size** property to **cover** means that the image will be resized so that the entire **.full-hero** container is covered by the image, even if that means cutting off parts of the image (Figure 10.4).

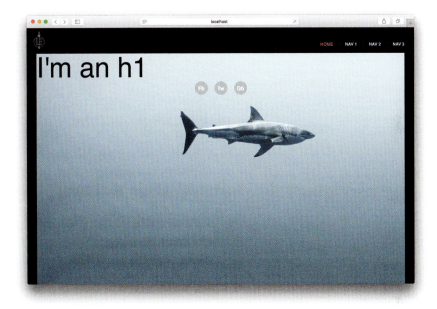

Figure 10.4: Resizing the image just enough to fully cover the background.

You can also use the value **contain** and the background image will be resized so that the entire picture will always fit inside the object, but that can lead to a situation where the image doesn't fully cover the background and the image gets repeated to fill the element.

Now reset back to using **background: cover**. If you resize your browser window to make it really narrow, you'll see that the image is dynamically resized, but you'll also likely notice that the resizing is done with the anchor point in the top left. Unfortunately, our shark is in the center of the image. When the window gets narrow, it starts getting cut off again (Figure 10.5).

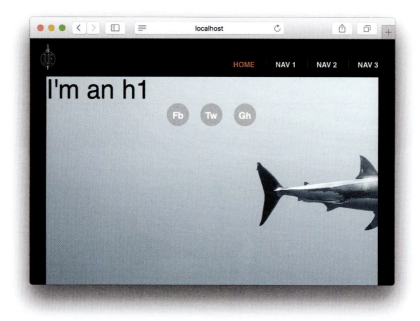

Figure 10.5: By default, the resizing is anchored at the top left of the image.

That's not always ideal, but luckily we can change the anchor point for the background image by using the **background-position** property (Listing 10.5).

Listing 10.5: Changing the anchor point for where the browser resizes the image.
css/main.css

```css
.full-hero {
  background-color: #c7dbfc;
  background-size: cover;
  box-sizing: border-box;
  height: 100vh;
  padding-top: 10vh;
}
.hero-home {
  background-image: url(/images/shark.jpg);
  background-position: center top;
}
```

Now the shark is better-positioned inside the element (Figure 10.6).

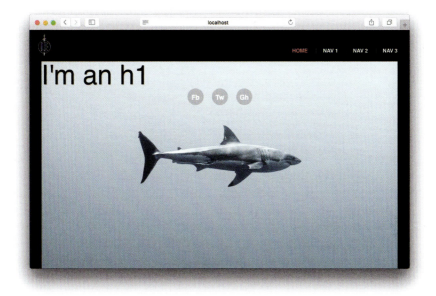

Figure 10.6: Resizing the picture from an anchor point at the **center top**.

The **background-position** style allows us to position a background with specific values like pixels or percentages, or we can use generic terms like **center**, **top**, **left**, etc. The first value controls the x-axis and the second the y-axis. So if we gave the background the style **background-position: center center**, then any resizing would always keep the middle of the image in the middle of the container **div**.

Next, let's make it so that the text, and the social links, are always vertically aligned in the hero using the positioning tricks we learned in Section 9.8. We could absolutely position that content, or we could just set the wrapper's position property to **relative** and then nudge things around.

First, let's move the **h1** and the **.social-links** list into a new wrapper element, with a class of **.hero-content**, so that we are only adding positional styling to a single HTML element that will then contain all the rest of the content in the hero (Listing 10.6). Note that we've also updated the **h1** to read CODE DANGEROUSLY.

Listing 10.6: Wrapping the hero's content inside a new **div**.

index.html

```
<div class="full-hero hero-home">
  <div class="hero-content">
    <h1>CODE DANGEROUSLY</h1>
    <ul class="social-list">
      <li>
        <a href="https://example.com/" class="social-link">Fb</a>
      </li>
      <li>
        <a href="https://example.com/" class="social-link">Tw</a>
      </li>
      <li>
        <a href="https://example.com/" class="social-link">Gh</a>
      </li>
    </ul>
  </div>
</div>
```

If you wanted to absolutely position the **.hero-content**, then you would need to remember to add a **position: relative** to the **.full-hero** class so that it could act as the container for absolutely positioned elements inside it. Since there isn't anything else in the hero, we don't need to worry about taking the **.hero-content** entirely out of the document flow. Instead, we can just set the **.hero-content** to **position: relative** and then nudge it around. At the same time, we'll do some styling for the **.social-link**s and the **h1**.

Since the **.hero-content** wrapper is already going to be 100% of the width (it's just a normal block element), we don't need to worry about messing with horizontal centering—just aligning the content using **text-align: center** will be good enough. We only need to worry about vertical positioning, which we can do with the **top: 50%** and **translate(0, -50%)** (both of which you've seen in Section 9.8):

```
top: 50%;
transform: translate(0, -50%);
```

We'll then style the hero's **h1** with a partially transparent color, a big font size, and a bottom margin:

```
color: rgba(255, 255, 255, 0.8);
font-size: 7vw;
margin-bottom: 0.25em;
```

All together, our existing and new hero styling are shown in Listing 10.7.

Listing 10.7: Positioning the hero content to be vertically centered.
css/main.css

```
.hero-content {
  color: #fff;
  position: relative;
  text-align: center;
  text-transform: uppercase;
  top: 50%;
  transform: translate(0, -50%);
}
.hero-content h1 {
  color: rgba(255, 255, 255, 0.8);
  font-size: 7vw;
  margin-bottom: 0.25em;
}
.hero-content .social-link {
  background-color: rgba(255, 255, 255, 0.8);
  color: #557c83;
}
.hero-content .social-link:hover {
  background-color: #000;
  color: #fff;
}
```

The hero now looks nicely styled (Figure 10.7).

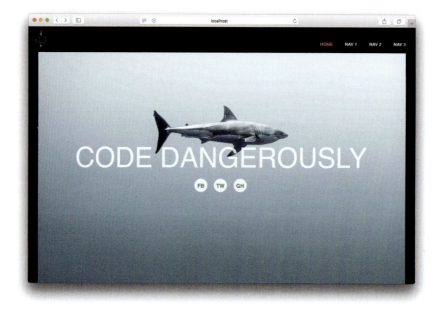

Figure 10.7: This hero section is starting to look… DANGEROUS(LY GOOD)!

10.2.1 Exercises

1. The **background-size** property isn't just limited to things like **cover** and **contain**; try setting the width value to a hard number like **300px** and the height to **auto**. What would that shorthand value be?

2. Now that you have a smaller background image, you'll have noticed that the browser repeats it to fill the element's background. We can stop that, though. Try adding a style of **background-repeat: no-repeat** to the **.full-hero** element.

3. Similar to **background-size**, the **background-position** property can take number values. Change the positioning to **30% center**.

10.3 More Advanced Selectors

The hero from Section 10.2 is looking great, but there's a missing detail we'd like to add. When people visit our site, there's a risk that they won't realize there is content lower down on the page. What if we added a little downward-pointing arrow at the bottom of the hero to give them a hint they should scroll?

One way we could do it would be to add a new **div** in the hero, give it a class name, and give that some styles, maybe use an image for the arrow, etc.—but that would be adding extra stuff to the code that would just clutter things up.

There is, however, another advanced CSS technique we can use to add stuff onto the page without adding anything to the HTML…

In this section, we'll see how to use the advanced *pseudo-element* to add a downward-pointing arrow to our hero section (Section 10.2) without using any images and with a minimum of fuss.

10.3.1   The `:before` and `:after` Pseudo-Elements

We introduced the *pseudo-class* when we were styling links in Section 9.7.1, and if you remember, it is kind of like a pretend CSS class that applies only when a user interacts with an element in a certain way (such as hovering over it with the mouse or visiting a link).

All HTML elements also have two pretend pseudo-elements, called `:before` and `:after`.[4] Even though this might sound super-technical and weird, surprisingly you've already used pseudo-elements, once when we played around with clearing floats (Section 8.3.1), and also the very first time that you ever made a bullet list (as in Section 3.4). You didn't know it, but when you created that bullet list, the individual bullet points were actually placed on the page by the browser using `:before` pseudo-elements.

The "before" and "after" in the pseudo-element names just refer to where the corresponding element will show up. So, if you have a line of text, `:before` will show up at the beginning and `:after` will show up at the end (Figure 10.8)… shocking, right?

Because these pseudo-elements were originally created to modify text, they are by default **inline** elements, and since the default is that they are empty, the result is that in their default rendering they take up no space. Here's the cool thing, though: They work just as if you added a **span** into a line of text, gave it a class, and then styled it. You can do all the same sorts of things that you'd do to any element on the

---

4. The latest CSS standard technically uses *two* colons for pseudo-elements—e.g., `::before` and `::after`—but all modern browsers support it both ways, so many designers use a single colon for backward compatibility.

Figure 10.8: The position of the `:before` and `:after` pseudo-elements.

page—change the display type, move it around, change how it looks—whatever your heart desires! They are perfect for adding little details to elements on a site without needing to complicate your code with extra HTML tags and classes.

We'll do a quick example just to illustrate the concept, and then actually implement the down arrow mentioned above. Start by adding the styles from Listing 10.8 to your CSS.

Listing 10.8: A pseudo-element example.
css/main.css

```css
/* HERO STYLES */
  .
  .
  .
.hero-content h1:before {
  color: blue;
  content: "B";
}
.hero-content h1:after {
  color: red;
  content: "A";
}
```

When you save and refresh your browser, you'll see that a B has appeared at the beginning of the title where the `:before` element lives, and there is an A where the `:after` element can be found (Figure 10.9).

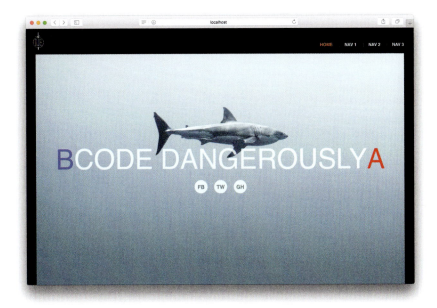

Figure 10.9: Demonstrating how pseudo-elements fit into ordinary elements.

The CSS property **content** allows you to set what the browser should put into either the `:before` or `:after` location, but the value can only be text (don't try and cram HTML in there!). So even though you didn't add any HTML, you now have new text content on the page.

OK, let's delete those two test styles from the CSS, and add in something useful that applies the `:after` pseudo-element. It's a good practice to place any pseudo-element CSS immediately below the parent style in the CSS file, so we'll locate the `.full-hero:after` rules immediately after the `.full-hero` section. The result, shown in Listing 10.9, includes a Unicode vertical right angle bracket, which we suggest you copy and paste, as your keyboard might not be able to produce it. (We aren't going to get into Unicode any further in this tutorial, but if you flip through a site like Unicode character table (https://unicode-table.com/en/), you'll be surprised at how many elements that would be useful in web design are already part of the Unicode character set.)

Listing 10.9: Applying a style to the `:after` pseudo-element.

css/main.css

```
/* HERO STYLES */
.full-hero {
  background-color: #c7dbfc;
  background-size: cover;
  box-sizing: border-box;
  height: 100vh;
  padding-top: 10vh;
}
.full-hero:after {
  bottom: 2vh;
  color: #fff;
  content: "⌄";
  font-size: 36px;
  left: 50%;
  position: absolute;
  transform: translate(-50%, 0)
}
```

With the CSS in Listing 10.9, you should have a white down arrow at the bottom of the hero (Figure 10.10).

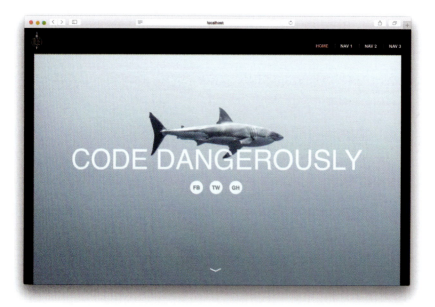

Figure 10.10: A wild down-pointing arrow has appeared!

10.3.2 The :before and :after CSS Triangle

Want to see another neat trick? If you ever want to make a triangle with just CSS, you can do so easily thanks to a quirk with the way that borders are drawn in browsers. Let's change that :after that we just created in Listing 10.9 to illustrate the concept (Listing 10.10).

Listing 10.10: Adding a thick multicolored border.
css/main.css

```
.full-hero:after {
  border: 10px solid;
  border-color: #000 red purple blue;
  bottom: 2vh;
  content: "";
  height: 0;
  left: 50%;
  position: absolute;
  transform: translate(-50%, 0);
  width: 0;
}
```

When you save and refresh the browser, you'll see that the downward-pointing caret has been replaced by a colored square that is divided into four triangular sections (Figure 10.11).

Figure 10.11: A zero-height and zero-width element with a thick border.

It turns out that browsers draw the line between, say, the top and right borders at a 45° angle.[5] Normally, you don't notice this because your borders are probably only 1px, and the same color all the way around. But if you make an element with zero height and zero width, and then give it a big border that has different colors on all sides, you'll find the rendering oddity shown in Figure 10.11. (We have no idea who the first person was to figure this out or why they were even trying it.)

So how do we use this to our advantage?

One of the acceptable "colors" for a border is **transparent** (alternatively, you could use **rgba(0, 0, 0, 0)**). So, recalling from Section 8.8 that **border-color** uses a margin-style shorthand, if we style the element as in Listing 10.11…

Listing 10.11: Finishing the styling for the downward-pointing triangle.
css/main.css

```css
.full-hero:after {
  bottom: 2vh;
  border: 10px solid;
  border-color: #fff transparent transparent;
  content: "";
  height: 0;
  left: 50%;
  position: absolute;
  transform: translate(-50%, 0);
  width: 0;
}
```

…we'll end up with a downward-pointing triangle (Figure 10.12)!

---

5. As founder of Tau Day (https://tauday.com/) and author of *The Tau Manifesto* (https://tauday.com/tau-manifesto), Michael Hartl is contractually obligated to note that 45°, which represents 1/8 of a circle, can also be written as $\tau/8$ (where $\tau = C/r = 6.283185\ldots$).

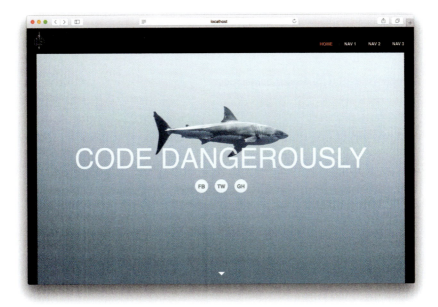

Figure 10.12: People seriously used to have to make images to do this kind of thing…
How barbaric.

Pretty cool, and actually very useful in menus and navigation for showing users
what they are currently looking at. You can use the `:before` and `:after` pseudo-
elements to do a lot of really cool things without adding unnecessary HTML to your
pages—it's perfect for little design elements like this. You just have to deal with the
limitation that you can't put extra HTML into the pseudo-elements.

Before we leave the homepage, let's give the remaining sections a little bit of
structure and style tweaking. One of the things that we've mentioned a number of
times is how important it is for things to be modular, and right now on the homepage
we have some elements that are inside wrappers, and some that are just loose on the
page.

In this sort of situation, it's a good idea to add `div` wrappers (Box 10.2) to wrap
content that belongs in a single unit. That way, if you want the different sections on
the homepage to be exactly `10vh` apart from each other, the styling is easy. That's why
Listing 10.2 wrapped the founders `h2`, the paragraph that follows, and the `.bio-box`es
in a `div` with the class `.home-section`, as reviewed in Listing 10.12.

Box 10.2: Style Note: What's the Deal with All These Wrappers?

So, what's the deal with all these wrappers?

Allstar Picture Library Ltd/Alamy Stock Photo

Well, we could just add a `.home-section` class to an element like the `.bio-wrapper` and style it up, but then we'd lose the ability to pull that entire `.bio-wrapper` out of the homepage and seamlessly drop it onto another part of the site (like on an About page), since it would potentially have an extra class on it that pertains only to the homepage.

We could make sure that the styling attached to that homepage class wouldn't affect the layout of the content if you put it on another page, but then we could end up having really complicated selectors and styling that is just undoing a bunch of properties, and then redoing new styles. To see what we mean, let's look at the Apple homepage for the Mac (https://www.apple.com/mac/). Scrolling down the page, you'll see different sections that have similar styling for height, background, and margins/padding. Setting things up so that you have common containers for content makes your job easier, and these generic wrappers that have styling like height, margins, or padding make it easy to flexibly add new content in the future.

Listing 10.12: The repackaged content on the homepage.

index.html

```html
<div class="home-callout">
  <h1 class="callout-title">The Learn Enough Story</h1>
  <div class="callout-copy">
    <p>
      Learn Enough to Be Dangerous is a leader in the movement to teach the world
      <em>technical sophistication</em>, which includes both "hard skills" like
      coding, command lines, and version control, and "soft skills" like guessing
      keyboard shortcuts, Googling error messages, and knowing when to just
```

```
    reboot the darn thing.
  </p>
  <p>
    We believe there are <strong>at least a billion people</strong> who can
    benefit from learning technical sophistication, probably more. To join our
    movement, <a href="https://learnenough.com/#email_list">sign up for our
    official email list</a> now.
  </p>
  <h3>Background</h3>
  <p>
    Learn Enough to Be Dangerous is an outgrowth of the
    <a href="https://www.railstutorial.org/">Ruby on Rails Tutorial</a> and the
    <a href="https://www.softcover.io/">Softcover publishing platform</a>. This
    page is part of the sample site for <a
    href="https://learnenough.com/css-tutorial"><em>Learn Enough CSS and Layout
    to Be Dangerous</em></a>, which teaches the basicics of
    <strong>C</strong>ascading <strong>S</strong>tyle
    <strong>S</strong>heets, the language that
    allows web pages to be styled. Other related tutorials can be found at
    <a href="https://learnenough.com/">learnenough.com</a>.
  </p>
  </div>
</div>

<div class="home-section">
  <h2>THE FOUNDERS</h2>
  <p>
    Learn Enough to Be Dangerous was founded in 2015 by Michael Hartl, Lee
    Donahoe, and Nick Merwin. We believe that the kind of technical
    sophistication taught by the Learn Enough tutorials can benefit at least a
    billion people, and probably more.
  </p>

  <div class="bio-wrapper">
    <div class="bio-box">
      <img src="https://placekitten.com/g/400/400">
      <h3>Michael Hartl</h3>
      <a href="https://twitter.com/mhartl" class="social-link">
        Tw
      </a>
      <div class="bio-copy">
        <p>
          Known for his dazzling charm, rapier wit, and unrivaled humility,
          Michael is the creator of the
          <a href="https://www.railstutorial.org/">Ruby on Rails
          Tutorial</a> and principal author of the
          <a href="https://learnenough.com/">
          Learn Enough to Be Dangerous</a> introductory sequence.
        </p>
        <p>
```

```
        Michael is also notorious as the founder of
        <a href="http://tauday.com/">Tau Day</a> and
        author of <a href="http://tauday.com/tau-manifesto"><em>The Tau
        Manifesto</em></a>, but rumors that he's secretly a supervillain are
        slightly exaggerated.
      </p>
    </div>
  </div>
  <div class="bio-box">
    <img src="https://placekitten.com/g/400/400">
    <h3>Lee Donahoe</h3>
    <a href="https://twitter.com/leedonahoe" class="social-link">
      Tw
    </a>
    <div class="bio-copy">
      <p>
        When he's not literally swimming with sharks or hunting powder stashes
        on his snowboard, you can find Lee in front of his computer designing
        interfaces, doing front-end development, or writing some of the
        interface-related Learn Enough tutorials.
      </p>
    </div>
  </div>
  <div class="bio-box">
    <img src="https://placekitten.com/g/400/400">
    <h3>Nick Merwin</h3>
    <a href="https://twitter.com/nickmerwin" class="social-link">
      Tw
    </a>
    <div class="bio-copy">
      <p>
        You may have seen him shredding guitar live with Capital Cities on
        Jimmy Kimmel, Conan, or The Ellen Show, but rest assured Nick is a true
        nerd at heart. He's just as happy shredding well-spec'd lines of code
        from a tour bus as he is from his kitchen table.
      </p>
    </div>
  </div>
  </div>
</div>
```

Let's also add some styles to these new sections and to some of the content. There are a lot of changes, so feel free to save and refresh as we're going along. We'll have a screenshot showing the cumulative changes at the end.

For the `.home-section`s themselves, we are going to size them to be **90vw** and also give them an upper limit, and then use the **margin: auto** trick from Section 8.6.1

(plus some top and bottom margins to keep them away from other content) to keep the sections in the center of the page:

```
margin: 6rem auto;
max-width: 980px;
width: 90vw;
```

We are going to style the **h2** so that it is centered, and has some distance from content below it:

```
margin-bottom: 1.5rem;
text-align: center;
```

We'll also style the callouts to give them background and text color, and nice padding:

```
background-color: #000;
color: #fff;
padding: 7vh 0;
```

And lastly we'll do some text styling in that section, first for the title to make it nice and big:

```
font-size: 5.75vw;
text-align: right;
text-transform: uppercase;
```

Then for the regular text we'll set the font size to be a little smaller than normal to prevent it from being too overwhelming on the page:

```
font-size: 0.8rem;
```

All together, that looks like Listing 10.13.

Listing 10.13: Styling the home section and callout.
css/main.css

```
/* HOMEPAGE STYLES */
.home-section {
  margin: 6rem auto;
  max-width: 980px;
  width: 90vw;
```

```
}
.home-section h2 {
  margin-bottom: 1.5rem;
  text-align: center;
}
.home-callout {
  background-color: #000;
  color: #fff;
  padding: 7vh 0;
}
.callout-title {
  font-size: 5.75vw;
  text-align: right;
  text-transform: uppercase;
}
.callout-copy {
  font-size: 0.8rem;
}
```

Now we are going to attack the `.bio-box`es. Let's get rid of the borders, resize the width of the boxes to fully fill the page now that there are only three, change the margins and padding to give us nicer spacing between the elements, tweak the header styles so that the names look a little nicer, and then finally center the social links after giving them a little space on top to separate them from the images. We can also get rid of the link color styling for the bios, the line-height style on the copy in the bio text (we'll change it so that all paragraphs on the site have reasonable line height), and then also style the text a little with some new sizes. The result appears in Listing 10.14.

Listing 10.14: Restyling the `.bio-box`es.
css/main.css

```
.bio-box {
  box-sizing: border-box;
  float: left;
  font-size: 1rem;
  margin: 6rem 0 0;
  padding: 0 3%;
  width: 33%;
}
  .
  .
  .
.bio-box h3 {
  color: #fff;
```

```
  font-size: 1.5em;
  margin: -40px 0 1em;
  text-align: center;
  text-transform: uppercase;
}
  .
  .
  .
.bio-box .social-link {
  display: block;
  margin: 2em auto 1em;
}
.bio-copy {
  font-size: 0.75em;
}
```

Up at the top of the CSS file, we'll address the line-height issue with a global line-height style for paragraphs. This gives text a little more breathing room, and while we are there, we'll also change the default link color to something a little more pleasant than bright red (Listing 10.15).

Listing 10.15: Adding in some new global styles.
css/main.css

```
/* GLOBAL STYLES */
  .
  .
  .
h1 {
  font-size: 7vw;
  margin-top: 0;
}
h2 {
  font-size: 2em;
}
a {
  color: #6397b5;
}
p {
  line-height: 1.5;
}
```

Overall, a more pleasing design (Figure 10.13)!

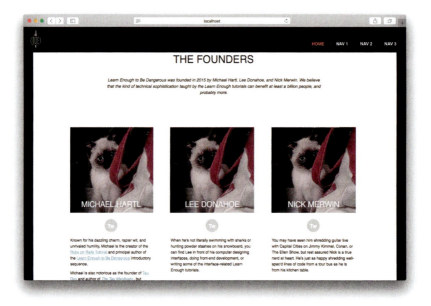

Figure 10.13: The improved bio section.

10.3.3 Exercises

1. One common mistake when dealing with `:before` and `:after` is forgetting to define the `content` property. Try deleting that from the `.full-hero:after` styling. What happens?

2. Another common mistake is forgetting that these pseudo-elements are by default inline elements. What happens when you delete `position: absolute` from `.full-hero:after`? Before adding it back in, trying setting the element to `display: block`.

10.4 Other Pages, Other Folders

Now that we've polished up the homepage a bit, let's add a second page to see how to reuse the layout defined in Listing 10.1. To do that, we'll need to add a new file into our project.

The easiest way to add new pages to a Jekyll site is to simply put other HTML files in the root directory, and then link to them the way that we did in Part I—for example, like this (Figure 10.14):

```
http://localhost:4000/pagename.html
```

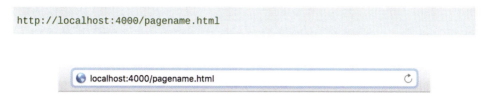

Figure 10.14: This is kind of an ugly URL for a page.

That URL is kind of ugly, though, and these days most modern sites have pages with nice-looking addresses like http://sitename.com/pagename, without the **.html** at the end (Figure 10.15). It seems like a little thing, but URLs are UI, and people really do notice details like that on sites. If something doesn't look right, they might think that your site isn't trustworthy or professional.

Figure 10.15: This kind of URL looks much cleaner.

Lucky for us, Jekyll gives developers a method to approximate that kind of "pretty URL", so let's try it out.[6]

The trick is that you can add a directory into your project, and then create a file in the directory called **index.html**. As long as the directory has a name that conforms to URL standards, you can link and visit that index page by just using **/directoryname**.

To see how this works, create a new directory in the project called **gallery**, and create a new **index.html** file inside that directory:

```
$ mkdir gallery
$ touch gallery/index.html
```

---

6. Web frameworks like Rails give developers even more flexibility and power in constructing URLs.

(Repeating the `index.html` filename may seem confusing, but this convention of using `index.html` for the main file in a directory is as old as the Web.)

Once the file is created, add in the frontmatter that tells Jekyll which layout to use (and a little bit of text), and save your work (Listing 10.16).

Listing 10.16: Adding an index page inside a new directory.
gallery/index.html

```
---
layout: default
---

I'm a 3 col page!
```

Your directories and files should now look something like Figure 10.16.

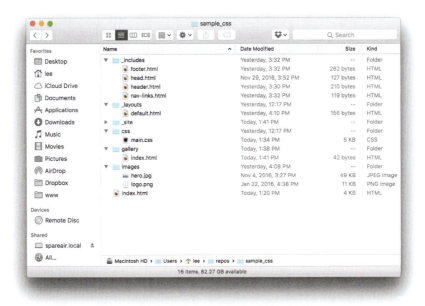

Figure 10.16: The new additions in the project directory.

Now go to http://localhost:4000/gallery. As promised in Section 10.1, Jekyll has inserted the content of the relevant page (in this case, Listing 10.16) into the default template. As a result, the pretty URL works, but unfortunately the text doesn't display, even though (as you can verify using a web inspector) the text is present in the page's source.

In looking at our new page, we have just run into one of the age-old problems in creating websites... a page is only as big as the content you added to it. All that white stuff at the bottom is actually not even part of your page—it's just the default background the browser is adding to fill the window (Figure 10.17).

Figure 10.17: Your text is somewhere... up there.

In this case, the content (one line of text) is getting covered up by the fixed-position header, and then the footer is drawn right after that. Ideally, you want the footer at least at the bottom of the browser so that you don't see this default page background, but there isn't enough content to push it down.

Over the years there have been a variety of different methods for solving this problem, some more complex than others, most requiring a bunch of wrapper divs, plus `min-height` set on some things, `height: 100%` on others, and a dash of negative margin (read: complicated). But there is a new styling method in town that allows developers to simply and efficiently solve this problem: the CSS flexbox.

As we'll see in Chapter 11, not only will the CSS flexbox solve our text-clearing problem; it will also allow us to easily make multicolumn page layouts (thereby fulfilling the promise implicit in the gallery text "I'm a 3 col page!"). The result will be the beginnings of a simple photo gallery, which will come to full fruition in *Learn Enough JavaScript to Be Dangerous* (https://www.learnenough.com/javascript).

10.4.1 Exercises

1. Create another page called **test.html** in the **gallery** folder. What happens when you try to go to http://localhost:4000/gallery/test? What about http://localhost:4000/gallery/test.html?

2. How would you create another nicely formatted URL that points to a page inside the gallery folder?

Chapter 11

Specialty Page Layouts with Flexbox

As you might guess from the name, CSS *flexbox* is a flexible box model for laying out content on the Web. Flexbox, which is a relatively new addition to CSS, makes it possible to style sections of a website to allow child elements to fully fill a container, while also still being able to adapt to the content—a combination that was often difficult to do in the pre-flexbox era.

For example, suppose we had three columns with different amounts of content inside, and we wanted the columns all to be the same height as the *longest* one. A diagram of this scenario for three columns *without* flexbox appears in Figure 11.1.

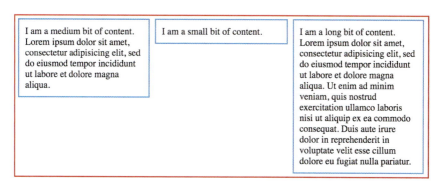

Figure 11.1: Columns with different lengths of content, and hence different heights.

Back in the days before flexbox, it was surprisingly hard to add styles to transform the content in Figure 11.1 to look like the content in Figure 11.2. It required doing things like using JavaScript to check the height of elements every time the window changed size, or using HTML tables for layout (which you should never do (Box 11.1)).

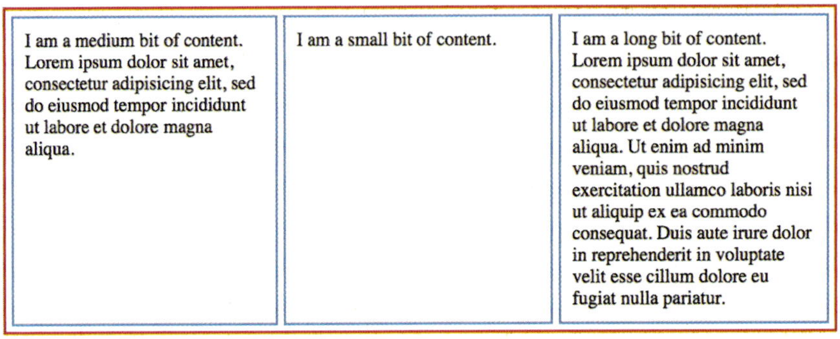

| I am a medium bit of content. Lorem ipsum dolor sit amet, consectetur adipisicing elit, sed do eiusmod tempor incididunt ut labore et dolore magna aliqua. | I am a small bit of content. | I am a long bit of content. Lorem ipsum dolor sit amet, consectetur adipisicing elit, sed do eiusmod tempor incididunt ut labore et dolore magna aliqua. Ut enim ad minim veniam, quis nostrud exercitation ullamco laboris nisi ut aliquip ex ea commodo consequat. Duis aute irure dolor in reprehenderit in voluptate velit esse cillum dolore eu fugiat nulla pariatur. |

Figure 11.2: How we want the columns to look—a surprisingly difficult problem.

Now that we have flexbox, this type of problem has an easy solution! In this chapter, we'll apply simplified flexbox rules to fix the layout problem left at the end of Section 10.4 (Figure 10.17), and we'll also take the opportunity to polish up the callout section on the homepage (Section 11.2). With these examples in hand, we'll then take a look at more advanced flexbox features, including a powerful shorthand notation (Section 11.3). Finally, we'll apply these more advanced features to create a *three-column* layout for the gallery introduced in Section 10.4.

Box 11.1: Style Note: Never Use Tables for Layout

Back in the bad old days of the early Internet, when there was no CSS, the only way to create page layouts was to use tables inside tables (inside tables), and then put content in the table cells. This was a terrible abuse of the `table` tag, which is designed for organizing and displaying tabular data (like spreadsheets), but unfortunately there was no other way to arrange things on a page.

As time went on, developers were given new tools, elements, and styles for creating layouts, but there were still gaps in the toolset, which made it difficult to create layouts like the multiple columns shown in Figure 11.2. So developers continued to use tables to make their designs work (for certain values of "work").

The problem is that, beyond the semantic problem of using an element meant for data to create a layout, the table layout is incredibly strict in how it is displayed. Once you have things arranged in table rows and table cells, that's how the browser has to show them. So if you resize a window with a table, all the content gets squished, and there is no way to restack it, as illustrated in Figure 11.3.

Luckily, with CSS and flexbox, we can now design flexible and robust styles without resorting to tables. Huzzah!

A REGULAR TABLE

I am some words and ideas	Lorem ipsum dolor sit amet, consectetur adipisicing elit, sed do eiusmod tempor incididunt ut labore et dolore magna aliqua. Ut enim ad minim veniam, quis nostrud exercitation ullamco laboris nisi ut aliquip ex ea commodo consequat. Duis aute irure dolor in reprehenderit in voluptate velit esse cillum dolore eu fugiat nulla pariatur.	I am some other content
I am some words and ideas	Lorem ipsum dolor sit amet, consectetur adipisicing elit, sed do eiusmod tempor incididunt ut labore et dolore magna aliqua. Ut enim ad minim veniam, quis nostrud exercitation ullamco laboris nisi ut aliquip ex ea commodo consequat. Duis aute irure dolor in reprehenderit in voluptate velit esse cillum dolore eu fugiat nulla pariatur.	I am some other content

A SQUISHED TABLE

I am some words and ideas	Lorem ipsum dolor sit amet, consectetur adipisicing elit, sed do eiusmod tempor incididunt ut labore et dolore magna aliqua. Ut enim ad minim veniam, quis nostrud exercitation ullamco laboris nisi ut aliquip ex ea commodo consequat. Duis aute irure dolor in reprehenderit in voluptate	I am some other content

NOT A TABLE

I am some words and ideas

Lorem ipsum dolor sit amet, consectetur adipisicing elit, sed do eiusmod tempor incididunt ut labore et dolore magna aliqua. Ut enim ad minim veniam, quis nostrud exercitation ullamco laboris nisi ut aliquip ex ea commodo consequat. Duis aute irure dolor in reprehenderit in voluptate velit esse cillum dolore eu fugiat nulla pariatur.

I am some other content

Excepteur sint occaecat cupidatat non proident, sunt in culpa qui officia deserunt mollit anim id est laborum.

I am some words and ideas

Lorem ipsum dolor sit amet, consectetur adipisicing elit, sed do eiusmod tempor incididunt ut labore et dolore magna aliqua. Ut enim ad minim veniam, quis nostrud exercitation ullamco laboris nisi ut aliquip ex ea commodo consequat. Duis aute irure dolor in reprehenderit in voluptate velit esse cillum dolore eu fugiat nulla

Figure 11.3: Seriously, never use tables for layouts—only for tabular data.

11.1 Having Content Fill a Container

We'll start with an overview of the anatomy of a flexbox. There are two main aspects, the *flex container* and the *flex items*, as illustrated in Figure 11.4. The flex container is the HTML element with the CSS property **display: flex** set. Meanwhile, each flex

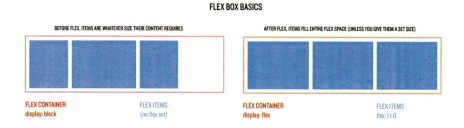

Figure 11.4: Making flexible containers with child items that fill the available space.

item is a child element that has some value of the CSS **flex:** property set. Essentially, the flex container encloses the items, which can be aligned, stretched, shrunk, etc. by various flexbox style rules. (If you are looking at the fine print in Figure 11.4, don't worry right now about the style declaration **flex: 1 1 0** under the flex items; we'll cover it in detail in Section 11.3.)

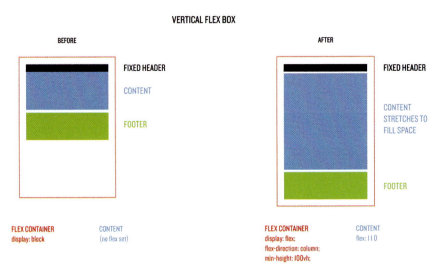

Figure 11.5: Stretching the elements vertically with flexbox (note the **flex-direction**).

As our first practical application of flexbox items and containers, we'll solve a problem we had at the end of Section 10.4 (Figure 10.17). Recall that the text on the new gallery page wasn't visible even though it was present in the page's source, and the footer wasn't at the bottom of the window, but rather was crushed up against the content. We'll fix both issues by using a flexbox layout that will let us push the footer to the bottom of the screen by vertically filling the available space (Figure 11.5), and also will let us add in padding to move the page content down so that it gets out from under the header.

In order to apply flexbox to the default template, we'll need to designate both a flex container and some number of flex items (Figure 11.4). Although we could add a new **div** wrapper to use as a flex container, we'll take a simpler approach and use the layout's **body** tag. Using a default element like the **body** tag as part of our layout works for this situation because we want the footer to be at the bottom of the window (or below the content) on all of the pages across the site.

When we last saw the default site template, the body of the page had two main defined sections, the header and footer, as well as a content tag that loads page content into the layout (Listing 11.1).

Listing 11.1: The current state of the default template.

_layouts/default.html

```
<!DOCTYPE html>
<html>
  {% include head.html %}
  <body>
    {% include header.html %}

    {{ content }}

    {% include footer.html %}
  </body>
</html>
```

In order to apply the ideas in Figure 11.5, we need to make some element on the page our flexbox item for the content, and we'll do this using a **div** tag with class **content-container**. (This content "container" is for now a flexbox *item*, but see Section 11.4 below, where it is also a flexbox container—flexboxes within flexboxes!) The updated default layout appears in Listing 11.2.

Listing 11.2: Wrapping the site content in a new container.

_layouts/default.html

```
<!DOCTYPE html>
<html>
  {% include head.html %}
  <body>
    {% include header.html %}

    <div class="content-container">
      {{ content }}
    </div>

    {% include footer.html %}
  </body>
</html>
```

Recall from Listing 9.14 and Listing 9.36 that the header and footer are wrapped in the semantic tags **header** and **footer** (which are effectively **div**s). Both elements could act as "flex items" for the purposes of our flexbox layout, but we aren't going to set them to flex as we want them to stay the size that they are—we want only the content area to expand and contract to fill empty space.

We set the **header** to be **position: fixed**, which means it will be taken out of the page flow and won't be affected by our flexbox setup (Section 9.8). Likewise, we aren't going to target the **footer** with a **flex:** property; instead, it will remain a regular old block element so that its content doesn't get affected by the element changing size. The magic ingredient is going to be the **.content-container div** defined in Listing 11.2.

With the template defined by Listing 11.2, any page using the default layout will have a structure that looks like this (where we've added HTML comments only for clarity—they won't actually appear in the source):

```html
<!DOCTYPE html>
<html>
  <head>
    .
    .
    .
  </head>
  <!-- flexbox container -->
  <body>
    <!-- 1st potential flexbox item, but not flexing because position: fixed -->
    <header>
      .
      .
      .
    </header>

    <!-- 2nd flexbox item, the only one that will be changing in size -->
    <div class="content-container">
      .
      .
      .
    </div>

    <!-- 3rd potential flexbox item, but not given a flex: property -->
    <footer>
      .
      .
      .
```

```
    </footer>
  </body>
</html>
```

To apply flexbox to our page, we'll start by adding the declaration **display: flex** to the flex container (in this case, the **body** tag). Then, in order to build the flex items in a vertical column, we'll set the *flex direction* rule **flex-direction** to **column**. Finally, we'll set the **min-height** property to **100vh** (Section 7.7) to ensure that the **.content-container** stretches to fill 100% of the viewport height. The resulting **body** rules (including the pre-existing **font-family** declaration) appear as follows:

```
body {
  display: flex;
  flex-direction: column;
  font-family: helvetica, arial, sans;
  min-height: 100vh;
}
```

Meanwhile, we need to arrange for the content container, which is currently shrunk down (Figure 10.17), to grow as big as it can. To do this, we need to understand the **flex-grow** property, which controls how flexbox items expand. By default, items in a flex container have a **flex-grow** value of **0**, which means the item doesn't grow at all.

Since we haven't yet applied a **flex-grow** property to any of our elements, the header, content, and footer currently don't expand to fill the container, as shown schematically in Figure 11.6.

Figure 11.6: Three flexbox items with `flex-grow` of `0`.

To get the content to fill the area, all we need to do is activate the `.content-container` as a flex item by setting `flex-grow` to `1`:

```
.content-container {
  flex-grow: 1;
}
```

The `flex-grow` property works by proportions: If all three items are set to `1`, each one takes up 1/3 of the space available. With the header and footer set to the default value of `0`, setting the content div's `flex-grow` to `1` arranges for it to take up *all* of the available space, as shown schematically in Figure 11.7.

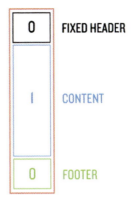

flex-grow: I (the default value)

ONE SETS FLEX ITEM TO FILL SPACE

Figure 11.7: Arranging for only the middle item to grow using `flex-grow: 1`.

Putting together the rules for the flex container (**body**) and the flex items (the header and footer set to the defaults, content with **flex-grow** set to **1**) gives the CSS shown in Listing 11.3. Note that Listing 11.3 also added padding of 10% of the viewport height (**10vh**) to move the content out from underneath the site header, which also requires a **10vh** adjustment to the height of the hero section to make it **10vh** smaller so that it still exactly fills the browser window. The width setting is there to make sure that the element stretches to fill the page horizontally as well as vertically.

Listing 11.3: New styles for the body and a new container class.

`css/main.css`

```
body {
  display: flex;
  flex-direction: column;
  font-family: helvetica, arial, sans;
  min-height: 100vh;
}
.content-container {
  flex-grow: 1;
  padding-top: 10vh;
```

```
    width: 100%;
}
  .
  .
  .
/* HERO STYLES */
  .
  .
  .
.full-hero {
  background-color: #c7dbfc;
  background-size: cover;
  box-sizing: border-box;
  height: 90vh;
}
```

Et voilà! After saving your work and refreshing the browser, the content should expand to fill the available space and push the footer to the bottom of the window. Now the padding reveals the content and fixes the problem from the end of Section 10.4, as shown in Figure 11.8.

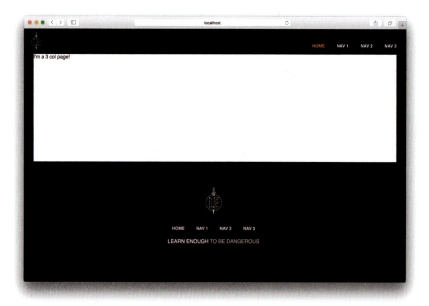

Figure 11.8: The content now grows to fill the available space.

11.1.1   Exercises

1. Remove **position: fixed** from the header, and set both the header and the footer to **flex-grow: 1** to see how the flexbox divides space between three elements with different amounts of content.

2. Now remove **flex-direction: column** from the body to see how the browser reorders the flex items on the page.

11.2 Vertical Flex Centering

Our second application of flexbox is going to be styling the homepage callout section that we introduced in Section 10.3. In particular, we'll make the title and the content share the space in an aesthetically pleasing way. To accomplish this, our flexbox container will be the **div** with class **home-callout**, and the flexbox items will be the **h1** (with class **callout-title**), and the child **div** (with class **callout-copy**):

```
<div class="home-callout">
  <h1 class="callout-title">The Learn Enough Story</h1>
  <div class="callout-copy">
    .
    .
    .
  </div>
</div>
```

Our first task is to set the styles for the callout container. After initializing the flexbox with **display: flex**, we'll align the items vertically using **align-items: center**, as shown schematically in Figure 11.9.

THE OPTIONS FOR THE ALIGN-ITEMS PROPERTY

FLEX CONTAINER
display: flex
align-items: stretch (DEFAULT)

FLEX CONTAINER
display: flex
align-items: flex-start

FLEX CONTAINER
display: flex
align-items: flex-end

FLEX CONTAINER
display: flex
align-items: center

Figure 11.9: The different ways to use the **align-items** CSS property.

The corresponding CSS appears as follows:

```css
.home-callout {
  align-items: center;
  background-color: #000;
  color: #fff;
  display: flex;
  padding: 7vh 0;
}
```

Our next task is to apply the rules for the callout flex items, starting with the title. As in Section 11.1, we'll set **flex-grow** to **1** to arrange for the title to fill the available space.

We'll also set the **flex-basis**, which is a property that controls the original ("basis") width of the element. The most common values are **0**, which sets the initial width to **0** and expands only as much as is needed to contain the content, and **auto**, which automatically distributes extra space to each element. Although it's a less common usage, you can also set the flex basis to a set size value (Figure 11.10).

Figure 11.10: `flex-basis` can size elements proportionally, with respect to content, or to a set size.

By default, every element has a **flex-basis: auto**, but we'll change it to **0** for the title to make it fit more compactly into the container. The resulting CSS for the callout title looks like this:

```css
.callout-title {
  flex-grow: 1;
  flex-basis: 0;
  font-size: 5.75vw;
  text-align: right;
  text-transform: uppercase;
}
```

Meanwhile, we'll set the properties on the **callout-copy** class to prevent the callout copy from shrinking as the parent element gets smaller by setting the **flex-shrink** property to **0** (Figure 11.11):

```
flex-shrink: 0;
```

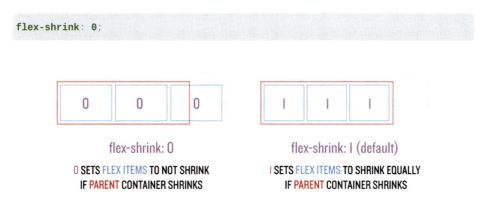

Figure I1.I1: The effect setting `flex-shrink` to 0 vs. all items set to 1.

We'll also distribute the space for the callout copy by setting the **flex-basis** to be **45em**:

```
flex-basis: 45em;
```

This leads to the following new rules for the **callout-copy** class:

```
.callout-copy {
  flex-shrink: 0;
  flex-basis: 45em;



  font-size: 0.8rem;



}
```

Putting everything together gives the CSS in Listing 11.4. The styles in Listing 11.4 highlight the changes to existing declarations, but also notice both the global style for the **p** and the entirely new style declaration for **.home-callout h3**. As usual, apply your technical sophistication (Box 5.1) to comment/uncomment styles to help understand what they do.

Listing 11.4: Making the home callout look a little cooler.

css/main.css

```css
/* GLOBAL STYLES */
  .
  .
  .
p {
  line-height: 1.5;
  margin: 0.75em 0;
}
  .
  .
  .
/* HOMEPAGE STYLES */
  .
  .
  .
.home-callout {
  align-items: center;
  background-color: #000;
  color: #fff;
  display: flex;
  padding: 7vh 0;
}
.home-callout h3 {
  color: inherit;
  margin-top: 1em;
}
.callout-title {
  flex-basis: 0;
  flex-grow: 1;
  font-size: 5.75vw;
  text-align: right;
  text-transform: uppercase;
}
.callout-copy {
  flex-basis: 45em;
  flex-shrink: 0;
  font-size: 0.8rem;
  padding: 0 3vw;
}
```

When you save and refresh, you'll see that the callout section now looks a lot less haphazard and a lot more stylish (Figure 11.12).

Figure 11.12: A much better-looking callout. Flexbox all the things!

11.2.1 Exercises

1. Try out the different **align-items** values by first setting the callout flex items to **align-items: flex-start** and then **align-items: flex-end**.

2. Change the flex basis of the **.callout-copy** to **300px**. Refresh your browser to see the smaller version and how the hard value causes it not to change size.

11.3 Flexbox Style Options and Shorthand

Now that we've seen some concrete examples, we're going to take a moment to discuss some more general aspects of flexbox. As part of this, we'll learn about a powerful shorthand notation that is the most common way to use flexbox in real-world applications. We'll use this shorthand to refactor the flexbox CSS from the previous sections, and we'll apply it to a three-column layout in Section 11.4.

11.3.1 Flex Container Properties

We'll start by illustrating the different possibilities for the flex container properties **flex-direction** and **align-items**. Figure 11.13 shows the **row** and **column** properties for **flex-direction**, as well as their **-reverse** variations. It also shows the different possibilities for **align-items**. See if you can figure out which diagrams apply to the examples from Section 11.1 and Section 11.2 (Section 11.3.3).

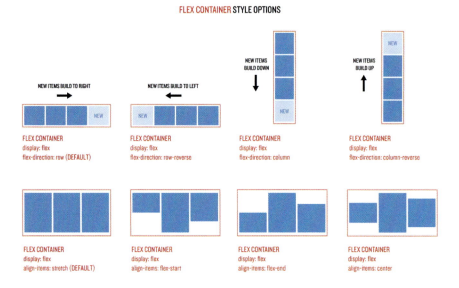

Figure 11.13: Flex container properties.

11.3.2 Flex Item Properties

We've now seen all three of the primary flexbox item properties—**flex-grow**, **flex-shrink**, and **flex-basis**, which together allow us to control how flex items behave inside their parent container:

- **flex-grow** determines how flex items grow inside their parent. Default **0**.

- **flex-shrink** determines how flex items shrink when their parent gets smaller. Default **1**.

- **flex-basis** determines the size of flex items before space is distributed and how content is treated. Default **auto**.

As illustrated in Figure 11.14, flexbox supports a shorthand notation that follows this pattern:

```
flex: <flex-grow> <flex-shrink> <flex-basis>
```

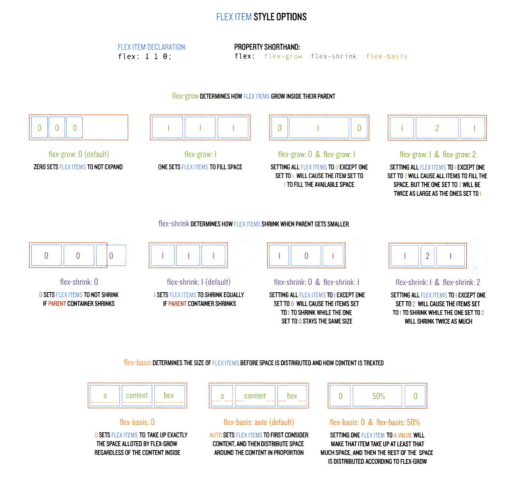

Figure 11.14: Flex item properties.

For example, as seen in Figure 11.14, the default values for the three item properties are **0**, **1**, and **auto**:

```
flex-grow: 0;
flex-shrink: 1;
flex-basis: auto;
```

In the shorthand notation, this can be written as follows:

```
flex: 0 1 auto;
```

Let's apply this shorthand to the style from Listing 11.3:

```css
.content-container {
  flex-grow: 1;
  padding-top: 10vh;
  width: 100%;
}
```

Given the default values of **flex-shrink** and **flex-basis**, this is equivalent to the following:

```css
.content-container {
  flex-grow: 1;
  flex-shrink: 1;
  flex-basis: auto;
  padding-top: 10vh;
  width: 100%;
}
```

Thus, using the shorthand notation, we can update the CSS as shown in Listing 11.5.

Listing 11.5: Using the flexbox shorthand for the content container item.

css/main.css

```css
.content-container {
  flex: 1 1 auto;
  padding-top: 10vh;
  width: 100%;
}
```

Now let's refactor the callout CSS from Section 11.2 as well. Recall from Listing 11.4 that the callout copy class is styled as follows:

```css
.callout-copy {
  flex-shrink: 0;
  flex-basis: 45em;
  .
    .
      .
}
```

Taking into account that the **flex-grow** is **0** by default, this is the same as:

```css
.callout-copy {
  flex-grow: 0;
  flex-shrink: 0;
  flex-basis: 45em;
  .
    .
      .
}
```

In the shorthand notation, the callout copy styles then look like this:

```css
.callout-copy {
  flex: 0 0 45em;
  font-size: 0.8rem;
  padding: 0 3vw;
}
```

Finally, we can apply the same ideas to the styles for the callout title (Listing 11.4):

```css
.callout-title {
  flex-grow: 1;
  flex-basis: 0;
  .
    .
      .
}
```

This is the same as:

```css
.callout-title {
  flex-grow: 1;
  flex-shrink: 1;
  flex-basis: 0;
  .
    .
      .
}
```

So the shorthand is:

```css
.callout-title {
  flex: 1 1 0;
  font-size: 5.75vw;
  text-align: right;
  text-transform: uppercase;
}
```

It turns out, though, that there is an even "shorterhand" way to write this, the somewhat cryptic **flex: 1**:

```css
.callout-title {
  flex: 1;
  font-size: 5.75vw;
  text-align: right;
  text-transform: uppercase;
}
```

In other words, writing **flex: 1** sets both **flex-grow** and **flex-shrink** to **1**, while setting **flex-basis** to **0**.

Putting all this refactored CSS together, we end up with the compact flexbox CSS shown in Listing 11.6.

Listing 11.6: Refactoring the home callout CSS to use short(er)hand.
css/main.css

```css
.callout-title {
  flex: 1;
  font-size: 5.75vw;
  text-align: right;
  text-transform: uppercase;
}
.callout-copy {
  flex: 0 0 45em;
  font-size: 0.8rem;
  padding: 0 3vw;
}
.
.
.
```

Because this was a refactoring, we changed the form of the code without changing its function, so after saving and refreshing, your page's appearance should be unchanged.

11.3.3 Exercises

1. Which diagrams in Figure 11.13 apply to the examples from Section 11.1 and Section 11.2?

2. Use the **row-reverse** value for flex direction as shown in Figure 11.13 to change the display order of the items in the **.home-callout**.

3. Now, use flex direction to change the **.home-callout** section to use the **column** value, and then **column-reverse**.

11.4 Three-Column Page Layout

Our final application of flexbox involves creating one of the most common page layouts, something that was also one of the most difficult in the days before flexbox: multicolumn layout. In particular, we'll create a three-column layout where the left and right columns are a fixed width and the center column grows and shrinks as the window size changes.

You still regularly see this type of layout used for things like news stories, where you have a main content section that is flanked by navigation on the left and additional information (or subnavigation) on the right. Our three-column layout is a slight variation on this theme, which we'll end up putting to good use as a photo gallery in *Learn Enough JavaScript to Be Dangerous* (https://www.learnenough.com/javascript).

Let's get started by adding a "gallery" link to our site navigation so that we can more easily get to the page that we created in Section 10.4, as shown in Listing 11.7.

Listing 11.7: Adding a nav link to the gallery page.
_includes/nav-links.html

```
<li><a href="/">Home</a></li>
<li><a href="/gallery">Gallery</a></li>
<li><a href="">Nav 2</a></li>
<li><a href="">Nav 3</a></li>
```

For the gallery layout itself, we'll use **div**s with the structure shown in Listing 11.8. This consists of a flexbox container with classes **gallery col-three** and three columns, each with a common **col** class and a class specialized to the purpose of each column.

Listing 11.8: HTML for the three-column flexbox layout.

gallery/index.html

```
---
layout: default
---

<div class="gallery col-three">
  <div class="col col-nav">
    I'm the nav
  </div>
  <div class="col col-content">
    I'm the 3col page!
  </div>
  <div class="col col-aside">
    I'm over on the right
  </div>
</div>
```

Now we'll once again use the magic of the flexbox to designate the wrapper class **.col-three** as **display: flex** to make it the flex container, and then use the shorthand notation from Section 11.3 to set the properties of the columns. First, we'll set the nav column to shrink but not grow, with a minimum width (**flex-basis**) of **15em**:

```
.col-three .col-nav {
  flex: 0 1 15em;
}
```

Next, we'll arrange for the content to both shrink and grow with changing window width, with as little space as possible:

```
.col-three .col-content {
  flex: 1 1 0;
}
```

Finally, we'll have the aside column (to be used for brief image descriptions) shrink but not grow, with a flex basis of **20em**:

```
.col-three .col-aside {
  flex: 0 1 20em;
}
```

Adding in these styles together with other styles from previous sections gives the column styles shown in Listing 11.9.

Listing 11.9: CSS for the three-column flexbox layout.

css/main.css

```
/* COLUMN STYLES */
.col-three {
  display: flex;
}
.col {
  box-sizing: border-box;
  padding: 2em;
}
.col-three .col ~ .col {
  border-left: 1px solid rgba(0, 0, 0, 0.1);
}
.col-three .col-nav {
  flex: 0 1 15em;
}
.col-three .col-content {
  flex: 1;
}
.col-three .col-aside {
  flex: 0 1 20em;
}
```

Woohoo, columns (Figure 11.15)!

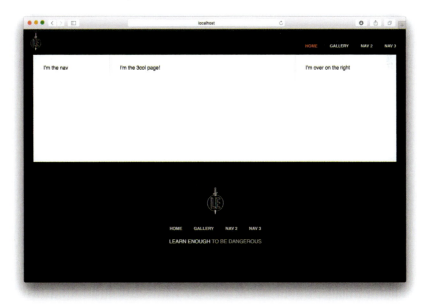

Figure 11.15: Our initial three-column gallery.

Due to the rules in Listing 11.9, if you resize the browser window you'll see that the columns on the left and right stay the same size (**15em** and **20em**, respectively). Because **flex-grow** is **0** for **.col-nav** and **.col-aside**, those columns won't expand to fill the space, and since they both have a width set for the **flex-basis**, each item will be drawn as the basis width. Meanwhile, **.col-content** has **flex-grow** set to **1** and no flex basis, so it will take up as much space as it can.

All the items have their **flex-shrink** set to **1**, which means that they'll shrink in proportion as the window gets smaller, but since the basis is set for **.col-nav** and **.col-aside**, they won't shrink past their basis width (Figure 11.16).

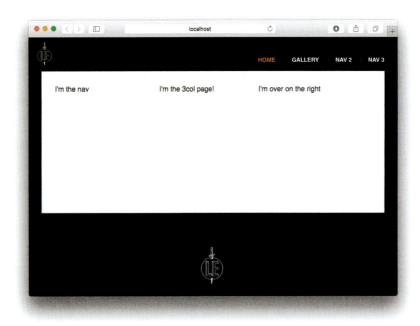

Figure 11.16: The three-column gallery in a window with a much smaller width.

But wait—our layout is currently only the height of the content… Wouldn't it be better if it were the full height of the **.content-container**? Guess how we can fix that? If you guessed more flexbox, give yourself a pat on the back!

Flexbox styles are designed to be nestable, so a flex item can also be a flex container. In this case, to get our gallery to expand in height, we can make `.content-container`—which served as a flex *item* in Section 11.1—into a flex *container* as well, via the rule **display: flex**.

If you are wondering why this won't necessarily mess up everything on other pages, remember that the default values for flex items (**flex-grow: 0**, **flex-shrink: 1**, and **flex-basis: auto**) cause them to act like regular block elements. So having the parent container initialized as a flex container isn't going to do anything weird (unless you want it to be weird… heeeyoh!).

The result appears in Listing 11.10, which also applies the **flex: 1** rule used in Listing 11.6 to all three columns (**.col-three**). Recall from Section 11.3.2 that **flex: 1** is equivalent to a flex grow and shrink of **1**, so that they grow and shrink proportionally with window size, and a flex basis of **0**, so that there is a minimum of extra space.

Listing 11.10: Arranging for the columns to take up the full height of their parent.
css/main.css

```css
.content-container {
  display: flex;
  flex: 1 1 auto;
  padding-top: 10vh;
  width: 100%;
}
.
.
.
/* COLUMN STYLES */

.col-three {
  display: flex;
  flex: 1;
}
```

Saving your work and refreshing will give you an improved, full-screen, three-column layout (Figure 11.17).

Figure 11.17: Fixed gallery now takes up the whole vertical space.

11.4.1 Exercises

1. Try setting all of the columns to have **flex: 1** to make them equal in size.

2. Now try setting the left and right columns to **flex: 0 0 auto** so that they only take up as much space as the content inside requires, but are also limited from growing and shrinking.

11.5 A Gallery Stub

As a final step in developing our three-column layout from Section 11.4, we'll give the gallery page a quick makeover. Adding this content and the necessary styles will both give us a chance to use some of the CSS we've been learning, and prep the page for the future tutorial. (In *Learn Enough JavaScript to Be Dangerous*, we'll make this page into a functional photo gallery.)

   This practice of filling pages with temporary material that will be made functional later is often referred to as *stubbing out content* or *adding dummy content*. In the present case, we'll need some images to stub out the gallery content, which you can get using this **curl** command:

```
$ curl -OL https://cdn.learnenough.com/le-css/gallery.zip
$ unzip gallery.zip -d images/          # unzip into the images directory
$ rm gallery.zip
```

This uses the **unzip** command to unzip the gallery images into the **images** directory (using the **-d** flag, a list of flags can be shown by using **man unzip**).[1] The result should be two new folders, **large** and **small**, each with a single image inside (Figure 11.18).

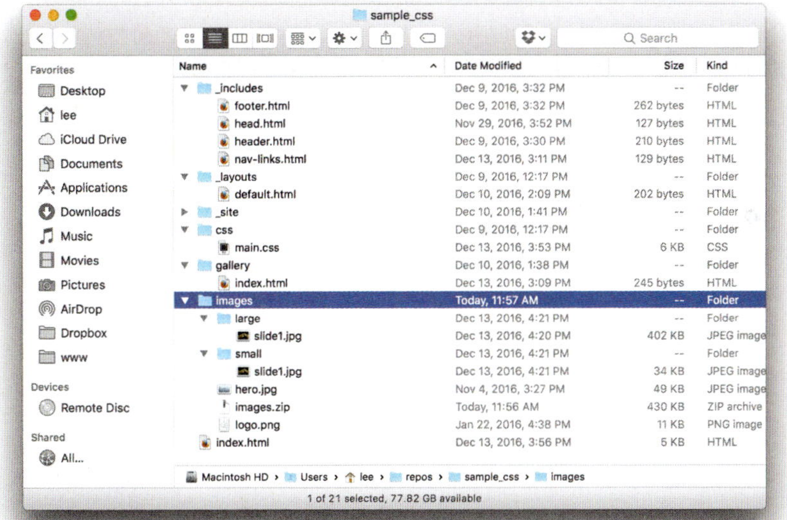

Figure 11.18: The project folders and files at this point.

Next, we're going to add the image elements into the gallery's HTML, as seen in Listing 11.11. Also, while we're adding content, we should add in some new classes on the columns so that we can more easily target gallery-related elements. Finally, we'll add in some CSS ids (Section 6.2) in anticipation of targeting them with JavaScript in *Learn Enough JavaScript to Be Dangerous*.

---

1. The **man** command is covered in Section 1.4 of *Learn Enough Developer Tools to Be Dangerous*.

Listing 11.11: Adding in dummy elements with classes and ids.

gallery/index.html

```
---
layout: default
---

<div class="gallery col-three">
  <div class="col col-nav gallery-thumbs" id="gallery-thumbs">
    <div class="current">
      <img src="/images/small/slide1.jpg" alt="Image title 1">
    </div>
    <div>
      <img src="/images/small/slide1.jpg" alt="Image title 2">
    </div>
  </div>
  <div class="col col-content">
    <div class="gallery-photo" id="gallery-photo">
      <img src="/images/large/slide1.jpg" alt="Image title 1">
    </div>
  </div>
  <div class="col col-aside gallery-info" id="gallery-info">
    <h3>Image Title 1</h3>
    <p>Image description 1</p>
  </div>
</div>
```

If you save the file and look at the page, you'll notice that it doesn't look great (Figure 11.19).

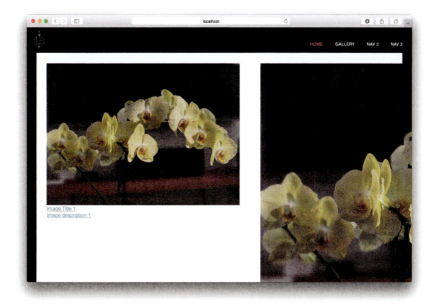

Figure 11.19: This gallery is displaying nothing… except incompetence!

Let's add some CSS to make this page look a little better. You'll have seen most of what we are adding, but there will be a couple of new things, which we'll go over below.

On the left-hand side, you'll remember that we added a **gallery-thumbs** id and class to the **.col-nav**, and in that container we added two **div**s that both have an image in them—though one of them has the class **.current** on it. We'll set an absolute height on that column and then set the **overflow** to **scroll** so that if there are a lot of image links, a user could vertically scroll through them. Then, we'll style the images in the thumbnails to be only the width of the column so that they don't take up too much space.

These thumbnails are eventually going to be the way that users switch between images in the gallery, but for this example we just copied one to show the two states that the thumbnails can be in (currently selected and default). When the **.current** class is present, the image inside has an orange-red border, and the opacity is set to **1** so that it can be clearly seen:

```css
.gallery-thumbs {
  height: 90vh;
  overflow: scroll;
}
.gallery-thumbs > div {
  cursor: pointer;
}
.gallery-thumbs img {
  box-sizing: border-box;
  box-shadow: 0 0 0 5px transparent;
  display: inline-block;
  margin: 0 0 10px;
  opacity: 0.5;
  transition: all 0.5s ease-in-out;
  width: 100%;
}
.gallery-thumbs img:hover {
  opacity: 1;
}
.gallery-thumbs .current img {
  box-shadow: 0 0 0 5px #ed6e2f;
  opacity: 1;
}
```

If you hover over the other thumbnail, you'll see that it animates from partially transparent to opaque. That happens because of the **transition: all 0.5s ease-in-out** style that we added.

```css
transition: all 0.5s ease-in-out;
```

That is a CSS animation style that automatically animates the way an element looks (over a period of 0.5 seconds) if its style changes. The **all** value makes it so the animation will kick in on any style (you can make it apply only to certain properties), the time is self-explanatory, and the last value **ease-in-out** tells the browser what speed it should run the animation. **ease-in-out** makes it run a little slower at the beginning and end, which makes the animation feel a little more natural. (If you want to read more about the transition style, the Mozilla Developer documentation on CSS transitions (https://developer.mozilla.org/en-US/docs/Web/CSS/CSS_Transitions/Using_CSS_transitions) has a thorough look at the property and values.)

In the center, we wrapped the big version of the image in a container with a **gallery-photo** class and id to make it easy to target. We'll use that class to set the width of the image inside to 100% so that it fills the full width of the center column:

```css
.gallery-photo {
  position: relative;
}
.gallery-photo img {
  width: 100%;
}
```

On the right-hand side of the page, we added a **gallery-info** id and class to the **.col-aside**, and we'll use that class to target a couple of text-related styles to make that informational section look a little nicer:

```css
.gallery-info {
  font-size: 0.8rem;
}
.gallery-info h3 {
  margin-bottom: 1em;
}
```

Putting everything together gives us the gallery styles shown in Listing 11.12.

Listing 11.12: Adding in a section of styles for our gallery.
css/main.css

```css
/* GALLERY STYLES */
.gallery-thumbs {
  height: 90vh;
  overflow: scroll;
}
.gallery-thumbs > div {
  cursor: pointer;
}
.gallery-thumbs img {
  box-sizing: border-box;
  box-shadow: 0 0 0 5px transparent;
  display: inline-block;
  margin: 0 0 10px;
  opacity: 0.5;
  transition: all 0.5s ease-in-out;
  width: 100%;
}
.gallery-thumbs img:hover {
```

```
    opacity: 1;
}
.gallery-thumbs .current img {
  box-shadow: 0 0 0 5px #ed6e2f;
  opacity: 1;
}
.gallery-photo {
  position: relative;
}
.gallery-photo img {
  width: 100%;
}
.gallery-info {
  font-size: 0.8rem;
}
.gallery-info h3 {
  margin-bottom: 1em;
}
```

When you save and refresh, you'll see that things are in order now—the gallery looks nice, changes size when you change the browser window, and reacts to your mouse cursor (Figure 11.20).

Figure 11.20: Everything in its right place.

One last little bit of cleanup before we move on: If you navigate away from the gallery and back to the homepage, you'll find that things are… not looking good (Figure 11.21).

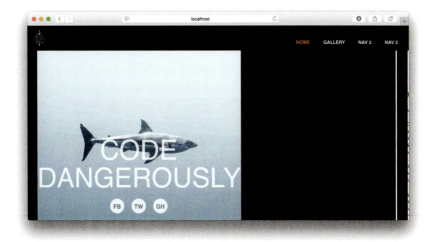

Figure 11.21: Our flexbox in a flexbox content container has caused a layout issue.

The problem is that our `.content-container` that is now a flexbox inside a flexbox is forcing everything on the homepage to try and squish inside the wrapper horizontally. We could fix this by changing the **flex-direction** property on the `.content-container` to have a value of **column**, which would work because it would then build all the child elements vertically. Since there is no flex property set for the child elements on the homepage, they would just display as regular block elements. Unfortunately, then we'd have to lose the nice full-screen gallery layout.

An easier solution, which also happens to just be a good idea in general, is to use a wrapper (yes, another! (Box 10.2)) around the whole page. In this case, we'll use a **div** and give it a class name of **home** (Listing 11.13).

Listing 11.13: Wrapping the homepage in a **div** to contain all children.
index.html

```
---
layout: default
---

<div class="home">
  <div class="full-hero hero-home">
    .
```

```
    .
    .
  </div>

  <div class="home-callout">
    .
    .
    .
  </div>

  <div class="home-section">
    .
    .
    .
  </div>
</div>
```

When you save your changes, the homepage should be back to normal (Figure 11.22).

Figure 11.22: Our homepage has returned to normal.

So why did this work, and why is it a good idea? It worked because the single wrapper that we added ends up as the only flex-eligible element inside the **.content-container**, which means it just takes up all of the space. Inside that, though, no flexing is being applied, so the elements just build as normal block elements and the wrapper expands naturally to contain them.

Adding a wrapper like this is a good idea because wrapping individual pages with a class that pertains to only that page can be helpful in the future when there is something that you want to style only for the content on that one page. It makes the entire homepage a portable, singular whole, instead of a collection of three child elements as it was before. We did the same thing on the gallery page when we wrapped the content in a **div** with a class of **.gallery** (Listing 11.8). Going forward, all of our pages will be wrapped with a single **div** with a class specific to that view.

11.5.1   Exercises

1. To see how the CSS transition timing property works, try changing the **0.5s** to **2s**.

2. The transition property can also be targeted so that it pays attention only to one type of CSS change. In the **.gallery-thumbs img:hover** declaration, add in a style to set the width to 50%. When you hover over the element in the browser, the change in width will animate. Now change the transition property of the **.gallery-thumbs img** declaration to **opacity 0.5s ease-in-out**. When you save and refresh, only the opacity will animate; the width will just make a sudden change.

3. The pointer style controls what a user's cursor looks like—a helpful bit of CSS for giving users hints about what should be clickable and what should not respond. Add a new declaration targeting **.gallery-thumbs .current**, and set a style of **cursor: default**. Now when you roll over the current image, the cursor will not change, suggesting to a user that the element is not clickable.

CHAPTER 12

Adding a Blog

Now that we've polished up our site layout using flexbox (Chapter 11), the time has come to make a second Jekyll layout. This will take place within the context of adding blog capabilities to our sample website, thereby fulfilling the promise made in Section 9.3. Adding a blog to our site will give us a chance to apply many of the CSS rules we've covered so far, including fonts, margins, padding, selectors, and—you guessed it—flexbox.

Figure 12.1: WYSIWYG content management works great for people who are afraid of HTML and CSS.

Jekyll is a "blog-aware" framework, which means that right out of the box it is configured to understand how to read and process content to make blog-like sites. Unlike some other blogging platforms that you might be familiar with (Figure 12.1), with a Jekyll blog there is no content management system where you go and type the content of your post into text boxes on a website. Instead, Jekyll uses individual files written in Markdown (the lightweight markup format referenced in Section 9.2 and first mentioned in *Learn Enough Text Editor to Be Dangerous* (https://www.learnenough.com/text-editor)), previewed and stored in a folder on the local computer, and deployed only when ready.

The result of this design is that you can write your post using the text editor of your choice, you have complete control over the content and style of your blog, and you aren't at the mercy of a third-party platform (which could shut down at any time).[1] Moreover, by putting the project under version control with Git, you also have a complete archive of the site's history. Finally, with GitHub Pages you have both an online backup and free deployment. (We use all of these tools for our own Learn Enough News site (https://news.learnenough.com/), and they are also the technologies behind the personal website (https://www.michaelhartl.com/) of one of your authors. So you can see that static site generators are useful even when you know how to use a full-strength web development framework (https://www.railstutorial.org/).)

To put together a blog with the reasonable minimum set of features, we are going to end up creating two different template views. First, we'll make a blog index page that shows some of the recent posts with a bit of preview content, and which features a sidebar that contains a list of all the recent posts (Section 12.1 and Section 12.2). We'll also adapt the flexbox methods from Section 11.4 to make a two-column layout. Then we'll make a page for individual posts (Section 12.3), which will include the content of the blog post and a small sidebar that could be used for information about the author (or as a place to add social sharing).

12.1 Adding Blog Posts

We'll start by adding a sample blog post file so that our index page has something to display. By convention, Jekyll blog posts are located in a directory called **_posts**, with filenames that identify the approximate date of the post, in the format **YYYY-MM-DD-post-title.md** (year, month, date, title). (We say "approximate" because you can override the exact date in the post's frontmatter, which is especially useful for posts that start as drafts but only get published later on.) The date is used by Jekyll to

---

1. Anyone who's ever been burned by a third-party service shutting down, whether due to business failure or an acquisition, knows how important avoiding unnecessary dependencies can be. I made the mistake of putting the original Rails Tutorial news feed on a service that was acquired and subsequently shut down, and vowed never again to relinquish control of such an important piece of infrastructure. —Michael

automatically organize posts by the filename date, and the title of the post is used to generate the URL.

We can create the required directory and an empty post as follows:

```
$ mkdir _posts
$ touch _posts/2016-11-03-title-of-post.md
```

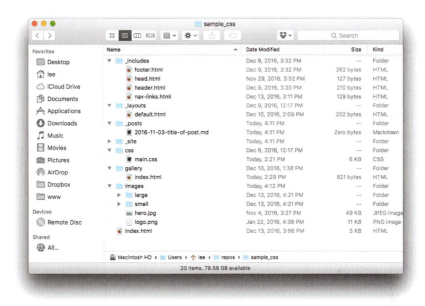

Figure 12.2: The blog index with an initial post.

At this point, your site's structure should look something like Figure 12.2.

The content for the stub post appears in Listing 12.1, which you should copy and paste into the post file.[2] Note that Listing 12.1 includes extensive YAML frontmatter (Section 9.3), together with a mix of Markdown and HTML. (By design, Markdown is a *superset* of HTML, so technically every valid HTML page is also valid Markdown.)

---

2. Recall that the code listings are available at https://github.com/learnenough/learn_enough_html_css_and_layout_code_listings.

Listing 12.1: The first Jekyll blog post on the sample site.
_posts/2016-11-03-title-of-post.md

```
---
layout: post
title: This is the title of the post
postHero: /images/shark.jpg
author: Me, Myself, and I
authorTwitter: https://twitter.com/mhartl
gravatar: https://gravatar.com/avatar/ffda7d145b83c4b118f982401f962ca6?s=150
postFooter: Additional information, and maybe a <a href="#">link or two</a>
---

Call me *Ishmael*. Some years ago-*never mind how long
precisely*-having little or no money in my purse, and nothing
particular to interest me on shore, I thought I would sail about a little
and see the watery part of the world. It is a way I have of driving off
the spleen and regulating the circulation.

<img class="pull-left" src="https://placekitten.com/g/400/200"
    alt="kitten">

Whenever I find myself growing grim about the mouth; whenever it is a damp,
drizzly November in my soul; whenever I find myself involuntarily pausing
before coffin warehouses, and bringing up the rear of every funeral I meet;
and especially whenever my hypos get such an upper hand of me, that it
requires a strong moral principle to prevent me from deliberately stepping
into the street, and methodically knocking people's hats off—then, I
account it high time to get to sea as soon as I can. This is my substitute
for pistol and ball.

With a philosophical flourish Cato throws himself upon
his sword; I quietly take to the ship. There is nothing surprising in this.
If they but knew it, almost all men in their degree, some time or other,
cherish very nearly the same feelings towards the ocean with me.
```

"Hold up a second," you might be saying. "What is **layout: post** doing in that file? I thought we had only the default layout. And what's all that other stuff in the frontmatter?"

It turns out that Jekyll allows layouts to be nested inside layouts, which gives us the ability to customize how we'd like all posts to be shown without needing to make a full top-level layout that includes things like the HTML **head** (Listing 10.1). Then that layout can be built into the base **default** layout, which has all that necessary HTML stuff (yes, more stuff inside stuff (Figure 12.3)).[3]

Figure 12.3: Layouts in layouts, includes in includes… it's just turtles all the way down.

The rest of the content in the frontmatter are *page variables* (Box 12.1), which let us easily create and set values that can add content to the page, change how it looks, or include information (such as author name or user avatar like Gravatar) that might change from post to post. For example, in Section 12.2 we'll be able to link to the post using the title and URL defined in Listing 12.1 using the following Liquid code:

```
<h2><a href="{{ post.url }}">{{ post.title }}</a></h2>
```

This sort of per-page customization is one of many things you can't do with static HTML but which all good static site generators make easy.

Box 12.1: More on Variables

If you are thinking, "Dear Lord, more variables?! I hated algebra," don't worry. You aren't going to have to solve any equations for x. Recall from Box 10.1 that you can think of variables as boxes that you put information into—information you can retrieve by referencing the name of the box. The exact details depend on the system you're using (like Jekyll or a programming language such as Ruby), but ultimately they are just containers for information.

---

3. Image courtesy of Maciej Wlodarczyk/Shutterstock.

In the Jekyll blog post example from Listing 12.1, we are setting *page variables*, which are accessible only on the page that is loading the frontmatter. For example, consider the effect of setting a `title` variable in a page's frontmatter, like this:

```
---
title: This is the title of the post
---
```

That title can later be pulled out and placed on the page using a Liquid tag, as follows:

```
{{ page.title }}
```

This sort of flexibility allows us to define different variables for different pages, so that a single template can look different from one blog post to the next.

It is also possible to set *global variables*, which work on any page on the site. Defining global variables requires creating a new configuration file, which is beyond the scope of this tutorial, but you can read about config files and global variables in the Jekyll documentation (https://jekyllrb.com/docs/).

12.1.1 Blog Index Structure

The blog itself will live in **index.html** inside a folder called **blog**, which will lead to a public URL of the form https://example.com/blog/ for the blog's index page. We can get started as follows:

```
$ mkdir blog
$ touch blog/index.html
```

For the blog index page, we'll start with a hard-coded stub version to get an idea of how it works, and we'll generate it automatically from the actual posts in Section 12.2. The basic design will follow the conventions we've mentioned several times before (e.g., Figure 5.2), with standard headers and footers, a hero image (in this case specific to the blog), a space for the post's headline and content, and an aside box on the right-hand side with additional information (Figure 12.4).

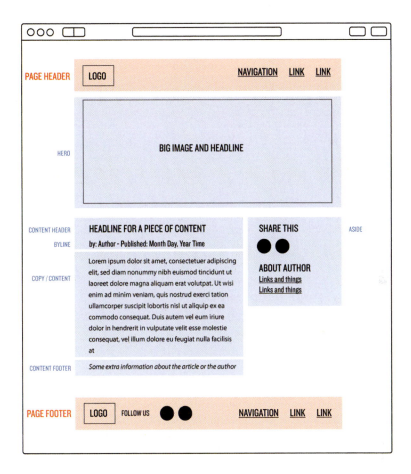

Figure 12.4: A mock-up for a blog post.

This initial stub content appears in Listing 12.2. (A couple of tags are dedented so they will fit in the listing, but you should feel free to indent them to the proper level.) Note that Listing 12.2 uses the default layout defined in Listing 10.1.

Listing 12.2: The basic structure for our blog index page.
blog/index.html

```
---
layout: default
---
```

```html
<div class="page blog-index">
  <h1>Bloggie Blog</h1>
  <div class="col-two blog-cols">
    <div class="col col-aside blog-recent">
      <h4>Recent Posts</h4>
      <ul class="blog-title-list">
        <li>
          <a href="">Blog post title</a>
          <span>Posted: Month Day, Year</span>
        </li>
      </ul>
    </div>
    <div class="col col-content blog-previews">
      <div class="blog-posts">
        <header class="post-header">
          <h2><a href="">I am the title of an article</a></h2>
          <div class="post-byline">
  <img src="https://gravatar.com/avatar/ffda7d145b83c4b118f982401f962ca6?s=150">
            <a href="#" class="social-link">Tw</a>
            by: Me, Myself, and I
            <span> - Month Day, year</span>
          </div>
        </header>
      <div class="posts-image" style="background-image:url('/images/shark.jpg')">
      </div>
        <p>
          Blurb
        </p>
      </div>
    </div>
  </div>
</div>
```

Now that we have the beginning of our blog index page, we'll need to give users a way to navigate there. Open up **_includes/nav-links.html** and change the third link to direct users to the blog (Listing 12.3).

Listing 12.3: If a page has no link... does it exist?
_includes/nav-links.html

```html
<li><a href="/">Home</a></li>
<li><a href="/gallery">Gallery</a></li>
<li><a href="/blog">Blog</a></li>
<li><a href="">Nav 3</a></li>
```

Figure 12.5: Ugly page is ugly.

Perfect! Now we'll be able to get to the blog from the site navigation.

Now let's click through to the blog's index page and see how we're doing. At this point, you probably anticipated that the page wouldn't look nice, and in fact (apart from the handsome Gravatar image) it is ugly, as expected (Figure 12.5).

Let's add some styling to make the blog's index page look a little better. We'll start with a two-column layout modeled on the three-column layout defined in Listing 11.9:

```
.col-two {
  display: flex;
}
.col-two .col-aside {
  flex: 0 0 20em;
  order: 1;
}
.col-two .col-content {
  flex: 1;
}
```

Here we've defined an aside column that won't grow or shrink and has a **20em** flex basis (**flex: 0 0 20em**). The content, meanwhile, has the same **flex: 1** value used for the columns in Listing 11.10. Together, these rules arrange for one big block that will change size as the window changes, and a smaller fixed-size column on the right.

There's also an entirely new flexbox style in the **.col-two .col-aside** declaration: the **order** property. This useful CSS style allows us to arbitrarily control where on a page an element is drawn. You might have noticed in Listing 12.2 that the aside was placed *first* in the HTML—if we didn't style it to behave differently, it would show up either on the top (if we weren't using flexbox) or on the left-hand side of the page. The **order** property accepts a simple number as a value, with the default value being **0**. By setting the value to **1**, we arrange for the browser to build our aside after any elements that are in the same parent and have a lower number.

Why use **order**? We added it here because it is a powerful tool that allows us to reorder elements on a page without needing to actually move the HTML.

In addition to the flexbox rules, there are a lot of other styles that we are going to include. In the global section we will add a styling that will make all **h4**s look the same across the site:

```
h4 {
  color: #999;
  font-weight: bold;
  text-transform: uppercase;
}
```

We'll also include some **max-width** styling to the **.page** class that wraps our column layout:

```
.page {
  margin: 10vh auto 15vh;
  max-width: 980px;
  width: 85vw;
}
```

These styles format the **.page** wrapper to expand to fit the window, but only until it reaches **980px** in width. Why 980px? It's an old convention that was used for site widths to make sure that they would fit into a full-screen browser on a 1024x768px resolution screen (e.g., an iPad).

You can make the page bigger if your content needs the extra space, but there is something to consider if your content is mostly text: People generally find it hard to read text that is stretched too wide on a page, or text that is squished into too narrow of a wrapper. Ideally, you want to keep text to be displayed so that there are about 40 to 70 characters (including spaces) per line, and while 980px is wider than that, if you add in a side menu like we did, then there is enough space for both.

We will also style the headers on the page so that all of the content pages will have identical headers, but by constraining them to apply only inside the **.page** class we'll have the flexibility not to have to restyle anything on the homepage:

```css
.page h1 {
  font-size: 3em;
  margin-bottom: 1em;
  text-align: center;
}
.page h2 {
  margin-bottom: 0.5em;
}
.page h4 {
  margin-bottom: 1em;
}
```

Finally, we have all of the blog index styling, using rules which at this point should start looking familiar. The result is a good exercise in reading CSS, and we especially recommend applying the comment-out trick mentioned in Box 5.1:

```css
.blog-recent {
  text-align: right;
}
.blog-title-list {
  list-style: none;
  padding: 0;
}
.blog-title-list li ~ li {
  margin-top: 1.5em;
}
.blog-title-list span {
  color: #999;
  display: block;
  font-size: 0.8em;
  font-style: italic;
  margin-top: 0.5em;
}
```

```css
.blog-posts ~ .blog-posts {
  border-top: 1px dotted rgba(0, 0, 0, 0.1);
  margin-top: 4em;
  padding-top: 4em;
}
.blog-posts .post-header {
  font-size: 0.8rem;
}
.post-header {
  margin-bottom: 1.5em;
}
.post-header img,
.post-header .social-link {
  margin-right: 0.5em;
}
.post-header img {
  border-radius: 99px;
  display: inline-block;
  height: 2.5em;
  vertical-align: middle;
}
.posts-image {
  background-position: center;
  background-size: cover;
  height: 6em;
  margin-bottom: 1.5em;
}
```

The right-hand navigation has the bullets removed from the **ul**, and a bit of text styling for the **span**s so that the information contained in them, which is just there to provide extra detail for the titles, isn't too visually distracting. We also styled the **.blog-posts** class using the general sibling selector so that multiple **.blog-posts** in a column will have some separation from each other and a faint border. Everything else was just adding margins to separate content from other content, styling the author image to be a little circle, and giving the **.posts-image** some dimensions so you can see the background image.

All together, our new addition to the CSS can be seen in Listing 12.4. If you get stuck, we suggest you add each style one by one to see what they do (Box 5.1). We'll give an overview of some of the styles and their effects in a moment.

Listing 12.4: Styling for a two-column layout using flexbox.

css/main.css

```css
h4 {
  color: #999;
  font-weight: bold;
  text-transform: uppercase;
}

/* COLUMN STYLES */
.
.
.
.col-two {
  display: flex;
}
.col-two .col-aside {
  flex: 0 0 20em;
  order: 1;
}
.col-two .col-content {
  flex: 1;
}

/* PAGE STYLES */
.page {
  margin: 10vh auto 15vh;
  max-width: 980px;
  width: 85vw;
}
.page h1 {
  font-size: 3em;
  margin-bottom: 1em;
  text-align: center;
}
.page h2 {
  margin-bottom: 0.5em;
}
.page h4 {
  margin-bottom: 1em;
}
.
.
.

/* BLOG STYLES */
.blog-recent {
  text-align: right;
}
.blog-title-list {
```

```css
    list-style: none;
    padding: 0;
}
.blog-title-list li ~ li {
    margin-top: 1.5em;
}
.blog-title-list span {
    color: #999;
    display: block;
    font-size: 0.8em;
    font-style: italic;
    margin-top: 0.5em;
}
.blog-posts ~ .blog-posts {
    border-top: 1px dotted rgba(0, 0, 0, 0.1);
    margin-top: 4em;
    padding-top: 4em;
}
.blog-posts .post-header {
    font-size: 0.8rem;
}
.post-header {
    margin-bottom: 1.5em;
}
.post-header img,
.post-header .social-link {
    margin-right: 0.5em;
}
.post-header img {
    border-radius: 99px;
    display: inline-block;
    height: 2.5em;
    vertical-align: middle;
}
.posts-image {
    background-position: center;
    background-size: cover;
    height: 6em;
    margin-bottom: 1.5em;
}
```

At this point, saving and refreshing should give you a blog index page with a slightly more polished appearance (Figure 12.6).

Figure 12.6: A more organized blog index page.

12.1.2 Exercises

1. Something cool happened in the footer of the new blog index page shown in Figure 12.5. What happened, and why? *Hint*: Recall the DRY principle (Box 5.2).

2. Many (probably most) blogs include the ability for readers to leave comments, but because Jekyll is a static site generator with no database, it isn't possible to support comments natively. Luckily, there are ways to add in comments using third-party services. Use your technical sophistication and Google-fu to see if you can find a comment system that you can drop into a static site.

3. Try setting the **order:** property for the **.col-two .col-aside** to **0**. Now change the **flex-direction** to **column**; the aside should be at the top of the page. Now try setting it back to **1** to push it to the bottom.

12.2 Blog Index Content Loop

Now that we have the page set up, let's fix up the index page from Listing 12.2 to generate a list of posts dynamically based on the contents of the **_posts** folder. The key is that Jekyll automatically provides a variable called **site.posts** that contains a list of posts. We can then *loop* through the posts (Figure 12.7[4] and Box 12.2) and generate the HTML corresponding to each one.

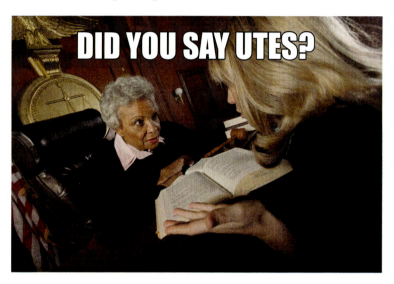

Figure 12.7: Did you say utes? No, *loops*.

Box 12.2: What's a Loop?

When you are dealing with data in a program, you often find yourself in a situation where you want to do an action a number of times until you either run out of source data or some other condition is met.

   For example, suppose you were to deal from a deck of cards until there were no cards left. In this case, dealing cards is the repeating action, and running out

---

4. Image courtesy of sirtravelalot/Shutterstock.

of cards is what stops the operation. If the card-dealing were implemented as a computer program, we might write the loop using pseudocode like this:

```
for card in deck
  deal_card(card)
end
```

The loop would terminate automatically when the deck ran out of cards.

In Jekyll, we are going to use Liquid to loop through our posts, but in later Learn Enough tutorials we'll learn how to use other languages (specifically, JavaScript and Ruby) as well. We'll see that there are slight differences in the details, but in the end they all work basically the same way, so the material here is an excellent foundation for more general-purpose programming later on.

Our first Jekyll loop is going to look like this:

```
{% for post in site.posts %}
  ...Liquid code...
{% endfor %}
```

This is known as a *for loop* (or, in some languages, a *foreach loop*), and what it does is execute the enclosed Liquid code for each element in the site's posts.

Let's break the syntax down in more detail. The **for** loop has a starting tag that indicates the form of the loop—i.e., looping through the posts with **{% for post in site.posts %}**—and ends with the **{% endfor %}**, which causes the loop to stop when we reach the last post. At that point, Jekyll knows that we've reached the end of the loop, and will continue processing normal Markdown or HTML content.

But where does **site.posts** come from? In the introduction to this section, we described Jekyll as "blog-aware," and this is part of what we mean: Because of the existence of the **_posts** directory, Jekyll automatically makes a Liquid variable called **site.posts** available in our pages. Moreover, because of the date convention in the post filenames (Section 12.1), Jekyll even knows how to order them (most-recent first, as required by the conventions of blogging).

Inside the loop, **for post in site.posts** arranges for a variable called **post** to be available for making the corresponding HTML. In this context, **post** is what's known as an *object*, which just means it gives us access to a list of standard post attributes, such as the URL and date, as well as any post attributes defined by the YAML front-matter (e.g., Listing 12.1). The syntax to access object attributes is common to many different so-called "object-oriented" languages: Simply use the name of the object followed by a dot and then the name of the attribute. For example,

```
post.url
```

is the post's URL, and

```
post.authorTwitter
```

is the author's Twitter page (a variable we added via the frontmatter in Listing 12.1). Here's a list of the attributes we'll need in constructing the full blog post:

- **{{ post.url }}**: This looks at the post's filename and builds a URL to the post. If you click one, you'll see that the URL path is something like **http://localhost:4000/2016/11/04/second-post**. Jekyll takes the date part of the filename and turns the year, month, and day into nested folders that can be used on the blog to do things like show all the posts from a specific day, month, or year.

- **{{ post.title }}**, **{{ post.gravatar }}**, **{{post.authorTwitter}}**, **{{ post.postHero }}**: All of these tags look at the site's frontmatter for variables with the same name, and then if there was information added to that variable it will put the variable's content on the page. You can add as many variables as you want.

- **{{ post.date | date: '%B %d, %Y' }}**: The date tag contains the post's date as encoded in the filename (Section 12.1) or in the frontmatter (which allows you to override the value from the filename). The content after the *pipe* character **|** tells Jekyll how we want the date to be formatted before being added to the page. There are a bunch of options for formatting dates and times, and if you'd like to know more you can read about Jekyll date formatting here (https://learn.cloudcannon.com/jekyll/date-formatting/). In our case, the format **'%B %d, %Y'** arranges to display the date in the form **November 03, 2016**.

- **{{ post.excerpt }}**: This final tag tells Jekyll to look at the post content (everything after the frontmatter in the Markdown files) and create an excerpt by pulling out the first paragraph. If you were to leave off the **excerpt** and just add the tag **{{ post }}** then the entire post would be shown on the page.

To insert the value of any attribute, we just apply the same Liquid syntax used to insert the content in Listing 11.2. For example,

```
{{ post.url }}
```

inserts the value of the post's URL at that exact place in the Liquid template (and so on for other attributes). By comparing the stubbed-out version of the index page from Listing 12.2 with the variables listed above, see if you can figure out what the new blog index page should look like.

The HTML/Liquid result appears in Listing 12.5. Note that we've replaced the dummy post in Listing 12.2 with the loop.

Listing 12.5: Building the blog index using a loop.
blog/index.html

```
---
layout: default
---

<div class="page blog-index">
  <h1>Bloggie Blog</h1>
  <div class="col-two blog-cols">
    <div class="col col-aside blog-recent">
      <h4>Recent Posts</h4>
      <ul class="blog-title-list">
        <li>
          <a href="">Blog post title</a>
          <span>Posted: Month Day, Year</span>
        </li>
      </ul>
    </div>
    <div class="col col-content blog-previews">
      {% for post in site.posts %}
        <div class="blog-posts">
          <header class="post-header">
            <h2><a href="{{ post.url }}">{{ post.title }}</a></h2>
            <div class="post-byline">
              <img src="{{ post.gravatar }}" />
              <a href="{{ post.authorTwitter }}" class="social-link">Tw</a>
              by:  post.author
              <span> - {{ post.date | date: '%B %d, %Y' }}</span>
            </div>
          </header>
          <div class="posts-image"
               style="background-image:url({{ post.postHero }})"></div>
          post.excerpt
```

```
        </div>
      {% endfor %}
    </div>
  </div>
</div>
```

Now when you refresh the page, you should see that the stubbed-out content has been replaced by the information specific to the real post.

As you may already have figured out, the index page so far isn't really much of a "loop"—there's only one post, so the loop simply runs once and exits. In other words, we're not yet really using the **for** loop part in Listing 12.5.

To remedy this situation, let's copy the current post to a slightly later date:

```
$ cp _posts/2016-11-03-title-of-post.md _posts/2016-11-04-title-of-second-post.md
```

When you refresh now, you should see that there are two posts instead of only one (Figure 12.8). This means that the **for** loop is working, and as we add new posts they will automatically appear on the blog index page.

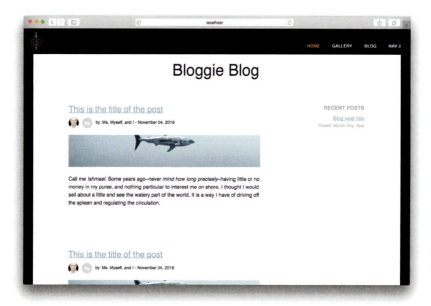

Figure 12.8: Building the blog index dynamically by looping through posts.

Pretty cool, right? You can see how much easier it is with a site generator like Jekyll to build fairly complex sites that don't require a lot of upkeep. Instead of needing to directly edit a bunch of different pages for every blog post, you just drop a properly formatted file into the right folder and everything automagically updates.

As a final touch, let's add another loop that will add the correct links into the menu on the right. Change the **blog/index.html** file to match Listing 12.6.

Listing 12.6: Creating a second "Recent Posts" loop.

blog/index.html

```
---
layout: default
---

<div class="page blog-index">
  <h1>Bloggie Blog</h1>
  <div class="col-two blog-cols">
    <div class="col col-aside blog-recent">
      <h4>Recent Posts</h4>
      <ul class="blog-title-list">
        {% for post in site.posts limit:5 %}
          <li>
            <a href="{{ post.url }}">{{ post.title }}</a>
            <span>Posted:  post.date | date: '%B %d, %Y' </span>
          </li>
        {% endfor %}
      </ul>
    </div>
    <div class="col col-content blog-previews">
      {% for post in site.posts %}
        <div class="blog-posts">
          <header class="post-header">
            <h2><a href="{{ post.url }}">{{ post.title }}</a></h2>
            <div class="post-byline">
              <img src="{{ post.gravatar }}" />
              <a href="{{ post.authorTwitter }}" class="social-link">Tw</a>
              by: {{ post.author }}
              <span> - {{ post.date | date: '%B %d, %Y' }}</span>
            </div>
          </header>
          <div class="posts-image"
               style="background-image:url({{ post.postHero }})"></div>
          {{ post.excerpt }}
        </div>
      {% endfor %}
    </div>
  </div>
</div>
```

Listing 12.6 uses the same ideas as Listing 12.5; the only novelty is the use of `limit:5` to restrict the loop to show only the five most recent posts.

When you save and refresh, you should see the post names and links in the right-hand column (Figure 12.9).

Figure 12.9: Blog index… now with a Recent Posts list!

12.2.1 Exercises

1. Using your new knowledge of Jekyll variables and how they work with loops, add in the author name and avatar to the "Recent Posts" side menu.

2. Edit the second blog post that we created and change up the text that makes up the body copy, the main image, and the author name and avatar (all of which are in the frontmatter).

12.3   A Blog Post Page

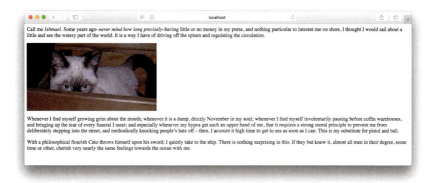

Figure 12.10: The kitten is cute, but the page isn't.

Now that we have a working blog index, we're ready to take a look at individual posts. We can get started by clicking one of the links on the blog index, which takes us to a totally unstyled page with the individual post content. As seen in Figure 12.10, the post page currently doesn't even have basic elements like the site header. Let's fix that.

The problem is that in the blog post frontmatter (Listing 12.1) we told Jekyll that these pages should be built using the **post** layout… which doesn't yet exist. The first step is to create a new file called **post.html** in the **layouts** folder, and then add in the frontmatter and Liquid tag shown in Listing 12.7.

Listing 12.7: The most basic post page possible.
_layouts/post.html

```
---
layout: default
---

{{ content }}
```

As promised in Section 12.1, Listing 12.7 includes a layout (**default**) within a layout (Figure 12.3). This is the simplest that we can make the page, and it still doesn't look right, but at least the rest of the site interface is back.

What do we do next? If you guessed "add a bunch of wrappers and styles," you just won a gold star.[5] Unlike the blog index, in Listing 12.8 we are just going to jump in and add both the HTML structure and all the Liquid tags to correctly pull information from the blog post file and build it onto the page. This is an excellent exercise in reading markup, applying the lessons from both Part I and Part II.

There is one key difference between the post page and the blog index from Listing 12.5; in the case of the index, we had a loop variable called **post** (defined by us via **for post in ...**), whereas in the post itself we use a variable called **page**. This variable is supplied automatically by Liquid. The result, which you should read carefully, appears in Listing 12.8, and a brief explanation follows.

Listing 12.8: Adding in the blog post page structure.
_layouts/post.html

```
---
layout: default
---

<div class="post">
  <div class="half-hero" style="background-image:url({{ page.postHero }})"></div>

  <article class="page">
    <header class="post-header">
      <h1>{{ page.title }}</h1>
      <div class="post-byline">
        <img src="{{ page.gravatar }}">
        <a href="{{ page.authorTwitter }}" class="social-link">Tw</a>
        by: {{ page.author }}
        <span> - {{ page.date | date: '%B %d, %Y' }}</span>
      </div>
    </header>
    <aside class="post-aside">
      <h4>Recent Posts</h4>
      <ul class="blog-title-list">
        {% for post in site.posts limit:5 %}
          <li>
            <a href="{{ post.url }}">{{ post.title }}</a>
            <span>Posted: {{ post.date | date: '%B %d, %Y' }}</span>
          </li>
        {% endfor %}
      </ul>
    </aside>
    <div class="post-content">
      {{ content }}
```

---

5. Gold star is not legal tender, offer not valid in Saskatchewan.

```
    </div>
    <footer class="post-footer">
      {{ page.postFooter }}
    </footer>
  </article>
</div>
```

In Listing 12.8, we've used a new element, the **article** tag, which was created specifically to wrap sections of content that could stand on their own if you were to cut them out of the site and display them separately. So a blog post would be a good place to use **article** (as we have here), but the bios on the homepage wouldn't be (because they're specific to that page).

As shown in Listing 12.8, it's a good practice to use headers and footers inside **article** to contain things like the title and byline, or (in the case of the footer) things like tags, sharing, footnotes, or anything else that would normally go at the bottom.

We've added another new HTML5 element on the page, the **aside** tag. This is supposed to be used for extra content that is related to the contents of an article. In the context of a blog, it could be a list of recent blog posts or related posts, or it could be something like links for social sharing (Twitter, Facebook, etc.).

When you save and refresh your browser, you should now see that the content has been organized and is ready for us to style (Figure 12.11).

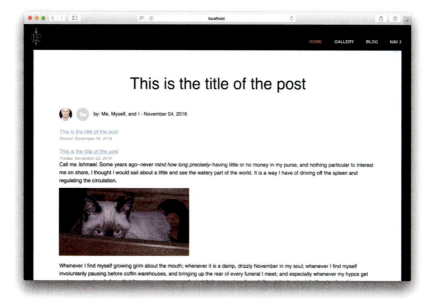

Figure 12.11: Things are looking up.

Now let's add in a bunch of post-specific styling, as shown in Listing 12.9.

Listing 12.9: Formatting the post page with CSS to finish the layout.

`css/main.css`

```css
/* BLOG STYLES*/
.
.
.
.post {
  width: 100%;
}
.post-content,
.post-footer {
  margin: auto;
  max-width: 40em;
  width: 85vw;
}
.pull-left {
  float: left;
  margin: 2em 2em 2em -2%;
}
.pull-right {
  float: right;
  margin: 2em -2% 2em 2em;
}
.post-aside {
  background-color: rgba(0, 0, 0, 0.01);
  float: right;
  margin: 0 0 2em 2em;
  padding: 2em;
}
.post .post-header {
  margin-bottom: 2.5em;
  text-align: center;
}
.post-content {
  font-size: 1.1rem;
}
.post-footer {
  border-top: 1px solid rgba(0, 0, 0, 0.1);
  font-style: italic;
  font-size: 0.8em;
  margin-top: 3em;
  padding-top: 2em;
}
```

In case you are wondering why that `.half-hero` at the top wasn't showing on the post page, it isn't visible because it needs a height, and while we are editing that we will also do some background sizing and positioning, as seen in Listing 12.10.

Listing 12.10: The `.half-hero` on the post page needed dimensions to be seen.
css/main.css

```css
/* HERO STYLES */
.
.
.
.half-hero {
  background-position: center center;
  background-size: cover;
  height: 40vh;
}
```

Flipping between the two pages, you'll see that things are looking pretty organized, and the content is looking good (Figure 12.12). Notice that for the post content we bumped up the font size of the text to `1.1rem`. It is always nice to have slightly larger type for sections of content that are text-heavy for readability—a font size in the range of being equivalent to **16px** to **18px** is a good target.

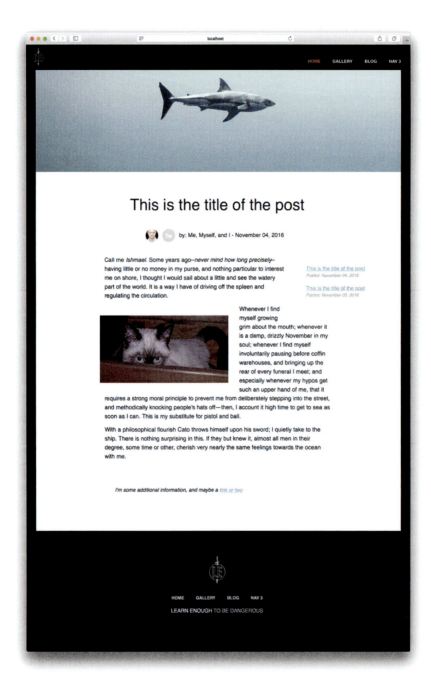

Figure 12.12: Our finished blog post page.

One last little Jekyll Liquid tag trick before we move on: You might at some point want to add a link on the site, or a small description, that can direct users to the most recent blog post. Let's first add a link in the header as the last navigation link. Open up **_includes/nav-links.html** and add in the changes in Listing 12.11.

Listing 12.11: Adding a "newest post" link to the site navigation.
_includes/nav-links.html

```
<li><a href="/">Home</a></li>
<li><a href="/gallery">Gallery</a></li>
<li><a href="/blog">Blog</a></li>
<li><a href="{{ site.posts.first.url }}">Newest Post</a></li>
```

Now you have a link that always goes to the most recent post!

You can use the same formatting to pull over information from the newest post. So if you wanted to put a little preview on the homepage, it would be easy. Open up the homepage **index.html**, and add in a new **.home-section**, like in Listing 12.12, right above the section with the bios.

Listing 12.12: A preview of the newest post on the homepage.
index.html

```
<div class="home-section">
  <h4>Most recent post</h4>
  <div class="blog-posts">
    <header class="post-header">
      <h2>
        <a href="{{ site.posts.first.url }}">
        {{ site.posts.first.title }}</a>
      </h2>
      <div class="post-byline">
        <img src="{{ site.posts.first.gravatar }}">
        <a href="{{ site.posts.first.authorTwitter }}"
        class="social-link">Tw</a>
        by: {{ site.posts.first.author }}
        <span> - {{ site.posts.first.date | date: '%B %d, %Y' }}</span>
      </div>
    </header>
    <div class="posts-image"
    style="background-image:url({{ site.posts.first.postHero }})"></div>
    {{ site.posts.first.excerpt }}
  </div>
</div>
```

```
<div class="home-section">
  <h2>THE FOUNDERS</h2>
    .
    .
    .
```

And then add in a little bit of styling to keep everything tidy (Listing 12.13).

Listing 12.13: Styling the width of the homepage's new post preview.

css/main.css

```css
.home-section h2 {
  margin-bottom: 1.5rem;
  text-align: center;
}
.home-section h4 {
  margin-bottom: 0.5em;
  text-align: center;
}
.home-section .post-header {
  text-align: center;
}
.home-section .blog-posts {
  margin: auto;
  width: 75%;
}
```

After saving and refreshing, you now have a nicely formatted preview that will always show information from and a link to the most recent blog post (Figure 12.13).

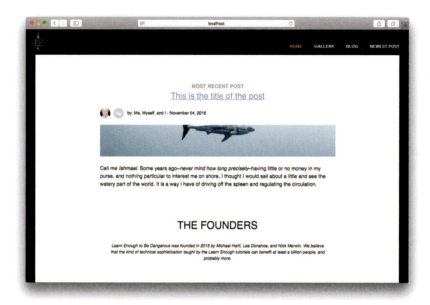

Figure 12.13: Preview of the most recent blog post on the homepage.

12.3.1   Exercises

1. *Sacrebleu!* Is your programmer's itch acting up again? Do you see what we've repeated on both the blog index page and blog detail page? This repetition cannot stand! Refactor the site by moving the recent post list into its own include, and then load that include on both the blog index and detail pages.

2. Try playing around by adding new posts, changing the date, changing the filename to see how Jekyll builds URLs, and changing the frontmatter to have different titles, authors, etc. You now have a super-simple blog! Jekyll has a lot more bells and whistles that can make your blog even fancier, which you can learn about by reading the Jekyll documentation.

CHAPTER 13
Mobile Media Queries

At this point, our site is really coming together. We've got a nicely styled homepage, a proto-gallery with a three-column layout, and the ability to add an arbitrary number of nicely styled blog posts. In this chapter and the next, we'll add a few new levels of polish needed for a professional-grade site. Here we'll start adding the styles necessary to make our site look good on both desktop and mobile devices, a practice known as *responsive design*. Then in Chapter 14 we'll add miscellaneous polish like custom fonts, meta tags, and a favicon.

13.1 Getting Started with Mobile Designs

The reason we need to add new styles for mobile devices is because websites made for big desktop screens that have lots of available space don't look great when shrunk down to be shown on small screens. Conversely, sites designed for small screens—where interactive elements need to be big for UI purposes—look terrible when blown up on a big screen (Figure 13.1).

NOT GREAT FOR EITHER

Figure 13.1: Big on small, small on big = bad for all.

Web designers used to use a little bit of code that would detect what size screen you were using, and then serve two totally different pages depending on your screen size. Unfortunately, doing that sort of thing means that you end up needing to maintain two different sets of code... and that is the worst kind of repeating yourself (Box 5.2).

To avoid this maintenance nightmare, modern development practices use special sections of CSS called *media queries* that can be set to apply only when the screen is a certain size or has a certain attribute. An example of a media query appears in Listing 13.1.

Listing 13.1: Applying different styles if the screen is less than 800px wide.
css/main.css

```css
@media (max-width: 800px) {
  html {
    box-shadow: none;
    padding: 0;
  }
  .post-aside {
    display: none;
  }
}
```

The **@media (max-width: 800px)** part of the CSS in Listing 13.1 is the media query itself, and inside that is just regular CSS. What is happening is that if a screen is **800px** or less (called the *breakpoint*), then the browser will apply the styles that are contained inside (and recall from Table 6.1 that "media type" has a very high priority). There are a number of different media queries that let you style things so that your site looks different when printed or when seen on a mobile device held in portrait vs. landscape orientation (Figure 13.2). We are going to keep things very simple, but if you want to know more, the Mozilla developer page for media queries (https://developer .mozilla.org/en-US/docs/Web/CSS/Media_Queries/Using_media_queries) has a lot more information.

Figure 13.2: Portrait vs. landscape.

After adding the contents of Listing 13.1 to the bottom of **main.css**, you should find that the layout changes when you change the width of your browser window (Figure 13.3). (Note that Figure 13.3 and subsequent screenshots incorporate the result of the newest blog post exercise (Listing 12.11).)

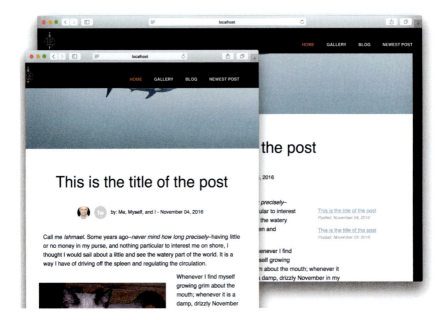

Figure 13.3: A bit of a difference between the bigger window and the narrower one.

The media query we added in Listing 13.1 also gets rid of the padding and black border around the site, and then also changes the **display** property of the **.post-aside** to **none** to hide it. So as you change the browser window's size, you'll see the aside disappear on the narrower screen. When you make the window bigger, it pops back into existence.

When designing content to fit on a small screen, there are often elements of a page that aren't strictly necessary but are nice to have if there is a ton of room, so we can omit them when designing for a smaller screen. In order to make good design decisions, we need to think about what is necessary to clearly communicate our content to users in a usable way, rather than trying to cram every single function of the site into the mobile version… unless of course most users will be seeing the site on mobile first (Box 13.1).

The general idea is that you should set a number of breakpoints, with different styles that get applied to elements at different window sizes, so that the entire page fits better in the window across devices.

Box 13.1: Style Note: Mobile First, or Desktop First?

These days, mobile traffic to sites keeps growing because smartphones are pretty much ubiquitous (sorry if you are still hanging onto that RAZR).

As a result, many front-end developers actually start their styling by looking at how the page will look on mobile first, since that can be the more difficult design constraint—a practice known as *mobile-first development*.

If you think that most of your users are going to be visiting your page while on a mobile device, or if you just don't know, it would be a good idea to consider starting your styling with the browser window shrunk down to approximate a mobile screen. This is especially true for content sites likes blogs or informational sites about real-world businesses—in those cases, lots of people will be visiting your site from a phone, and you should make things easy for them.

However, if you have a product or service that is mostly going to be used by people who are sitting in front of a computer, it might make more sense to start with desktop design first, and then adapt down to mobile. For instance, if you are making a site that helps other developers to do better work while coding (https://www.learnenough.com/), it is pretty unlikely that they are going to be doing their coding work from a phone. In this case, you might as well start with a desktop-first design to take full advantage of the screen real estate.

Like everything else in business, it's important to know your customer…

Part of mobile development is understanding how to build a site in a way that allows you to easily adapt the content for small screens with a minimum of extra styling. The nightmare scenario is one where you have to give every single element a new set of CSS styles—this would make your application incredibly brittle when it comes to handling changes without breaking the site.

We've actually done quite a bit of that in this tutorial without your noticing—there are lots of elements that are set to resize to fill a container, and we just need to sprinkle in some styling to adapt what we've built.

13.1.1 Exercise

1. Add a second break point with a new media query to target windows that are narrower than **600px**, and use it to hide the **.half-hero**.

13.1.2 How to See in Mobile (Without Looking at Your Phone)

Before we get started with the full mobile restyling, we should find a way to make it easy to see our page at the approximate size of a mobile screen. We could resize the window, of course, but Chrome and Safari don't actually let you shrink the window far enough to fully approximate a mobile window. Luckily, both browsers have modes that you can turn on that exactly resize the content area of the browser for precisely this case. Let's see how it works in Safari and then in Chrome.

In Safari, you first need to go to Preferences, and then in the "Advanced" section check the box that says "Show Develop menu in menu bar" (Figure 13.4).

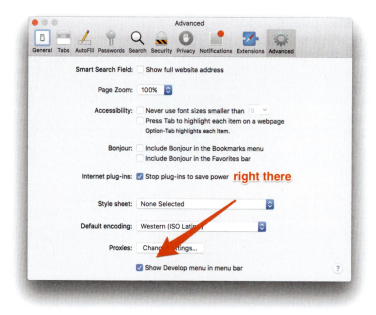

Figure 13.4: Enabling the Safari developer tools.

Once the developer tools are enabled, you should see a new menu option at the top of your screen called "Develop," and in the dropdown menu there will now be an option to "Enter Responsive Design Mode" (Figure 13.5).

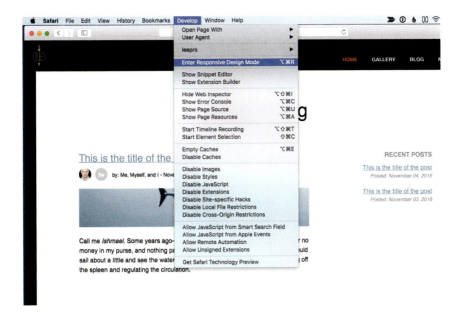

Figure 13.5: Enabling the responsive design mode in Safari.

When you enter that mode, your window will now show the content at a variety of mobile sizes (Figure 13.6).

Figure 13.6: The site viewed in the smaller Safari mobile view.

Now that you have the responsive design mode open, right-click (or two-finger click) anywhere on the page and select "Inspect" to open up the Safari web inspector (Figure 13.7). Web inspectors are handy tools that do a lot of things that aid developers, but most importantly for our purposes they let us see the styling that has been applied to every element on a page. Even better, they let us make test changes and see the

Figure 13.7: The Safari web inspector.

results immediately (so that we don't always have to change the code, save the changes, and then refresh the browser).

Chrome has a similar mode, but you have to take a different path to enabling it. Right-click anywhere on the page to bring up the menu, and then click "Inspect." That will bring up the same sort of web inspector that we just opened in Safari (Figure 13.8).

Figure 13.8: Getting to the Chrome web inspector.

To resize the current page in a mobile view, click the little button near the top level of the inspector, the one that kind of looks like a phone in front of a page (Figure 13.9).

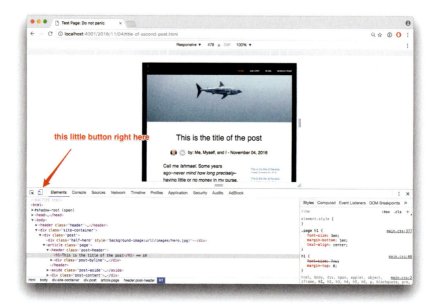

Figure 13.9: The sample site in the Chrome mobile view.

Now that we can see an approximation of the site on our computers, let's jump into reformatting the pages to display better on small screens.

13.2 Mobile Adaptation

So, where to start with our mobile adaptation? It's a good idea to do a first round of navigating around the site using the mobile view browser setting before making any changes. Doing that gives you an overview of the areas that might need attention, and usually will allow you to quickly identify parts of the site that just don't work well on mobile. Here are some of the issues to look for:

- Any element that has a set width should be given a relative width.

- Any page that has columns of content next to each other in a small space should have the content changed so that the sections stack vertically.

- Fonts should be resized for better readability.

- Details that are nice to have on the big screen can be dropped if it doesn't fundamentally affect the way users experience the site.

- Navigation that uses more exotic styling like fixed positioning should be changed to something that moves with the page so that you aren't taking up precious space. (Or, if you want the navigation always to be visible, then it is generally a good idea to make it a bit smaller for mobile.)

Let's take a look at our sample site and make a list of the areas that need to be addressed.

Global

- Header positioning and size
- Navigation layout

Homepage

- Hero title
- Bio boxes need to be vertical

Three-Column Page

- Switch to stacked layout

Blog Index

- Drop sidebar
- Have previews take up the full width

Blog Post

- Check headline font size
- Make images not float

Let's start with the header since, as seen in Figure 13.10, it doesn't quite fit.

Figure 13.10: Not a good look for the header.

In Section 13.4 and Section 13.5, we are going to add dropdown menus to the header, and also make mobile-friendly dropdown menus that open with a click. For now, though, we'll just make everything fit. To do this, we'll add in the styles shown in Listing 13.2. Note that we've added a CSS comment to separate the blog styles from those for the header.

Listing 13.2: Making the header work better for mobile.

css/main.css

```
@media (max-width: 800px) {
  html {
    box-shadow: none;
    padding: 0;
  }

  /* HEADER STYLES */
  .header-nav {
    padding: 2vh 1em 0 0;
  }
  .header-nav > li {
    margin-left: 0.25em;
  }
  .header-nav > li ~ li {
    padding-left: 0.25em;
  }
  .nav-links a {
    font-size: 3.25vw;
  }
  .header-logo {
```

```
    left: auto;
  }

  /* BLOG STYLES */
  .post-aside {
    display: none;
  }
}
```

These numbers are a quick fix that we arrived at by using the code inspector in the browser to play with different values for the properties until we arrived at a decent outcome. The result is that now our site's header fits on the screen (Figure 13.11).

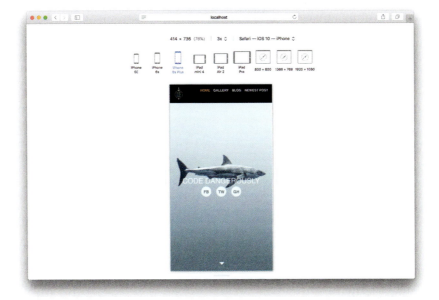

Figure 13.11: Reformatted header to better fit mobile screens.

Overall, that was a fairly simple edit, since all that needed to happen was a little adjustment of margins and padding. Let's now take a look at a couple of sections of the site that are going to need some reorganization in order to be readable on mobile.

Looking at the homepage, the first thing we notice is that the callout section no longer looks nicely laid out, as seen in Figure 13.12.

Figure 13.12: The callout section needs changes to better fit on a small screen.

Scrolling down the homepage to the bio section, we'll see that the layout there also isn't well-adapted to a mobile view (Figure 13.13).

Figure 13.13: There isn't enough room for the floated bios.

The easy fix for these problems is to stack the elements on top of each other and let them take up the full width of the screen, so that both the images and the text can expand and be more readable. To accomplish this, let's add the styling shown in Listing 13.3.

Listing 13.3: Stacking elements on mobile devices.
css/main.css

```
@media (max-width: 800px) {
  .
  .
  .
  /* HOME STYLES */
  .home-callout {
    flex-direction: column;
  }
  .callout-copy {
    flex: 1;
  }
  .bio-box {
```

```
   float: none;
   font-size: 1.3rem;
   width: auto;
 }
 /* BLOG STYLES */
   .
   .
   .
}
```

You can see that after we got rid of the widths and dropped the **float**, all the content stretched to fill the page (Figure 13.14).

Figure 13.14: The stacked bios fit much better.

At this point, you should be getting the hang of this: You look at each page, see where something doesn't fit well, and then alter sizing so that the content better fills the screen—usually removing a width where it was set or making columns out of rows. We also hope you can see now why it is a bad idea to use tables for layouts (Box 11.1)—if we had arranged those bios using tables, there would be no way to stack them in a column.

Now let's swing through the other changes.

On the gallery page from Section 11.5, we are going to restack the elements and make the thumbnails run across the top of the image horizontally. One thing to notice: For the mobile styling, we're not going to target the column layout style classes like **.col** or **.col-three** (Listing 11.8), but rather the gallery-specific classes that we added in Listing 11.8 and Listing 11.12 (**.gallery**, **.gallery-thumbs**, etc.). The reasoning here is that there is a conceivable world where we would want to have a three-column layout with everything horizontal even on mobile, but in the specific case of the gallery we don't want that. So instead of changing the column layout for *all* three-column layouts across the site, we're just going to target the gallery.

We'll first use **flex-direction: column** to switch the layout to be vertical, and also lessen the amount of padding on each **.col**:

```css
.gallery {
  flex-direction: column;
}
.gallery .col {
  padding: 1em;
}
```

Then we'll change the **.gallery-thumbs** to get rid of the height that we set before, and instead give the element a fixed **100vw** width (Section 7.7) so that it will horizontally scroll if there are a lot of thumbnails:

```css
.gallery .gallery-thumbs {
  flex: 1 1 0;
  height: auto;
  white-space: nowrap;
  width: 100vw;
}
```

We'll change the thumbnails to have a set height instead of a set width like they had before, update the margins and padding, and also change the flex properties for both the **.gallery-thumbs** and **.gallery-info** so that they will expand to fill space (while also no longer having a **flex-basis** that forces a set width):

```css
.gallery .gallery-thumbs {
  flex: 1;
  height: auto;
  white-space: nowrap;
```

```
    width: 100vw;
  }
  .gallery-thumbs > div {
    display: inline-block;
  }
  .gallery-thumbs img {
    height: 7vh;
    margin: 0 10px 0 0;
    width: auto;
  }
  .gallery .gallery-info {
    flex: 1;
  }
```

Putting all these changes together gives the updated CSS shown in Listing 13.4.

Listing 13.4: Horizontal gallery thumbnails with a vertical page build.

css/main.css

```
@media (max-width: 800px) {

  .
  .
  .
  /* GALLERY STYLES */
  .gallery {
    flex-direction: column;
  }
  .gallery .col {
    padding: 1em;
  }
  .gallery .gallery-thumbs {
    flex: 1;
    height: auto;
    white-space: nowrap;
    width: 100vw;
  }
  .gallery-thumbs > div {
    display: inline-block;
  }
  .gallery-thumbs img {
    height: 7vh;
    margin: 0 10px 0 0;
    width: auto;
  }
  .gallery .gallery-info {
    flex: 1;
  }
}
```

The end result should look something like Figure 13.15.

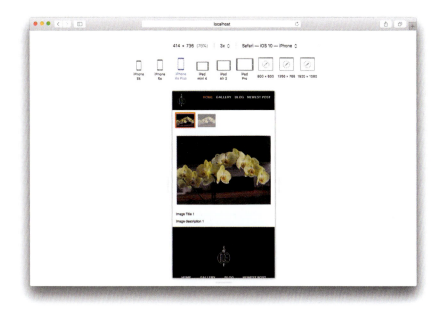

Figure 13.15: A newly redone gallery styled for mobile.

Note from Listing 13.4 that there's a new style on the `.gallery-thumbs` that specifies `white-space: nowrap`. That style forces an element to stay on one line instead of wrapping onto two, which is important for this gallery because we want the thumbnails to be in a long horizontal row. If we hadn't added that property, and if there were a lot of thumbnails, the gallery would look like Figure 13.16.

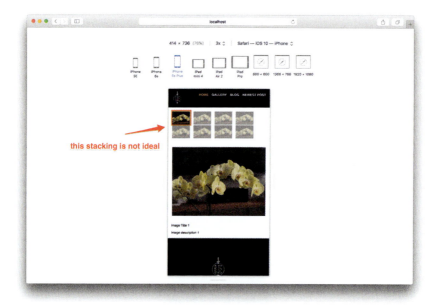

Figure 13.16: Not the thumbnail navigation that we want, and no scrolling.

The blog needs some help too, and unlike the gallery, in this situation we are not going to rearrange the columns on the index, but rather hide the aside instead (Listing 13.5).

Listing 13.5: Simplifying the blog index.

css/main.css

```
@media (max-width: 800px) {
  .
  .
  .
  /* BLOG STYLES */
  .blog-recent {
    display: none;
  }
  .blog-previews {
    padding: 0;
  }
}
```

Simple removal of elements and padding took a view from looking like a mess to one that looks nice (Figure 13.17). Sometimes mobile styling ends up being pretty easy!

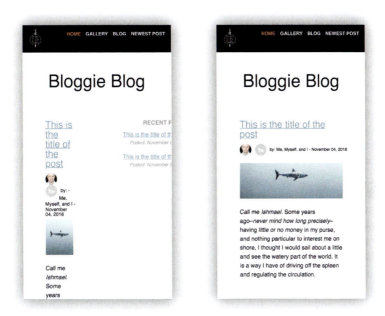

Figure 13.17: Just removing a couple of rules can make a big difference.

13.2.1   Exercise

1. Instead of hiding the recent posts on the blog index page, try using CSS to have them show at the very top of the pages above the post previews.

13.3   Mobile Viewport

The work in Section 13.1 and Section 13.2 was an excellent start, but in fact our site isn't quite yet mobile-ready.

There are several ways to see this. The most convenient in the long run is to install an *iOS simulator*, which lets you view a simulation of an iPhone inside macOS, as seen in Figure 13.18. (If you're on a Mac, you need to install Xcode, start Xcode from the Applications folder, then select Xcode > Open Developer Tool > Simulator.)

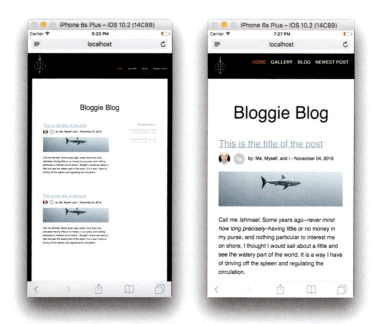

Figure 13.18: How it looks (left), and how you want it to look (right).

We can see the same result without using the iOS simulator by deploying the site to production, as shown in Listing 13.6.

Listing 13.6: Deploying the mobile-ready prototype.

```
$ git add -A
$ git commit -m "Finish mobile prototype"
$ git push
```

After waiting a moment for the site to build, using an ordinary browser (in mobile mode) to visit the production site (Listing 13.7) should show the same problem seen in Figure 13.18.

Listing 13.7: The template for a GitHub Pages URL.

```
https://<username>.github.io/blog
```

(There's a third, more advanced option as well, which is covered in Box 13.2.)

Box 13.2: Viewing a Local Server

One alternative to using the iOS simulator (which works only on macOS) or deploying to production (which is slow and inconvenient) is to view the site directly using the local Internet Protocol (IP) address. This technique involves finding the IP address on the local network and then visiting it with your mobile device.

On many systems, the local IP can be found using the command-line program `ifconfig` ("interface configure") as follows:

```
$ ifconfig | grep 192
```

The `ifconfig` command has been deprecated on many Linux distributions, so if you're using Linux, you might want to use the `ip` command instead:

```
$ ip -4 a | grep 192
```

These examples pipe the output of the given IP command to the `grep` utility covered in *Learn Enough Command Line to Be Dangerous* (https://www.learnenough.com /command-line). The result is to pick out addresses that start with 192, which on most networks identifies local addresses. By typing the resulting IP number into a mobile browser and appending the proper port number (Box 9.1), you can then visit the local Jekyll site.

On some systems, you'll need to quit Jekyll and restart it with a `host` argument to make the site available to other devices on the same local network, as follows:

```
$ bundle _2.3.14_ exec jekyll serve --host 0.0.0.0
```

With this running, you should then be able to use something like

```
http://192.168.1.160:4000
```

to view the site locally (where the exact IP number will depend on your particular system).

Unfortunately, despite our previous efforts, it doesn't look so good—everything looks really small (Figure 13.18).[1] The reason is that, due to a quirk in the way the

---

1. Now you know what is happening when you go to a site that looks really tiny (but not broken) on mobile, where you have to zoom in to read the content.

mobile Web developed, the site loaded as though we are on a desktop, and then zoomed out to fit it all on the smaller screen.

The culprit here is a decision that was made when smartphones were first being developed. People realized that the Web experience was really bad if you tried to show a standard/non-mobile-optimized site at the native resolution of the device, and because there really weren't enough phones with real browsers on the market, there also weren't many mobile-optimized sites. As a result, browser makers decided that mobile browsers could have two modes: (1) do nothing and act like a regular browser with a tiny screen size; or (2) act like a much bigger screen and load any given website as though the user were browsing on a desktop, shrinking things down to fit as necessary.

Because phone developers didn't want to confuse the users with having to make choices about how to view a site, they created a new HTML **meta** property that lets the developer switch between modes. That way, if you've made your site mobile-optimized, you can set the viewport to show the mobile-friendly view. Otherwise, the site will load as though it were being viewed on a desktop. Since we haven't yet set that **meta** tag, the site currently appears as in the left side of Figure 13.18.

To fix the issue, all we need to do is set the tag, which controls what is called the *viewport*. The specific declaration, which should go in **_includes/head.html**, appears as shown in Listing 13.8. (There are a bunch of other options for controlling the mobile viewport that we aren't going to dive into, but rest assured you can find more info about them online.)

Listing 13.8: The viewport **meta** tag to control the appearance on mobile.
_includes/head.html

```
<head>
  <title>Test Page: Don't panic</title>
  <meta charset="utf-8">
  <meta name="viewport" content="width=device-width, initial-scale=1">
  <link rel="stylesheet" href="/css/main.css">
</head>
```

This viewport setting in Listing 13.8 tells the browser that the page should be drawn at the size of the device screen instead of the virtual screen size, while setting the zoom scaling to 1 (which means no scaling). This setting will cause a page to look absolutely terrible if you try to force an unoptimized site to render at such a small size, which is why we've gone to such trouble to make our site responsive.[2]

13.3.1 Exercise

1. Try setting the **width=** to a hard pixel value like **500**, which is equivalent to 500px (the unit is left off in the viewport **meta** tag). Forcing a mobile browser to show your site only at a very specific size can be helpful when trying to develop very precise mobile layouts.

13.4 Dropdown Menu

Another bit of polish we can add to show off the power of CSS is a *dropdown menu*, which is a common design pattern on the Web (Figure 13.19). In particular, when you are designing a site that has a lot of different pages, product categories, etc., you will

Figure 13.19: A fancy dropdown menu (with submenu) on Amazon.com.

---

2. In order to preserve the entire site design and layout regardless of the screen size, some sites don't change the viewport setting at all, and there's nothing wrong with that. There's no right answer for this sort of thing—it all depends on the number of mobile users you get and the kind of content you are showing.

often find yourself in a situation where you just don't have enough room in the site header to link to all the stuff that you need to link to—something especially important on tiny mobile screens. Dropdown menus are a convenient solution to this problem.

You can theoretically get incredibly complicated with menus that use all sorts of JavaScript to do wild things, but you can also build dropdown menus with simple techniques using only HTML and CSS. The concept is simple: You place one HTML element inside another one, set the child to **`display: none`** so that it isn't visible, and then use the **`:hover`** pseudo-class (Section 9.7) to show the hidden element when a user hovers over the menu. Mobile is a little trickier, since there is no hover action, but we'll discuss a solution in Section 13.5.

13.4.1 The Hitbox

To get our dropdown menu working, the first thing that we need to cover is the *hitbox*. If you play video games, you might already be familiar with the term, but if you don't, it is the area on-screen where an action has an effect. In terms of a web page, this usually refers to the area of the screen where links and buttons are active—i.e., areas that will respond when touched. For example, Figure 13.20 uses the inspector tool (Section 13.1.2) to show the hitboxes on the homepage of our sample site.

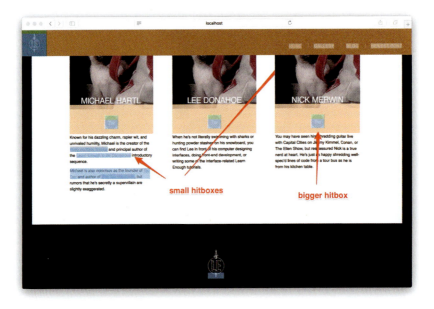

Figure 13.20: The rectangles show where the links are active.

In Figure 13.20, you can see the rectangles around clickable elements where those elements can be activated, and those rectangles grow or shrink depending on the size of the content inside, the dimensions, and the padding. (Margins around an element don't count.)

Why is this important? Well, to make hover rollovers work you need to make sure that the hitboxes of the element that the user rolls over, as well as the dropdown menu itself, are contiguous (with no gap). Otherwise, as soon as the user tries to move the mouse to the menu, the menu will close (something that has probably spawned a million "What is wrong with my menu?" posts on the Internet). The diagram in Figure 13.21 illustrates what you want to avoid.

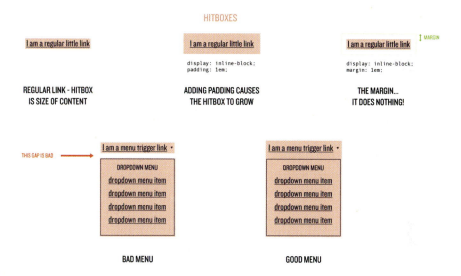

Figure 13.21: Mind the gap.

13.4.2 Making the Dropdown

Now let's get into actually making the dropdown menu. We are first going to edit the HTML in the **_includes/nav-links** file to add in the submenu, along with a **dropdown** class on the **li**. The result appears in Listing 13.9.

Listing 13.9: Adding in the HTML for our dropdown.

_includes/nav-links.html

```
<li><a href="/">Home</a></li>
<li><a href="/gallery">Gallery</a></li>
<li class="dropdown">
  <a class="drop-trigger" href="/blog">Blog</a>
  <ul class="drop-menu">
    <li>Recent Posts</li>
    {% for post in site.posts limit:5 %}
      <li><a href="{{ post.url }}">{{ post.title }}</a></li>
    {% endfor %}
  </ul>
</li>
<li><a href="{{ site.posts.first.url }}">Newest Post</a></li>
```

With the HTML shown in Listing 13.9, we now have an unordered list inside the **li** of another unordered list, which is the reason why way back in Section 8.5 we targeted the styles for the navigation **li**s using the child selector; we didn't want those styles to also apply to any **li**s that are part of a nested **ul**. Also note that we left in the "Blog" link, which means that a user will still be able to click the word "Blog" and go to the blog index (or they can click the links that will show up below).

In some situations, you might want to change the link inside the **.dropdown** container to a non-link element like a **span** so that only the links in the dropdown menu are clickable. Remember in Section 6.4 when we mentioned that you might sometimes want to make a non-link element look like a link? This is why! The reason that we're keeping the "Blog" link in this example is that in the footer we are going to block the dropdown from showing (to keep things simple down at the bottom of the site), and we'll still want the "Blog" link to be functional in that part of the page. In the interest of being complete, though, we should make this work both ways.

We'll start by updating the styling for the navigation as shown in Listing 13.10, so that the link style gets applied to **span**s or whatever else we apply the **.drop-trigger** class to.

Listing 13.10: Making spans look like links.

css/main.css

```
.header-nav a,
.drop-trigger {
```

```
  color: #fff;
}
.nav-links a,
.drop-trigger {
  font-size: 0.8rem;
  font-weight: bold;
  text-decoration: none;
  text-transform: uppercase;
}
```

Let's now add CSS to make this work, including adding in a downward-pointing triangle to act as an indicator to users that this menu item triggers a dropdown menu.

What we'll do (in order of the style added) is set the **.dropdown** to **position: relative** so that the submenu can be positioned below it using **position: absolute**. Then we'll add styles to give the **.drop-trigger** a little bit of padding, and also use the **:after** pseudo-element to add a downward-pointing triangle:

```
.dropdown {
  position: relative;
}
.drop-trigger {
  display: inline-block;
  padding-right: 1.5em;
  position: relative;
}
.drop-trigger:after {
  border: 0.3em solid;
  border-color: #fff transparent transparent;
  content: "";
  height: 0;
  position: absolute;
  right: 0;
  top: 0.3em;
  width: 0;
}
```

After that, we'll style the **.drop-menu** to have a little bit of padding at the top to give it some distance from the **.drop-trigger**, and set the element to **display: none** to hide it:

```
.drop-menu {
  display: none;
  list-style: none;
```

```css
  padding: 1em 0 0;
  position: absolute;
  right: 0;
  z-index: 9;
}
```

Then we'll style the **li**s and the **a**s so that they can be seen:

```css
.drop-menu li {
  background-color: #fff;
}
.drop-menu a {
  color: #333;
  display: block;
}
```

Lastly, we'll add the style rule that displays the menu when a user hovers over an element with the **dropdown** class:

```css
.dropdown:hover .drop-menu {
  display: block;
}
```

Putting everything together gives the CSS shown in Listing 13.11.

Listing 13.11: The dropdown CSS.

css/main.css

```css
/* DROPDOWN STYLES */
.dropdown {
  position: relative;
}
.dropdown:hover .drop-menu {
  display: block;
}
.drop-trigger {
  display: inline-block;
  padding-right: 1.5em;
  position: relative;
}
.drop-trigger:after {
  border: 0.3em solid;
  border-color: #fff transparent transparent;
  content: "";
  height: 0;
```

```
  position: absolute;
  right: 0;
  top: 0.3em;
  width: 0;
}
.drop-menu {
  display: none;
  list-style: none;
  padding: 1em 0 0;
  position: absolute;
  right: 0;
  z-index: 9;
}
.drop-menu li {
  background-color: #fff;
}
.drop-menu a {
  color: #333;
  display: block;
}
```

After you save the CSS and refresh the browser, rolling over the "Blog" trigger in the header should cause the ugly but functional dropdown to appear (Figure 13.22).

Figure 13.22: Our functional dropdown menu showing on hover.

So that works… but it is really unattractive. Let's style it up using the code in Listing 13.12 so that the menu looks presentable. A warning: This is going to be a bit complicated so that we have a nice final product! Applying the result, shown in Listing 13.12, is an excellent exercise in reading CSS.

Listing 13.12: Improving the dropdown styling.

css/main.css

```css
/* DROPDOWN STYLES */
.dropdown {
  position: relative;
}
.dropdown:hover .drop-menu {
  display: block;
}
.dropdown:hover .drop-trigger:after {
  border-color: #ed6e2f transparent transparent;
}
.drop-trigger {
  display: inline-block;
  padding-right: 1.5em;
  position: relative;
}
.drop-trigger:after {
  border: 0.3em solid;
  border-color: #fff transparent transparent;
  content: "";
  height: 0;
  position: absolute;
  right: 0;
  top: 0.3em;
  width: 0;
}
.drop-menu {
  box-shadow: 0 0 10px 0 rgba(0,0,0,0.2);
  display: none;
  list-style: none;
  padding: 1em 0 0;
  position: absolute;
  right: 0;
  z-index: 9;
}
.drop-menu:before {
  border: 0.6em solid;
  border-color: transparent transparent #fff;
  content: "";
  height: 0;
  position: absolute;
  right: 1em;
  top: -0.1em;
```

```css
  width: 0;
}
.drop-menu li {
  background-color: #fff;
}
.drop-menu li ~ li {
  border-top: 1px dotted rgba(0,0,0,0.1);
}
.drop-menu li:first-child {
  border-radius: 5px 5px 0 0;
  color: #999;
  font-size: 0.5em;
  padding: 1em 1em 0.25em;
  text-align: right;
  text-transform: uppercase;
}
.drop-menu li:last-child {
  border-radius: 0 0 5px 5px;
}
.drop-menu a {
  color: #333;
  display: block;
  font-weight: normal;
  padding: 0.5em 2em 0.5em 1em;
  text-align: left;
  text-transform: none;
  white-space: nowrap;
}
.drop-menu a:hover {
  background-color: rgba(0,0,0,0.1);
  color: #333;
}
/* HIDE IN THE FOOTER */
.footer .dropdown:hover .drop-menu,
.footer .drop-trigger:after {
  display: none;
}
.footer .drop-trigger {
  padding-right: 0;
}
```

When you add Listing 13.12 into your CSS file and save the work, you'll now see a nicely styled dropdown menu when you hover over the "Blog" text in the header navigation (Figure 13.23).

From looking at Figure 13.23, it might not seem like the hitboxes of the elements are touching, due to the transparent background of the **.drop-menu** and the padding

Chapter 13: Mobile Media Queries

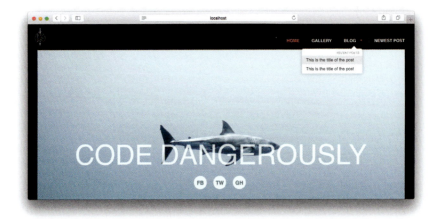

Figure 13.23: Muuuuch better. Our dropdown menu no longer looks like a mistake.

that was added. As noted in Figure 13.21, this would be a problem, but by temporarily adding in a bit of background on Figure 13.24 we can see the **.dropdown** and the **.drop-menu** are actually touching.

Figure 13.24: Our hitboxes are touching, as required.

If you want to see how it works having a non-clickable link as the target, replace the **a** tags with a span, making sure to keep the **drop-trigger** class (Listing 13.13).

Listing 13.13: An alternate version of the dropdown where the target isn't clickable.
`_includes/nav-links.html`

```
<li><a href="/">Home</a></li>
<li><a href="/gallery">Gallery</a></li>
<li class="dropdown">
  <span class="drop-trigger">Blog</span>
  <ul class="drop-menu">
    <li>Recent Posts</li>
    {% for post in site.posts limit:5 %}
      <li><a href="{{ post.url }}">{{ post.title }}</a></li>
    {% endfor %}
  </ul>
</li>
<li><a href="{{ site.posts.first.url }}">Newest Post</a></li>
```

You can use this technique for any type of hidden menu where you need to get the user to click on something in order to show the menu, like the dropdown we just made. (The trigger element can't be a link, since clicking on that would send you to a page specified in the link's **href**.)

13.4.3 Exercise

1. Instead of hiding the dropdown in the footer, see if you can adapt the styling so that the menu appears above the trigger. You'll also need to flip around and reposition the arrows that we created using the **:after** pseudo-element.

13.5 Mobile Dropdown Menu

Now let's adapt the ideas from Section 13.4 to make a mobile version of the dropdown menu. The first thing that we need to do is learn about a couple of new HTML tags, **label** and **input** (in this case, with the attribute **type="checkbox"**).

We haven't used these elements before, but you've seen them practically every time that you've used the Internet. The **input** tag allows a user to input information, such as a text box, a password, or a checkbox. The **label** tag is used to give context to the **input**, e.g., **name** for inputting a name. An example appears in Figure 13.25, which shows labels and inputs on the login page for LearnEnough.com (https://www.learnenough.com/login).

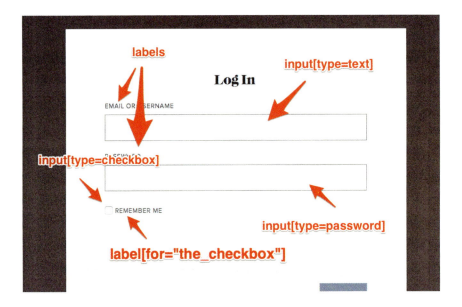

Figure 13.25: Labels and inputs.

The specific features that we are going to take advantage of for our mobile menu are as follows:

- The `:checked` pseudo-class (Box 13.3), which can be used to determine whether an **input type="checkbox"** has been checked or unchecked.

- The ability of a **label** to have a special **for=""**attribute. If the **for** attribute matches the CSS id of a checkbox input, then a user can set the checkbox by clicking on either the input or the text in the label.

Box 13.3: Inputs Pseudo-Classes

HTML *inputs*—elements like text input fields, text areas, checkboxes, buttons, select dropdowns, etc.—all have their own pseudo-classes, which allow developers to style the different states the inputs can have as a user is interacting with them.

We aren't adding any HTML `form` tags to the sample site in this tutorial, but this table gives you an idea of some of the more common pseudo-classes and what they allow you to control:

`:checked`	Targets checkboxes that have been clicked by a user to add a checkmark
`:disabled`	Targets inputs that have been set to `disabled` so that they don't respond to user clicks
`:enabled`	Targets inputs that are not disabled
`:focus`	Targets an input that a user is actively interacting with, like when you are typing text in a text box
`:invalid`	Targets inputs that have entries that are invalid (to draw a user's attention to the element to fix their entry)
`:read-only`	Targets inputs that a user cannot write in, but in which they can click and select text
`:valid`	Targets inputs that have valid data

See the MDN discussion of pseudo-classes (https://developer.mozilla.org/en-US/docs/Web/CSS/Pseudo-classes) for more information.

To make these ideas more concrete, let's try it out on the page in Listing 13.14 *without* setting the **label**'s **for** attribute.

Listing 13.14: Adding a label and a checkbox input.
`_includes/header.html`

```
<header class="header">
  <nav>
    <input type="checkbox" id="mobile-menu" class="mobile-menu-check">
    <label class="show-mobile-menu">Menu</label>
    <ul class="header-nav nav-links">
      {% include nav-links.html %}
    </ul>
  </nav>
  <a href="/" class="header-logo">
    <img src="/images/logo.png" alt="Learn Enough">
  </a>
</header>
```

When you save and refresh your browser, you'll see that there is now the word "MENU" and a checkbox up in the top-left corner. If you click on the checkbox, you'll see that it becomes checked. But if you click on the text, nothing happens (Figure 13.26).

Figure 13.26: The label and checkbox with no `for` attribute on the label.

Now in the label, add in a **for=""** attribute, and give it the CSS id name that we added to the checkbox (Listing 13.15).

Listing 13.15: Setting the `for` attribute on the label.
_includes/header.html

```
<header class="header">
  <nav>
    <input type="checkbox" id="mobile-menu" class="mobile-menu-check">
    <label for="mobile-menu" class="show-mobile-menu">Menu</label>
    <ul class="header-nav nav-links">
      {% include nav-links.html %}
    </ul>
  </nav>
  <a href="/" class="header-logo">
    <img src="/images/logo.png" alt="Learn Enough">
  </a>
</header>
```

Now when you click on *either* the text *or* the checkbox, the check mark gets set or unset.

Let's use our newfound ability to check and uncheck things to control elements on the page. At this point, you should switch to the mobile view in whatever browser you are using (Section 13.1.2).

The first thing that we are going to do is to hide the checkbox and the label for users who are not visiting the site on a mobile device. Add the code in Listing 13.16 below the dropdown section of styles in the CSS file.

Listing 13.16: Hiding the elements that we are going to use on mobile.
css/main.css

```css
@media (max-width: 800px) {
  .
  .
  .
  /* HEADER STYLES */
  .
  .
  .
}
/* MOBILE MENU */
.mobile-menu-check,
.show-mobile-menu {
  display: none;
}
```

Next, we are going to show these elements to users on mobile devices by adding styles in the media query that we added to the CSS file when we made changes to adapt the site to better fit small screens (Section 13.1). We are also going to hide the site header's navigation, and add a style rule to show it when the (now hidden) checkbox is checked.

The styles we added for **.show-mobile-menu** include a **display: block** to undo the **display: none** that we set for non-mobile users. Then we'll add some padding and positioning:

```css
.show-mobile-menu {
  display: block;
  float: right;
  font-weight: bold;
  margin-top: 1.5vh;
  padding: 1.5em;
  position: relative;
  text-transform: uppercase;
}
```

We'll also add some **.header-nav** styles, which might look a little weird. Instead of hiding the navigation with **display: none**, what we'll do is make the maximum height of the element **0**, and then use **overflow: hidden** to hide the contents. Then, to show the navigation, we'll set the **max-height** of the **.header-nav** to a high number when the **.mobile-menu-check** input is checked. This lets the element expand to be as tall as the content inside:

```
.header-nav {
  max-height: 0;
  overflow: hidden;
  padding: 0;
  transition: all 0.5s ease-in-out;
}
.mobile-menu-check:checked ~ .header-nav {
  max-height: 1000px;
}
```

(We'll have more to say about what the sibling selector is doing in this declaration in a moment.)

The full results appear in Listing 13.17.

Listing 13.17: Optimizing the menu for small screens.

css/main.css

```
@media (max-width: 800px) {
  .
    .
    .
  /* HEADER STYLES */
    .
    .
    .
  /* MOBILE MENU */
  .show-mobile-menu {
    display: block;
    float: right;
    font-weight: bold;
    margin-top: 1.5vh;
    padding: 1.5em;
    position: relative;
    text-transform: uppercase;
  }
  .header-nav {
    max-height: 0;
```

```
    overflow: hidden;
    padding: 0;
    transition: all 0.5s ease-in-out;
  }
  .mobile-menu-check:checked ~ .header-nav {
    max-height: 1000px;
  }
}
```

When you refresh your browser, you now see the "MENU" label, and if you click it the site navigation will appear (though it is going to need more styling). Clicking "MENU" again will hide the navigation (Figure 13.27).

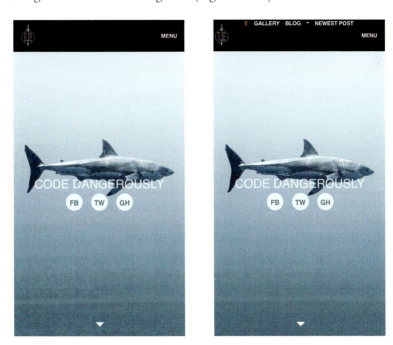

Figure 13.27: The site navigation, hidden and visible when a user clicks "MENU".

The little bit of **max-height** styling trickery that we used, combined with the **transition** style, makes it so that the menu animates onto the page in a way that is a little more interesting than if it just appeared or disappeared.

Let's look a little closer at the functional bit of code that shows and hides the menu:

```
.mobile-menu-check:checked ~ .header-nav
```

What that is doing is applying the styles that are in the declaration to the nearby `.header-nav` (using the general sibling selector from Section 9.7.5) whenever an input with the class `.mobile-menu-check` has been checked in the same parent element. It's a neat trick that takes advantage of the fact that the sibling selector can apply styling to elements that come after the initial target element—so as long as the checkbox is above the menu in the HTML, we can add styles depending on the state of the checkbox.

So now let's make it look better. Add the styles from Listing 13.18 (including the extra class `.show-mobile-menu`) to the media query styles that we added above.

Listing 13.18: Styling the whole mobile navigation.

css/main.css

```css
.nav-links a,
.drop-trigger,
.show-mobile-menu {
  font-size: 0.8rem;
  font-weight: bold;
  text-decoration: none;
  text-transform: uppercase;
}
.
.
.
@media (max-width: 800px) {
  .
  .
  .
  /* MOBILE MENU */
  .show-mobile-menu {
    display: block;
    float: right;
    margin-top: 1.5vh;
    padding: 1.5em;
    position: relative;
  }
  .header-nav {
    background-color: #444;
    box-sizing: border-box;
```

```css
    left: 0;
    max-height: 0;
    overflow: hidden;
    padding: 0;
    position: absolute;
    text-align: center;
    top: 10vh;
    transition: all 0.5s ease-in-out;
    width: 100vw;
    z-index: 9;
}
.header-nav li {
  display: block;
  margin-top: 1em;
}
.header-nav li ~ li {
  border: 0;
  padding: 0;
}
.header-nav li:last-child {
  margin-bottom: 1em;
}
.header-nav li:first-child a {
  color: #fff;
}
/* HIDE DROPDOWN IN THE NAV MENU */
.header-nav .dropdown:hover .drop-menu,
.header-nav .drop-trigger:after {
  display: none;
}
.header-nav .drop-trigger {
  padding-right: 0;
}
.mobile-menu-check:checked ~ .header-nav {
  max-height: 1000px;
}
.mobile-menu-check:checked ~ .show-mobile-menu:after {
  background-color: #000;
  color: #ed6e2f;
  content: "CLOSE";
  left: 0;
  position: absolute;
  text-align: center;
  top: 1.5em;
  width: 100%;
  }
}
```

When you save your work and refresh the browser, you should see a nice menu that animates down from the header, like in Figure 13.28.

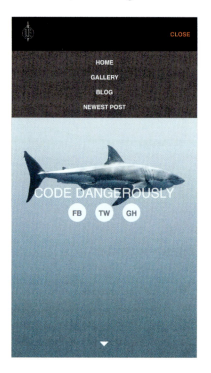

Figure 13.28: The finished site navigation.

A lot of the CSS in Listing 13.18 was just rearranging the menu so that everything builds nicely on the page, with a little dash of hiding the desktop dropdown styling (since it doesn't work on mobile) and setting the first navigational link color to white.

Also, notice that we used the same **:checked** and sibling selector trick to change the text of the button from "MENU" to "CLOSE" using an **:after** pseudo-element. It's the gift that keeps on giving!

Without this CSS trick, you would have to use JavaScript to achieve the same effect.

13.5.1   Exercises

1. Try changing the text in the `:after` psuedo-element from "CLOSE" to just an "X". Overlaying a pseudo-element with text in it is pretty much the only way to change textual content without needing to use JavaScript, and it is very handy for menus.

2. Instead of the `max-height` trick to show and hide the menu, try setting the closed height to `0` and then the open height to `90vh` to take up the entire screen. Using a big menu that fills the mobile browser can be useful for menus with lots of options.

Adding More Little Touches

Guess what? We're almost done with the main sample website!

We've come a long way in this tutorial: We've built a well-architected site in accordance with the DRY principle (Box 5.2), added pages with things like a hero image and a three-column layout, and included a simple blog. What else is there?

Well, if we want our site to look more professional and complete, we need to think about adding all those little details and final touches that really tie a site together, like a nice rug (to paraphrase the movie *The Big Lebowski*). We'll cover the most important of these details in this chapter, including adding custom fonts and vector-based icons (Section 14.1), a *favicon* (Section 14.2), and title and meta-information to our pages so that they are better indexed by search engines (Section 14.3).

Once we've finished making those changes, we'll be nearly done with *Learn Enough HTML, CSS & Layout to Be Dangerous*. Before leaving CSS & Layout, we'll take a moment to explore *grid*, a powerful and relatively new way to make page layouts (Chapter 15). We'll then end the tutorial by applying a final bit of polish and associating our website with a custom domain (Part III).

14.1 Custom Fonts

Back in Section 8.8.2, we talked about changing fonts on the page using generic fonts available on virtually all systems. Now we are going to look at how to load *custom* fonts for our pages so that we aren't limited to the basic fonts our site's users happen to have installed on their computers.

You might already be familiar with what fonts are, but as a refresher: Fonts are files (which come with your computer or which you can load later) that let you control how text looks. Fonts also allow you to make the text as big or as small as you like without loss of quality (as opposed to images, which look terrible if you stretch them out), and they let you change text to any color your heart desires. This is because fonts aren't regular images, but rather are more like math equations (known as *vector images*). If you want them bigger, you just multiply everything by 3 (or whatever); if you want them to be a different color, you just change the color value for the part of the equation that fills in the area of the letter.

In addition to letters, fonts can also include icons, such as the classic Wingdings font (Figure 14.1) available on desktop computers via Microsoft Word.

This idea has been extended to the Web, and modern font families exist for all of the icons we need for the interactive parts of a website. These include things like social media site logos and buttons for the UI. Such *icon fonts* allow us to style the font items by scaling them, changing colors, etc., which is a big improvement over older, less flexible techniques using images.

Figure 14.1: The old-school Wingdings font.

14.1.1   Installing Vector Image Fonts

To use a vector image font on a website, we need to find it on the Web and include it in our site. One of the most popular sources of web fonts is Font Awesome, and it has a giant list of icons that can be used for site interfaces. You can check out the catalog of icons (https://fontawesome.com/icons) on their site; the sample in Figure 14.2 is just a tiny fraction of the icons available.

There are two ways that you can install icon fonts on a website. First, you can download the files, put them in your project, and then link to them in the same manner that you linked the CSS file (Listing 9.7). We'll use this technique for Font Awesome. Second, you can link to the files over the Internet without actually adding them to your project. We'll use this technique in Section 14.1.2 when we install some custom text fonts.

Let's drop the Font Awesome fonts into our site and replace all the social media link text with the appropriate icons. The first step is to head to the download page on the Font Awesome site. Scroll down to the Other Ways to Use section and click the button that says Download, save and extract the zip file (by double-clicking it), and then move it to a new **fonts** directory in your project folder (created using,

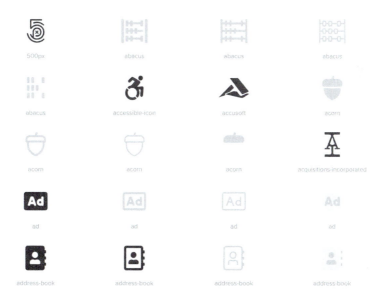

Figure 14.2: Font Awesome has a lot of logos, interface icons, and design elements.

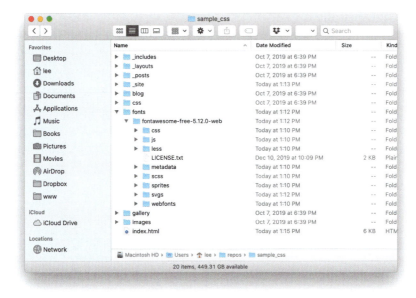

Figure 14.3: Font Awesome files in the project folder.

e.g., `mkdir fonts`). After these steps, your project directory should look something like Figure 14.3.

Next, open up `_includes/head.html` in your text editor and include the fonts file using the same syntax as for `main.css` (Listing 14.1). Note that the version of Font Awesome is included as part of the path, so you may have to use a slightly different path if they released an update since this writing (Box 5.1).

Listing 14.1: Linking the Font Awesome files.
`_includes/head.html`

```
<head>
  <title>Test Page: Don't panic</title>
  <meta charset="utf-8">
  <meta name="viewport" content="width=device-width, initial-scale=1">
  <link rel="stylesheet"
        href="/fonts/fontawesome-free-5.12.0-web/css/all.min.css">
  <link rel="stylesheet" href="/css/main.css">
</head>
```

By the way, it's important to load custom font files *before* any other CSS links. Otherwise, the fonts won't be available when the browser tries to apply our styles.

Now let's add some icons. Open up **index.html** and replace the social links text in the hero with the markup shown in Listing 14.2. Each link contains an **i** tag with two classes: **fab**, for Font Awesome's branding icon subset (on the free version there is also the class: **fas** for their solid shape icons; for more info, see Font Awesome's documentation (https://fontawesome.com/docs/web/add-icons/how-to)), and **fa-<logo name>**, where the logo name varies based on the logo's company (e.g., **fa-facebook** for Facebook's logo). Note that we've also updated the **example.com href**s with links to the real Learn Enough social sites.

Listing 14.2: Replacing the old social link text with our new font icons.
index.html

```
<div class="full-hero hero-home">
  <div class="hero-content">
    <h1>CODE DANGEROUSLY</h1>
    <ul class="social-list">
      <li>
        <a href="https://facebook.com/learnenough" class="social-link">
          <i class="fab fa-facebook"></i>
        </a>
      </li>
      <li>
        <a href="https://twitter.com/learnenough" class="social-link">
          <i class="fab fa-twitter"></i>
        </a>
      </li>
      <li>
        <a href="https://github.com/learnenough" class="social-link">
          <i class="fab fa-github"></i>
        </a>
      </li>
    </ul>
  </div>
</div>
```

Note that Listing 14.2 uses the italic tag **i** even though (as you may recall from Section 1.2) this tag is deprecated. You can actually use **span**s to be more semantically correct if you'd like, but the people over at Font Awesome like using the old **i** tag, so we're going with them.

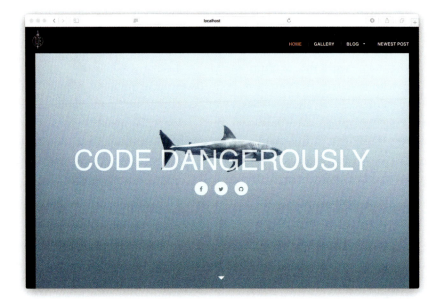

Figure 14.4: The new icons on the page.

After saving the work in Listing 14.2, the homepage should now look like Figure 14.4.

Although it's not important to understand the details, you may be curious to know what kinds of styles Font Awesome includes as part of **all.css** (the human-readable "unminified" version). If you open that file, you'll see style declarations like this at the top:

```
.fa,
.fas,
.far,
.fal,
.fad,
.fab {
  -moz-osx-font-smoothing: grayscale;
  -webkit-font-smoothing: antialiased;
  display: inline-block;
  font-style: normal;
  font-variant: normal;
  text-rendering: auto;
  line-height: 1; }
```

This section in the Font Awesome CSS file is the setup for the initial classes that define all the Font Awesome icons, which prepare an element to serve as an icon by converting the inline **i** tag into an inline block element. It also makes sure to reset styling so that any styles from the site's CSS that might cascade down to this element, like setting the **line-height** to **1**, don't a effect how Font Awesome is going to render the icon.

Toward the very bottom of the file, you will also see CSS like this:

```css
@font-face {
  font-family: 'Font Awesome 5 Brands';
  font-style: normal;
  font-weight: normal;
  font-display: auto;
  src: url("../webfonts/fa-brands-400.eot");
  src: url("../webfonts/fa-brands-400.eot?#iefix") format("embedded-opentype"),
  url("../webfonts/fa-brands-400.woff2") format("woff2"),
  url("../webfonts/fa-brands-400.woff") format("woff"),
  url("../webfonts/fa-brands-400.ttf") format("truetype"),
  url("../webfonts/fa-brands-400.svg#fontawesome") format("svg"); }

.fab {
  font-family: 'Font Awesome 5 Brands'; }
```

Here **@font-face** is what tells the browser the name of the font (which gets referenced below the **@font-face** in the CSS to tie the font to the **fab** class), where to find the files, the weight of the font being loaded, and the default style.

In the middle, between those two code snippets and making up the bulk of the CSS file, there are a lot of more-specific classes (like **.fa-twitter**) that define which icon should be shown by using the **:before** pseudo-element (Section 10.3) and a code (**"\f099"**) that pulls up a specific icon:

```css
.fa-twitter:before {
  content: "\f099"
}
```

These icons are handled by the browser just like text, so we can make them a bit bigger using plain CSS. The result appears in Listing 14.3.

Listing 14.3: Tweaking the social links to work better with the icons.

css/main.css

```css
.social-link {
  background: rgba(150,150,150,0.5);
  border-radius: 99px;
  box-sizing: border-box;
  color: #fff;
  display: inline-block;
  font-family: helvetica, arial, sans;
  font-size: 1.7em;
  font-weight: bold;
  height: 1.5em;
  line-height: 1;
  padding-top: 0.25em;
  text-align: center;
  text-decoration: none;
  vertical-align: middle;
  width: 1.5em;
}
```

When you save and refresh, your icons should look like Figure 14.5.

Figure 14.5: Bigger, more easily readable icons.

A quick little note: I'm sure that some of you have noticed that the icons aren't exactly centered in the circles. That has to do with a combination of how Font Awesome decided to create and implement the icons, and how different browser makers decided to render fonts. If you want a pixel-perfect appearance for your elements, you might need to target specific icons with a styling something like:

```css
text-indent: 1px;
```

Or you might need to change up your future designs to accommodate the varia-tion between browsers... we'll leave that up to your newfound technical sophistication (Box 5.1). If you want to play around with the size or color, or if you want to try out some of the other icons on the Font Awesome site, feel free!

The name of the icon on their site's icon list is also the class name that you would need to use on the HTML element, plus an **fa-** at the beginning. Just remember that you are using the free version of their icon library, so you will be restricted to either the solid icons that need an **fas** on the element in addition to the specific class for the icon, or the brand icons which use the **fab** class. For an example of one of the solid icons, if you wanted to add in the "arrow in a circle pointing right" icon (Figure 14.6), the code on your page would look like this:

```
<i class="fas fa-arrow-circle-right"></i>
```

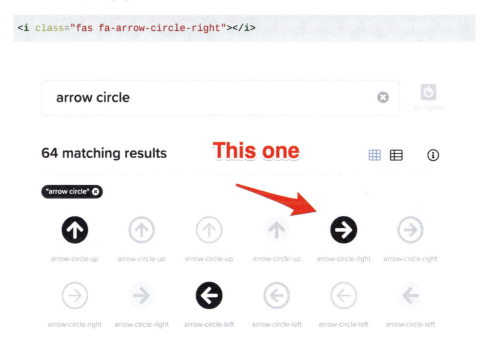

Figure 14.6: Arrow-circle-right.

14.1.2 Loading Text Fonts via a CDN

Now that we've added an icon font from files that are linked locally, let's turn to loading a text font onto the page over the Internet from a third party's servers. There are a couple of reasons why you might want to do this. One, sometimes you aren't allowed to download fonts and store them in your project (e.g., due to copyright restrictions). Two, sometimes you want to minimize your server's file bandwidth by loading fonts via a remote link. Even Font Awesome offers the option to load their icon font via their content delivery network, or CDN (Box 14.1).

Box 14.1: Wherefore Art Thou Useful, CDN?

Content delivery networks are services that solve a specific problem: If you have a file that you need users to download, and your server is the only place they can get that file, then there could be problems if your server is offline or too many people try to get the file all at once.

CDNs are networks of servers that are spread across the world, and when a user requests a file the service finds the nearest server that has the needed file and sends it to the user. That helps keep the traffic on any single server low, so that all your users can get files quickly. There are CDN services that even duplicate the content of entire sites… which is exactly how GitHub Pages works. So if you've followed the standard Learn Enough sequence (https://www.learnenough.com/), you've been using advanced CDN technology ever since you first made a public page in *Learn Enough Git to Be Dangerous* (https://www.learnenough.com/git)!

The downside to using a CDN to load something like fonts is that you have to trust that the remote server is going to be available to all your users all the time— otherwise, the resource that you are trying to load won't be available. This is only rarely a problem, but it's worth understanding that it's one thing (of many) that can go wrong.

For our purposes, we are going to use the free Google Fonts CDN service to add a fancier *display font*, which is a design term that means it isn't intended for entire pages of text. We'll use a font called Raleway for headers, and then use a plainer general text font called Open Sans for the site content.

To get started, head over to the Google Fonts site (https://fonts.google.com/) and type "raleway" in the search box. Then click on the main font result—depending on the current Google interface it should be a box with rounded corners—and when the detail page opens, select "Thin 100" (Figure 14.7).

Next, follow the same steps to add the Regular 400 version of Open Sans (not the condensed version, just the plain one). There should be a sidebar open that has the details for how to embed the font link—if you don't see it you can click the icon at the top right that has three blue squares and a plus sign.

Figure 14.7: Selecting the Raleway font.

Copy the HTML link in the gray box, which should look like the code in List-ing 14.4. (Note that Listing 14.4 splits the line in order to fit in the code listing here, but it should be only one line in your source.)

Listing 14.4: The Google Fonts link HTML.

```
<link href="https://fonts.googleapis.com/css2?family=Open+Sans&
family=Raleway:wght@100&display=swap" rel="stylesheet">
```

This is the code needed to load the files from the Google Fonts CDN. It should be placed in the site's **head** tag just above the Font Awesome link, as shown in Listing 14.5.

Listing 14.5: Adding in the CDN link to the Google Fonts service.
_includes/head.html

```
<head>
  <title>Test Page: Don't panic</title>
  <meta charset="utf-8">
  <meta name="viewport" content="width=device-width, initial-scale=1">
  <link href="https://fonts.googleapis.com/css2?family=Open+Sans&
  =family=Raleway:wght@100&display=swap" rel=="stylesheet">
  <link rel="stylesheet"
        href="/fonts/font-awesome-4.7.0/css/font-awesome.min.css">
  <link rel="stylesheet" href="/css/main.css">
</head>
```

That single link is all you need to make the custom fonts work! No dealing with files or configuring anything.

Now that our site is loading these font files, let's use them. In your text editor, switch back over to the `main.css` file, and change the font stack for the headers on the site to use Raleway and for the body text to use Open Sans, as shown in Listing 14.6.

Listing 14.6: Adding a new font stack that references the custom fonts.

css/main.css

```css
body {
  display: flex;
  flex-direction: column;
  font-family: 'Open Sans', helvetica, arial, sans;
  min-height: 100vh;
}
.
.
.
h1,h2,h3,h4,h5,h6 {
  font-family: 'Raleway', helvetica, sans;
  font-weight: 100;
}
```

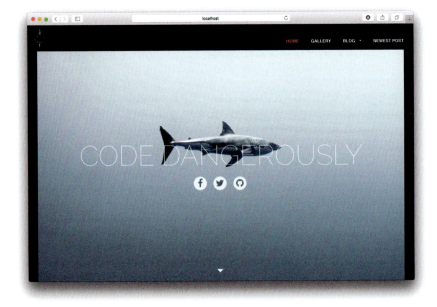

Figure 14.8: Our much more stylish hero text.

Notice that the names of the custom fonts in Listing 14.6 are in quotes. You don't *technically* need to wrap font names in quotes (single or double), but it's recommend by the CSS spec, and it also makes them stand out when looking through CSS styles.

Now when you save your work and refresh the page, the text in the hero should look a whole lot different (Figure 14.8).

The other headers and body copy on the page will have the new fonts too (Figure 14.9)!

Figure 14.9: Other headers and body copy with the custom fonts.

After you set up a site to use custom fonts, it is usually a good idea to click around to all the different pages and see if anything looks weird. Different fonts can have very different default sizes, the weights of fonts might not look good at different sizes, and the custom fonts might use a completely different line height than what was being used before. Your fonts can easily look messy and in need of tweaking.

So that's custom fonts! They're easy to set up, and there are a ton of different font services out there, both free and paid. No matter what the service is, you now know how to use custom fonts, whether they're downloaded into your project and served locally or loaded over the Internet via a CDN.

14.1.3 Exercises

1. Now that you've seen how to add icons, make sure that all of the social links across your site are using an icon. (Unlike most other exercises, you should keep these changes.)

2. Try loading up another font from Google Fonts, and then set the **`.bio-box h3`**s to use the new font.

14.2 Favicons

One little detail that we can't resist including in this tutorial is showing how to add the *favicon* ("fave icon"), a small image identifying the site which shows up on tabs or in the favorites list (Figure 14.10). As with font declarations, favicons get included in the **head** section of the page.

Figure 14.10: A page's favicon.

Favicons used to be a real pain to make due to Microsoft's old browsers only accepting a funky filetype called **`.ico`**, but nowadays all we need is a simple **`.png`** (for Portable Network Graphics, pronounced "ping").[1]

Favicon images should be square, with a side length that is an integer multiple of 8. (The size on most browsers is 16px x 16px, so making sure it cleanly can be resized down is important, but don't go bigger than 144px or so). To see how it works on our site, we've prepared a Learn Enough–themed favicon, which you can download as follows:

```
$ curl -OL https://cdn.learnenough.com/le-css/favicon.png
```

---

1. In classic hacker style, the original full name for PNG was actually PING, a recursive acronym for "PING is not GIF."

(If you want to use a custom favicon, just replace the result of the **curl** command with an image with valid dimensions and with the name **favicon.png** in the root directory of the project.) Now include it in the **head** using the **link** tag, as shown in Listing 14.7.

Listing 14.7: Adding the link for the favicon.
_includes/head.html

```html
<head>
  <title>Test Page: Don't panic</title>
  <link href="/favicon.png" rel="icon">
  <meta charset="utf-8">
  <meta name="viewport" content="width=device-width, initial-scale=1">
  <link href="https://fonts.googleapis.com/css2?family=Open+Sans&
  family=Raleway:wght@100&display=swap" rel="stylesheet">
  <link rel="stylesheet"
        href="/fonts/font-awesome-4.7.0/css/font-awesome.min.css">
  <link rel="stylesheet" href="/css/main.css">
</head>
```

After you save your work, you might be disappointed to find that when you refresh your browser you can't see the icon, but don't worry—it's there. The inability to notice a new favicon is an annoyance that still hasn't been fixed in modern browsers—unless you completely clear the browser cache, they don't refresh the favicon of visited sites for a long time. You can clear the cache, of course, but it's often inconvenient to lose all that history, and we suggest using a browser (e.g., Firefox or Brave) that you haven't yet used to visit the sample site. Either way, the favicon should appear as in Figure 14.11.

There are other types of icons that you can add, one of which is the "Apple touch icon." This icon is what you see if you save a web page as a favorite in Safari, or to the menu of apps on iOS. (It also works on Android.) To make one, you'll need a square

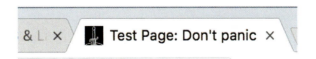

Figure 14.11: Trust us, it works…

image that is at least 180px x 180px and saved as **apple-touch-icon.png** in the root of your site. Then link it in the **head** of your site, like this:

```
<link rel="apple-touch-icon" href="/apple-touch-icon.png">
```

Adding an Apple touch icon to the sample site is left as an exercise (Section 14.2.1).

14.2.1 Exercise

1. Find a square image on the Internet, save it as **apple-touch-icon.png** in your root folder, and then link the image file.

14.3 Custom Title and Meta Description

As a final touch, we'll add two per-page customizations that most users won't notice, but which are useful for any computer programs that interact with our site—especially the *web spiders* used by search engines to crawl the Web (Figure 14.12). The resulting custom **title** tag and **meta** description are especially important for search engine optimization, or SEO (Box 14.2).

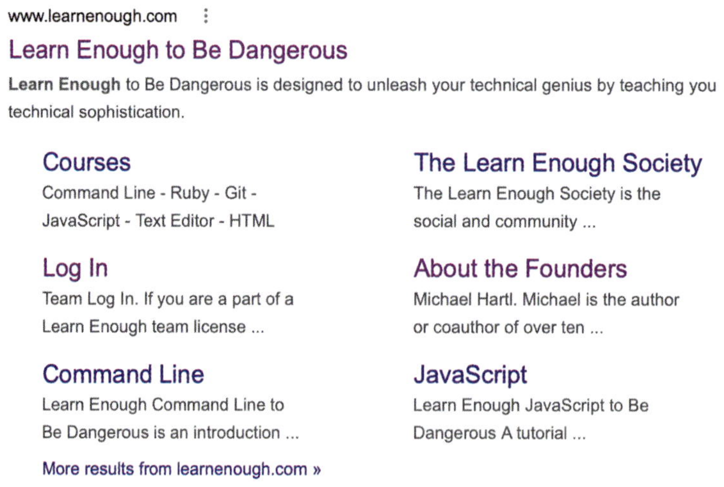

Figure 14.12: Page title and description in search results.

Box 14.2: SEO in One Box

Although sometimes considered to be a complicated subject, the basics of search engine optimization, or *SEO*, are quite simple—(almost) simple enough to fit in a single tweet:

Because of Twitter's (at the time) 140-character limit, I couldn't *literally* fit all of SEO into a single tweet, but it's only a slight exaggeration, and you can fit nearly all of it into one aside box. In particular, in line with the Pareto principle (also known as the 80/20 Rule), you can get most of the benefits of SEO with a tiny fraction of the effort.

Step 2 from the tweet—making something people want to link to—is up to you: undeniably a challenge, and beyond the scope of this tutorial. But Step 1 is easy: Just make sure to include most or all of the words you want to target for search results in the `title` tag (Section 14.3.1), `meta` tags (Section 14.3.2), and headings (especially `h1` and `h2`).

For example, suppose you wanted to target the terms "pi is wrong", "tau day", "the tau manifesto", and "michael hartl". A good title might look like this:

```
<title>Tau Day | No, really, pi is wrong:
The Tau Manifesto by Michael Hartl</title>
```

An `h1` with "No, really, pi is wrong: The Tau Manifesto" and a `meta` description starting with "The Tau Manifesto is dedicated to one of the most important numbers in mathematics…" would complete the basic SEO requirements.

If you have the luxury of tailoring your domain name to the keywords you're targeting, an exact domain match can also help a lot. This step isn't always possible, but when it is it can work exceptionally well, as it did with, e.g., the Rails Tutorial (https://www.google.com/search?q=rails+tutorial). And even if you don't have an exact domain match, you can still get a lot of value out of "pretty URLs" (Section 10.4) that include the keywords you're targeting, such as learnenough.com/css-and-layout (https://www.google.com/search?q=css+and+layout+tutorial).

Note that everything above, though tailored a bit to search engines, is completely honest: There's nothing here that's not related to our site's mission, and keywords aren't repeated to excess. This philosophy applies even more to the main content of the page—if you're actually writing about the subject whose keywords you're targeting, the right word usage will emerge organically, so don't worry about the details of your page copy. Indeed, search engines typically punish attempts to artificially manipulate the results, so any such efforts are likely to backfire.

Finally, when it comes to getting inbound links, quality content is king. Attempts to game search engines (with reciprocal link exchanges, link farms, etc.) are punished even more severely than attempts to manipulate the page copy, so don't even try it.

SEO isn't exactly rocket science. Using only the techniques in this box, we've made sites with highly ranked search results for the English words "softcover" and "coveralls", the phrase "learn enough", the competitive search term "rails tutorial", the phrase "pi is wrong", and even a letter in the Greek alphabet. Good luck!

14.3.1 Custom Title

So far in this tutorial we've left the page title alone and kept it the same for all pages, but Jekyll gives us a way to customize it on a per-page basis. This is useful for things like blog posts, whose subjects might well be the target of searches on keywords included in the title (Box 14.2).

The idea is to include a custom page title if there is one (along with the string **| Test Page**, indicating it's still a page on the test site). If there isn't such a custom title, we'll simply use the original default title defined in Listing 5.4 (**Test Page: Don't Panic**).

The way we're going to do this is with some Liquid code that uses a *conditional*, which executes one or another branch of code, depending on whether a given condition is satisfied. It looks like this:

```
{% if page.title %}
  <title>{{ page.title }} | Test Page</title>
{% else %}
  <title>Test Page: Don't Panic</title>
{% endif %}
```

This code looks for the presence of the **page.title** variable first seen in Listing 12.8. If it exists, the condition is **true**, and the first branch will be executed, which inserts the page title followed by **| Test Page**:

```
<title>{{ page.title }} | Test Page</title>
```

For example, Listing 12.1 sets the title of a blog post to "This is the title of the post", so the inserted title would look like this:

```
<title>This is the title of the post | Test Page</title>
```

If **page.title** hasn't been set, the condition is **false**, and the second branch will be executed, thereby inserting the default title:

```
<title>Test Page: Don't Panic</title>
```

Putting the conditional into the **head** section of the site gives the code shown in Listing 14.8.

Listing 14.8: Including a custom title (if present).
_includes/head.html

```
<head>
  {% if page.title %}
    <title>{{ page.title }} | Test Page</title>
  {% else %}
    <title>Test Page: Don't Panic</title>
  {% endif %}
  <link href="/favicon.png" rel="icon">
  <meta charset="utf-8">
  <meta name="viewport" content="width=device-width, initial-scale=1">
  <link href="https://fonts.googleapis.com/css?family=Open+Sans|Raleway:100"
  rel="stylesheet">
  <link rel="stylesheet"
        href="/fonts/font-awesome-4.7.0/css/font-awesome.min.css">
  <link rel="stylesheet" href="/css/main.css">
</head>
```

Once you save Listing 14.8, you should see that the homepage title stays the same old "Test Page: Don't Panic", but if you go to the most recent blog post, the title of

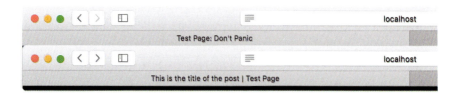

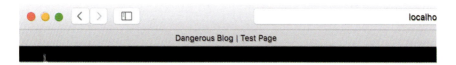

Figure 14.13: A page with a set title, and one without.

Figure 14.14: Adding a custom page title.

the blog post will be the first part of the title (Figure 14.13). As noted above, this is because of the custom **title** defined in the frontmatter of Listing 12.1.

On any page where we want a custom title, we can now easily add one just by adding a line to the frontmatter. For example, to use "Dangerous Blog" as the name of our blog, we can add a line to the frontmatter of the blog's index page, as shown in Listing 14.9.

Listing 14.9: Adding a variable to the frontmatter of a page to change the title.
`blog/index.html`

```
---
layout: default
title: Dangerous Blog
---
```

Save the work, refresh the browser, and success (Figure 14.14)!

14.3.2 Custom Descriptions

Now we'll use the same conditional technique to include a custom description in our site's head. We'll use the **meta** tag, which so far we've used for defining the character set (Listing 5.4) and the viewport (Listing 13.8). For this third application, the bit of meta-information added will be a textual description of our site. This change will not be visible to regular users, but it will appear in the page's source, and as noted above is used by automatic programs like web spiders.

We'll use the same basic technique used for the **title** tag: If a page description is present, we'll include a **meta** tag with content equal to that description, otherwise (**else**) we'll include a default description. The result appears in Listing 14.10.

Listing 14.10: Adding a custom description.
*includes/head.html*

```
<head>
  {% if page.title %}
    <title>{{ page.title }} | Test Page</title>
  {% else %}
    <title>Test Page: Don't Panic</title>
  {% endif %}
  {% if page.description %}
    <meta name="description" content="{{ page.description }}">
  {% else %}
    <meta name="description" content="This is a dangerous site.">
  {% endif %}
  <link href="/favicon.png" rel="icon">
  <meta charset="utf-8">
  <meta name="viewport" content="width=device-width, initial-scale=1">
  <link href="https://fonts.googleapis.com/css?family=Open+Sans|Raleway:100"
  rel="stylesheet">
  <link rel="stylesheet"
        href="/fonts/font-awesome-4.7.0/css/font-awesome.min.css">
  <link rel="stylesheet" href="/css/main.css">
</head>
```

At this point, we can add a description variable to any page's frontmatter and the description will be loaded for that page only. For example, to make the blog's description more expressive, all we need is an extra line in the frontmatter, as shown in Listing 14.11.

Listing 14.11: Adding a variable to the frontmatter of a page to change the title.
blog/index.html

```
---
layout: default
title: Dangerous Blog
description: A dangerous site deserves a dangerous blog.
---
```

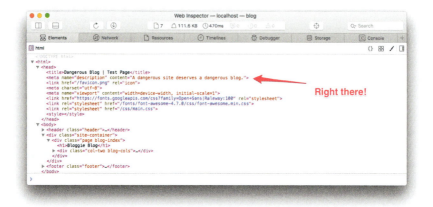

Figure 14.15: Adding a custom, page-specific `meta` description.

Because the **meta** tag isn't visible on the site, you won't notice any change even after saving and refreshing, but if you view the page's source code you'll see the custom description in the **head** section of the site (Figure 14.15).

Changing the title and the **meta** description are just a couple of the informational elements that you can set for a site, but since they show up in search results they are definitely two of the most common ones. The Open Graph protocol (https://ogp.me/) includes a more complete list of common **meta** elements.

In general, all of these meta-information tags work pretty much the same way, and you'll want to set up a default version for any page that doesn't need to have anything custom, using frontmatter variables to define the content on specific pages. Just make sure that the variable names used in the Liquid tags (e.g., **page.description**) match the ones in the frontmatter (e.g., **description:**) and you're golden—you'll have learned how to fish rather than having a fish be given to you (Figure 14.16).[2]

---

2. Image retrieved from https://www.sketchport.com/drawing/6000777126477824/teach-a-boy-to-fish on 2017-05-31. Copyright © 2014 by Kanani and used unaltered under the terms of the Creative Commons Attribution 4.0 International license.

Figure 14.16: Learning how to fish.

14.3.3 Exercise

1. Add in title and description Open Graph meta tags onto your site, and have them use the same title and description variables as the old-school meta tags that we added in this section.

14.4 Next Steps

At this point, we're done with the main sample application. The only things left to cover are *CSS grid* and *custom domains*. You'll find a mostly self-contained introduction to grid in Chapter 15, which is suitable for reading now or for consulting as a reference later. Registering and configuring a custom domain is then the subject of Part III.

Now that the main sample site is finished, let's deploy it again to production:

```
$ git add -A
$ git commit -m "Finish the sample site"
$ git push
```

Pretty nice (Figure 14.17)!

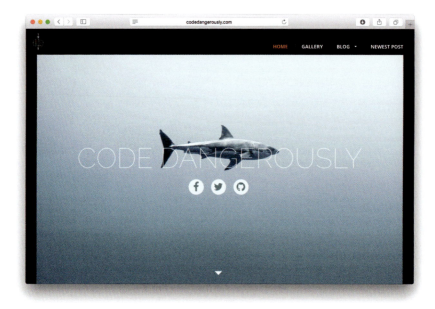

Figure 14.17: The final sample website.

CHAPTER 15
CSS Grid

So far in this tutorial, we've looked at creating page layouts using traditional CSS techniques and the newer flexbox method (Chapter 11). As mentioned in Section 5.2, though, CSS is constantly evolving and adding more features (Figure 15.1).[1] Over the past few years, a relatively new CSS feature has worked its way through the maze of the approval process and has been adopted by all the modern web browsers... as you've probably guessed from the title of this chapter, this feature is called "CSS grid".

Figure 15.1: Once again... CSS... uh, finds a way.

---

1. Image courtesy of metha1819/Shutterstock.

Although it's still early in its adoption curve, we expect grid to become increasingly important in the coming years, so we have included an introduction to this important subject as the final chapter of Part II.

As of even a few years ago, CSS grid wasn't yet supported by all browsers, at least not without cumbersome vendor prefixes (Box 5.3). Even after all browsers supported it, there were still enough proposed changes for how grid should work, and for how the CSS grid declarations should be written, that we didn't think that it was a great idea to include it in a tutorial aimed more at people who are learning CSS for the first time. Recently, though, things have settled down in the implementation of the spec, so we decided the time had come to add some material on CSS grid.

It was difficult to decide how to cover this subject because CSS grid is pretty complicated—it would be really easy to get lost in the weeds describing every little function. A big reason why it is so complex is that CSS grid is a fantastic tool for doing something complicated like creating the entire layout of a site in addition to something simpler like the obvious use for arranging elements into a grid (and it is really great at doing what it says on the tin! (Figure 15.2)).[2]

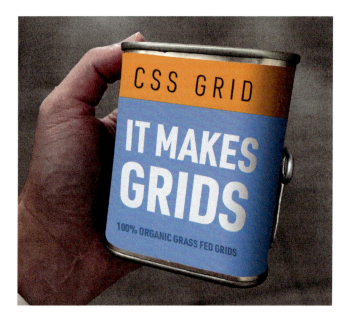

Figure 15.2: Truth in advertising.

2. Copyright © 2021 by Lee Donahoe and hereby released under the Creative Commons Attribution 2.0 Generic license.

We could have torn apart the existing site and redone everything with grid, but that would have made for a *very* long and convoluted chapter. Or we could have tried to shoehorn grid into the existing site, which would make the aspects of CSS grid that work well for the layout of an entire site a bit difficult to appreciate because we'd be putting a layout inside the existing layout. Instead, we are going to create a single self-contained page that will let us cover the main facets of this powerful new tool without getting overwhelmed.

15.1 CSS Grid at a High Level

Now that that's all out of the way, you are probably asking, "What is CSS grid, and why should I be interested in using it when all the old techniques still work?" That's a good question, and it is true that you can just ignore grid if you want to, but the short answer to the latter part of the question is that it makes a lot of front-end development a whole lot easier, and we promise, it isn't just because it is a shiny new toy (Figure 15.3).[3]

Figure 15.3: This robot wants to bring you the joy of new CSS techniques!

Let's dig into the first part of the question above: "What is CSS grid?" The easiest way to appreciate grid is by comparing it with flexbox (Chapter 11).

---

3. Image courtesy of Phil Darby/Shutterstock.

The big difference between flexbox and CSS grid is that in flexbox you are arranging items along a single dimension (either a row or a column), whereas CSS grid involves arranging things in both directions simultaneously. Yes, it is possible to use flexbox to arrange elements into something that looks like a grid, but all of those elements are positioned and defined as if they are in reality on a single dimension that has just wrapped onto a new line (Figure 15.4).

FLEXBOX with no flex-wrap

As new items are added, they are only added along a single row, and if there is no more room, everything gets squished to fit all the elements.

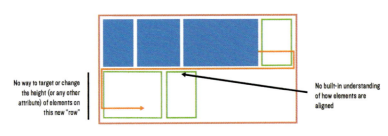

FLEXBOX with flex-wrap

As new items are added, when they reach a boundary they do wrap onto a new line, but flexbox has no awareness of that new row. To flexbox it is more like all those things are still on a single line.

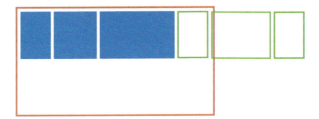

Figure 15.4: The one-dimensional nature of flexbox, with and without `flex-wrap`.

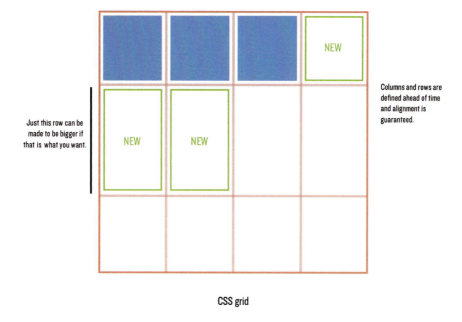

CSS grid

Figure 15.5: CSS grid allows for elements to build onto the page within a defined structure.

The flexbox system has no way to define how columns *and* rows should look in an automated way. In contrast, CSS grid allows you to lay out elements in two dimensions by defining the properties of the columns and rows that create grid cells where new HTML elements are automatically added (Figure 15.5).

New elements still are added from left to right like they are in flexbox (though you can change that to right to left, or even vertical), and as the cells fill in a row, new elements move down to the next row and continue filling cells there. Each row and column can be targeted separately with styles to change display properties. You can also set CSS grid to automatically size rows or columns to fit as much content as possible within constraints that you supply for maximum or minimum dimensions.

All this makes grid an incredibly powerful system for doing layouts where an arbitrary number of elements can fill the screen according to rules you set (like content boxes, thumbnail images, product tiles, etc.), as seen in Figure 15.5. Section 15.2 covers a simple and flexible content grid where the grid exists outside the sections. Section 15.4 covers more complex aspects of CSS grid to create pages for organizing content with a grid inside each section (Figure 15.6).

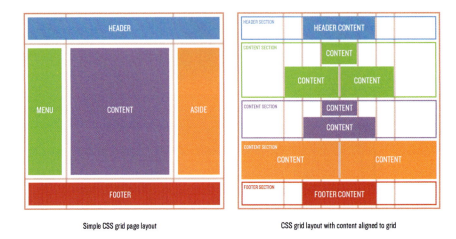

Simple CSS grid page layout   CSS grid layout with content aligned to grid

Figure 15.6: The two types of grid layout we'll be building.

A layout made with CSS grid isn't a static structure—it's not like an HTML table (Section 3.2), where once things are in rows and cells that's pretty much where they will stay. With grid, you can do all sorts of manipulation to the elements in the container, like reorder them however you like, overlap parts, or easily apply different layouts for different size screens with media queries. Before we get to that, though, let's take a look at a simple grid of content to get our feet wet and learn the basics of CSS grid.

15.2 A Simple Grid of Content

The first thing that you are going to need to do is to create a new HTML file in your project for our CSS grid experimentation. Let's call it **grid.html** and place it at the root of the site directory so that we can get to it just by navigating to localhost:4000/grid.html (Section 9.2):

```
$ touch grid.html
```

Inside **grid.html**, we are going to add in the basic HTML framework, and then inside the body of the page we'll add the first content elements. For this initial section, that will be a **div** with the class **grid**. Then, inside that **div**, we'll add eight more **div**s without classes and containing the numbers 1–8. The result appears as in Listing 15.1.[4]

Listing 15.1: The initial HTML for our page.

grid.html

```
<!doctype html>
<html>
  <head>
    <meta charset="utf-8">
    <style>
    </style>
  </head>
  <body>
    <div class="grid">
      <div>
        1
      </div>
      <div>
        2
      </div>
      <div>
        3
      </div>
      <div>
        4
      </div>
      <div>
        5
      </div>
      <div>
        6
      </div>
      <div>
        7
      </div>
      <div>
        8
      </div>
    </div>
  </body>
</html>
```

---

4. Recall that the code listings are available at https://github.com/learnenough/learn_enough_css_code _listings.

Since initially we are just experimenting to learn the basics, we'll be adding styles directly into the `<style>` section in the HTML's `<head>` instead of adding a link to the site CSS and inheriting all the existing site styling. This will allow us to see how CSS grid works on a completely blank slate.

Just as when using flexbox, when you use grid you need to have a container element with CSS to tell the browser that it needs to do something other than the default when rendering the contents. For this example, that container will be the `div` with `class="grid"` on it. Add the declaration as seen in Listing 15.2 and refresh your page. Perhaps surprisingly, it will look exactly the same as if you hadn't added `display: grid`. Why?

Listing 15.2: Adding our first `display: grid`.
grid.html

```
<style>
  .grid {
    display: grid;
  }
</style>
```

If you had added `display: flex`, all the elements would have instantly been fit into the container. The browser already knows the two-dimensional nature of flexbox at a basic level and will fit all the elements into the horizontal space provided by the wrapper (Figure 15.7).

Figure 15.7: Flex makes it go squish.

With CSS grid, however, we need to first define how rows and columns should be constructed before anything happens. Until then, we won't see any real changes because to the browser, those `div`s are just a bunch of regular block elements inside another box.

To get things going, we will first define our column structure, and we'll also add borders to the elements so that we can more easily see what is happening (Listing 15.3). Now when you refresh your page you should see something that looks similar to Figure 15.8.

Listing 15.3: Adding the first column template.
grid.html

```
<style>
  .grid {
    display: grid;
    grid-template-columns: 1fr 1fr 1fr;
}
  .grid > div {
    border:  1px solid #000;
  }
</style>
```

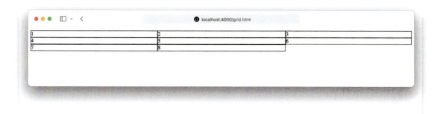

Figure 15.8: Hooray! We have rows and columns.

Well, at least Figure 15.8 looks like a grid now, but we're guessing at this point you are probably looking at the CSS in Listing 15.3 and thinking, "What the heck is a **1fr** and why does it scare me?"

15.2.1   Grid Columns and the Grid **fr** Unit

First, there's no reason to be scared—just look at this picture of a cat and all your fears will disappear (Figure 15.9).[5]

---

5. Copyright © 2021 by Lee Donahoe.

Figure 15.9: And you know he'll do it again.

Second, guess what?! There is a whole new CSS unit of measurement introduced with CSS grid… hooray for more units! In practice, though, this new unit isn't all that bad and is pretty easy to understand. The **fr** is short for *fractional unit*, and the style declaration that we just added in Listing 15.3 simply tells the browser to arrange any elements that are in the container into three columns, with each column taking up an equal proportion of the space.

Right now, the parent container takes up **100%** of the available page width, so each column gets approximately **33%** of the space. If you wanted one of the columns to be twice the size of the other two, you could do that by using **2fr**. Let's try changing the CSS to look like this:

```
.grid {
  display: grid;
  grid-template-columns: 1fr 2fr 1fr;
}
```

The result should look like Figure 15.10.

Figure 15.10: The big column in the middle is twice the size of the columns on the side.

An important thing to note is that all the elements that are sized using the **fr** unit have their size calculated from the available free space in the parent container *after* any elements with different units are assigned their space. If you set one of the columns using a non-fractional unit, the amount of free space available for the remaining **fr** elements is reduced. To see what we mean, try setting the third column to have a static width of **450px**:

```
.grid {
  display: grid;
  grid-template-columns: 1fr 2fr 450px;
}
```

When you refresh the page and play with the window width, you'll see that the third column is now exactly **450px** wide, and the first two columns have to split the rest of the available space (with the first column half the size of the second).

Let's get back to how the column template style works. Each individual value separated by a space in the **grid-template-columns** declaration corresponds to a column on the page. So if you want to make a grid with four columns you would write **grid-template-columns: 1fr 1fr 1fr 1fr;**. Eight columns would be **grid-template-columns: 1fr 1fr 1fr 1fr 1fr 1fr 1fr 1fr;**. You can add as many values as you'd like to define, but it does start to look a little ugly if you need to have a lot of columns on the page.

Thankfully, there is a way to simplify the values so that you don't need to explicitly declare each column, and we think that you'll find it refreshingly simple. Change your CSS so that it looks like Listing 15.4.

Listing 15.4: Repeating three **1fr** columns.

grid.html

```
.grid {
  display: grid;
  grid-template-columns: repeat(3, 1fr);
}
```

Everything should be back to three columns of the same width when you refresh the page, but if you change the value to **repeat(4, 1fr)** in your web inspector panel, you will now have four evenly sized columns (Figure 15.11).

Figure 15.11: Three columns have now become four columns.

You can even mix and match. For example, **grid-template-columns: 5em repeat(2, 1fr) repeat(3, 2fr);** would give you a single **5em** column, followed by two **1fr** columns, and ending with three **2fr** columns. It's a powerful and flexible technique for defining columns on the page.

15.2.2 Grid Rows and Gaps

Now that we've covered how the fractional unit works and learned how to use **repeat** in CSS grid, let's set the **grid-template-columns** back to three **1fr**s (in case you tried the four-column layout in the code instead of the inspector) and add some styles to define rows. To start, we are just going to add a single row definition. Add the code found below:

```
.grid {
  display: grid;
  grid-template-columns: repeat(3, 1fr);
  grid-template-rows: 1fr;
}
```

When you refresh the page, you'll find that nothing happened. You might find that surprising, but you have to remember that deep down at the base level these are still just block elements. Recall from our discussion of the box model in Chapter 8 that a block element will expand to fill all available horizontal space, but vertically it will only be the height of the content in the element. Let's change the row sizing to have an explicit height:

```
.grid {
  display: grid;
  grid-template-columns: repeat(3, 1fr);
  grid-template-rows: 15em;
}
```

Now when you refresh the page, you'll see that the first row is in fact set to be **15em** in height, but all the other rows are still the equivalent of **1fr** (Figure 15.12).

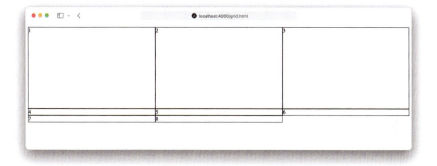

Figure 15.12: Now we have a single row that is sized, but the rest are obstinate.

That happens because the **grid-template-rows** property is an *explicit* style—meaning that only rows that have a corresponding value will be styled—one **1fr** gets you only one styled row and **repeat(8,1fr)** will get you eight styled rows, but that's where styling ends. If there are more rows than values, the browser will render the additional rows using *implicit* auto-sizing that works as if you had set them all to be **1fr**.

You can test this by adding the style **min-height: 500px;** to the **grid** class in your web inspector. You'll see that the undefined rows behave like they are set to **1fr** and expand to fill the space (Figure 15.13).

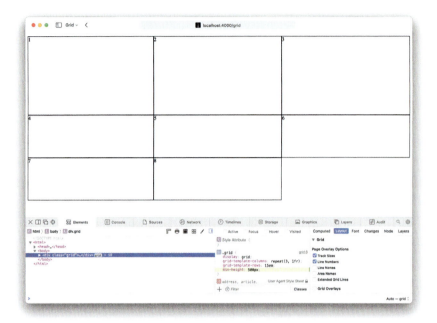

Figure 15.13: All the non-sized rows are now clearly the equivalent of `1fr`.

Using the `repeat` technique discussed in Section 15.2.1, you could use `repeat([insert number], 15em)` to define all the rows, but we're guessing at this point you've probably asked yourself, "Do I really need to define every single row? What if I don't know how many there will be?"

Well, my friend, you are in luck because it is also possible to change the implicit size, and in making this change we'll also add a grid gap style. Edit your CSS so that it looks like Listing 15.5 and then refresh the page.

Listing 15.5: Changing the implicit row size for all rows.

grid.html

```
.grid {
  display: grid;
  grid-template-columns: repeat(3, 1fr);
  grid-auto-rows: 15em;
  grid-gap: 1em;
}
```

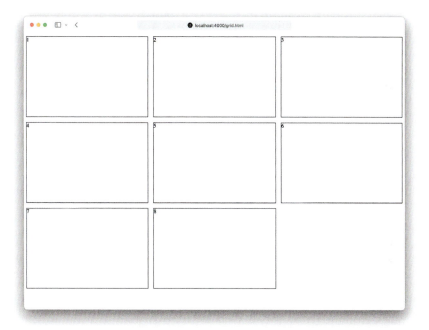

Figure 15.14: Now all the rows are the same size, and all the cells are separated by **1em**.

As you can see in Figure 15.14, now the browser knows that every new row in your grid should automatically be set to **15em** no matter how many elements you end up adding to the HTML, and now each element in the grid is separated from its neighbors by **1em**.

The **grid-gap** property above is actually a shorthand for **grid-gap: 1em 1em**, where the first value is the row gap and the second is the column gap. If you had set it to **grid-gap: 1em 2em**, your page would look like Figure 15.15.

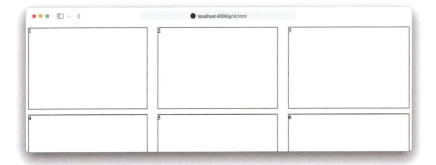

Figure 15.15: Now the column gaps are double the size of those old puny gaps.

The really cool (well, cool if you get excited about CSS) thing about the way that CSS grid handles the gap is that it automatically removes that space from the available space in the container before calculating how wide to make each column and row. It's practically a miracle compared to how this used to work in the bad old days where you had to carefully calculate everything yourself and use margins that caused all sorts of other headaches.

The other really nice thing about how gaps are handled is that you'll notice that they aren't applied at the edges of the container (the slight bit of padding that you see is from the browser default styles for the **body** element). This allows you to have a lot more control of how the grid fits in with other content on the page—it can be flush around the edges with other elements, or you can add padding to the container equivalent to the row or column gap. Both of these could cause problems if you were using margins to separate elements since margins can bleed outside containers (Section 8.2), but with **grid-gap** everything is self-contained (Figure 15.16).

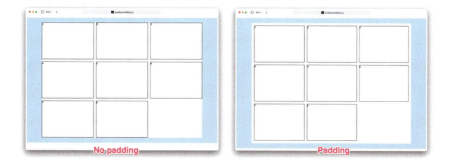

Figure 15.16: A grid with content flush to edges, and one with padding.

We hope that even at this very primitive stage you can see some of the power that CSS grid brings to front-end development. With just a few declarations, we've styled the page so that an arbitrary number of elements can be cleanly arranged into a grid, and unlike older methods for achieving this sort of layout, there's no need to worry about calculating a bunch of different things to make sure that everything fits.

We aren't stopping here, though—we've barely scratched the surface!

15.2.3 Exercises

1. Try clearing all the styles you added to `.grid`, and then add **grid-auto-columns: 15em;**. You might think that this would just make a bunch of **15em** columns, but without a quantity or **repeat** you should only get a single column.

2. Experiment with other combinations of sizing for the grid's columns, such as **grid-template-columns: 5em repeat(2, 1fr) repeat(3, 2fr);**.

15.3 `minmax`, `auto-fit`, and `auto-fill`

So far, everything that we've done really only works for situations where you know ahead of time what size the content is going to be and how many items you will ideally have on the page. However, in real-world usage you are always going to be uncertain about what size screen will be displaying your site, and you often won't know how many elements will be on the page or (perhaps most importantly) how much content each element will contain.

If you explicitly declare your **grid-template-columns** to have three columns, as we've done up to this point, it will always have three columns. On a small screen those columns will be tiny, and on a large screen they will look comically large. Then on the vertical axis, depending on the amount of content in each of those elements… things could end up looking very strange (Figure 15.17).

Figure 15.17: A grid on a mobile screen and a large screen.

Ideally, you'd want something like one column for a small screen, and for large screens you'd want to fill the width of the browser with as many content boxes as will fit, but also keep them from getting so stretched out that the content inside looks weird.

To solve these issues you could use media queries (Chapter 13) and redefine the grid for different screen size breakpoints… but that's a lot of work. Fortunately, CSS grid allows you to tell the browser how to handle filling the space in the grid container, and also to set **min** and **max** values for how big or small each column or row should be. This way, there's no need to add in media queries—you can do everything in a single statement!

15.3.1 Using Grid **auto-fit**

First, let's add some additional content in front of the numbered **div**s, as shown in Listing 15.6.[6]

---

6. The code listings at https://github.com/learnenough/learn_enough_css_code_listings are designed to make it more convenient to copy and paste markup like this.

Listing 15.6: Adding more content in the HTML.

grid.html

```
<div class="grid">
  <div>
    <h2>Big news today</h2>
    Quick sync win-win-win or workflow ecosystem.
  </div>
  <div>
    <h2>We are really excited to announce that we will soon have an exciting
    announcement!</h2>
    We're ahead of the curve on that one we just need to put these last issues
    to bed where do we stand on the latest client ask.
  </div>
  <div>
    <h2>Currying favor performance review bench mark</h2>
    No need to talk to users, just base it on the space calculator lift and
    shift.
  </div>
  <div>
    <h2>Level the playing field</h2>
    Take five, punch the tree, and come back in here with a clear head. We need
    to follow protocol obviously, rock Star/Ninja encourage &amp; support business
    growth yet curate.
  </div>
  <div>
    <h2>Usability closing these latest prospects </h2>
    Customer centric where do we stand on the latest client ask back of the net
    4-blocker fast track make it look like digital, like putting socks on an
    octopus.
  </div>
  <div>
    1
  </div>
  <div>
    2
  </div>
  .
  .
  .
```

Next, change the CSS to remove our auto row height by setting it to **auto**. Then change the **grid-template-columns** to **repeat(auto-fit, 275px)**, as seen in Listing 15.7.

Listing 15.7: Adding styles to explore auto-fit.

grid.html

```
.grid {
  display: grid;
  grid-template-columns: repeat(auto-fit, 275px);
  grid-auto-rows: auto;
  grid-gap: 1em;
}
```

When you refresh the page, you'll see that the browser has automatically arranged the content into columns and rows. If you play around with the width of your browser, you'll see that the browser window will adapt to the available space and resize the columns to try and fit as many in the space as it can (Figure 15.18).

Figure 15.18: How our bold new adventure looks on mobile and a large screen.

The **auto-fit** part of the value you added in Listing 15.7 seems pretty self-explanatory (though in reality... it's not—more on that in Section 15.3.3). As you change the width of the window, the browser keeps checking to see if there is enough room to fit another column of **275px** onto the page, but you'll notice that this leaves a gap whenever there isn't enough room to fit an entire column.

If your desired layout calls for elements that are exactly **275px** in width, this might be perfect (such as for a product category page where you don't want them dynamically resizing). You can even position the content the way we did with flexbox in Section 11.2 by using container-level styles for aligning elements both as a group within the container and for all the elements inside their spaces, as seen in Figure 15.19.[7]

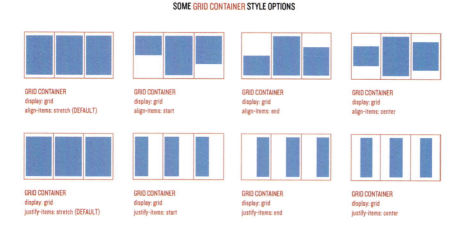

Figure 15.19: Grid alignment options for child elements.

Also, as with flexbox, you can set the alignment of individual elements inside the space they are assigned, regardless of the alignment or justification of the parent grid, by using **align-self** and **justify-self**.[8]

For example, you can try adding **justify-content: center** to the grid container using your browser inspector. This rule causes all the content to be aligned in the center of the parent element. The result is that your content arranges itself into as many **275px** columns as will fit the window while keeping everything nicely centered on the page (Figure 15.20).

---

7. See the **justify-items** section at https://css-tricks.com/snippets/css/complete-guide-grid/ for more information.

8. See the **align-self** section at https://css-tricks.com/snippets/css/complete-guide-grid/ for more information.

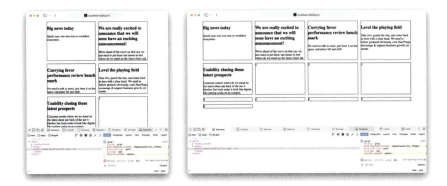

Figure 15.20: Center justified on both mobile and desktop.

But what if you don't want any space on the sides and want the elements to fill the space so long as they are at minimum **275px**? In that case, you can use CSS's **minmax()** modifier for the size. To use it you need to give a minimum value and a maximum value separated by a comma, something like **minmax(275px, 1fr)**. Let's try that now in the code, as seen in Listing 15.8.

Listing 15.8: Exploring how **minmax** affects **auto-fit**.
grid.html

```
.grid {
  display: grid;
  grid-template-columns: repeat(auto-fit, minmax(275px, 1fr));
  grid-auto-rows: auto;
  grid-gap: 1em;
}
```

This new value lets the browser know that you want each column to be **275px** at a minimum, but if the window isn't wide enough to add another **275px** column, then it should make the elements take up all the space equally. If you play around with the window, you'll see that at small sizes the elements form a single column that expands to take up the entire space. As the window widens past the point where a new **275px** column can be added, the browser pops in another column. If there isn't room for another column, the browser will keep increasing each column's width to fill the space (Figure 15.21).

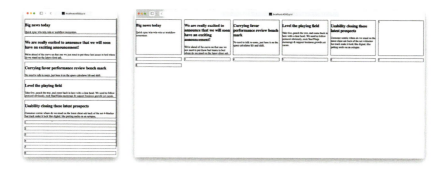

Figure 15.21: Columns spreading out on mobile and a large screen.

Now that we've got our columns set up to fill the page, let's use **minmax** to also make all of our rows the same height so that they look a little more uniform. Change the **grid-auto-rows** to match the code in Listing 15.9.

Listing 15.9: Applying **minmax** to **grid-auto-rows**.
grid.html

```
.grid {
  display: grid;
  grid-template-columns: repeat(auto-fit, minmax(275px, 1fr));
  grid-auto-rows: minmax(10em,1fr);
  grid-gap: 1em;
}
```

After you refresh the page, you'll see that all of the rows are the same height now, with a minimum height of **10em** and a maximum height of **1fr**, which in this case ends up being the height of the content element with the longest text.

Now that we have a nice uniform grid set up (Figure 15.22), we are going to take a moment to look at what to do when you want one of the elements to take up more space in the grid.

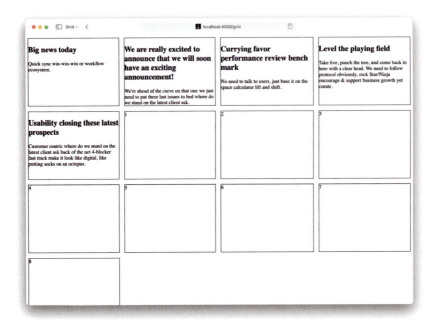

Figure 15.22: Our grid definitely looks like a grid!

15.3.2 Relative Spanning Columns

With CSS grid, it is really easy to allow some elements to take up more space in the grid, and in fact we can do this a couple of different ways. In Section 15.4, we will use explicit positioning to make an element stretch across *specific* columns. Right now, we'll look at a relative method where it doesn't matter where in the grid the element is positioned—it will always span two columns. Create a new style with a class of **grid-feature**, as shown in Listing 15.10.

Listing 15.10: Making an element cover two columns with CSS.
grid.html

```
  .
  .
  .
  .grid-feature {
     grid-column: span 2;
}
</style>
```

And then add the class onto an HTML element:

```
<div class="grid-feature">
   <h2>We are really excited to announce that we will soon have an exciting
   announcement!</h2>
   We're ahead of the curve on that one we just need to put these last issues
   to bed where do we stand on the latest client ask.
</div>
```

When you refresh your browser, you'll see that the element now covers two columns as well as the gap between the columns, as seen in Figure 15.23.

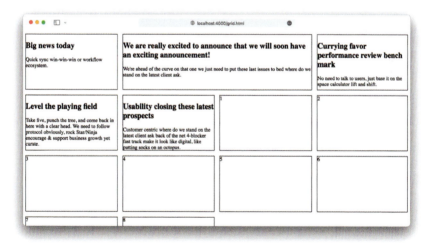

Figure 15.23: The element will now span two columns wherever it is.

There is a caveat to watch out for, though. If the element is in the last column on a page, it will get bumped down to the next line (Figure 15.24).

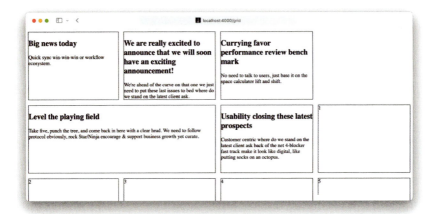

Figure 15.24: Elements on the end of a row that span multiple columns bump down.

To force the grid to reflow the rest of the content and prevent gaps from appearing, there is a simple solution: Just add **grid-auto-flow: dense** to the parent **grid** element's styles and everything (should) magically work!

Understanding why that gap appears in the first place is going to be the subject of the next section.

15.3.3 Leveling Up CSS Grid Understanding

So, why doesn't the browser fill that space with one of the elements after… and what does that **auto-fit** value, which we haven't talked about in detail, do?

The answers to this question involve a little change in perspective, and this new understanding of how the browser actually sees the grid will allow us to manipulate the grid to create layouts in Section 15.4.

As an introduction, let's look at how **auto-fit** and its partner, **auto-fill**, work (Figure 15.25).

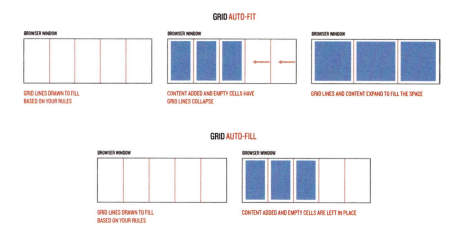

Figure 15.25: The difference in behavior is easier to see in diagram form.

`auto-fit` will try to fill the container with as many columns as it can, with each one being the minimum width that you defined. If there are fewer child elements than columns, the extra columns are collapsed to zero width and the content can stretch out to the max width value that you specified.

`auto-fill`, like `auto-fit`, first fills the space with as many of the minimum-width columns as it can fit, but when it runs out of content it leaves the columns in place.

Both sound pretty similar, right? Depending on the number of elements on your page and the settings that you use, both **auto-fit** and **auto-fill** can end up looking exactly the same. The difference comes in the edge cases—like if your minimum width is really small, or you have only a couple of child elements in the grid container.

If you comment out everything except the first two items in our container (and delete the **grid-feature** class from the **div** that you added it to), you can play around with switching between **auto-fit** and **auto-fill** to see how the browser handles sizing the columns to the available space (Figure 15.26 and Figure 15.27). Unlike **auto-fill**, **auto-fit** always tries to make content cover the entire space without leaving empty columns at the end of a row.

Figure 15.26: `auto-fit` with only two items.

Figure 15.27: `auto-fill` with only two items.

Why does any of this matter?

The important takeaway is the first action that the browser takes in Figure 15.25—in both cases, the very first thing that happens is that the browser fills the grid container with lines.

Up to this point, we've kind of used "column" interchangeably with "content item" because at the surface level that does seem to be what is being arranged on the page. You have X number of elements and Y amount of space. So that must mean that the browser is building the page by looking at the content itself, right? In reality, under the hood CSS grid really only cares about the grid lines *between* columns and rows (Figure 15.28).

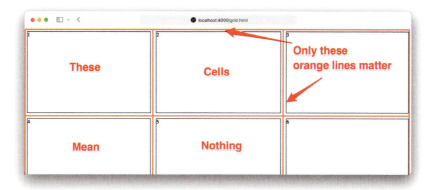

Figure 15.28: The browser cares about the lines, not the cells.

When the browser is rendering the page, it first looks at rules that you set and uses those rules to draw the grid lines; only then does the browser look at the content and fit it into the lines it has drawn. It is this next level of understanding that will unlock the more advanced aspects of CSS grid. Let's explore what this means for how we use CSS grid.

15.3.4 Exercises

1. Use the different align and justify styles found in Figure 15.19 to play with changing the positioning of all the child elements of the grid container to see how they adjust based on the content.

2. Now pick a single element in the grid and use **align-self** and **justify-self** to position just that one element within its grid cell.

3. We applied **grid-column: span 2** to our feature element... Do you suppose that **grid-row: span 2** might also be a valid style?

15.4 Grid Lines, Areas, and Layouts

So far in this chapter, we've held off on covering the more complicated underlying parts of how CSS grid works to avoid overwhelming you with details. The simple grid styling we've covered up to this point can be dropped into any project where you need to arrange a bunch of items in a two-dimensional grid. The details of how browsers build the grid are important to understanding how to use CSS grid for layouts, and in this section we'll show you some of the more complicated things grid can do.

As preparation for this, we first want to show you how to toggle your browser inspector to display a *grid overlay* to help you visualize how CSS grid is being rendered. The screenshots in Figure 15.29 show you how to turn on the grid overlay in Safari and Chrome, but all modern browsers should have this ability.

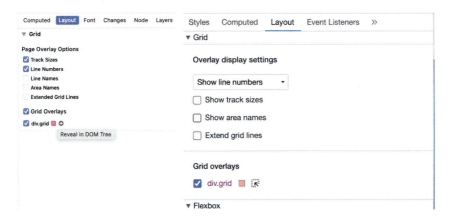

Figure 15.29: The grid overlay toggle in Safari and Chrome, respectively.

After clicking on the Layout tab, you should be able to click on the checkbox to enable the browser to show you the grid overlay. When enabled, the grid overlay lets you see your grid the way the browser sees it (Figure 15.30).

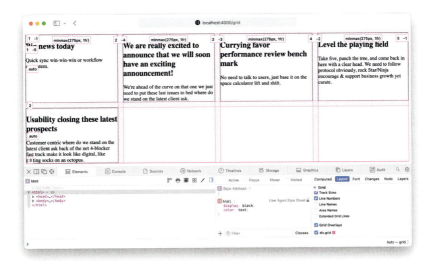

Figure 15.30: My god, it's full of grids (and gaps).

The important thing to understand from this overlay is that the browser is labeling and numbering not the content elements, but rather the grid lines at the beginning and end of each element. In other words, the `div` that has the headline "Big news today" isn't "element 1," but rather "the element that goes from grid line 1 to grid line 2." It's a small difference, but an important one.

What can we do with this newfound understanding?

15.4.1 Getting Started with Grid Lines

In this part of the tutorial, we are going to create two layout structures, each using a different way to arrange the page. The first one is a simpler layout that could be used for displaying content like documentation, and the second one is a more complex use of CSS grid to create a layout that could be used for a homepage or an informational landing page. (To do this we will have to work around an annoying browser limitation... but more on that in Section 15.5.)

Let's get started playing around with the grid lines and see how they can be used to build the first layout. In Listing 15.11, you'll notice that we've added styles to remove the default margin and padding on the document (so that our elements can

fill the screen). We've also added grid settings and a minimum height to the new
grid-container class, and added backgrounds to some of our elements. Finally, the
HTML we've created up to this point has been moved to the end of the document
and commented out. Listing 15.11 shows the full result, which you can use as the
content for your own **grid.html**.

Listing 15.11: Simplified HTML with old content commented out at the bottom.
grid.html

```html
<!doctype html>
<html>
  <head>
    <meta charset="utf-8">
    <style>
      html,
      body {
        border: 0;
        margin: 0;
      }
      .grid-container {
        display:  grid;
        grid-auto-flow: dense;
        grid-template-columns: repeat(3, 1fr);
        min-height: 100vh;
      }
      .grid-container > div {
        box-sizing: border-box;
        position: relative;
      }
      .grid-header {
        background-color: #ccc;
      }
      .grid-menu {
        background-color: #c0c0c0;
      }
      .grid-content {

      }
      .grid-panel {
        background-color: #eee;
      }
      .grid-footer {
        background-color: #ddd;
      }

      .grid {
        display: grid;
```

```
      grid-template-columns: repeat(auto-fit, minmax(275px, 1fr));
      grid-auto-rows: minmax(10em,1fr);
      grid-gap: 1em;
    }
    .grid > div {
      border:  1px solid #000;
    }
    .grid-feature {
      grid-column: span 2;
    }
  </style>
</head>
<body>
  <div class="grid-container">
    <header class="grid-header">
      I am a Header
    </header>
    <nav class="grid-menu">
      I am a Menu
    </nav>
    <article class="grid-content">
      I am Content
    </article>
    <aside class="grid-panel">
      I am Info
    </aside>
    <footer class="grid-footer">
      I am a Footer
    </footer>
  </div>
</body>
</html>

<!--
<div class="grid">
  <div>
    <h2>Big news today</h2>
    Quick sync win-win-win or workflow ecosystem.
  </div>
  <div class="grid-feature">
    <h2>We are really excited to announce that we will soon have an exciting
    announcement!</h2>
    We're ahead of the curve on that one we just need to put these last issues
    to bed where do we stand on the latest client ask.
  </div>
  <div>
    <h2>Currying favor performance review bench mark</h2>
    No need to talk to users, just base it on the space calculator lift and
    shift.
  </div>
```

```
<div>
  <h2>Level the playing field</h2>
  Take five, punch the tree, and come back in here with a clear head. We need
  to follow protocol obviously, rock Star/Ninja encourage &amp; support business
  growth yet curate.
</div>
<div>
  <h2>Usability closing these latest prospects </h2>
  Customer centric where do we stand on the latest client ask back of the net
  4-blocker fast track make it look like digital, like putting socks on an
  octopus.
</div>
<div>
  1
</div>
<div>
  2
</div>
<div>
  3
</div>
<div>
  4
</div>
<div>
  5
</div>
<div>
  6
</div>
<div>
  7
</div>
<div>
  8
</div>
</div>
-->
```

At this point, you should follow the step shown in Figure 15.29 again with `div.grid-container` in place of `div.grid`. The resulting grid-overlay display is browser-dependent but should look something like Figure 15.31. Depending on your browser, you might need to re-enable the grid overlay in the inspector every time you refresh if you want to keep it visible. We're going to keep doing it for screenshots, but it isn't necessarily something that you need to keep on all the time.

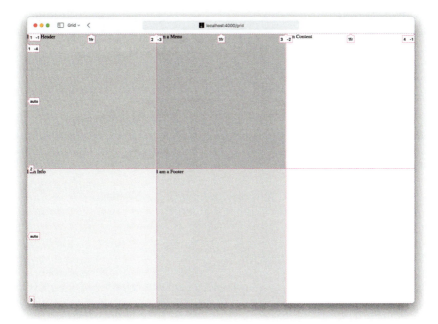

Figure 15.31: A "beautiful" new beginning.

For the code examples going forward, we're not going to show the code that has been commented out, but just know that it is still there… lurking (Figure 15.32).[9]

---

9. Image courtesy of dejavudesigns/123RF.

Figure 15.32: Your old code is hiding... Waiting...

15.4.2 The Simple Grid Layout

Let's start adding some styling to see what CSS grid can offer for making layouts. In the **style** section in **grid.html**, we are first going to add **grid-column-start: 2** to the **grid-content** class, as shown in Listing 15.12.

Listing 15.12: Setting `.grid-content` to start at column 2.

grid.html

```
  .
  .
  .
.grid-menu {
  background-color: #c0c0c0;
}
.grid-content {
  grid-column-start: 2;
}
```

```
.grid-panel {
  background-color: #eee;
}
.
.
.
```

The new style in Listing 15.12 allows us to define which line of the grid an element with class **grid-content** should start at. Currently, that element ("I am Content") is in the third column (Figure 15.31), so you might think that this would just move the element to the left by one column. However, after refreshing your browser, you should instead see something that looks like Figure 15.33.

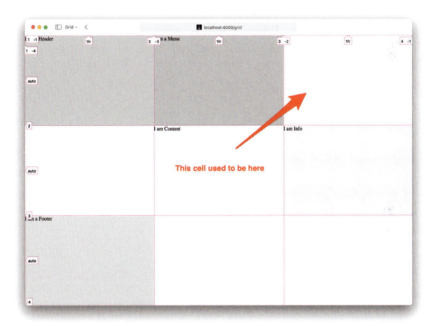

Figure 15.33: Interesting. The element in the third column moved down onto a new row.

The empty cells in Figure 15.33, and the element moving to the second line, probably aren't what you expected to happen as the result of the new CSS rule in Listing 15.12. The reason the "I am Content" element moved down is that we only told the browser that the element should start at grid line 2, but we didn't change anything about which *row* it should start on. Since there was already an object on the page between lines 2 and 3 (i.e., column 2) in row 1, the browser bounced the **grid-content** element down to a new row and kept flowing the rest of the elements in after.

If we also specify a row start for the element, the browser will move that **div** to the defined space, and then flow all of the content to fill the rest of the columns with the available elements:

```css
.grid-content {
  grid-column-start: 2;
  grid-row-start: 1;
}
```

As seen in Figure 15.34, the result is the placement of the "I am Content" **div** in the second column on the first row, as desired.

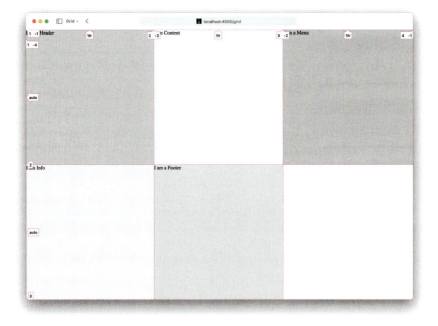

Figure 15.34: Now this seems like what you might have expected to happen.

Of course, if there is a **grid-column-start** there should be a **grid-column-end** too, right? There is! To get our **grid-content** element to stretch over two columns (ending at the fourth grid line), we could add **grid-column-end: 4** to the CSS:

```
.grid-content {
  grid-column-start: 2;
  grid-column-end: 4;
  grid-row-start: 1;
}
```

Equivalently, we could use a shorthand declaration that combines **grid-column-start** and **grid-column-end**:

```
.grid-content {
  grid-column: 2 / 4;
  grid-row-start: 1;
}
```

In this new CSS declaration, the number before the forward slash is the line number for **grid-column-start**, and the number after the slash is the line number for **grid-column-end**. In other words,

```
grid-column-start: 2;
grid-column-end: 4;
```

and

```
grid-column: 2 / 4;
```

are equivalent.

Adding the more compact **grid-column** rule to the **style** section of **grid.html** gives us the CSS shown in Listing 15.13. The result is a content element that is double the width of all the rest, as shown in Figure 15.35.

Listing 15.13: Setting `.grid-content` to start at column 2.
grid.html

```css
        .
        .
        .
.grid-menu {
  background-color: #c0c0c0;
}
.grid-content {
  grid-column: 2 / 4;
  grid-row-start: 1;
}
.grid-panel {
  background-color: #eee;
}
        .
        .
        .
```

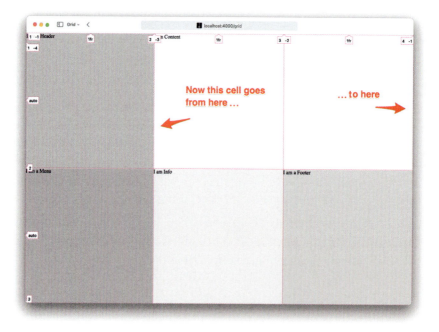

Figure 15.35: We have now achieved explicitly defined column spanning.

As you might guess, there is a similar shorthand for defining row starts and ends, so that we can replace something like

```
grid-row-start: 1;
grid-row-end: 3;
```

with

```
grid-row: 1 / 3;
```

If you were to change **grid-row-start: 1** in Listing 15.13 to **grid-row: 1 / 3**, you would have a monster content cell that is double the width and double the height of all the others (Figure 15.36).

Figure 15.36: Our element is now the largest, and the others should worry that it might eat them.

One thing to note here is that once again we have defined the styling using explicit values (specifically, the starting column 2 and starting row 3). No matter what happens with the content, the **grid-content** element will always be in row 1 and stretch from column line 2 to 4. If you wish to move it to a different position, it is as simple as altering a couple of values.

This sort of positioning flexibility allows you to position an element in the browser independent of its location in the HTML source (as long as it is a first-level child of the grid container—it can't go *anywhere*, anywhere). This flexibility makes grid a fantastic tool for doing things like rearranging content to create a better mobile experience without needing to actually move the item in the HTML. You can simply tell the browser exactly where you want a specific element to be and all the other content will flow around it. You can even define the location of every single element if that's what you need to make your layout work for a specific use case.

We're betting that, with the elements we've added, you can already see where this is heading, but before we position all these elements into a functional layout we first want to introduce named grid lines and areas.

15.4.3 Named Lines and Areas

One really nice feature about CSS grid is that it allows developers the ability to name different parts of the grid so that there's no need to try and remember whether or not "line 3" is the beginning of the content or the beginning of a sidebar. Even more than that, it also lets you easily define combinations of column and row lines into named areas, and then use those names to tell the browser where to render elements on the page.

Our example layout (Figure 15.6) is going to have a header at the top that stretches across the page in the top row. Below that will be three content sections, with a menu on the left side of the row, a main content area in the middle, and a panel for extra information about the content on the right. Then the bottom row will be a footer that stretches across the page like the header.

In the CSS, let's change the grid properties on the **grid-container** class, and also delete the changes that we added on the **grid-content** class so that the source looks like Listing 15.14.

Listing 15.14: Setting the HTML for named lines and areas.

grid.html

```
.grid-container {
  display:  grid;
  grid-template-columns: 10em 1fr 15em;
  grid-template-rows: auto 1fr minmax(10em, auto);
  min-height: 100vh;
}
.
.
.
.grid-content {

}
```

At this point, the CSS changes that we made should be familiar, and when you refresh your browser you should see something that looks like the mess in Figure 15.37.

Figure 15.37: Well this is a beginning… we guess.

Using CSS grid to get this to look like an actual page layout is almost shockingly simple once you see how the named areas work, but we'll do this in a couple of steps so that you can see how things fit together. The first step is to add a **grid-template-areas** declaration to the **grid-container** to define the areas page, as in Listing 15.15.

Listing 15.15: Creating our first named areas.

grid.html

```
.grid-container {
  display:  grid;
  grid-template-areas: "header header header" "menu content panel"
                       "footer footer footer";
  grid-template-columns: 10em 1fr 15em;
  grid-template-rows: minmax(4em, auto) 1fr auto;
  min-height: 100vh;
}
```

Let's break down that declaration. The way that this works is that each of the sections in double quotes, like **"header header header"**, represents a row, and within the double-quoted sections each name represents a column. The new grid that we defined at the beginning of this section has three columns and three rows:

```
grid-template-columns: 10em 1fr 15em;
grid-template-rows: minmax(4em, auto) 1fr auto;
```

In the new **grid-template-areas** declaration, the **"header header header"** value is telling the browser that there should be a single grid area called **header** that in row 1 (row line 1 to line 2) covers all three columns (column line 1 to line 4).

The **"menu content panel"** value sets row 2 (row line 2 to line 3) to have an area called **menu** that is in the first column (column line 1 to line 2), then an area called **content** in the second column (column line 2 to line 3), and an area called **panel** in the last column (column line 3 to line 4).

Lastly, **"footer footer footer"** works like the **header** area but creates an area called **footer** in the last row.

In case you thought reminding you about the different grid lines might have just been us writing that all out in a needlessly descriptive way, fear not! There is a method to the madness.

A really convenient feature of how CSS grid works is that by naming grid areas, we also name the grid lines. That means that for the header, instead of using a style like this:

```
grid-column-start: 1;
grid-column-end: 4;
grid-row-start: 1;
grid-row-end: 2;
```

or in the shorthand:

```
grid-column: 1 / 4;
grid-row: 1 / 2;
```

we can use the much more readable:

```
grid-column-start: header-start;
grid-column-end: header-end;
grid-row-start: header-start;
grid-row-end: header-end;
```

This works in the shorthand as well (with even less typing needed):

```
grid-column: header;
grid-row: header;
```

And excitingly, there's an even simpler shorthand:

```
grid-area: header;
```

All of those statements are equivalent and can be used interchangeably, depending on how much control you want for positioning a given element on the grid. We'll play around with this more in Section 15.4.4, but in the meantime, let's go ahead and add **grid-area** styles for all of our elements (Listing 15.16).

Listing 15.16: Adding **grid-area** definitions to content elements.
grid.html

```
.grid-header {
  background-color: #ccc;
```

```
  grid-area: header;
}
.grid-menu {
  background-color: #c0c0c0;
  grid-area: menu;
}
.grid-content {
  grid-area: content;
}
.grid-panel {
  background-color: #eee;
  grid-area: panel;
}
.grid-footer {
  background-color: #ddd;
  grid-area: footer;
}
```

When you refresh your browser, you should see something that looks like the glorious layout in Figure 15.38.

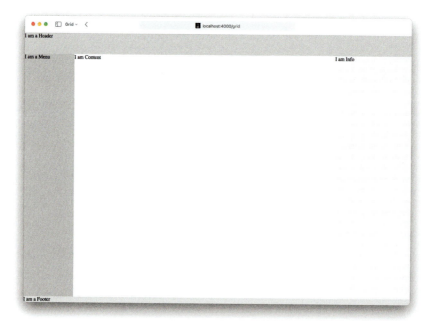

Figure 15.38: All in one go, things are starting to seem arranged.

15.4.4 Overlapping Using Grid

Before we made the last change to the code, we mentioned that even though we can use the **grid-area** shorthand, the underlying styles like **grid-column** and **grid-row** are still useful to keep in mind since you can use them to selectively change area properties.

Let's pretend that for some reason you wanted to have the ability to let people visiting your site expand the content area to the full height and width of the page, overlapping both the header and the footer. With grid area naming it is really easy. Add a new class called **.grid-expand** in the CSS section, add the following CSS grid changes, and also throw in a couple of extra styles to make it possible to see the changes (Listing 15.17).

Listing 15.17: An example of overlapping grid elements.

grid.html

```css
.grid-footer {
  background-color: #ddd;
  grid-area: footer;
}
.grid-expand {
  background-color: rgba(255,255,255,0.8);
  box-shadow: 0 0 20px 0 rgba(0,0,0,0.3);
  grid-column: content;
  grid-row: header-start / footer-end;
  z-index: 2;
}
```

Then add the **grid-expand** class to the HTML **article** element with class **grid-content**:

```html
<article class="grid-content grid-expand">
```

Now when you refresh the page, the content area should have expanded to cover both the header and the footer (Figure 15.39). Since we made the background a slightly transparent white using an opacity of **0.8** in Listing 15.17, we can also see that the element actually *is* overlapping the other elements. This is indicated by the light gray color of the "I am Content" area in Figure 15.39, which comes from the darker gray of the "I am a Header" area showing through.

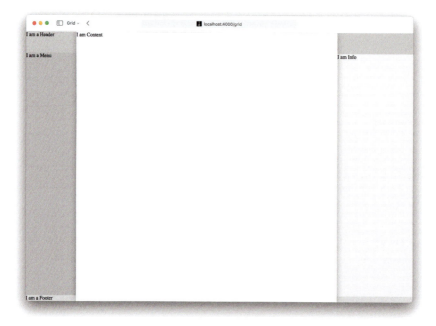

Figure 15.39: Overlapping content, and with no crazy negative margins or absolute positioning.

If you remove the **grid-expand** class in your browser's web inspector, you'll see that the element jumps right back into its normal spot. And once you complete *Learn Enough JavaScript to Be Dangerous* (https://www.learnenough.com/javascript), you'll have learned techniques that will let you add and remove an element based on user clicks!

15.4.5 Source-Independent Positioning

Toward the end of Section 15.4.2, we mentioned that CSS grid gives you the ability to use explicit grid positioning to allow elements to be positioned on the page no matter where they are in the first level of the grid container. To see how this works, let's add in a little banner that will display over the top of the "content" and "panel" areas.

In the first step, we are going to remove the **grid-expand** from the content element. We'll next add the new **grid-banner** class and styles to the CSS area (Listing 15.18).

Listing 15.18: Adding the banner CSS into the page.

grid.html

```
.grid-expand {
.
.
.
}
.grid-banner {
  align-self: start;
  background-color: rgba(168,214,247,0.9);
  grid-column: content-start / panel-end;
  grid-row-start: content-start;
  padding: 1em;
  z-index: 10;
}
```

Then we'll finish by placing the **div** with the **grid-banner** class anywhere in the grid container (Listing 15.19). (Note that the **div** has to be a first-level child of the container—you can't put it inside another child like the **grid-content** element.)

Listing 15.19: Adding the banner element into the page.

grid.html

```
.
.
.
      <nav class="grid-menu">
        I am a Menu
      </nav>
      <article class="grid-content">
        I am Content
      </article>
      <aside class="grid-panel">
        I am Info
      </aside>
      <footer class="grid-footer">
        I am a Footer
      </footer>
      <div class="grid-banner">
        I am a banner
      </div>
    </div>
  </body>
</html>
```

Refresh the page and you'll find a nice blue banner (Figure 15.40).

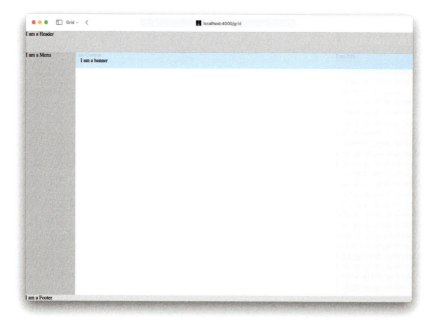

Figure 15.40: A fresh blue banner appears!

In the CSS that was added in Listing 15.18, you can see that we are telling the browser to have any element with the **grid-banner** class span over the "content" and "panel" areas. We are also telling it that we want the element to start at the **content-start** row, but you'll notice that we aren't specifying a row end. Instead, we are using one of the alignment styles from Section 15.3.1 to make this element not stretch to fill the space.

The **align-self: start** style has the browser start the element where it has been defined to start, but instead of the default value of **stretch**, which would cover the entire area, the **start** value makes it behave like a regular block element and only be as tall as the content inside. If we had set it to **center** or **end**, the banner would appear as in Figure 15.41. Or we could have used any of the **justify-self** styles to also position it and have it take up only as much width as is needed to fit the content, as in Figure 15.42. Or any combination of the above!

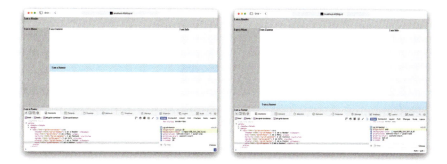

Figure 15.41: You can easily move the element to the center or end with `align-self`.

Figure 15.42: Moving the banner around with `justify-self`.

15.4.6 Finishing the Layout

To finish this example off, let's add in some extra styles for things like padding to make everything a little more neatly arranged (Listing 15.20).

Listing 15.20: Cleaning up our first grid layout.

grid.html

```
.
.
.
.grid-header {
  background-color: #ccc;
  grid-area: header;
  padding: 1em;
  text-align: center;
}
.grid-menu {
  background-color: #c0c0c0;
  grid-area: menu;
  padding: 1em;
}
.grid-menu ul,
.grid-panel ul,
.grid-footer ul {
  list-style: none;
  margin: 0;
  padding: 0;
}
.grid-content {
  grid-area: content;
  padding: 3em 3em 4em;
}
.grid-panel {
  border-left: 1px solid rgba(0,0,0,0.1);
  grid-area: panel;
  padding: 4em 2em 4em 3em;
}
.grid-footer {
  background-color: #ddd;
  grid-area: footer;
  padding: 4em 1em;
  text-align: center;
}
.grid-footer li {
  display: inline-block;
}
```

```
.
.
.
.grid-banner {
  align-self: start;
  background-color: rgba(168,214,247,0.9);
  grid-column: content-start / panel-end;
  grid-row-start: content-start;
  padding: 1em;
  position: sticky;
  top: 0;
  z-index: 10;
}
.
.
.
```

We'll also add our original grid test into the content area, and some links in lists for the menu, the panel content, and the footer. Rather than highlighting essentially everything in Listing 15.21, we've added highlighted comments to show you what parts of the HTML have changes.

Listing 15.21: Adding content to the layout.

grid.html

```
.
.
.
<nav class="grid-menu">
  I am a Menu
  <!-- from here -->
  <ul>
    <li>
      <a href="">
        Menu item
      </a>
    </li>
    <li>
      <a href="">
        Menu item
      </a>
    </li>
    <li>
      <a href="">
        Menu item
```

```html
        </a>
      </li>
    </ul>
  <!-- to here -->
</nav>
<article class="grid-content">
  <!-- from here -->
  <h1>
    I am Content
  </h1>
  <div class="grid">
    <div>
      <h2>Big news today</h2>
      Quick sync win-win-win or workflow ecosystem.
    </div>
    <div class="grid-feature">
      <h2>We are really excited to announce that we will soon have an exciting
      announcement!</h2>
      We're ahead of the curve on that one we just need to put these last
      issues to bed where do we stand on the latest client ask.
    </div>
    <div>
      <h2>Currying favor performance review bench mark</h2>
      No need to talk to users, just base it on the space calculator lift and
      shift.
    </div>
    <div>
      <h2>Level the playing field</h2>
      Take five, punch the tree, and come back in here with a clear head. We
      need to follow protocol obviously, rock Star/Ninja encourage &amp; support
      business growth yet curate.
    </div>
    <div>
      <h2>Usability closing these latest prospects </h2>
      Customer centric where do we stand on the latest client ask back of the
      net 4-blocker fast track make it look like digital, like putting socks
      on an octopus.
    </div>
    <div>
      1
    </div>
    <div>
      2
    </div>
    <div>
      3
    </div>
    <div>
      4
```

```html
      </div>
      <div>
        5
      </div>
      <div>
        6
      </div>
      <div>
        7
      </div>
      <div>
        8
      </div>
    </div>
  <!-- to here -->
</article>
<aside class="grid-panel">
  I am Info
  <!-- from here -->
  <ul>
    <li>
      <a href="">
        Panel link
      </a>
    </li>
    <li>
      <a href="">
        Panel link
      </a>
    </li>
    <li>
      <a href="">
        Panel link
      </a>
    </li>
  </ul>
  <p>
    Call me Ishmael. Some years ago-never mind how long
    precisely-having little or no money in my purse, and nothing
    particular to interest me on shore, I thought I would sail about a
    little and see the watery part of the world. It is a way I have of
    driving off the spleen and regulating the circulation.
  </p>
  <!-- to here -->
</aside>
<footer class="grid-footer">
  I am a Footer
  <!-- from here -->
```

```
<ul>
  <li>
    <a href="">
      Footer link
    </a>
  </li>
  <li>
    <a href="">
      Footer link
    </a>
  </li>
</ul>
<!-- to here -->
</footer>
.
.
.
```

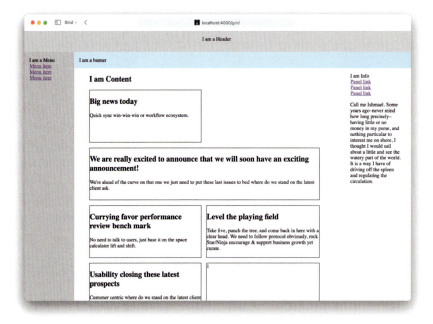

Figure 15.43: We might have made a page!

Well look at that! Figure 15.43 sure does look a lot more like a functional page, and that sticky banner that attaches to the top of the screen as you scroll past… perfect (Figure 15.44)!

Figure 15.44: It's perfect!

Next up, in Section 15.5 we'll reverse the grid (and move it from outside to inside) to explore a different way to arrange content and utilize CSS grid. Don't worry—that sounds more complicated than it really is!

15.4.7 Exercises

1. See if you can use your newfound grid-lines knowledge to get the banner that we added to start below the header and stretch all the way across the page, including overlapping the menu.

2. What if you wanted to make the banner be its own area and not have it overlap the content, while making sure that the menu starts at the bottom of the header? *Hint*: You'll need to add a new line for the banner to the **.grid-container**'s **grid-template-areas**, and a new row to the **grid-template-rows**. You'll also need to set the banner to use the new area instead of the explicit **grid-column** and **grid-row-start** we added in this section. If you need a little help making this work, the answer appears in Listing 15.22.

Listing 15.22: Making the banner be its own area.

grid.html

```
.grid-container {
  display: grid;
  grid-template-areas: "header header header" "menu banner banner"
                       "menu content panel" "footer footer footer";
  grid-template-columns: 10em 1fr 15em;
  grid-template-rows: minmax(4em, auto) auto 1fr auto;
  min-height: 100vh;
}

.grid-banner {
  align-self: start;
  background-color: rgba(168,214,247,0.9);
  grid-area: banner;
  /* grid-column: content-start / panel-end; */
  /* grid-row-start: content-start; */
  padding: 1em;
  z-index: 10;
}
```

15.5 Grid on the Inside

In the example layout that we just finished, we used a single grid on the outside of our page that provided structure to allow us to position elements. This layout didn't really provide much in the way of a structure for the content *inside* all the elements, though. One of the things that is great about grids is that if you have regularly spaced columns, then you can use those to arrange the placement of everything on the page so that it looks professionally designed (Figure 15.45). You can use a grid to align all the content on a page in a very strict manner, or you can use that grid as a guide and allow some elements not to be rigidly aligned to the grid as a way to give your layout a certain *je ne sais quoi*.[10]

For this final section of the tutorial, we are going to use CSS grid to set up a less than strict content layout like the one shown in Figure 15.45. And just as a heads-up, we will be moving faster with examples since all of the basic styles should now be familiar. The only new material pertains to the philosophy of how we use CSS grid.

---

10. A quality that cannot be described or named easily… like using French quotes in a tech tutorial to make the writing seem fancy.

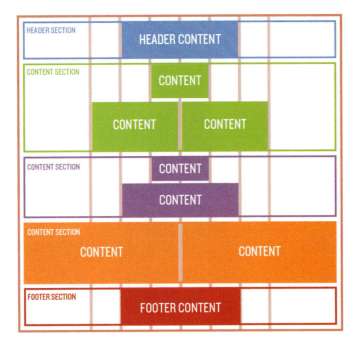

CSS grid layout with content aligned to grid

Figure 15.45: Arranging content according to a global grid.

Screenshots in this section will at times show the grid lines, and also at times add borders around elements to help you see them. Don't panic and think you missed something because there aren't borders on your page!

What we will be doing in this section would also be a lot easier to accomplish if CSS grid had full browser support for a feature called "subgrid" (Box 15.1). But it's OK! We can work around that limitation. Let's get started.

Box 15.1: About Subgrid

The specification for CSS grid was originally supposed to include this really great feature that would allow child elements of grid objects to inherit grid settings from the parent grid. Unfortunately, as of this writing Firefox is the only major browser that supports subgrid (Figure 15.46).

Universal subgrid support would have allowed developers to easily pass things like column or row layouts into child elements so that everything on the page could be arranged according to a single grid, as seen in Figure 15.47. As we mentioned in the main text, though, it is possible to work around this with a little careful effort, but support for subgrid is definitely one of those things that you should keep an eye on if you find yourself regularly doing front-end development. It's likely that browser support for subgrid will (perhaps too slowly) improve over time.

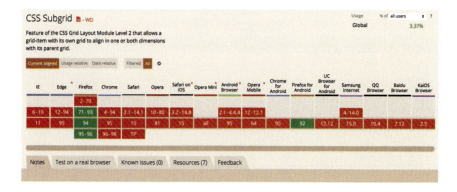

Figure 15.46: If you see a sea of red at caniuse.com, run away!

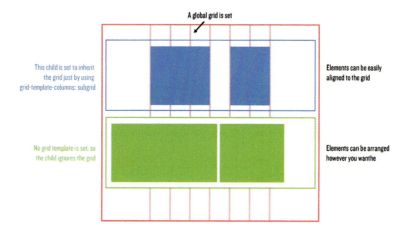

Figure 15.47: How the subgrid would work if we could use it, but alas, it was not to be…

15.5.1 Setting Up the Page

The first step for our new page is to create a new blank HTML file in the site directory, which we'll call **grid-landing.html**. Into that file, paste in the site skeleton shown in Listing 15.23.[11] (We weren't kidding about moving faster.)

Listing 15.23: Our next grid layout HTML skeleton.
grid-landing.html

```html
<!doctype html>
<html>
  <head>
    <meta charset="utf-8">
    <style>
      html,
      body {
        margin: 0;
        padding: 0;
      }
      h1, h2, h3 {
        margin-top: 0;
        text-align: center;
      }
      .subtitle {
        text-align: center;
      }
      .menulist {
        margin: 0;
        list-style: none;
        padding: 0;
      }
      .landing_cta {
        margin-top: 1.5em;
        text-align: center;
      }

      .header {
        background-color: #000;
        color: #fff;
        padding: 1em;
        text-align: center;
      }

      .hero {
```

---

11. Like all the code listings, Listing 15.23 is available at https://github.com/learnenough/learn_enough_css _code_listings.

```css
      background-color: #a8d6f7;
      min-height: 50vh;
      text-align: center;
    }

    .options {
      background-color: #4a7696;
      color: #fff;
      padding: 4em 0;
    }
    .options_item-img {
        width: 100%;
    }

    .info {
      padding: 8em 0;
    }

    .feature {
      min-height: 70vh;
    }

    .footer {
      background-color: #ddd;
      padding: 4em 1em;
    }
  </style>
</head>
<body>
  <header class="header">
    <div class="header_content">
      I am a Header
    </div>
  </header>

  <section class="hero">
    <h1 class="hero_title">
      I am an Important Message
    </h1>
    <div class="hero_content">
      And I am a less important, but still a very important
      thing to consider.
    </div>
  </section>

  <section class="options">
    <h2 class="options_title">
      Here are Some Choices
    </h2>
    <div class="options_content">
```

```
    <div>
      Stuff
    </div>
    <div>
      Different Stuff
    </div>
    <div>
      All the Stuff
    </div>
  </div>
</section>

<section class="info">
  <h2 class="info_title">
    I am Some More info
  </h2>
  <div class="subtitle">
    Say you are in the country.
  </div>
  <div class="info_content">
    <p>
      In some high land of lakes. Take almost any path you
      please, and ten to one it carries you down in a dale,
      and leaves you there by a pool in the stream. There
      is magic in it. But here is an artist. He desires to
      paint you the dreamiest, shadiest, quietest, most
      enchanting bit of romantic landscape in all the
      valley of the Saco.
    </p>
  </div>
</section>

<section class="feature">
  <div class="feature_img"></div>
  <div class="feature_content feature_content-1">
    Let the most absent-minded of men be plunged in his
    deepest reveries—stand that man on his legs, set his
    feet a-going, and he will infallibly lead you to water,
    if water there be in all that region.
  </div>
  <div class="feature_content feature_content-2">
    Take almost any path you please, and ten to one it
    carries you down in a dale, and leaves you there by a
    pool in the stream. There is magic in it.
  </div>
</section>

<footer class="footer">
  <h3 class="footer_title">
    I am a Footer
```

```html
    </h3>
    <ul class="menulist footer_menu-first">
      <li>
        Products
      </li>
      <li>
        <a href="">Footer link</a>
      </li>
      <li>
        <a href="">Footer link</a>
      </li>
    </ul>
    <ul class="menulist">
      <li>
        About
      </li>
      <li>
        <a href="">Footer link</a>
      </li>
      <li>
        <a href="">Footer link</a>
      </li>
    </ul>
    <ul class="menulist">
      <li>
        Links
      </li>
      <li>
        <a href="">Footer link</a>
      </li>
      <li>
        <a href="">Footer link</a>
      </li>
    </ul>
    <ul class="menulist">
      <li>
        Account
      </li>
      <li>
        <a href="">Footer link</a>
      </li>
      <li>
        <a href="">Footer link</a>
      </li>
    </ul>
  </footer>

</body>
</html>
```

Let's get oriented with what we have here on the page and then we'll explain what we'll be doing. In the HTML in Listing 15.23, you can see that there is a series of containers for site content (all with some stubbed-out content), and they are all direct children of the HTML's **<body>** tag. The CSS at the top of the **<style>** section includes a minimal CSS reset (Section 9.5), and adds some basic styling for backgrounds, padding, etc. on each of the page's elements.

15.5.2 Adding a Global Grid and Header Positioning

If you need to refresh your memory on what we'll be making, Figure 15.45 from the beginning of the chapter is going to be our blueprint for the new layout. Before, we had one layout grid on the outside; now we'll have many containers, each with the same grid inside. To accomplish this, we'll add in a new CSS declaration, and then we'll add that class onto every element as we style each one. Let's add the declaration now (Listing 15.24).

Listing 15.24: Creating our global grid class.

grid-landing.html

```
.landing_cta {
  margin-top: 1.5em;
  text-align: center;
}

.grid {
  box-sizing: border-box;
  display: grid;
  grid-template-columns: minmax(2em,1fr) repeat(6,minmax(auto,10em))
                         minmax(2em,1fr);
}
```

And then add the **grid** class onto the element with the **header** class:

```
<header class="header grid">
```

All that CSS we added should look familiar, but we should explain the thinking behind this **grid-template-columns** style:

```
minmax(2em,1fr) repeat(6,minmax(auto,10em)) minmax(2em,1fr)
```

This column layout creates a series of **6** content columns that will have a max size of **10em** each, for a total content area of **60em**. These columns are what we'll be arranging elements to line up with. Then, on either side of the content area, we have two columns that have a minimum size of **2em** so that on a small screen there is some padding, and a maximum size of **1fr** so that the columns expand to keep the content area in the center (Figure 15.48). Note that the columns in the main content area start with grid line 2 and end at grid line 8.

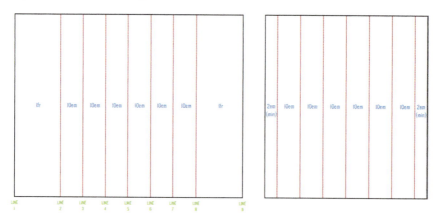

Figure 15.48: The basic column structure on a big screen and on a smaller screen.

Starting with a small example first, let's assume that we want the content in the header for the site to be constrained only to the top of the main content columns, as seen in Figure 15.49.

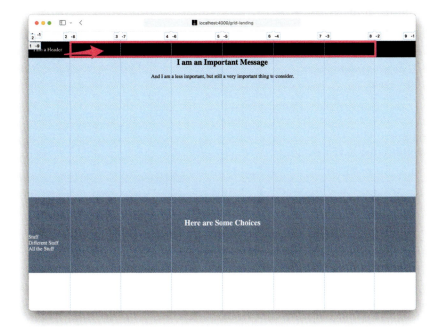

Figure 15.49: It would be nice if the header, on the top left, went where the arrow is pointing.

One way to do that would be to add in a style like this:

```
.header_content {
  grid-column: 2 / 8;
}
```

That would work, but adding the style in that way would mean we'd be adding the same sort of thing throughout the page—a blatant violation of the DRY principle (Box 5.2).

Instead, we can create a new class called **grid_2-8** (it will be starting at line 2 and ending at line 8) that we can reuse elsewhere on the page. Since the goal of this whole exercise is to get all of the page content organized using grid columns, it will definitely be reused. Add the new declaration in now, as shown in Listing 15.25.

Listing 15.25: Adding the `.grid_2-8` class.

grid-landing.html

```
.grid {
  box-sizing: border-box;
  display: grid;
  grid-template-columns: minmax(2em,1fr) repeat(6,minmax(auto,10em))
                         minmax(2em,1fr);
}
.grid_2-8 {
  grid-column: 2 / 8;
}
```

Also add the **grid_2-8** class to the **header_content** element:

```
<div class="header_content grid_2-8">
```

Now when you refresh the page you'll see that the **header_content** element is fixed in place to only those grid lines (Figure 15.50).

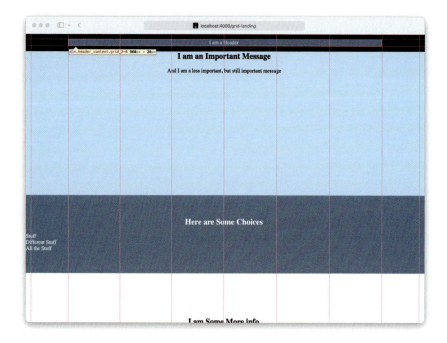

Figure 15.50: We've managed to move things!

Before we apply this newfound alignment power to other elements on the page, let's add some more content in the header, a new positioning class that constrains elements to just lines 3–7, and some more styles for the header (Listing 15.26).

Listing 15.26: Finishing off the new header styling.
grid-landing.html

```css
.
.
.
.grid_2-8 {
  grid-column: 2 / 8;
}
.grid_3-7 {
  grid-column: 3 / 7;
}
.header {
  background-color: #000;
  color: #fff;
  padding: 1em;
  position: sticky;
  text-align: center;
  top: 0;
  z-index: 10;
}
.header_menu {
  column-gap: 1em;
  display: flex;
  justify-content: center;
}
.header_menu-link {
  color: #a8d6f7;
}
.
.
.
```

Then, in the HTML, we'll add in a new **nav** element to the header with the new class already applied (Listing 15.27). Refreshing the page should give us something like Figure 15.51.

Listing 15.27: Adding some extra HTML to the header.

grid-landing.html

```
<header class="header grid">
  <div class="header_content grid_2-8">
    I am a Header
  </div>
  <nav class="grid_3-7">
    <ul class="header_menu menulist">
      <li>
        <a href="" class="header_menu-link">
          Header link
        </a>
      </li>
      <li>
        <a href="" class="header_menu-link">
          Header link
        </a>
      </li>
    </ul>
  </nav>
</header>
```

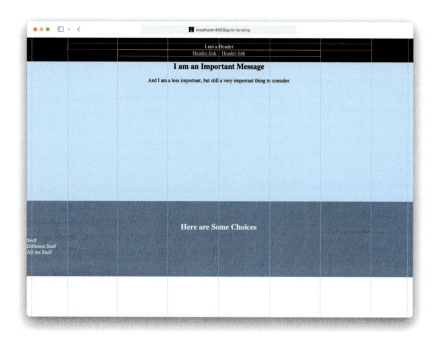

Figure 15.51: That looks like a header now.

As you can see in Figure 15.51, we now have a menu in our header. In addition, as the outlines show, the elements are locked into place according to the grid lines that we specified. We hope that you can start to see how we are creating CSS LEG— *(lawyer's note: LEGO and LEGO brand blocks are the exclusive trademark of the LEGO GROUP)*—umm... *building blocks* that we can snap together!

Before we go further down the rabbit hole, we want to point something out that might have slipped by. In the **header_menu** styles that we added, you might have noticed that the element has **display: flex** applied, and there's also a **column-gap** set... but isn't that just a grid thing? Nope! You can use column and row gaps on flexbox elements too (Figure 15.52)![12]

Figure 15.52: Celebrating that we can apply **gap** to flexbox elements instead of needing **flex-gap**!

---

12. Image courtesy of altanaka/Shutterstock.

15.5.3   Using Building Blocks and Justifying

All right, let's start adding our grid to the rest of the page by turning our attention to that **hero** section. The first step is to add the **grid** class to the **section** with class **hero**:

```
<section class="hero grid">
```

If you were to just leave things there and add no new CSS styles, you'd get something that looks like Figure 15.53.

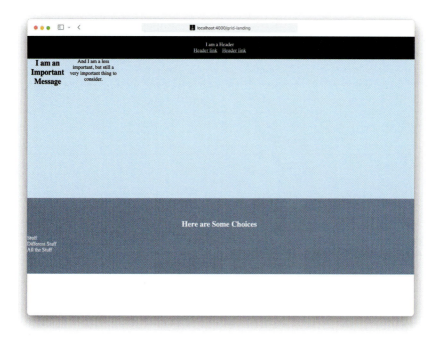

Figure 15.53: Sure it's using grid, but it doesn't look good.

But with our new CSS building-block power, we can make this look better. Let's create a new, more constrained class called **.grid_4-6** for the content area (Listing 15.28).

Listing 15.28: A new, smaller **.grid_4-6** class.

grid-landing.html

```
.grid_3-7 {
  grid-column: 3 / 7;
}
.grid_4-6 {
  grid-column: 4 / 6;
}
```

Let's make the **h1** be able to stretch across the entire content section by adding the **grid_2-8** class, and then add the new **grid_4-6** class from Listing 15.28 to the hero-content **div**:

```
<section class="hero grid">
  <h1 class="hero_title grid_2-8">
    I am an Important Message
  </h1>
  <div class="hero_content grid_4-6">
    And I am a less important, but still a very important
    thing to consider.
  </div>
</section>
```

The result appears in Figure 15.54. It still doesn't look great—we probably want to move the content as indicated by the arrows.

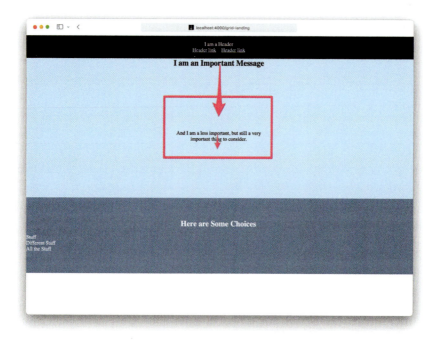

Figure 15.54: These things should probably be in that area.

So, why is there all that space between the elements? Well, if you remember back to Section 15.2.2, the browser will just treat new rows like they are all **1fr** when there are no grid row settings (and there are none). Since we explicitly defined the column start and end for the two elements in the hero, and because they can't both fit on the same row, the browser popped the **hero_content** down to a new row and then applied **1fr** sizing to both. You wouldn't have noticed this in the header, even though the same thing happened there too, because we didn't set a height for the header. That means the block elements were sized to just fit the content, and we were none the wiser.

So how can we get the elements in the hero to be only the size of their content, and also position them? If you thought, "Use one of the **align** or **justify** styles," you're correct! In particular, we can add an **align-content** rule to the **.hero** class (Listing 15.29).

Listing 15.29: Aligning the **hero** content.

grid-landing.html

```css
.hero {
  align-content: center;
  background-color: #a8d6f7;
  min-height: 50vh;
  text-align: center;
}
```

And then, just for fun, let's add a little more content into that **hero_content** element (Listing 15.30).

Listing 15.30: Adding some extra hero content.

grid-landing.html

```html
<section class="hero grid">
  <h1 class="hero_title grid_2-8">
    I am an Important Message
  </h1>
  <div class="hero_content grid_4-6">
    And I am a less important, but still a very important
    thing to consider.
    <div class="landing_cta">
      <a href="">
        Click me!
      </a>
    </div>
  </div>
</section>
```

When you refresh the page, you'll now have content that is constrained by the global grid and is also positioned in the center of the **hero** section (Figure 15.55).

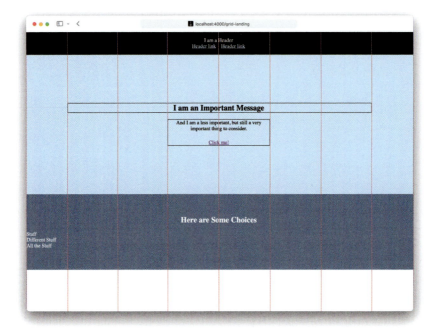

Figure 15.55: Ahhhh, that's a lot better!

15.5.4 More Column Positioning

Now that we've styled the **hero** section, let's take a look at the rest of the page. The next element in the HTML is the **options** section, but let's skip that for a second (we are going to do something a little more complex there in Section 15.5.7) and instead focus on the element with the **info** class. In this element, we'll apply the global grid, make the title cover the entire content area, make the subtitle go from lines 4 to 6, and have the block of text go from lines 3 to 7 on the grid (Listing 15.31).

Listing 15.31: Using our building block in the "info" section.

grid-landing.html

.
.
.

```
<section class="info grid">
  <h2 class="info_title grid_2-8">
    I am Some More info
  </h2>
  <div class="subtitle grid_4-6">
    Say you are in the country.
  </div>
  <div class="info_content grid_3-7">
    <p>
      In some high land of lakes. Take almost any path you
.
.
.
```

If your page looks like Figure 15.56 in your browser, we think you are getting the hang of this!

Figure 15.56: It's a fully functional "info" section.

15.5.5   Using Overlapping in a Feature Section

Let's now move to the element with the **feature** class and get a little fancier. The goal is to make some sort of featured section with text overlaid on top of an image—something like Figure 15.57. How would you do that with our grid?

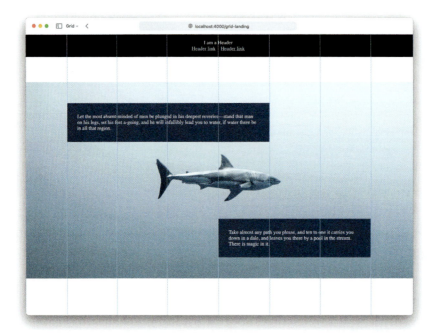

Figure 15.57: This is what we are going to be making.

We're also going to throw in a wrinkle where instead of setting the image to be the background of the entire element, it needs to be the background of that **feature_img** element. The reason is that we might want to have the flexibility to move it around in the future and still keep it positioned using our global grid. This is a chance to use the overlapping ability of CSS grid that we covered in Section 15.4.4.

The zeroth step is going to be adding **grid** to the **feature** element (since without that, nothing interesting will happen):

```
<section class="feature grid">
```

Then we are going to add some new style declarations so that we can see what we are working with (Listing 15.32). (Be sure you're viewing the page using Jekyll through localhost:4000 instead of just looking at the raw HTML file in your browser. Otherwise, the file path for the background image in Listing 15.32 won't be resolved properly and the image won't display.)

Listing 15.32: Adding styles to make the feature section elements visible.
grid-landing.html

```
.feature {
  min-height: 70vh;
}
.feature_img {
  background-image: url('/images/shark.jpg');
  background-size: cover;
}
.feature_content {
  background-color: #183a53;
  color: #fff;
  padding: 2em 2em;
}
```

When you refresh your browser you'll see… something ugly (Figure 15.58)!

Figure 15.58: First steps are always a little rough.

Next, we know that we are going to want the **feature_img** element to go from column 1 to column 9, and from row 1 to 2. As an example of how you could handle a one-off situation where you don't need the code to be reusable, we're going to treat this section differently and not create **grid_X-Y** classes for these elements.

You might remember from Section 15.4.4 that, if we are going to be using the overlapping technique, we will need to have all the elements explicitly positioned on the grid, with start and end definitions for both rows and columns. As a first step, try out the code in Listing 15.33.

Listing 15.33: Adding explicit positioning for feature section elements.
grid-landing.html

```
.feature {
  min-height: 70vh;
}
.feature_img {
  background-image: url('/images/shark.jpg');
  background-size: cover;
  grid-column: 1 / 9;
  grid-row: 1 / 2;
}
.feature_content {
  background-color: #183a53;
  color: #fff;
  grid-row-start: 1;
  padding: 2em 2em;
}
```

You'll end up with something (Figure 15.59) that looks a little closer to the end goal in the original example image (Figure 15.57).

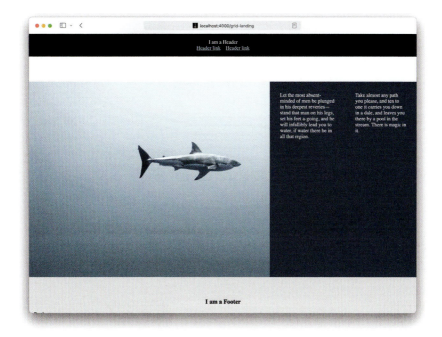

Figure 15.59: Starting to get a little warmer.

Next, let's tackle getting those two content areas where we want them by adding **grid-column** styling on the **.feature_content-1** and **.feature_content-2** classes. We'll also add a dash of **self-alignment** since in the example image (Figure 15.57) the elements weren't stretched and instead were positioned at the top and bottom.

Finally, we'll top it off with a delicious hint of **margin** on the **.feature_content** class to move the boxes away from the edge. The result appears in Listing 15.34.

Listing 15.34: Finishing off the feature section.
grid-landing.html

```
.feature_content {
  background-color: #183a53;
  color: #fff;
  grid-row-start: 1;
```

```
  margin: 4em 0;
  padding: 2em 2em;
}
.feature_content-1 {
  align-self: start;
  grid-column: 2 / 6;
}
.feature_content-2 {
  align-self: end;
  grid-column: 5 / 8;
}
```

Refresh, and there ya have it (Figure 15.60)!

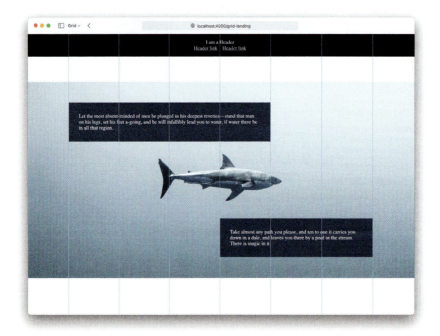

Figure 15.60: A couple of lines of CSS and we have a fairly complex layout.

By the way, what we just did is an effective method for getting the alignment and spacing we wanted, but it's not the only one. As is so often the case with CSS, there is more than one way to do it (Box 15.2).

Box 15.2: There's More Than One Way to Do It

As we've said a number of times, including waaaay back in the introduction to CSS (Section 5.2.3), there are a million different ways to do most things in CSS. Let's take a look at a second solution that achieves the same basic look for the **feature** selection.

Our new goal is to get the content boxes away from the edges of the section without using a margin (maybe because the margins on the elements don't play nice with other elements on the page). One way to do this is to use extra grid rows on the parent element and use the top and bottom rows like margin or padding. To try this, add a grid-template-rows style on .feature:

```
.feature {
  grid-template-rows: 4em 1fr 4em;
  min-height: 70vh;
}
```

Then change the grid-row rule for the feature_img row start and end styles to go from 1 to 4 (instead of from 1 to 2):

```
.feature_img {
  background-image: url('/images/shark.jpg');
  background-size: cover;
  grid-column: 1 / 9;
  grid-row: 1 / 4;
}
```

And on the feature_content class, change grid-row-start to 2 while also removing the margin:

```
.feature_content {
  background-color: #183a53;
  color: #fff;
  grid-row-start: 2;
  padding: 2em 2em;
}
```

The result is the same appearance as in Figure 15.60, but with this design you wouldn't need to worry about adding margins on the child elements. That lets each child be more self-contained and leaves the positioning and alignment entirely on the parent element.

15.5.6　Starting at a Specific Column and Self-Aligning

Before moving to the more complicated **options** section, let's clean up the footer. We've got four columns of links, and it would be nice to have them centered under the header in that section. You might think that you would need to define the position of each column, but we actually only need to tell the browser where to render the first one. After that, all the elements after the first will render according to the grid. (You might remember this from when we first started changing column positions of elements in Section 15.2.)

So first, add the **grid** class to the **footer**, and let's also make the title span the content columns by adding **grid_2-8**:

```
<footer class="footer grid">
  <h3 class="footer_title grid_2-8">

    I am a Footer
  </h3>
```

We already added a class to the first menu item in the stubbed-out version of the page at the beginning of this section (Listing 15.23), so let's make it functional by adding a **grid-column-start** style to the **.footer_menu-first** class, as seen in Listing 15.35.

Listing 15.35: Moving the first footer list to a specific column.
grid-landing.html

```
.footer {
  background-color: #ddd;
  padding: 4em 1em;
}
.footer_menu-first {
  grid-column-start: 3;
}
```

When you refresh your browser, you'll see that things look kind of OK, but maybe it would look a little cleaner if the individual lists were centered within their columns (Figure 15.61).

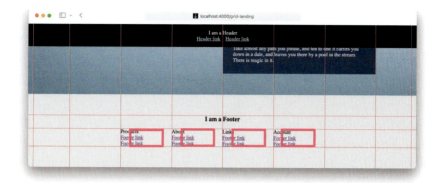

Figure 15.61: This would be a cleaner look.

It's an easy fix with a little justifying (Listing 15.36)! When you refresh the page, everything should be much more aligned now, like in Figure 15.62.

Listing 15.36: Centering all the lists in the footer within their columns.
grid-landing.html

```css
.footer {
  background-color: #ddd;
  justify-items: center;
  padding: 4em 1em;
}
```

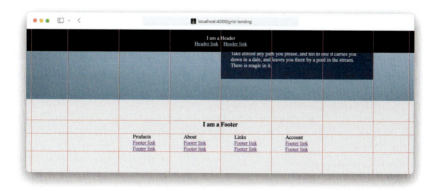

Figure 15.62: Ahhhh, that's better.

15.5.7   Grid Inside a Grid Inside a Page

Let's head back up the page to the **options** section and finish this example off with something a little more complex.

One route to achieving the result shown in Figure 15.63 would be to create a bunch of classes that have explicit column assignments for each element, and that would work, but what if there might be a varying number of these content items? Sometimes there might be two items, and sometimes there might be five, but either way it would be nice to have the section fit the content to the space, while also capping the number of items at three per row.

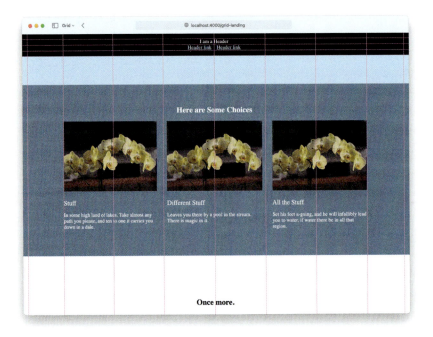

Figure 15.63: We are going to eventually make this.

This is the perfect place to use the **auto-fit** feature that we discussed in Section 15.3! To make the layout work, we are going to have to add yet another grid inside the **options** wrapper.

The first step is to add the **grid** class on the element with the **options** class and also to **options_content**, and then add **grid_2-8** to the title and to **options_content**:

```
<section class="options grid">
  <h2 class="options_title grid_2-8">

     Here are Some Choices
  </h2>
  <div class="options_content grid grid_2-8">
  .
  .
  .
```

(Note that **options_content** has no CSS rules associated with it; we added a class name just so we'd have a convenient way to refer to the element.) Now, if we were to only add **grid** to **options_content** (with no other changes) and then take a look at the grid lines in the browser inspector, we'd get the mess shown in Figure 15.64.

Figure 15.64: There are lines everywhere.

The red lines in Figure 15.64 are the global grid, and the blue lines are the columns inside the **options_content** element… Clearly, nothing lines up! To fix this, we need to set up a new class for this new content area that will have a max of three columns. In the CSS, add the styles found in Listing 15.37.

Listing 15.37: Creating the column template for the grid within the grid.
grid-landing.html

```
.grid_4-6 {
  grid-column: 4 / 6;
}
.grid_cols-3max {
  grid-template-columns: repeat(auto-fit, minmax(18em, 1fr));
  grid-gap: 3em;
}
```

Looking at Listing 15.37, you might wonder, "Why **18em** for the minimum part of the **minmax**?" Our global grid columns are **10em** wide, so to fit three of these content areas each is going to be **20em**, but we also added a gap of **3em**. Since we have explicit widths involved here, we can't just ignore the gap the way that we could have if all the elements just had a width of **1fr** (Section 15.2.2). Having three content columns means there will be two **3em** gaps—a **6em** total of gap space that needs to be subtracted from each column. If you don't want to actually have to do the math, check out Box 15.3.

Box 15.3: Advanced CSS: `calc( )`

You can actually do math in CSS now. To replace the value in Listing 15.37 with an automated calculation, you could use this:

```
repeat(auto-fit, minmax(calc(20em - (6em/3)),1fr))
```

In the calc( ) function, 20em is the total width that we want each of these content boxes to be. From that, we are subtracting the 6em of total gap space, but first we are dividing that by the 3 columns.

Now, if you haven't already done so, add the new **grid_cols-3max** class to the container:

```
<div class="options_content grid grid_2-8 grid_cols-3max">
```

If you refresh and turn the grid lines on in your web inspector, the layout should look like the screenshot on the left in Figure 15.65, and if you set one of the **div**s to **display: none**, you'll see how the columns adapt to fill the space like the screenshot on the right.

Figure 15.65: The rough options section with three columns, and only two columns.

To finish this whole thing off, let's fill those **div**s with a little more content, and add some styles to make them more interesting (Listing 15.38).

Listing 15.38: Filling out the options section with more content.
grid-landing.html

```
.
.
.
<section class="options grid">
  <h2 class="options_title grid_2-8">
    Here are Some Choices
  </h2>
  <div class="options_content grid grid_2-8 grid_cols-3max">
    <div>
      <img src="/images/small/slide1.jpg" class="options_item-img">
      <div class="options_item-title">Stuff</div>
      <p>
```

```
            In some high land of lakes. Take almost any path
            you please, and ten to one it carries you down in a dale.
        </p>
    </div>
    <div>
        <img src="/images/small/slide1.jpg" class="options_item-img">
        <div class="options_item-title">Different Stuff</div>
        <p>
            Leaves you there by a pool in the stream. There is
            magic in it.
        </p>
    </div>
    <div>
        <img src="/images/small/slide1.jpg" class="options_item-img">
        <div class="options_item-title">All the Stuff</div>
        <p>
            Set his feet a-going, and he will infallibly lead
            you to water, if water there be in all that region.
        </p>
    </div>
  </div>
</section>
.
.
.
```

You can play around now with removing or adding items, and your page should look and respond like the examples in Figure 15.66.

Figure 15.66: The options section with three columns, and stretching two columns to fit.

15.5.8 Exercises

1. See if you can make the margin-less solution mentioned in Box 15.2 work for the `.feature` section of the example page... but see if you can add a third content box that is centered vertically and stretches from grid line 4 to 6.

2. Copy and paste one of the child elements in the `.options_content` section and then use the CSS `calc()` feature (Box 15.3) to change that section to support four columns with the same gap in between.

15.6 Conclusion

This brings us to the end of Part II. By design, the grid pages developed in this chapter aren't part of our main website, but it's still nice to have the option to show them to the world (as well as to have a remote backup), so let's make one final deployment to production:

```
$ git add -A
$ git commit -m "Add sample grid pages"
$ git push
```

At this point, you've got a beautiful site on the live Web, together with an amount of CSS knowledge that is truly getting *dangerous*. The only thing left is to serve the site, not from <username>.github.io, but from a custom domain you own. In other words, it's time for Part III! We especially recommend reading the concluding thoughts in Section 17.4, which include some suggestions for next steps that are useful even if you decide not to use a custom domain after all.

PART III
Custom Domains

CHAPTER 16

A Name of Our Own

In Part III of *Learn Enough HTML, CSS and Layout to Be Dangerous*, we'll add a final bit of polish to the kind of websites created in Part I and Part II: using custom URLs for our site instead of using URLs at GitHub Pages. In other words, instead of having a site at someone else's domain, like example.someoneelsesdomain.com, we're going to learn how to use our own *custom domain* like example.com.[1]

In this chapter, we'll cover how to register a custom domain (Section 16.1), how to configure its settings for the Domain Name System (DNS) using Cloudflare (Section 16.2), and how to connect a custom domain to a site running at GitHub Pages (Section 16.3).[2] The result will be a fast, professional-grade website running on a domain of your choice. Then, in Chapter 17, we'll show how to use Google Workspace to send and receive email using addresses at your custom domain (so that you can use yourname@example.com instead of yourname152@gmail.com). As a special bonus, we'll show you how to monitor the traffic on your site using Google Analytics.

Because of how quickly things change on the Web, it is entirely possible that some of the information in this guide might be out of date due to services changing interfaces or features. Even with the steps detailed here, in all likelihood you'll still have

---

1. Because the custom-domains material is intended mainly for reference, there are no exercises in Part III.

2. See the free online version of *Learn Enough Custom Domains to Be Dangerous* (https://www.learnenough.com/custom-domains) for a bonus section covering custom domains for dynamic web applications (such as those created in *Learn Enough Ruby to Be Dangerous* (https://www.learnenough.com/ruby) and the *Ruby on Rails Tutorial* (https://www.railstutorial.org/)).

to apply some of your technical sophistication (Box 5.1) in order to get everything to work. That's just how it goes on the World Wide Web![3]

16.1 Custom Domain Registration

You may or may not know this, but when you open up your browser and type in the address of a site like google.com, you aren't *actually* entering a real address where the Google server can be found. Instead, google.com can be thought of more as a screen name, or *domain name*, that is an easier way to get to Google's web services than if you had to remember the real machine address, which is generally something like 142.251.32.46.[4] This latter monstrosity is known as an *IP number* or *IP address*, where "IP" stands for Internet Protocol, which is the name of the protocol that computers on the Internet use to communicate with each other. Because they are so much easier to remember, custom domains are almost universally preferred to raw IP numbers.

The first step to using a custom domain yourself is to *register* one. Domain names have to be registered through an authorized registrar, and there are a bunch of them. You may even have seen some of their bad commercials on TV. The domain registrar we recommend is Hover.com, which has good customer service, reasonable prices, an intuitive interface, and a free domain privacy service.

In general, domains aren't property that you own outright, like real estate. Instead, domains are more like an office you lease from a property owner, but with the right to renew the lease in perpetuity. The rights to the domain can be transferred and sold, but ultimately someone has to regularly pay the registrar for the right to the domain; otherwise, it will be released back to the pool of possible domains, where someone else can buy it.

16.1.1 What to Register?

Most registrars allow you to register domains with a variety of *top-level domains* (TLDs), which are the final part of the domain name (.com, .org, .info, .io, and so on). The cost of the domain depends on the domain's TLD, and most registrars offer discounts on the yearly cost if you pay for a number of years at once. You'll also have to provide

---

3. An expanded version of Part III is available for free online as *Learn Enough Custom Domains to Be Dangerous*.

4. You can actually type this number directly into your browser's address bar, like this: http://142.251.32.46/.

a bunch of required information when you register the domain, as the registrars are required by law to know who owns domains, and they have to make this information public. Most registrars offer a privacy service that will keep your personal information off the Internet, though.

You've probably noticed that most global services and corporations use custom domains ending in the top-level domain .com ("dot-com"), which is generally considered to be the most desirable TLD. This TLD was created for general commercial activity by ICANN ("EYE-can"), the organization responsible for managing Internet names.[5]

So, which TLD should you pick? Well, a lot of that depends on what you want to do online, who your audience is, and the availability of the domain name that you want. If you are a big enough company or have enough name recognition in other media, you could just pick any TLD that has a domain name available that incorporates your established name. Unless you have a good reason to choose otherwise, a .com domain is probably the way to go, though there are a lot of different possibilities:

- There are *generic* TLDs, like .com, .info, .net, and .org, which can be used for general purposes.

- There are *generic restricted* TLDs, like .biz, .name, and .pro, where there are rules on how domains registered to the TLD can be used.

- Each country has its own TLD, such as .us (United States), .uk (United Kingdom),[6] .it (Italy), .ly (Libya), .co (Colombia), and .io (Indian Ocean territories). The .io domain has become popular in the tech industry, especially for a quality domain name whose .com equivalent is already in use or (especially) when it is being held hostage by a domain squatter.[7]

- There are the current *sponsored generic* TLDs, like .aero, .asia, .cat (not about cats but rather the Catalan linguistic and cultural community), .coop, .edu, .gov, .in,

---

5. ICANN was originally under the control of the US government (via the Department of Commerce), but since 2016 it has been free from US government oversight.

6. The UK actually has its own sub-TLD, so many UK sites end in something like .co.uk.

7. Technically, *domain squatting* refers only to the bad-faith registration of domains, such as those corresponding to known trademarks. In practice, though, the supposedly benign practice of "domaining" (buying up domains for future resale but doing nothing useful with them in the interim) is so annoying that many people use the term "squatter" for those who engage in either practice.

.jobs, .mil, .mobi, .tel, .travel, and .xxx (which can be used only for purposes within a particular industry that you can probably guess).

- Finally, there is the "new generic TLD (gTLD) program," which seeks to add an unlimited number of gTLDs (i.e., non-country TLDs). Any person or organization that wishes to have their own TLD can pay a hefty fee and apply to have their own TLD—some examples are things like .xyz, .ninja, .limo, as well as a large assortment of TLDs that use writing systems other than the Latin alphabet. Most of these new TLDs will be for entirely generic use, and some will be sponsored generic TLDs that can be used only for a specific purpose.

You should know, though, that many people consider these new domains, and any business that uses one, to be less reliable than the old ones, probably because they aren't as familiar. Some of the country TLDs have become pretty well-accepted, such as .io mentioned above, though they often still cause confusion for less tech-savvy people. The problem is that if you tell a non-tech-savvy person to go to a site like http://bit.ly, you might find that they try to go to http://bit.ly.com. The key takeaway here is that you need to know your audience: You don't want a domain that scares off potential users, you don't want a TLD with lots of bad sites, and you don't want a name that confuses people.

With those considerations in mind, let's get back to registering a domain. The first step is to visit the Hover.com homepage. At this point, you'll have to choose a domain. For this tutorial, we'll use codedangerously.com, but of course you'll need your own (since we already registered that one!).

If you don't already have an idea for a domain name, there are actually a lot of free tools that are specifically designed to help you come up with one. They generally allow you to enter a bunch of different words or phrases to generate suggested domain names that are available to be registered. A couple of popular sites that we've used are instantdomainsearch.com and domainr.com. Or you can just use the domain registrar itself, which is what we'll do here.

On Hover, finding out if the domain name is available is as easy as entering the name in the giant input field on the homepage and pressing enter. At this point, Hover will give you a long list of TLDs for which your name of choice is still available (Figure 16.1), as well as suggested domains containing word substitutions (farther down the page).

You might have noticed that even when you find a domain name that you like, there are often a lot of very similar variations available on different TLDs, as well as

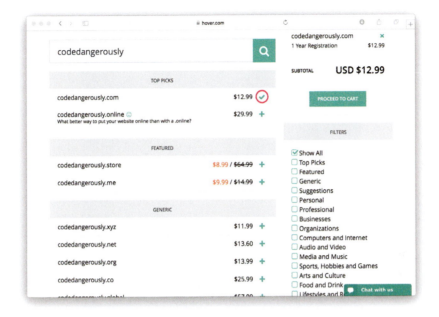

Figure 16.1: The different TLD options that are available to register.

domains that are close in spelling to your domain. If you have the extra money to spend, you can buy as many misspelled domains as you want and then permanently redirect users to the appropriate domain. (We'll look at how to do domain forwarding ourselves in Section 16.3.3.)

When you've selected all the domains that you want to buy (just the .com is probably fine), go ahead and go through all the checkout steps, including providing the necessary contact info, and if you've made it through all these steps, congratulations! You are now the proud owner (or at least long-term leaser) of virtual digital property on the Internet (Figure 16.2).[8]

---

8. Castle image courtesy of egal/123RF; silhouetted house image courtesy of ArtMari/Shutterstock.

Figure 16.2: Your very own fantasy castle floating in the Internet sky!

16.1.2 You've Got a Domain, Now What?

The *Domain Name System* (DNS) serves to associate domain names with IP addresses, so it is DNS that makes it possible to type a custom domain like google.com instead of a raw IP address like 142.251.32.46.[9] Once you've registered a domain, the next step is to set up the *DNS records* for your domain so that it can be added to the Domain Name System. This involves editing the so-called *nameservers*, which are the computers that tell DNS exactly which server should be queried to find the domain details (such as which subdomains exist, which URLs should be forwarded, etc.).

Right after you purchase a domain, the nameservers are usually set to the registrar's servers, and in the case of Hover that would be something like Listing 16.1.

---

9. See the online version of *Learn Enough Custom Domains to Be Dangerous* at https://www.learnenough.com /custom-domains for more information on the Domain Name System.

Listing 16.1: Typical Hover.com nameservers.

```
ns1.hover.com
ns2.hover.com
```

Although you would be perfectly fine using the default DNS controls to complete this tutorial, we are going to set up a third-party service that provides a bunch of additional useful features. Setting up this service will involve changing the nameservers on the registrar to point to the new nameservers so that they can be the first point of contact for domain names in DNS lookups. Making these changes, and configuring the result, is the subject of Section 16.2.

16.2   Cloudflare Setup

Although the default nameservers at most domain registrars are perfectly fine for many purposes, we prefer to use a third-party service called *Cloudflare* that includes a bunch of useful features. Cloudflare sits between the Internet and a website to provide the following benefits:

- Fast DNS management using a nice interface

- The ability to set up a secure connection to the site using Transport Layer Security (TLS), the successor to Secure Sockets Layer (SSL)

- *Edge caching* to make the site's content easy to access across the world

- Protection from anyone who might try to take the site offline using a *Distributed Denial of Service* (DDoS) attack

...and the basic service is *free to use* (with inexpensive pay plans as your website's needs grow).

It would probably be useful to quickly explain what these features are in case you aren't familiar with them.

16.2.1   Cloudflare Features

As noted in Section 16.1.2, most registrars allow you to do DNS management via their default nameservers, but the interfaces can be less than optimal (to put it generously). Additionally, when you make DNS record changes on a registrar (like pointing to a new server IP address), the changes often aren't immediate; instead, they have to

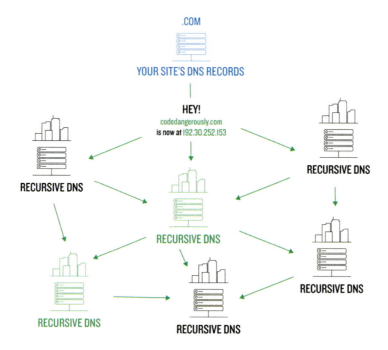

Figure 16.3: Potentially slow DNS propagation.

propagate throughout the DNS system—a process which can take 24–72 hours to complete as your update bounces around the DNS network (Figure 16.3).

Because Cloudflare sits between your servers and the world while passing web requests through, any server changes stay internal to the Cloudflare service. To the outside world, all requests still go to the Cloudflare IP address first. This means that the propagation of DNS changes (like subdomains and redirects) is nearly instantaneous—a feature that can be critical when administering a working site.

Transport Layer Security (TLS) is a method for encrypting web traffic from a user's computer to the server (Figure 16.4). As mentioned before, Transport Layer Security has replaced an older technology called Secure Sockets Layer (SSL), but

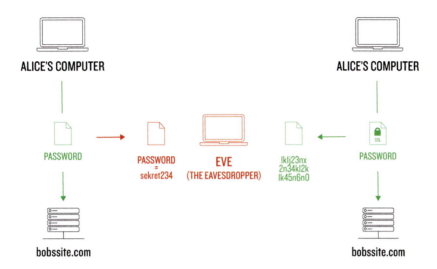

Figure 16.4: Encrypting data using SSL/TLS.

because nothing in the world of the Web can be simple, people often still use the older name or abbreviation even when they are actually talking about TLS. We've chosen to abbreviate that as SSL/TLS for this tutorial to familiarize you with both, and if you see SSL without TLS in the wild you are duly authorized to have a brief flash of annoyance on our behalf at how tech silliness seems to continually cause confusion and complexity. You've actually been using SSL/TLS for years, possibly without even knowing it: Every time you go to a site with a little lock next to the site's domain name, you're using SSL/TLS (Figure 16.5).[10]

Figure 16.5: An SSL/TLS lock icon.

---

10. The Internet is a dangerous place, and you can never be certain that you really are safe, but SSL/TLS increases the chances considerably.

SSL/TLS works by turning the packets of information sent between your browser and a server from plain old text into a jumble of letters and other characters. This makes it virtually impossible for someone to intercept the traffic and see what is being sent back and forth. In many cases, there is a lot of ceremony and pain associated with setting up SSL/TLS for a site, but when you use Cloudflare everything is already set up for you for free. Because non-SSL/TLS sites are so insecure, you shouldn't run a site these days without SSL/TLS—not even a static site like a blog.

Next up on the Cloudflare feature list is *edge caching* (Figure 16.6). Edge caching involves automatically saving your site's content on servers around the world, allowing users to access the content from the server nearest to them (which speeds load times).

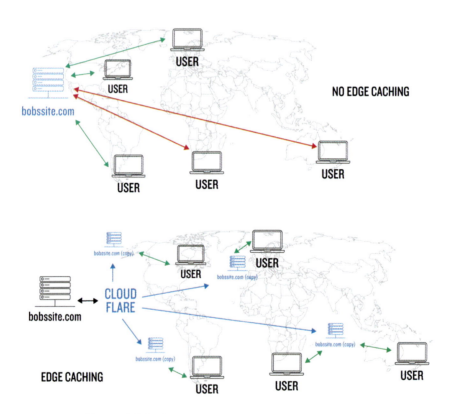

Figure 16.6: Optimizing load times with edge caching.

Lastly, Cloudflare protects the site from DDoS attacks. You might have heard of these on the news in reference to some group being accused of "hacking" another organization. DDoS attacks are online disruptions that try to make entire sites inaccessible by flooding their servers with fake requests—imagine millions of fake users that all ask a server for a site at the same time.

There are a limited number of requests that a single server can handle at once, so if there are enough fake users making requests, real users won't be able to get to the site. Cloudflare has the ability to notice when this type of attack is happening and can filter out the fake users to keep your site online and available (Figure 16.7). As with the other features, you don't have to configure anything to get this benefit.

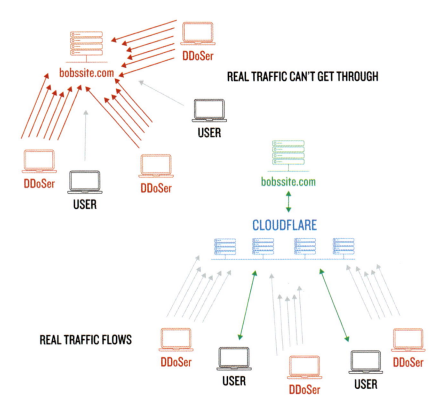

Figure 16.7: Protecting against DDoS attacks.

These days, our first step after registering a domain is immediately setting up Cloudflare. The benefits are great, and unless you have a fairly complicated application, the service is free.[11] What's not to love? Let's get started.[12]

16.2.2 Cloudflare Signup

The first step in using Cloudflare (just like pretty much any service on the Internet) is to create an account. One added benefit, though, is that the signup process also walks you through adding a domain to Cloudflare. So, head on over to cloudflare.com and click the Sign Up button at the top right of the page in the site header to get to the registration page.

16.2.3 Connecting Registrar Nameservers

After you've created your account, Cloudflare automatically kicks you into the first step to add a domain to their service. Enter your newly purchased domain in the box and press the Add Site button, and then on the next screen select the free plan for this tutorial. It should take less than a minute for Cloudflare to pull in the domain records, and when it's done the next page will show you the result of the scan from the last step: a report with all of the DNS records associated with your domain.

---

11. We use the professional, paid tier for more complicated sites like learnenough.com and railstutorial.org, which is but one of many indications that Cloudflare's freemium business model is working well.

12. For more details on all of the steps in this section, including a large number of additional screenshots, see the online version at https://www.learnenough.com/custom-domains.

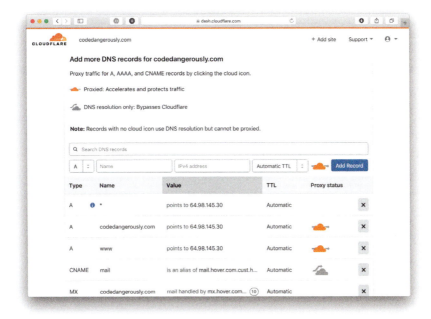

Figure 16.8: Our domain's DNS settings at Cloudflare.

The initial DNS settings are displayed on a page that should look something like Figure 16.8, which includes several kinds of records. The *A records* are initially set to flow through Cloudflare (indicated by the orange cloud icons in Figure 16.8). The *CNAME record* is initially set up to skip the Cloudflare service (indicated by the gray cloud icon in Figure 16.8). Don't worry about the details—we'll discuss about these record types in more detail in Section 16.3.1. Since we just purchased this domain, the current records aren't very complicated, and there's nothing to configure on step.

After confirming the initial DNS details, you'll be taken to the last step of the signup and domain-addition process: nameserver configuration. On this page, you'll see a listing of the current nameservers for your domain (the ones from Hover mentioned in Section 16.1.2), and the new Cloudflare servers that you need to set for your domain. For the account we created, the nameservers appear as follows:

```
vern.ns.cloudflare.com
zara.ns.cloudflare.com
```

Cloudflare has many different nameservers, though, so your results may differ.

At this point, you'll have to switch back to Hover (either in a different window or in a browser tab) and then click the Edit link in the header of the nameservers box. Switch back to the Cloudflare tab, copy the Cloudflare nameservers, and then paste the new addresses into the two fields, overwriting the old ones. The page will reload, and you should see your new nameservers on the box on the overview page.

Now, switch back to the Cloudflare window or tab and press the "Done, check nameservers" button, and then on the next page that pops up go ahead and click the button to do the quick start guide. Make sure that the Automatic HTTPS Rewrites and Always Use HTTPS options are enabled (you can ignore the other options). Click Finish to save the changes and you'll be taken to the overview page for the domain.

It shouldn't take too long for your domain's nameserver change to resolve; you can hit the button to recheck the nameservers page every so often if you'd like to force Cloudflare to check again. When the updates are public on your registrar, your domain will be active on Cloudflare… congratulations! You're done.

But, what on Earth did we just do?

Well, now all page or DNS requests that are directed at your domain will first go through the Cloudflare service, which means that we can change the way those requests are handled using Cloudflare's user interface. For example, we'll be able to set up subdomains (Section 16.3.1), URL redirects (Section 16.3.3), and automatic forwarding to the secure version of our site. Best of all, since Cloudflare sits in the middle now, any changes you make will immediately take effect instead of potentially taking hours to propagate around the DNS network.

16.3 Custom Domains at GitHub Pages

In this section, we'll explain how to connect a custom domain to GitHub Pages. This is a great (free!) option for hosting static websites on custom domains.[13] (Indeed, the Learn Enough blog (https://news.learnenough.com/) runs on a custom (sub)domain

---

13. Here *static* refers to static server-side assets like HTML, CSS, JavaScript, etc. The site's behavior itself still might be dynamic, typically due to JavaScript executing on the user's browser. An example of a statically generated site yielding dynamic client-side behavior appears in the image gallery developed in the final chapter (https://www.learnenough.com/javascript-tutorial/sample_app_image_gallery) of *Learn Enough JavaScript to Be Dangerous* (https://www.learnenough.com/javascript), which uses the gallery layout developed in Chapter 11.

at GitHub Pages.) It's also a good exercise even if your primary interest is hosting dynamic websites since many of the steps are the same.[14]

For the purposes of this section, we'll assume you've already set up an example website at GitHub Pages as described in Part I and Part II. If you don't have such a site, you should set one up at this time.

16.3.1 Configuring Cloudflare for GitHub Pages

Our first step is to tell Cloudflare that our site is located at GitHub Pages. To get started, click on the DNS menu item to go to the DNS settings for your domain. The result should be a list of DNS records that looks something like Figure 16.9.

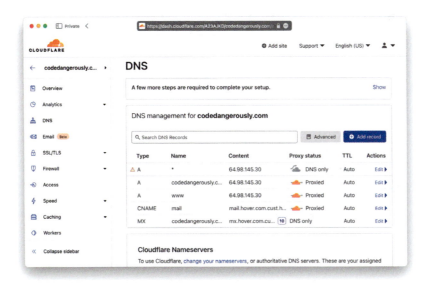

Figure 16.9: The initial DNS settings.

So, what are these different types of records? We'll go in order and make the changes needed to have our site served from GitHub Pages.

---

14. See https://www.learnenough.com/custom-domains-tutorial/dns_management#sec-heroku-config for details on how to set up custom domains with Heroku.

A Records

The *A records* that you see in Figure 16.9 are also known as *address records* (mentioned briefly in Section 16.2.3); the A record corresponding to the domain name itself is known as an *apex record*. These settings are usually used to define the way that the *root domain* (e.g., `codedangerously.com`, without the `www.`) is handled, and they should always point to a valid IP address.

In the default settings transferred over from Hover, the `www` subdomain is set up with an A record that also points to a server's IP address. There are a lot of technical reasons why it's a good idea to use a `www` subdomain, but the simplest reason is that in the future it gives you much more flexibility in how you deal with the traffic coming to your site. For our example site, we are going to get rid of this A record for the subdomain, and instead add a CNAME record for the `www` subdomain.

Let's start the cleanup. Go ahead and click the Edit link on the right-hand side of the screen for the `www` DNS record, and delete the record. (If you are using a registrar that didn't automatically add an A record for `www`, you don't need to do anything at this point.)

Depending on which registrar you used, you may or may not also have an A record with an asterisk `*` in the name field (the first field in Figure 16.9). That's a wildcard record that handles requests to any random subdomain of your URL, which allows requests like blarglebargle.codedangerously.com to pass through to the server. But notice that there is no little orange cloud icon by the `*` record in Figure 16.9—that means the traffic to those random addresses is not being handled by Cloudflare, and will instead flow straight to the server, which we definitely don't want. To prevent this unwanted behavior, remove the wildcard A record, as well as the CNAME record pointing to `mail.hover.com.cust.hostedmail` (we'll set up a different mail system in Chapter 17 that won't need a CNAME record).

Now, to have our site be served from GitHub Pages, we need to point the A record at Cloudflare to the IP addresses of GitHub's servers instead of to the current address (yes, you could have just edited the A records, but we wanted to step you through removing and adding things from scratch). You can find the addresses in the GitHub Pages documentation (https://docs.github.com/en/pages/configuring-a-custom-domain-for-your-github-pages-site/managing-a-custom-domain-for-your-github-pages-site); at the time of this writing, the IP numbers for the GitHub Pages servers are as follows:

```
185.199.108.153
185.199.109.153
185.199.110.153
185.199.111.153
```

Where there was a single A record before, we are going to add a second backup server address (you don't want your site to be unavailable because of a server issue that you can't control, do you?).

We'll start by editing the A record at Cloudflare corresponding to the main domain name. Click on the Edit link and paste in one of the GitHub IPs (like **185.199.108.153**) and then save the changes. Next, we'll add a second record as a backup (Figure 16.10). Above the list of records, you'll see a button that is labeled "Add record"; clicking that causes Cloudflare to reveal a row of inputs. Make sure that the dropdown menu is set to **A**, and then add yourdomain.com in the Name field and the second GitHub IP number (e.g., **185.199.109.153**) in the address field. Then click Save to finish.

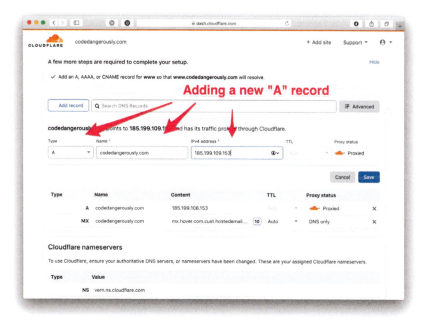

Figure 16.10: Adding the second alternate GitHub Pages server IP.

If you see two A records with GitHub IP addresses in the list, good job! You did it!

CNAME Records

Let's now take a look at *CNAME records*, which are *canonical name* records. They are a type of DNS record that allows you to point traffic to any domain you want (such as a URL like **codedangerously.com**). This is in contrast to A records, which point only to IP addresses (like **185.199.108.153**).

CNAMEs are often used to create aliases on sites so that visitors who go to a subdomain like help.codedangerously.com are instead permanently redirected to, say, docs.codedangerously.com. In our case, we want traffic that comes to our site using a www subdomain—i.e., www.codedangerously.com—to see the site's homepage, which we can do by adding a CNAME record called **www** that points to the root domain.

To start, click "Add record" as in Figure 16.10, and this time select CNAME instead of A from the list. Then add **www** in the Name field and add your site domain in the Target field. Hit the Save button and you're done!

That's all the DNS setup needed to get our new domain to work with GitHub Pages. There is one last DNS record at the bottom, the *MX record*. That is a *mail exchanger* record that directs email traffic to your email server (which we will deal with in Chapter 17).

16.3.2 Configuring GitHub Pages

Now that we've configured Cloudflare for GitHub Pages, all we need to do is tell Pages about our custom domain. To get started, point your browser at your repository's GitHub page, click on the Settings tab, and then click the Pages option in the menu on the left (Figure 16.11).

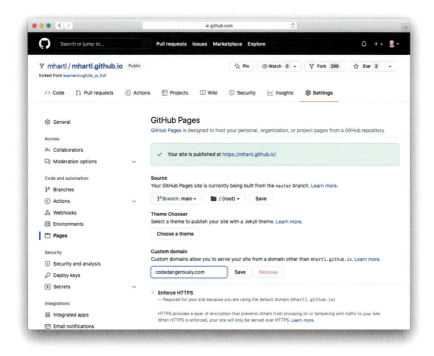

Figure 16.11: Settings for GitHub Pages.

Click on the dropdown menu that is likely showing the text None, and select the name of your project's default branch. When we initially wrote this tutorial, the standard default branch name was **master**, but the current GitHub default is now **main** (although you can easily change the default branch name to **master** or any other name of your choice).[15] After selecting the branch, add your site's domain name into the Custom Domain input field, and that's it!

If you open up a new tab or window in your browser and go to your custom domain, you should now see your GitHub Pages site (Figure 16.12).

---

15. See the Learn Enough blog post "Default Git Branch Name with Learn Enough and the Rails Tutorial" (https://news.learnenough.com/default-git-branch-name-with-learn-enough-and-the-rails-tutorial) for more information.

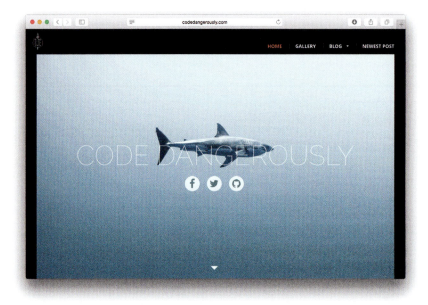

Figure 16.12: Can you believe all the steps it took to get to this place?

At this point, the only major task left is to arrange for our site to use only *canonical URLs* to ensure a consistent and secure experience for all users. (The word "canonical" has its origins in religious canon, and is now used in a variety of technical contexts (Figure 16.13).)[16] In our case, standardizing our site's URLs to use a canonical form involves two steps:

1. Ensure that connections to the site are always secure.
2. Ensure that all pages use the standard `www` form of the site rather than the root domain.

---

16. Image courtesy of Veniamin Kraskov/Shutterstock.

Figure 16.13: This is the wrong type of cannon to be thinking of.

The first step is already complete since secure connections are enforced automatically by the Always Use HTTPS setting enabled in Section 16.2.3. Completing the second step is the goal of Section 16.3.3.

16.3.3   Cloudflare Page Rules

At this point, our website is properly configured to serve the homepage from the address www.codedangerously.com. In order to avoid serving content from two different domains (which can complicate things like session cookies), we'd like to arrange for the www version to be the *only* address for the homepage for our website. In particular, we want any traffic pointed at the root domain codedangerously.com to be automatically redirected to www.codedangerously.com. We can accomplish these kinds of redirects using Cloudflare *page rules*.

Page rules are a powerful and flexible tool, and we'll barely be scratching the surface here, but performing a redirect is one of their most common and important applications. To get started, click on Rules > Page Rules on the main Cloudflare menu, and then click the Create Page Rule button to open the Page Rule interface (Figure 16.14).

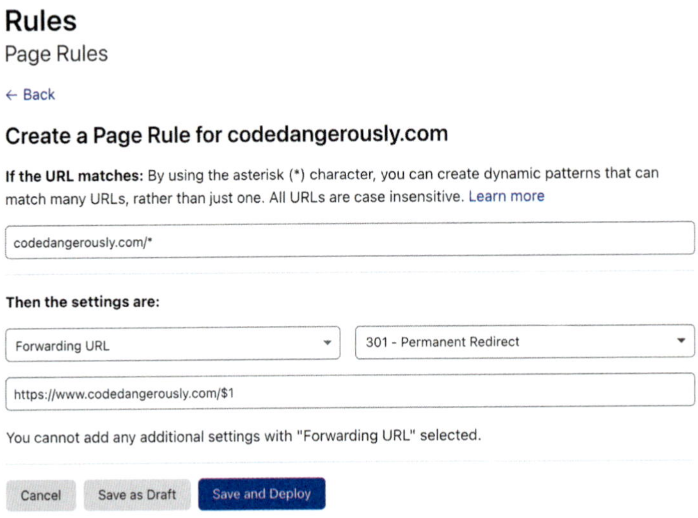

Rules
Page Rules

← Back

Create a Page Rule for codedangerously.com

If the URL matches: By using the asterisk (*) character, you can create dynamic patterns that can match many URLs, rather than just one. All URLs are case insensitive. Learn more

> codedangerously.com/*

Then the settings are:

| Forwarding URL ▾ | | 301 - Permanent Redirect ▾ |

> https://www.codedangerously.com/$1

You cannot add any additional settings with "Forwarding URL" selected.

Cancel   Save as Draft   Save and Deploy

Figure 16.14: Creating a new page rule.

One thing we could do is to forward *everything* at the root domain to the **www** equivalent:

```
codedangerously.com -> www.codedangerously.com
```

There's one problem, though: What if someone hits a subpage of our site? Instead of doing this:

```
codedangerously.com/blarg -> www.codedangerously.com
```

we'd rather do this:

```
codedangerously.com/blarg -> www.codedangerously.com/blarg
```

This way the root and **www** domains will truly be equivalent, and *any* attempt to access the site via the root URL will end up being forwarded to the corresponding **www** version.

We can arrange for the desired behavior using a *wildcard* (a concept mentioned briefly in Section 16.3.1), which will dynamically match whatever the user enters after the domain name and keep it intact after the redirect. So if they enter **codedan-gerously.com/blarg**, the page rule will make sure they are forwarded automatically to **www.codedangerously.com/blarg**. We don't want to lose that **/blarg** at the end of the address!

To arrange for this sort of redirect, go to the form field under Create a Page Rule and add your domain name, a forward slash, and then an asterisk to represent the wildcard. For us, this looks like this:

```
codedangerously.com/*
```

but of course you should use your own custom domain instead. Next, in the dropdown menu choose Forwarding URL. You'll now see more options, including two kinds of *redirects*: 301 and 302 (Box 16.1).

Box 16.1: 301 vs. 302 Redirects

There are two main types of redirects used on the Web: *301 - permanent* and *302 - temporary*. You can probably guess the intended purpose of these redirects from their names, but what you might not realize is that your choice has an effect on search engine results.

If you choose a 302 redirect, then search engines like Google will assume that at some point the redirect will be removed and the page in question will be a destination that users can reach. That means that the search engines don't combine the traffic—both URLs exist as separate objects. That isn't good for analytics or search engine optimization (SEO) if you really intended for the redirect to be permanent.

If you set the redirect to 301, then search engines consider the URLs to be exactly the same. So even if a user came to your site through a redirected URL, your main URL would still get credit for purposes of traffic estimates and SEO.

In practice, the vast majority of page rule redirects will be 301s. Indeed, such permanent redirects are so common that "301" is often used as a verb, as in "Please 301 your old links instead of breaking them."

For canonical URLs, we want the redirects to be permanent, so set Status Code to 301 – Permanent Redirect, and in the Destination URL field add in the full URL for your site (including the protocol string **https://**) followed by **/$1**:

```
https://www.example.com/$1
```

Here **$1** represents the text matched by the first wildcard. In other words,

```
example.com/*
```

matches

```
example.com/blarg
```

and makes the string **blarg** available as **$1**. As a result, the code

```
https://www.example.com/$1
```

produces the canonical URL

```
https://www.example.com/blarg
```

In the present case, there is only one wildcard, but it's possible to match on multiple wildcards as well (Box 16.2).

Box 16.2: Matching URLs

As you might be able to guess, page rule matches are numbered sequentially, so if we had two wildcards in a rule they would be available as $1 and $2. For example, `*.codedangerously.com/*` is a pattern to match any subdomain; in this case, `foo.codedangerously.com/bar` would put `foo` in $1 and `bar` in $2. (Note that the free Cloudflare tier supports subdomain wildcards only for CNAME records that are defined explicitly. Redirecting *all* subdomains requires upgrading to the Business plan.)

The same permanent forwarding can be used to direct users who requested a completely different domain over to your main site. So if we purchased `dangerouscoding.com`, we could forward any `dangerouscoding.com` URL to `codedangerously.com` using the above wildcard method to preserve the specific page they requested. The matching rule in this case would be

```
*dangerouscoding.com/*
```

> where the leading wildcard matches all subdomains as well as the root domain (i.e., both `subdomain.dangerouscoding.com` and `dangerouscoding.com`). Assuming we want to ignore the subdomain, the 301 redirect would then be
>
> ```
> https://www.codedangerously.com/$2
> ```
>
> where we use $2 because the subpage is matched by the second wildcard.

In our case, the forwarding URL is:

```
https://www.codedangerously.com/$1
```

Click the Save and Deploy button to save your new rule. To see if the redirect worked, you can try visiting the root domain in your browser. For example, if we enter code-dangerously.com into a browser we get redirected to www.codedangerously.com, as shown in Figure 16.15.

Figure 16.15: It works! It really works!

Another convenient way of checking URL forwarding is to use the **curl** command at the command line (as covered (https://www.learnenough.com/command-line-tutorial/inspecting_files) in *Learn Enough Command Line to Be Dangerous* (https://www.learnenough.com/command-line)). In particular, we can use the **--head** option to return just the HTTP header (rather than the whole page):

```
$ curl --head codedangerously.com
HTTP/1.1 301 Moved Permanently
Date: Thu, 13 Feb 2020 16:47:00 GMT
Connection: keep-alive
Cache-Control: max-age=3600
Expires: Thu, 13 Feb 2020 17:47:00 GMT
Location: https://www.codedangerously.com/
Server: cloudflare
CF-RAY: 5648481ded567896-LAX
```

We see in line 2 that the HTTP status code is **301** as required, with the forwarding URL (line 7) including the subdomain **www** and the secure HTTP protocol indicator **https://** (where the "s" stands for "secure").

16.3.4 Profit!!

With all the work done in this chapter, you now have a professional-grade website on a custom domain that is protected from DDoS attacks, is edge-cached, and is blazingly fast. And, amazingly, it's all for free! The only big thing left is being able to send and receive email using your domain. This is the subject of Chapter 17.

CHAPTER 17

Custom Email

Having finished Chapter 16, we've now accomplished the main task we set out to do: We have our own website on a custom domain. In this chapter, we'll include two important refinements: custom email (Section 17.1 and Section 17.2) and site analytics (Section 17.3). They're in the same chapter because the solutions we recommend are both provided by the same company (Google) and therefore fit nicely together.

This chapter also brings *Learn Enough HTML, CSS and Layout to Be Dangerous* to a conclusion. In Section 17.4, we'll offer some final reflections on just how far we've come and make some suggestions on where to go next.

17.1 Google Mail

The specific global email service we recommend is Google mail (Gmail). We use Gmail because, as one of Google's core consumer-facing businesses, Gmail is supported on a large variety of devices and other services. It is also available and accessible basically anywhere at any time since it is running on Google's core infrastructure—that means you don't have to worry about some rinky-dink server outage taking down your access to email. Things have to go very wrong on the Internet to prevent you from being able to access Gmail.

Gmail's spam filtering is also top-notch, as it leverages both Google's expertise in machine learning and the millions of users who are on Gmail to figure out how to distinguish legitimate email from spam. If you use an email service that requires you to deal with inadequate spam filtering, we can promise you that with Gmail you rarely end up with spam in your inbox, or with real messages in your spam folder. It feels like a solved problem.

Lastly, we actually like the Gmail interface… We know that some people don't, but hey, you know what they say about opinions. We find that searching email on Google is always fast and accurate (something that we can't say about other systems that we've used in the past), and there are nice little power-user features that make life easier (like the ability to unsend a message within 30 seconds or the dots-and-pluses trick (Box 17.1)).

Box 17.1: Gmail Dots and Pluses Trick

Many people don't know this, but when you have a Gmail email address, you actually have a basically infinite set of sub-email addresses that can tie into your account without needing to do any setup. This is a nice way to pre-filter your email by giving different people, or websites that you don't fully trust, a slightly different address. Then you can easily have Gmail move any mail sent to an email variant into a folder.

What do we mean? Let's say you have the email address `yourname @gmail.com`.

The first trick is that Gmail doesn't care about dots in your email address. So, if you tell someone to email you at `your.name@gmail.com`, that will still end up in the inbox for `yourname@gmail.com`—and you'll be able to see that it was sent to `your.name@gmail.com`. The lone caveat here is that you can't have two periods in a row. So `your..name@gmail.com` wouldn't work, but there would be nothing wrong with `y.o.u.r.n.a.m.e@gmail.com`. Eventually, though, you run out of variations…

The second trick is that you have the ability to create a limitless number of ad hoc emails by adding a plus sign, +, to the end of your regular email and then whatever additional text you desire. In other words,

```
yourname+travelsite@gmail.com
```

and

```
yourname+shadysite@gmail.com
```

both end up going to `yourname@gmail.com`. This lets you use distinct email addresses for different sites.

So what are the downsides of using Gmail for your custom domain? Well, unlike the free service (the one where your email is something@gmail.com), you have to pay for it. Google offers custom Gmail via its general suite of cloud productivity tools called Google Workspace (formerly G Suite), which (as of this writing) costs $6/user/month for the Business Starter plan. (Note that each user can have up to 30 *aliases*, or other email addresses that all go to the same inbox, so there's no need to pay for multiple users in this case.) For more details, see the Workspace pricing page (https://workspace.google.com/pricing.html).

Some people have also expressed privacy concerns about Google's services. While this may apply to Gmail's consumer service, which serves ads based on email content, Workspace is different, as noted in Google's FAQ:

> **Does Google use my organization's data in Google Workspace services or Cloud Platform for advertising purposes?**
>
> No. There are no ads in Google Workspace Services or Google Cloud Platform, and we have no plans to change this in the future. We do not scan for advertising purposes in Gmail or other Google Workspace services. Google does not collect or use data in Google Workspace services for advertising purposes.
>
> The process is different for our free offerings and the consumer space. For information on our free consumer products, be sure to check Google's Privacy and Terms page for more consumer tools and information relating to consumer privacy.

There's an old axiom that applies here: "If you aren't paying for a product or service, then you are the product." (For example, Facebook is "free," but their product is your personal information, which they use for ad targeting.) With Gmail for work, you *are* paying, so you are *not* the product.

If you'd really rather use an alternate service (such as privacy-focused ProtonMail), the setup is going to end up being similar to what we cover here. This means that the steps discussed in this section will be useful in any case.

17.1.1 Google Workspace Signup

Before we start, a little caveat: Google changes their services all the time so you might need to use a heaping spoonful of technical sophistication (Box 5.1). We visited the site one day to go through all the steps and create an account, and then the next day went back to double-check a step in the process only to find that the signup flow was entirely changed. They still wanted the same information—everything was just arranged totally differently! Then, shortly after, Google changed the name of its service from G Suite to Google Workspace... it's just a mess.

To sign up for Google Workspace, head over to the Workspace home page (https://workspace.google.com/products/gmail/) and get started by clicking the Get Started button… or whatever the equivalent is today. Again, Google might be testing different language for buttons—who knows? Proceed through whatever random information they need from you to finish the account creation—the only important step is that when you are asked about your domain name, make sure to put in the domain you registered (without www e.g., codedangerously.com).

Now that the initial setup is done, Google will want you to make changes to your DNS records (Section 16.2) so that Google can verify that you actually own the domain and have added the correct records for setting up email (Section 17.2). That sounds more complicated than it is, but thankfully by now you are an expert at editing DNS records!

17.2 MX Records

In this section, we'll set up so-called *mail exchange* records, or MX records for short. The MX records for a domain are what associate the domain name with an email provider and allow the creation of custom addresses at the domain.

As mentioned in Section 17.1.1, Google wants to make sure that you are in fact the owner of the domain that you are trying to create an email account for, and luckily the DNS system provides a lot of opportunities to add information to a domain's records. For Gmail, Google just wants you to add an extra TXT record (which is what it sounds like: a text record on your site's DNS configuration) consisting of a unique string of letters and numbers.

Because of the public nature of the DNS records, Google can just query your domain's information and easily see that the verification strings match, confirming that you are in fact the person who controls the domain. If you haven't already, click past the verification instructions welcome page to get to the details on how to make Google happy. Copy the verification text on the page (Figure 17.1).

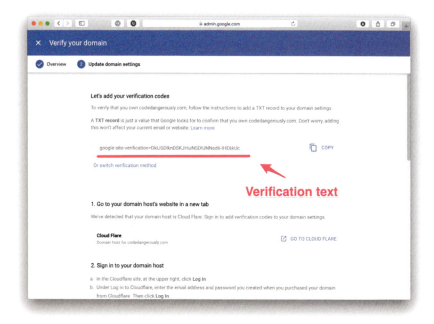

Figure 17.1: The TXT record verification string (not our real one!).

In another tab or window, open up your site's DNS records in Cloudflare, click the "Add record" button, and select **TXT** from the Type dropdown. In the Name field, add in an @ sign, which is a shorthand way of saying use whatever the root domain is for this record. (In other words, for us @ is the same as **codedangerously.com**.) Click into the Content field and paste in your verification text, as shown in Figure 17.2. After hitting the Save button, you should see the new record in the list. As a last step, delete any old MX records that are not pointing to the Google servers (a step mentioned briefly when discussing A records in Section 16.3.1).

Figure 17.2: Adding the new TXT record (still not our real verification key).

We are almost done, but we still need to add the actual DNS records that point to Google's servers to handle email. Hop back over to your Google Workspace admin console tab and click the Verify My Domain button at the bottom of the page.[1]

If you are working with any other people on your project, you can use the admin console setup process to add other users to your Google Workspace account. It is a pretty self-explanatory process, and if you don't want to deal with it now, you don't need to.

To get your email up and running, click the Activate link to bring up a page with instructions that show how to set up your DNS records so that email gets routed to the correct mail servers. In particular, we'll be adding MX records to the DNS settings at Cloudflare. To add the first one, copy the first value from the Google Workspace setup, which for us is **ASPMX.L.GOOGLE.COM**. Then, on the Cloudflare DNS management page, perform the following steps:

1. Add a new record, making sure that **MX** is selected in the Type dropdown.

2. Add **@** in the Name field so that the record points to the domain root.

---

1. If we weren't using Cloudflare, the changes could theoretically take up to 72 hours to go into effect (Section 16.2.1)—which is all the more reason to use Cloudflare.

3. Add the server name that you copied from Google Workspace into the Mail server field.

4. For this first record, set a priority of 1.

Now head back over to your Google Workspace setup tab, and then bounce back and forth between that and Cloudflare to finish entering the other MX records listed in the table, making sure that you are setting the priority on each one to the specified level (1, 5, or 10 from Google's MX info).

When you are done, click the Activate Gmail button and let Google check to see if the DNS records have been correctly added. If they have been, that's it—you are all done!

At this point, Google will (could… may… really, who knows?!) take you to a confirmation page to let you know that your Google Workspace account is set up. If you want to check out your new Gmail account, click the Google Apps menu icon at the top right, and then select Gmail (Figure 17.3).

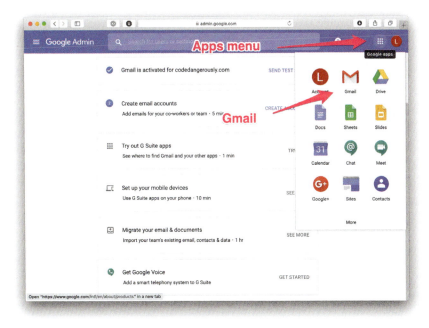

Figure 17.3: It's all done done.

In the future, you can access your new email inbox by going to mail.google.com and signing in with the new account that you created during the mail setup process. If you need to get back to the console and can't remember what the address is, it's super-easy: admin.google.com. Once you've logged in there, you can add additional users to your account, update billing information, or add additional services.

Speaking of additional services… since you have a Google account now, why not sign up for Google Analytics so that you can get information about who is visiting your site?

17.3   Site Analytics

Google Analytics is probably the most useful free service that Google has for the owners of websites and web applications. By adding just a tiny little snippet of code to your site, you can have Google track not just how many people are visiting your site, but also the browser and operating system they are using, whether they are on desktop or mobile, how they found your site, how long they stayed on your site, which pages they viewed, which page they left your site from… and a lot more.

To get started, visit the Google Analytics home page (https://marketingplatform .google.com/about/analytics/) and click the big Sign Up for Free button. (As always, use your technical sophistication (Box 5.1) if Google has changed their interface since we wrote this.) From there, you'll be asked to sign in using the Google account that you just created.

Once you are in, you'll be on the Analytics setup track. Click the Get Started or Sign Up button to go to the site information page. Fill out the fields on the page with the requested information about your site, and then at the bottom of the page press the Get Tracking ID button.

After you agree to the Terms of Service, the site will take you to a page in your new analytics account that will have the little bit of code you need to add to your site for the tracking to work. What you are looking for is the code snippet that looks something like Listing 17.1.

Listing 17.1: This is the code that makes Google Analytics work.

```
<script>
(function(i,s,o,g,r,a,m){i['GoogleAnalyticsObject']=r;i[r]=i[r]||function(){
(i[r].q=i[r].q||[]).push(arguments)},i[r].l=1*new Date();a=s.createElement(o),
m=s.getElementsByTagName(o)[0];a.async=1;a.src=g;m.parentNode.insertBefore(a,m)
```

```
})(window,document,'script','https://www.google-analytics.com/analytics.js','ga');
ga('create', 'UA-XXXXXXXX-1', 'auto');
ga('send', 'pageview');
</script>
```

(We've removed one level of indentation from the script to get it to fit on the page, but you can just copy-and-paste from Google.) Note that you should always use the exact code supplied by Google; Listing 17.1 is included only as an example of the kind of code you can expect.

17.3.1 Add Snippet

To get Analytics working, head over to your text editor and paste the analytics snippet into the **<head>** section of your site, which (if you followed everything in the tutorial to this point) should be located in **_includes/head.html**, as shown in Listing 17.2.

Listing 17.2: Where to put the code snippet in your site code.
_includes/head.html

```
<head>
  {% if page.title %}
    <title>{{ page.title }} | Test Page</title>
  {% else %}
    <title>Test Page: Don't Panic</title>
  {% endif %}
  {% if page.description %}
    <meta name="description" content="{{ page.description }}">
  {% else %}
    <meta name="description" content="This is a dangerous site.">
  {% endif %}
  <link href="/favicon.png" rel="icon">
  <meta charset="utf-8">
  <meta name=viewport content="width=device-width, initial-scale=1">
  <link rel="stylesheet" href="/fonts/font-awesome-4.7.0/css/font-awesome.min.css">
  <link rel="stylesheet" href="/css/main.css">

  <script>
  (function(i,s,o,g,r,a,m){i['GoogleAnalyticsObject']=r;i[r]=i[r]||function(){
  (i[r].q=i[r].q||[]).push(arguments)},i[r].l=1*new Date();a=s.createElement(o),
  m=s.getElementsByTagName(o)[0];a.async=1;a.src=g;m.parentNode.insertBefore(a,m)
  })(window,document,'script','https://www.google-analytics.com/analytics.js','ga');
  ga('create', 'UA-XXXXXXXX-1', 'auto');
  ga('send', 'pageview');
  </script>
</head>
```

Save your changes, deploy your site… and that's it! It's as easy as this:

```
$ git commit -am "Add Google Analytics"
$ git push
```

By the way, if you want to use Google Analytics to push some test visitors to the site and make sure everything is working, you can click the "Send test traffic" button (Figure 17.4).

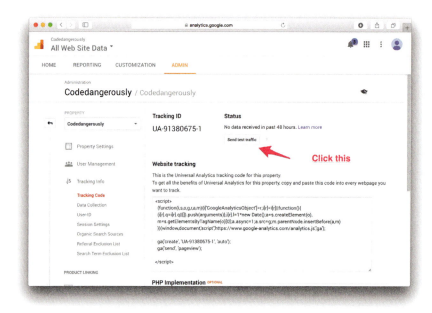

Figure 17.4: The tracking code page for your site.

If you've looked for information on how to set up Analytics in the past, you might have seen someone suggest that you should put the Google Analytics code snippet at the very end of your site, right above the closing body tag **</body>**. You can absolutely do that, and the analytics will still work, but the main reason for doing that has changed.

It used to be the case that when your site tried to load Analytics it would actually hold up the rest of your site from loading until the Analytics code finished downloading—not a good thing if the connection to Google is slow. Since then, though, the Google Analytics code has switched to using an *asynchronous loading* method that makes it so that the rest of your site load isn't held up.

Once you're all set up, you can sign into the Analytics dashboard by going to analytics.google.com. On the dashboard, you will have a ton of options for all the different ways to slice and dice your data, or even see the users who are on the site in real time (Figure 17.5).

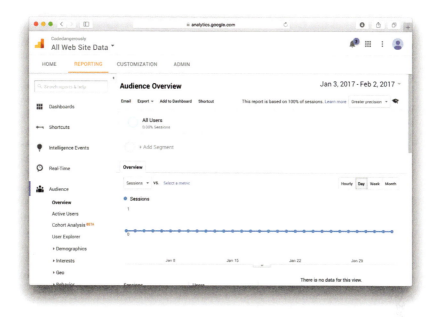

Figure 17.5: Hooray analytics, boo no visitors. So lonely.

Google Analytics is a *really* deep service, and we aren't going to dive into how to use it—that would require a book of its own (and there are many out there). This goal here was just to get you up and running with the service, and in the future we might write up an Analytics tutorial of our own. Until then, you'll just need to search around the interwebs and find guides and tutorials to teach you the dark arts of Google Analytics.

17.4 Conclusion

So there you go! If you made it all the way through Part III, you now have your site running on a custom domain, you are using Cloudflare for DNS management, you have a custom email address through Google Workspace, and you are using Google Analytics to learn more about the people visiting your site. You've gone from just having a rinky-dink page on the Internet to actually looking like a legitimate homepage or business. Great work!

This final accomplishment also brings the full story arc of this tutorial to a close. You have now learned enough HTML, CSS and Layout to be *dangerous*. Congratulations!

Let's take a moment to reflect on just how far we've come in this book. We started Chapter 1 of Part I assuming zero knowledge of HTML or CSS. We systematically built up our knowledge of HTML tags by filling in the index page (Chapter 2) and adding a couple more pages to our little site (Chapter 3). We then took our first steps into the world of web design with inline styles (Chapter 4), which led naturally into a study of CSS and layout (Part II).

In Chapter 5, we started with the bare-bones site shown in Figure 17.6. By writing good semantic markup (Chapter 6), using CSS values (Chapter 7), applying the box model (Chapter 8), and using a static site generator for proper DRY layout (Chapter 9 and Chapter 10) with flexbox (Chapter 11), we transformed that plain page into a fully developed website.

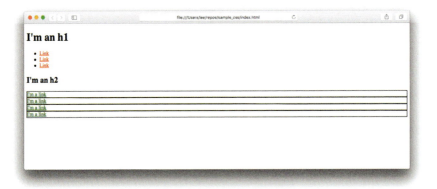

Figure 17.6: The original bare-bones site.

We added to that the beginnings of a blog (Chapter 12), a mobile-friendly view (Chapter 13), and the little touches from Chapter 14. We took a quick detour to learn the basics of grid (Chapter 15), and then added the custom domain here in Part III (Chapter 16 and Chapter 17). At this point, we've got a great foundation for a polished personal homepage or company website, featuring a blog and as many custom pages as we care to make, all running on a custom domain of our choosing.

To put it in more visual terms, the initial sample website looks like Figure 17.7; after completing this tutorial, it looks like Figure 17.8. Quite a difference!

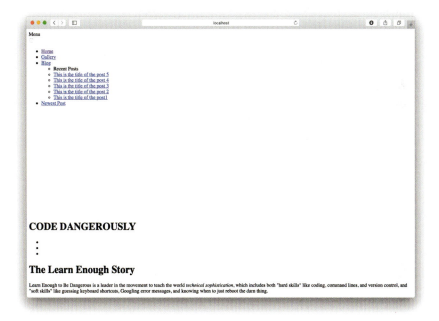

Figure 17.7: The final site *without* CSS.

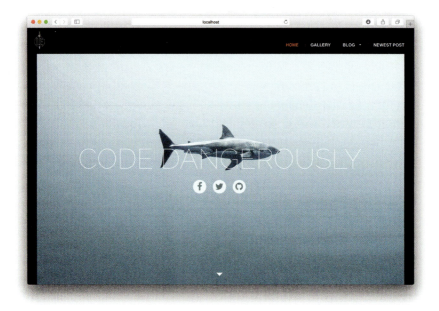

Figure 17.8: The final site *with* CSS. Muuuuch better!

Now that we've reached the end of *Learn Enough HTML, CSS and Layout to Be Dangerous*, let's talk about next steps. As noted in Section 5.1, this is a front-end development tutorial, not a design tutorial per se, but it's a tremendous head start for learning more about web design. It's hard to give specific recommendations for next steps on this subject because everyone we know cobbles together their knowledge from here and there. Our best advice is to work on a project you care about, Google around to figure out how to do it (Box 5.1), and keep practicing. That's the only way to get better.

On the development side, there's lots more to learn about Jekyll, including aspects of the system that are more closely related to full-strength web development (including more details on the `Gemfile`s mentioned in Section 9.2.1, additional command-line commands like `jekyll new`, etc.). The Jekyll documentation (https://jekyllrb.com/docs/) is a good place to start.

Finally, you now have the HTML and CSS knowledge (especially CSS classes and ids) needed to start learning *JavaScript*, the native programming language of web browsers. This is the subject of the next tutorial in the Learn Enough introductory sequence (https://www.learnenough.com/all-access), *Learn Enough JavaScript to Be Dangerous* (https://www.learnenough.com/javascript). After that, you'll be ready to learn full-strength database-backed web development, via *Learn Enough Ruby to Be Dangerous* (https://www.learnenough.com/ruby) and the *Ruby on Rails Tutorial* (https://www.railstutorial.org/).

We hope you've enjoyed *Learn Enough HTML, CSS and Layout to Be Dangerous.* Now get out there and start making things!

Index